Ta Eben wrote and self-published his first book in 2018 titled: *A Journey to the World: Reminiscences and Moments*, which was revised in 2020 and was a huge success. This book, *In Search of a Future* is his second book. Before becoming a budding author after his retirement in 2003, Ta Eben was many things at different times: a veterinarian, a rubber planter in the plantations, a researcher in the CGIAR, a university don, a UN international civil servant, etc. etc. He earned a Ph. D. degree in February, 1978. He has written and published extensively in international journals and consulted and advised on a wide range of agricultural development and socioeconomic policy issues.

To his parents,
Ta Ako-aragbor (Mansa) and Mama Rose Ayuk-ebet.
You prepared Don well for the journey to broaden his horizons and search for
a future.

Ta Eben

DON HARRIS OBEN: IN SEARCH OF A FUTURE

AUSTIN MACAULEY PUBLISHERS®

LONDON * CAMBRIDGE * NEW YORK * SHARJAH

Ordering Information
Quantity sales: Special discounts are available on quantity purchases by corporations, associations, and others. For details, contact the publisher at the address below.

Publisher's Cataloging-in-Publication data
Eben, Ta
Don Harris Oben: In Search of a Future

ISBN 9798889108726 (Paperback)
ISBN 9798889108733 (Hardback)
ISBN 9798889108740 (ePub e-book)

Library of Congress Control Number: 2024907156

www.austinmacauley.com/us

First Published 2024
Austin Macauley Publishers LLC
40 Wall Street, 33rd Floor, Suite 3302
New York, NY 10005
USA

mail-usa@austinmacauley.com
+1 (646) 5125767

I would like, first and foremost, to express my sincere appreciation to Dr. Don Harris Oben for giving me the opportunity and privilege to write and publish his life story. I cherish the long hours, days, weeks, and months I spent with him listening to his fascinating stories and going over lots of papers, files and images, to select relevant material and information for the book.

Quite a number of people made the publication of this book possible. Don Jr. helped me with selecting, arranging, and scanning the images of relevant material for this book especially images of family members. Vanessa helped me with some microsoft word program functions for proofreading documents. A few friends read and corrected the initial manuscripts. I'm grateful to them. I also appreciate all Don's family members and friends who helped me in one way or another during the writing of this biography.

On Don's behalf, I would like to acknowledge his father, Ta Ako-aragbor, for the fascinating stories he told him when he was a little boy which invoked in him a burning desire to undertake his own journey to 'broaden his horizons'. I also acknowledge his mother, Ma Rose Ayuk-ebet, who not only gave birth to him, but also ensured that he survived his infancy and childhood to undertake this journey. He owes a debt of great love and gratitude to them. Finally, I acknowledge his lovely wife, Dr. (Mrs.) Dorothy Ebot Oben who accompanied and gave him unwavering support during this journey which turned out to be long, difficult, and protracted.

Don couldn't have undertaken such a long and enduring journey without the strong financial support of the Mamfe Town and Area Council, the West Cameroon Government, the Government of the Federal Republic of Cameroon, and the Rockefeller and Ford Foundations of the United States of

America. His heart will forever remain grateful to them for their respective scholarships and fellowships.

But his greatest debt is to God almighty who, through His abundant Grace, not only enabled him to undertake the journey, but kept him alive and able to have his journey and story published more than a decade after it ended.

Table of Contents

A Footprint

In early 1984, while still a young staffer at the UN Economic Commission for Africa (ECA), in Addis Ababa, Ethiopia, Don Oben and a colleague, Godfrey Coker were asked to go to Rome to use FAO's up-to-date data and prepare a 'Report on the Situation of Food and Agriculture in Africa'. This Report was for presentation by the ECA, to the ECA Conference of Ministers of Planning due in April 1984. Based on their analysis of the food situation and outlook, Don, an agricultural economist and his colleague, a statistician, WARNED in the Report, of an impending FOOD CRISIS in Africa and URGED African member states and the international community to take all necessary measures to AVERT it. For this timely warning supported by rigorous analysis of FAO most current data, they were berated by a high official in FAO's Assistance Planning Service. He accused Don and his colleague of being 'alarmists'.

"Food crisis, food crisis, food crisis, where is the food crisis?" he asked. "It's true there are pockets of crop failure here and there and areas of food shortages. But that does not mean that there is a food crisis," he asserted, advising strongly that they delete all reference to an impending food crisis in Africa in the report.

Don and his colleague refused to back down and submitted their Report to the ECA. The Commission accepted and presented it to the 9th Meeting of the ECA Conference of Ministers of Planning in April 1984. Most African member states and the international community, for whatever reasons, did not take the required actions to avert the impending catastrophe.

It was not long before Africa was engulfed in one of the most devastating food crisis in the continent's history. The African food crisis of the late 1980s and early 1990s and the widespread hunger, famine and starvation which accompanied it, captured the attention of the whole world as never before, prompting a global response to save lives......

The above abstract from the archives provides an insight into one of several footprints that Don Oben left behind on the sands of time during his epic journey, *In Search of a Future.*

Abbreviations/Acronyms

AAF-SAP African Alternative Framework to Structural Adjustment Programs

AATPO Association of African Trade Promotion Organizations

ACMAD African Center of Meteorological Applications for Development

AEC African Economic Community

AMU Arab Maghreb Union

AOCRS African Organization for Cartography and Remote Sensing

APPER Africa's Priority Program for Economic Recovery

ARCEDEM African Regional Center for Engineering Design and Manufacturing

ARCT African Regional Center for Technology

ARSO African Regional Organization for Standardization

ATRCW African Training and Research Center for Women

AU African Union

AUC African Union Commission

BCI Banca Commerciale Italiana

CAFRAD Centre Africain de Formation et de Recherche Administratives pour le Développement/African Training and Research Center in Administration for Development (ATRCAD)

CAREL Centre Audio-visuel de Royan pour l'Etudes de Langues

CASIN Center for Applied Studies in International Negotiations

CEMAC Communaute Economique et Monetaire d'Afrique Centrale (Customs and Economic Union of Central Africa)

CGIAR Consultative Group for International Agricultural Research

CILLS Intergovernmental Committee for Combating Drought in the Sahel

CRTO Centre Regional de Teledetection

CUD Centre Universitaire de Dschang/Dschang University Center

DALF Diplôme Approfondi de Langue Française

DELF Diplôme d'Études en Langue Française

DPCSD Department of Policy Coordination and Sustainable Development

ECA Economic Commission for Africa

ECCAS Economic Community of Central African States

ECE Economic Commission for Europe

ECOSOC Economic and Social Council

ECOWAS Economic Community of West African States

ECLAC Economic Commission for Latin America and the Caribbean

ENSA École Nationale Supérieure d'Agriculture (Higher National School of Agriculture)

EPLF Eritrian Peoples Liberation Front

EPRDF Ethiopian People's Revolutionary Democratic Front

ESAMI Eastern and Southern African Management Institute

ESCAP Economic and Social Commission for Asia and the Pacific

ESCWA Economic and Social Commission for Western Asia

ESL English as a Foreign Language

FAO Food and Agriculture Organization

GATT General Agreement on Tariffs and Trade

GTZ German Agency for Technical Cooperation

HRO Human Resources Officer

IAW International Alliance of Women

IBRD International Bank for Reconstruction and Development (World Bank)

ICRISAT International Crops Research Institute for the Semi-Arid Tropics

IDDA Industrial Development Decade for Africa

IDEP Institute for Development and Economic Planning

IFAD International Fund for Agricultural Development

IFDC International Fertilizer Development Center

IFPRI International Food Policy Research Institute

IIASA International Institute for applied Systems Analysis

IITA International Institute for Tropical Agriculture

ILCA International Livestock Center for Africa

IMF International Monetary Fund

ISNAR International Service for National Agricultural Research

ITA Institut Technique Agricole

LPA Lagos Plan of Action

LUTH Lagos University Teaching Hospital

MULPOC Multinational Programming and Operational Center

NEPAD New Partnership for Africa's Development

NRD Natural Resources Division

OAU Organization of African Unity

ODG Overseas Development Group

OGSS Owerri Government Secondary School

OHRM Office of Human Resources and Management

PTA Preferential Trade Area

RCSSMRS Regional Center for Services in Surveying, Mapping and Remote Sensing

RECs Regional Economic Communities

RECTAS Regional Center for Training in Aerospace Surveys

RIPs Regional Institute for Population Studies

SADC Southern Africa Development Community

SAP Structural Adjustment Program

SERPD Socioeconomic Research and Policy Division

SRO Subregional Office

SSA Sub-Saharan Africa

TEPCOW Technical Preparatory Committee of the Whole

TCD Transport and Communication Division

TGE Transitional Government of Ethiopia

TPLF Tigray Peoples Liberation Front

UCH University Teaching Hospital

UN United Nations

UNCTAD United Nations Conference on Trade and Development

UNDP United Nations Development Program

UNGA United Nations General Assembly

UNICEF United Nations International Children's Emergency Fund

UNIDO United Nations Industrial Development Organization

USSR Union of Socialist Soviet Republics

WASC West African School Certificate

WBI World Bank Institute

WFC World Food Council

WFP World Food Program

WHO World Health Organization

Part 1
In Search of a Future:
Before the Journey

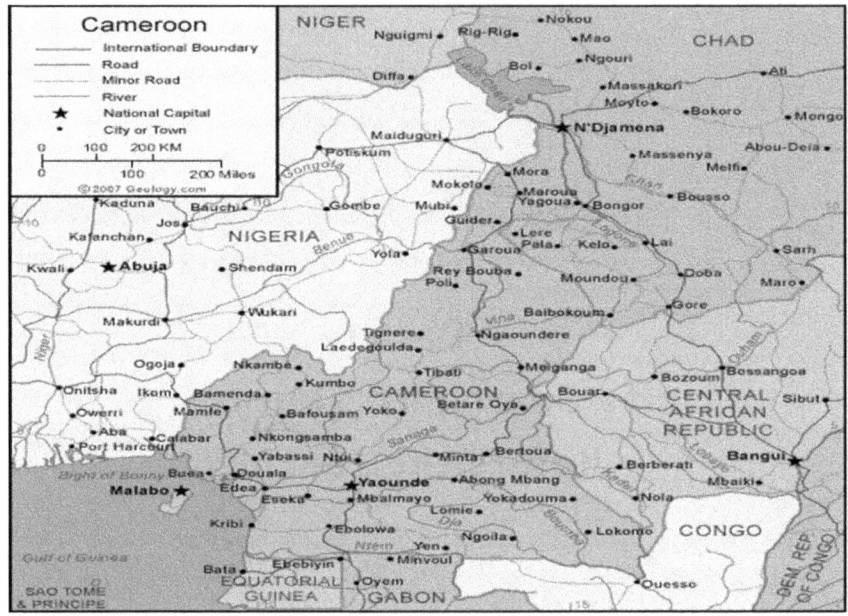

Fig 1 (above): The map of Cameroon and part of Nigeria showing some prominent towns along Don's early journey. Below, left: Map of Southern Cameroon showing some prominent towns. Below, right: Map of Nigeria showing the position of Southern Cameroon, Northern Cameroon and Republic of Cameroon.

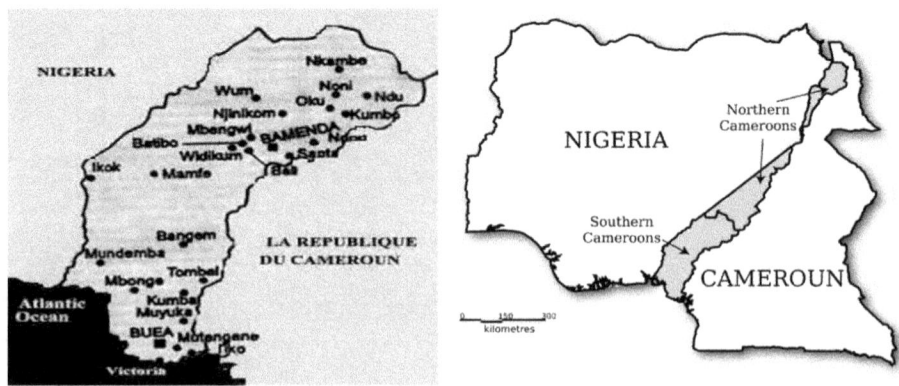

Chapter 1
Introduction

After Don retired from the United Nations in 2003 and relocated in Buea, Cameroon, he had an increasing urge to write a book about himself even though he was very much engaged in many other activities including consultancies with the African Union (AU) and other organizations. But a voice within him always created an inertia that prevented him from getting started. "Are you a world leader, a former head of state or a charismatic freedom fighter? Only these people write autobiographies for more money, more fame and greater POWER," the voice would counsel him.

Don did get started however, but stopped after a few months. He needed some inspiration, some re-assurance or something to help jerk him from this inertia. And what he needed, came very unexpectantly. The organizer of a small seminar for retirees which he attended about that time and for no apparent reasons, (having participated in several previous and much bigger similar workshops at the UN), in his closing remarks urged the retirees present not only to spend their time on money-making ventures, but also to write books about themselves and their experiences. "Everyone has a story to tell and no one is too small to tell his or her story. Each story is different, and each story has an audience," he concluded.

Wow! So Don could tell his story. But could he tell it well? As Don pondered this question in his mind, he remembered what his long-time friend and old classmate, Prof. Anthony Ikpi always said about him whenever someone told him a story that Don had narrated to him. "Trust Don for telling a good story." Then Don's children came to mind. He remembered when they were young what they used to say after he had told them a story for the umpteenth time. They would wink at each other and in the manner of that woman in Crocodile Dundee, they would chuckle: "Dad, this story gets better and better each time you tell it."

This acknowledgement that he could tell a good story not only gave Don the motivation, confidence and re-assurance that he had experiences to offer and share, but that he could also convey them to his readers in the manner of a good story teller. It rekindled his interest and inspired him to go back to his book. When he completed the manuscript and Xlibris LLC provided the services and tools that transformed it into a well-designed, customized, and well-published book, 'A Journey to the World: Reminiscences and Moments', Don realized that the book and its author had become much larger than he ever imagined. Among the several readers who called Don or sent messages after the first edition was released, one had this to say about the book. "It is 2 am now and I am still reading your book. I cannot put it down. You are one hell of a writer."

The book is about Don Oben who, as a little boy used to listen attentively to the fascinating stories his father told him about his travels in Nigeria during the colonial era. These stories invoked in little Don a burning desire to undertake his own journey to 'broaden his horizons'. Don's father served and traveled widely with European administrators as a chief steward. He could write and speak English and some German; His lifestyle, comportment and industriousness set him apart from his illiterate peers in the small town of Mamfe in the former Southern Cameroons. Don is convinced that the socio-cultural environment in Nigeria where he had lived had a profound impact on him.

As a frail lad of 14, he sets out in a mammy wagon accompanied by an uncle to attend a privileged but highly competitive government secondary school in Eastern Nigeria, having declined offers of admission from schools in Cameroon. This marks the start of his journey into the unknown to broaden his horizons which later turns into an epic journey that lasts 46 years 'in search of a future'.

In this book, *Don Harris Oben: In Search of a Future*, I look at Don's journey through my own lens and narrate Don's story in my own words and I am not holding back. I do not stop at Don's journey to 'broaden his horizons.' I follow him as he journeys further and further and narrate how, now with a wife and five 3rd – culture kids, he navigates through a bewildering world in his search for a future.

I want to share with a diverse audience, Don's vast experiences, opportunities, challenges and frustrations, the costs of his journey to himself, his family and his friends, as well as the remarkable footprints he left behind along the journey. I also unveil the human frailties and the ethical issues that they raise to provide lessons and food for thought to my esteemed readers.

Some of the most memorable moments I had with Don were when he recounted stories of some events and most endearing moments along his journey. These stories are simply hilarious, bewildering, mind-boggling or all three together. I have included twenty-eight (28) of these short stories in the last chapter of this book. Four of these stories are new and unbelievable and were not recounted by Don in his Autobiography. These are *The Ethiopian Letter, Credit History, Declaring His Age,* and *Welli Wegbe For PRO.* Some stories will cause contagious laughter; Some will evoke much pity for Don; others will keep the reader exclaiming "Oh My God!" (OMG), while others will cause one to wonder whether these are true stories. Yes, these stories are all TRUE and reflect the type of terrain Don had to navigate through. More importantly, they reflect the kinds of human behavior and character – the Good, the Bad, and the UGLY, Don had to contend with during his journey that was as epic as that of Jason and the Argonauts in "quest of the Golden Fleece" in Greece in 1300 BC. These 28 stories will undoubtedly be of profound interest especially to the media – radio, TV, and movie industry.

Chapter 2
Growing Up in Mamfe Town:
The Early Years

Mamfe Town in the 1950s

Sarah Ban Breathnach[1] once wrote, "Life is not made up of minutes, hours, days, weeks, months, or years, but of moments. You must experience each one before you can appreciate it." Life in Mamfe town, where Don was born and grew up, was full of moments in the 1950s. Those moments are worth reminiscing about and Don often found himself doing so with much pleasure.

Mamfe Town is where he started his journey. In the 1950s, it was the headquarters of Mamfe Division of the Southern Cameroons, a trust territory administered along with Nigeria by the British colonial powers. Sitting at the junction of three major road arteries, it enjoyed a lot of road traffic from Kumba and Victoria in the south, Bamenda in the north, and from Nigeria in the west. It was thus a very lively town in the 1950s, in fact, much more than it is now in the 2000s.

Don remembers in particular, Tuesdays, Thursdays, and Saturdays, when mammy wagons and other passenger vehicles and trucks arrived from Bamenda and Kumba and from Onitsha via Enugu, Abakaliki, and Ikom in Nigeria. The town bustled with activity. As each vehicle blared its horn on arriving at Main Street, onlookers and bystanders would let out shouts of 'No Condition Is Permanent' or 'God's Case, No Appeal' or whatever name was written on the vehicle. These vehicles all had very philosophical names.

Don was always elated, going round in the evenings, reading these names as the vehicles lined up along Main Street, unloading and preparing for the next day's journey. There they were: No Condition Is Permanent; God's Case, No Appeal; Watch and Pray; God's Time Is the Best, which all plied the

Nigeria-Cameroon route, and Mandu[2] (Little by Little), Semoh Sengoh (Let's Try and See), Mandem Achi (God Is Great), and Save Me O God (S.M.O.G), which arrived from Kumba and Bamenda.

Because the roads were not wide enough for traffic to go both ways conveniently and safely to and from Mamfe to Kumba and Bamenda, it had been decided that on certain days of the week, traffic would go one way, and on other days, it would go the other way. So there came into being days known as 'Mamfe come down' and 'Mamfe go up' when traffic came to Mamfe or went to Kumba and Bamenda respectively.

On those days in the 50s, Mamfe town usually came alive as from four o'clock in the afternoon, when the passenger lorries started arriving from Nigeria and from Kumba and Bamenda. Women would be selling food in roadside canteens, boys and girls hawking various wares, and truck pushers and 'bambe' boys (porters) fighting to carry passengers' luggage to their homes. The hustle and bustle always continued right into the night under moonlight or candlelight or light from dozens of kerosene lanterns.

Sitting also on the banks of the Cross River that straddles the border between South-western Cameroon and Southeastern Nigeria, Mamfe town enjoyed the status of an important river port in the 1950s. During the rainy season, the Cross River became another hub of activities, in fact, a lifeline in Mamfe town. During this season, the river overflowed its banks and became a very important trading route between Calabar in Nigeria and Mamfe town. This was the season when the two mini river ports in Mamfe town came to life with activity as small ships brought cargo from Europe via Nigeria to supply the warehouses of the United Africa Company (UAC) and the John Holt Co. Ltd. As each ship approached the town but was still miles away, it would blow its horn to announce its impending arrival.

Almost immediately, Mamfe town would be overwhelmed by an almost contagious excitement—an excitement deriving from the knowledge that the arrival of the ships heralded a small economic boom for the town and its people: small new jobs would be created, people would make some quick money, new supplies of consumer goods would arrive from abroad, and there would be more eating and drinking and happy times. In a twinkle of an eye, the whole town had drifted to the UAC harbor which was called 'UAC beach' where the UAC premises and warehouses were located. As the ships approached the harbor and their names could be read, shouts of *A.A. Cawan*[3] or *James Frettin* would rise from the excited crowds. Many of the people who rushed there came for work, but many came just to marvel at such 'gigantic canoes' that came to those waters only *at the height of the rainy season.*

A lot of people, however, came to watch the flurry of activities that would follow. These included lighters (rafters containing goods) being towed to the shore, names of overseers and headmen who had many days earlier been recruited as supervisors being called; porters being recruited, and the main work of off-loading cargo from the ships to the warehouses getting underway. This cargo included bags of salt, building materials (cement, corrugated iron sheets, etc.), household/consumer goods, bales of cloth, fuel, etc. Those activities would continue right into the night, under the supervision and watchful eyes of Mr. S. A. Akpey, a Ghanaian businessman who had settled in Mamfe.

After days of unloading the goods destined for the UAC warehouses, the ships would steam a mile up the river to a second port/harbor called John Holt beach, which housed the warehouses of the John Holt Company Ltd., to deliver its own supplies. Similar activities would take place there for the next week or two, after which the ships would set sail back to Calabar and on to the United Kingdom, carrying the country's exports of cocoa, coffee, timber, palm oil and palm kernels, etc.

The Cross River was not only a transport route. With its four beaches, the UAC, Otto-bonne, John Holt, and the D.O beaches, about a mile apart from each other, it was the lifeline of the inhabitants of Mamfe town. Afikpo men (Nigerian nationals from Afikpo) resident in Mamfe made their living fishing and selling fresh and smoked fish caught in the Cross River. The inhabitants of Mamfe bathed and swam there, washed their clothes there, carried out some fishing there, sometimes defecated along the banks, and carried their drinking water from there. During weekends in particular, the John Holt beach was like a picnic ground. And as the river flowed from the D.O Beach downward through the John Holt, Ottoborne, and UAC beaches and onward toward Calabar, so did it carry all the pollution from bathing, laundry, and defecation through these beaches. And it was this river that was the main, if not the only source of drinking water, except in the rainy season, in those days.

It is a miracle that the inhabitants did not die in the hundreds of typhoid, diarrhea, cholera, and other water-borne diseases from drinking contaminated water! It is probable that after decades of drinking from this river, they must have acquired immunity from these diseases.

This was the town where Don's mother had brought him as a little boy many years earlier from Besongabang village, her home village some four miles from Mamfe town, to rejoin her husband, Don's father after their long stay there. It is the town where he was born and grew up. He remembers Mamfe town and most of what went on there in the early 1950s because he was a part of this milieu at an early age. He remembers the days of 'Mamfe come down' and 'Mamfe go up'; He remembers the names of the passenger vehicles which plied the routes. Their bodies were built of wood and attached to the chassis, and they had names which were boldly written above the windscreens.

Most days when Main Street was a beehive of activities, when food sellers sold food by the roadside, when vendors hawked their wares, when music blared from loudspeakers from roadside shops and porters with head loads struggled for rite of passage through the "choked" street, he was part of it all. He hawked cigarettes. The popular brands in those days were 'Bicycle' and 'Craven A.' And he did portering, carrying passengers' luggage. When the ships arrived, he was also there; he carried small bags of salt from the 'lighters' to the UAC and the John Holt warehouses to earn a few pennies. For young active boys, hawking little wares and portering were lucrative jobs. They earned a few pennies which could buy a plate of rice and stew at school during lunch break—rice and stew, which, in those days, they were privileged to eat only at Christmas. And he washed clothes, and swam in, and fetched drinking water from the Cross River at the John Holt and Ottoborne beaches. So he was there in the good old days of Mamfe town.

A Conversation with His Mother

Yes, Mamfe town was the town to which Don's mother, Ma Rose Ayuk-ebet had brought him after her long stay in Besongabang, her paternal and his father's maternal village. He must have been about two or three years old. He remembers the day when his mother had told him her story, why she had to return to Small Mamfe sooner than she had anticipated. His father, Ta Ako-Aragbor, had left her with his maternal people in Besongabang village to rest and recuperate for some time after she had given birth to Don, but he visited them regularly in Besongabang.

29

At the time Don was born, he was establishing himself in his father's compound and farmlands in Small Mamfe, the part of Mamfe town owned and inhabited by the natives, which extended from the John Holt Road/Main Street roundabout to the boundary with Egbekaw village. He had just recently returned home after an extended period of duty in Nigeria.

According to Don's mother, he was always sick and frail right from the time he was brought to Besongabang village, and she always feared he would die. She had every reason to believe so. "You better return to Mamfe before some village people kill your child," some people had advised his mother, so she had recounted to Don during one of their conversations much later in life.

"Why would some village people want to kill me?" he had asked.

"It's a long story." His mother sighed.

"Then let me hear it, tell me," he responded, adjusting his stool to face her more directly as they sat in the sitting room of her house.

She cleared her throat and began. "You think you are my first child. You are not," she said with much difficulty, and a sad shadow crossed her face.

"What!" Don exclaimed, having known and believed all his life that he was her first child.

"You are not my first child—"

"Wait a minute," Don cut in, wondering whether he heard her well. "Did you say I am not your first child?"

"Yes. Neither are you the second, nor third—"

"What?" He jumped up, surprised. "I am not even the third? What are you saying, Mama?"

Covering her face and heaving a big sigh of anguish, she broke down, almost sobbing. "You are not even the fourth nor fifth nor sixth."

For a long while, Don could not talk. He just stared at her with his mouth wide open. "So if I am not the fourth nor the fifth nor the sixth, then I am what?" he asked, still in shock.

"You are, in fact, my seventh child," she finally said, wiping a tear.

"Then what happened to the other children, my siblings? Where are they?" he asked when he was finally able to recover himself.

"Beautiful children they were. They died," she said slowly. "Each passed away in infancy before the next was born. Some died a few days after birth, some a few months, and one or two a few years after. None survived the age

30

of four or so. Some passed away after a little fever or convulsion in 'bright daylight.' Some died suddenly without even being sick."

Don stared at her, unable to speak for a while.

"My first child, Enowraw, was a plump, handsome, healthy boy whom we gave birth to in Nigeria. He took my complexion but was much lighter, like a white child. He died mysteriously and suddenly one afternoon in broad daylight. I was heartbroken," his mother continued.

"It was believed that all the children were being taken by witchcraft by some witches in the village because they died during times when I was spending time in the village. And they were now after you. You were not sickly after you were born. But you became sickly, thin, fragile, and losing weight when we came to Besongabang. No one could diagnose what was wrong with you. Many people in the village thought that you would go the same way as your six siblings before you. Hence the advice that I should leave Besongabang and take you to your father's village where the evildoers will not be able to see or reach you. So I took you to Mamfe to rejoin your father," his mother finished.

Don was stunned, dumfounded. "And did you believe that people could use witchcraft on me?" he finally asked.

"Whether I believed or not, I would do anything to save your life. In any case, I was to be in the village just for a while. I was also feeling your father's absence and believed it was time I left to join my husband, your father. So I took you and left."

How she continued to have children, hoping that the next will survive, was beyond Don's comprehension. She continued until the seventh baby eventually did survive. And that was him. She must have been a woman of *faith*. Two other siblings came after him and also survived: his sister Eunice Besem (now Mrs. Nzo-nguty) and Brother, James Agbortar (now of late). James was cute but born with a cleft lip, a birth defect that occurs when a baby's lip does not form properly during pregnancy. Because such birth defects had probably not been seen before, baby James was often a source of curious attention wherever his mother took him.

Don remembers the embarrassing questions her fellow women often asked her:

"What kind of child is this?"

"What happened to his mouth?"

Others would just stare at her and the baby and sneer. Many were sympathetic and understanding though. But his mother never got offended. She always smiled and told them proudly he was her baby and that is how God had given him to her. She was proud of him, and she loved him. She was probably happy that her ninth child, now the third alive, had not died like the first six children.

Don believes his mother was a woman of faith because she experienced another major tragedy or happening in her life. This one caused her so much pain and left her blind in one eye for more than half of her lifetime. Early in life, as a young mother, she had gone to the farm to harvest cassava tubers. As she was cutting the cassava stems, one with a pointed end plunged into her right eye. He and his sister, Eunice, were too young then, but they felt the agony and pain she was going through as she cried and groaned every day, especially when the eye was being subjected to all kinds of traditional treatment.

Don recounts that he doesn't remember ever having seen eye drops or any Western medication administered into her eye. Rather, only traditional concoctions of herbs mixed sometimes with pepper were squeezed into the eye three times daily amidst her wailing. It was one of the saddest points in their lives, as they watched helplessly as their mother's eye turned red, shrank, deteriorated, and she eventually lost sight in that right eye. It was really very devastating for her to lose one eye at the prime of her youth.

Left with only one eye, she lived her life still fulfilling her chores and thanking God for his abundant grace. But that period was one of the saddest for both her, his sister and himself, as they struggled to help her with cooking and other household chores during their childhood.

Don's Father

According to family history, Don's father, Joseph Ako-Aragbor Oben, started work as a houseboy to some German colonial administrators in Cameroon at the time when the country was under German rule. Each time the tour of one German 'master' came to an end, he handed his father to his successor, and that went on until the Second World War broke out. However, before the last one left the country, he left a note about his father, and in it, he included his name and the address at which he could be found. He left that note for the benefit of any incoming officer. After the end of the war, when Southern

Cameroon became a trust territory administered by the British, a messenger appeared one day at his father's door with a summons for him to appear at the new administration's office in Mamfe.

The summons was for him to commence work as a steward to the new administrators. This time, he was to serve a British doctor as a steward. Thus, his father started a second tour/service with a number of British officers, which took him from Mamfe, his hometown, to several other stations/towns, including Kumba and Bamenda in Cameroon and to Okigwi and other towns in Nigeria. The last of them was one Dr. Wilson, a medical doctor.

Don's father could not read or write when he started serving those Europeans. Early in his service, when his master realized that he was illiterate, he admonished him and advised him to go to school during the months when he was away on leave in England. His father therefore enrolled himself in primary school each time his master was away and returned to work when he came back from home leave. That went on until his father had a total of three years of primary school education, i.e., he had reached standard 1 before he stopped. By that time, he could read and write, but by the time Don grew up and knew him, they thought he had finished primary school, judging from the way he read, wrote, and spoke English and kept his records.

According to him, he got much of his education also from reading and through his interactions with others in the performance of his duties. In fact, in the evenings, he told them stories and fairy tales like Cinderella, Little Red Riding Hood, Rumpelstiltskin, etc., and sang nursery rhymes such as 'Humpty Dumpty'. These are fairy tales and rhymes which their own children were to learn in nursery schools in the 1970s and 1980s! That was amazing and demonstrates how well-read he was in the 1950s when most of his peers were illiterates.

The end of Don's father's service came when his latest master at the time, Dr. Wilson, whom he liked very much and who really loved him, retired and returned finally to Britain. His father also decided it was time he too retired and returned to Cameroon. They were in Nigeria at the time. So he was discharged and given a certificate exempting him from paying tax when he returned to Cameroon. And he never paid any tax. Don was not born then.

By the time Don became aware of his environment several years after his father retired and relocated to Small Mamfe, he found himself growing up in a large compound in Small Mamfe that consisted of a big front house occupied by tenants, his father's house, and a long rectangular thatched house housing five women—his father's widowed sister, Aunty Susanah Ebai-nso, and his four wives: Ma Alice Takor (the first wife), Mama Rose Ayuk-ebet (Don's mother, his second wife), Ma Alice Ayuk Mbuoh (his third wife), and Mama Manyi (the fourth). He later married a fifth wife, a much younger woman called Nancy, who didn't last long in the marriage. Aunty Susanah had five children, Ma Alice Takor and Don's mother had three children each while Mama Manyi and Ma Alice Ayuk Mbuoh each had two children. One of his wives had died when Don was still a child, leaving behind a son, Nathaniel. Ma Nancy had one child, a son called Ojong.

Altogether, Don's father had about twelve children when he was growing up.[4] His sister's children were like his children, and they all grew up together like brothers and sisters. In fact, it was much later when they were teens that they came to realize that Aunty Susanah was their father's sister and not one of his wives and that her children were their cousins. But that did not change anything. Except for those children who were in attendance in colleges outside Mamfe, each child stayed with his or her mother. Ma Alice Ayuk Mbuoh had brought with her three young children from her previous marriage and her younger brother, Victor. Ma Manyi had also brought with her two children from her previous marriage. So they must have been more than fifteen children living together in the compound as one large family at any one time.

They regarded their aunty and all their father's wives as their mothers, and all his children and their mothers' nephews and nieces who had come to live with them as their brothers and sisters. Likewise, he loved and treated all his children, nieces, and nephews as his children. His sister, Aunty Susana, was his confidante. He sought her advice on most issues on his mind. I shall return to Don's father later.

Below left, Don's father. *Below right,* Don's father, Don, and his mother.

Below left, Don's mother in her youth and his mother in later years *(right).*

Chapter 3
Preparing for the Journey

Don's Years in Primary School in Mamfe

Don's early recollection of school was when he was about seven years old and in infant 2, the second year in primary school in the Government School Mamfe. It is from that time that he recollects the events in his life. He remembers they had a little white boy of his age in their class, something which was very rare in those days. He was probably the son of the expatriate doctor. While they wore green khaki shorts and white shirts and no shoes, he was always dressed in black shorts, white short-sleeved shirt and tie, and black shoes with white socks. He was chauffeur-driven to school in a black car every day.

At 10:00 every morning, while they were on short break, the same car would arrive with a steward and any child still in the classroom would be sent out; a table would be laid out, covered with a small white tablecloth, and the boy would quietly and gently have tea and a sandwich while the steward stood in attendance and the driver waited in the car. The rest of them would climb on top of the short classroom walls to watch in amazement at the dignified **manner** in which he ate his sandwich and drank his tea and wondered whether what he ate was enough to satisfy a hungry boy.

Afterward, when he joined them in the playground after his tea, they would bombard him with questions regarding what food it was that he always ate, and at the slightest opportunity, they would not hesitate to give him some knocks on the head for being so privileged and 'selfish'. At closing time, the same car would come to pick him up while they marched home barefooted. His stay in the school was very short, for they never saw him again after sometime.

Don was funny as a little boy. He could dance and make people laugh. The teachers probably took notice of that because he was always given acting roles that would make him cause laughter. In those days, the school always put up some entertainment for the public at the end of term or end of year, which involved singing and acting. Pupils were selected or volunteered to take part in those performances. In one of those plays, Don was made to act the part of an akara seller (bean cake seller). He would lay down my wares by the roadside or at the market place and dance some funny gigs to attract buyers. People would gather and clap and laugh their lungs out. Such scenes were hilarious. However, as he grew older, he stopped being funny.

Don learned to draw early in primary school. He would rather say it was a natural gift because he was never taught pencil drawing. By the time he got to standard 1 and standard 2, he was good at drawing. He spent a lot of his spare time with a classmate, Thomas Ako-njang, drawing pictures of boxers like Hogan Bassey, the British featherweight boxing champion at the time; pictures of cars; animals, trees, houses, etc. In fact, in standard 2, his class teacher, Mr. Nyukechen, one morning during the time for manual labor, gave Don a large cardboard paper to draw a human skeleton from a biology book. Any student of biology knows how complicated and difficult a human skeleton is, and for a nine-year-old to be asked to produce an enlarged drawing of a human skeleton from a small photograph was not funny. However, he produced what seemed like a masterpiece to the delight of the whole school because the picture was hung on the classroom wall for teaching purposes.

But Don was not aware that he wasn't an academically bright child in his early years in primary school. It was not until he was sent from standard 2 to standard 3 on 'trial' at the end-of-year exams in 1952 that that became a big issue. Had he not been doing well? Why did he not know before then that he was not doing well in school? In those days, promotional exams were held at the end of the school year, and the results were read on the last day of school in a general assembly and in full view of all the teachers and pupils. The results were written on special examination results registers kept by each class teacher.

Beginning with infant 1 right up to standard 6, each teacher would step forward when it was his or her turn, and read the class results amidst thunderous shouting and clapping for those who did well. After the names of those who passed were read, the names of those who were sent on 'trial', if any, were then read. Those who did not hear their names were considered to have failed.

Don remembers that morning in December 1952 very vividly. When it was the turn of the standard 2 results to be read, Mr. Nyukechen stepped forward. Don's name was not among those who passed. He gasped for breath and covered his face with his hands. Then the teacher cleared his throat and said that he was sending one boy on 'trial' to standard 3. His name is Oben Oben (that was how Don was called in primary school). In those days, a pupil was sent on 'trial' to the next class if he/she failed the promotional exams but there was a probability that he/she could improve if given a chance to proceed to the next class. So, the child was promoted with the proviso that if he/she did not show any marked improvement in the next class, he/she would be sent back to his previous class after the first term.

Hell broke loose when Don got home and his father heard that he had been sent to the next class on 'trial'. According to his father, education is the foundation on which every child must build his or her life—if not other children, his own. So, the greatest irresponsibility a child could show is not being academically bright. Don was to learn in later years that the surest way to his father's heart was to be a bright student. In fact, to his father, being brilliant was not just passing exams but being at the top. He felt Don was sent to standard 3 on 'trial' out of pity and that was a disgrace. For putting himself in a situation to be pitied, he declared he would not pay Don's school fees anymore. He had better things to do with his money than waste it on a dull boy.

When Don broke the news to his mother that Papa was not going to pay his fees any longer, she told him not to worry. "Why should I not worry?" Don asked his mother. "How am I going to pay my fees if Papa is not going to give me money?" he continued, quite upset.

"I have cassava in my farms. We will make gari and sell. We can also sell some tubers. I can make plantains and koki (beans pudding) and you will hawk it in the market and on Main Street during 'Mamfe come down'. We will get enough money to pay your fees if only you will do what is required, which I know you will," his mother consoled him. She was not going to let her first surviving child drop out of school because of fees.

And so they planned. During the Christmas holiday, she made gari and they sold it. They also harvested and sold cassava tubers in the Saturday markets. He also hawked plantains and koki. By January 1953, they had made enough money to pay Don's first term's fees.

In standard 3, Don underwent a transformation which he himself could not understand or explain. School suddenly started to make sense. He became aware of his presence in class. He started to enjoy the mental arithmetic tests which were administered first thing every morning. He particularly loved history, Roman and Greek history—Leonidas, Alfred the Great, Julius Caesar, Constantinople, the 300 Spartans—as well as John Bunyan, John Wesley, the Quakers of America, etc. His teacher felt his presence in class; everyone felt his presence. He was alive! He couldn't explain the source of the sudden transformation. Had he just matured?

In April of that year after they had taken the first term's exam and before the results were announced, Mr. Nyukechen, who had sent Don on 'trial', called him to his class, sat him down, and after looking long with half-closed eyes, asked him how he found standard 3 classes. Don hadn't the faintest idea why he was asking that question. He simply shrugged his shoulders. When it was the turn of Mr. J. A. Akhimien, Don's class teacher and a Nigerian from the Midwest state to read his class results at the school assembly the following day, he read, "The third out of thirty pupils is Oben Oben…"

"This is the kind of performance I expect from my children," Don's father complimented and said he would start to pay his fees again. But Don's love and gratitude went to his mother. Without her determination and effort, he probably might have dropped out of school.

Either his father was too difficult to satisfy or he thought that his children just had to be brilliant. When in the following term Don took the second position and expected even more compliments from him, he just said, "Well done." But later in the evening when Don had brought him a hot kettle of boiling water for his tea, he asked him to sit down. Then as he was making his tea, he looked at Don with a smile and asked, "The boy who came first in your class, I think he has two heads or is it two horns that he has growing out of his head?"

"Why do you think so?" Don asked, rather amused by what his father had just said. "Of course, he is an ordinary boy, just like me. Papa, how can he have two heads or two horns growing out of—"

"Then if he is an ordinary boy just like you, why should you allow him take the first position and you take the second?" he cut in.

From standard 3 until Don finished primary school, he always took the second or third position in class except for one term in standard 5 when he was seventh. But try as he may, he could never come first. One exceptionally bright Nigerian classmate and his friend, Sunday Egozi, monopolized that position until he left at the end of standard 5. Don was later in life to learn that he went on to become a medical doctor in the Cross River State of Nigeria, owning a private clinic in Calabar.

Given his own experience during his work and travels in Nigeria, Don's father tried to instill in his children the importance of education and the need to attain the highest possible level in whatever field they chose. He could never compromise education and hard work. Thus, Don and his other siblings, including his aunt's children, were brought up together to appreciate the value of education and hard work as well as honesty. All of them, both boys and girls, had to learn to do all tasks, and all tasks were considered gender-neutral. So all of them learned to cook, clean the compound, wash their clothes, fetch water from the river, work on the farm, harvest and sell crops, take care of their younger siblings, etc.

Their father tried to provide them with their school needs. They would pay their fees by dehusking and selling coconuts. Their father had planted coconut trees all over the large compound, and these were already producing coconuts when they were in primary school. So when the time for paying fees came, he would get somebody to climb and harvest all the dry coconuts, after which he would share them among all the school-age children according to the amount of fees each of them had to pay. As far as he was concerned, he had paid their fees after sharing out the coconuts. Each child (boy or girl), was then responsible for dehusking and hawking his or her coconuts in the market on market days or in the evenings along Main Street. The proceeds from the sales were thus used to pay his/her school fees and buy his/her school supplies, including exercise books, pens, readers, etc.

Their father provided them with uniforms—two blue dresses with white bands round the neck and arms for each girl-child, and two pairs of green khaki shorts and two white short-sleeved shirts for each boy-child. School children didn't wear shoes in those days, and so none were provided. Similarly, their father did not consider any clothes apart from uniforms as a necessity. So if they needed shoes and such clothes, it was their responsibility or that of their mothers. Their mothers thought differently. Through the sale of cassava and other foodstuffs which the children helped them to harvest from their farms, they were often able to provide them with these other clothes and an occasional pair of shoes at Christmas.

Their uniforms were always sewn by Mr. J. B. Ajagbor, a Nigerian who was their father's tenant and who occupied more than half of the big house he gave out on rent. Don remembers he was from the small town of Apiapun in the former Cross River State. Don knew it because he was a friend to Mr. Ajagbor's wife's brother, Egbara, who was also Don's age.

Mr. Ajagbor's billboard by the road side on Main Street carried the inscription, 'Mr. J. B. Ajagbor, Lagos Trained Master Tailor'. His workshop was always crowded with apprentices, customers, and orders. He seemed to have specialized in European wear and he sew the latest fashion suits, shirts, trousers, etc. The elite and anybody who was somebody had to come to him for his services. And Don and his siblings were privileged to have his services because their father was his landlord. All they did was to go to his shop and have their measurements taken after their father must have bought the material and given to him. They had no voice in choosing the style for their uniforms. He would not even listen to them. His contract was with their father, and he was always too busy.

Mr. Ajagbor was not only an expert tailor, he was also an expert ballroom dancer. That was quite surprising for a tailor because, not only could he dance, but he was also organizing dancing classes for senior civil servants and undergraduates from the university of Ibadan. On the days when he held his classes, which often were on late afternoon on Saturdays, Don and some other children would stand below and watch him as he taught his students the various steps on the large rectangular verandah at the back of the big house. With the right hand on his chest and the left hand stretched out at almost forty-five degrees, he would say, "Slow, slow, quick, quick, slow. Slow, quick, quick, slow," as he moved briskly across the floor. And then he would engage a man or woman, and they would jump or skip and swing and run around the floor together in unison.

Don and his friends saw him teach different dances, which he called the waltz, quick step, foxtrot, and cha-cha-cha with music coming from what he called a gramophone. Each dance had a different style, a different tempo. Don remembers some of his students. There was his eldest brother, Njang Ako Oben, from the University College, Ibadan, and his sister Janet from Queen's School Ede, Lagos, and their friends, Mr. S. E. Eyong and Mr. S. E.

Takunchung. It was amazing. He marveled how two people could dance together, running and jumping and swinging in such a synchronized manner. He was simply blown away and it made an impression on him. And he never missed being around to watch them each time they practiced.

After Mr. Ajagbor and his students had practiced and left, they, in the manner of children, would go up to the dance floor and try to imitate what they had watched them do. "Slow, slow, quick, quick, slow." they would mimic until someone would come and drive them away. Little did Don know that he would, in later years, dance in ballroom circles around the world. Looking back now, he realizes that they were barely just doing the basics.

After Mr. Ajagbor returned to Nigeria, their father rented the house to one Mr. Benebo from what is now the Rivers State of Nigeria and who was posted to Mamfe to work in the Public Works Department (PWD). Don remembers him quite well because his first child, a boy about his age named Tari, became his friend. Mr. Benebo had two wives and two children. Don remembers that when he was promoted to senior service, he bought a small, nice car. There was much celebration. He was later allocated a house at the PWD quarters at Besongabang Road, and he moved out of their father's house. Then the house was rented to one Mr. Njoku, a nurse, who had just been transferred from Eastern Nigeria to work in the general hospital in Mamfe. One of his little sons, Chima, and Don soon became friends. Mr. Njoku was an Ibo from Owerri-nta.

At the time Mr. Ajagbor was renting the larger part of the big house, another tenant was renting the smaller apartment at the other end of the house. He was Mr. Obians (full name Obianime), a photographer. He was from Okrika in the Rivers State of Nigeria. He lived in the house with his young wife and his younger brother, David Obianime who was attending the Roman Catholic School in Mamfe Town. He and Don were good friends.

Mr. Obians stayed in the house until the late 1950s/early 1960s and became quite famous in Mamfe. His billboard by the roadside read, "Obians Photo Studios, P.O. Box Mamfe." And below in smaller letters was written: "Ensure Your Shadow Ere It Fades." Everybody in Mamfe Town knew him and anybody who wanted their photograph taken went to him. He was most popular with students from the Queen of the Rosary College, (QRC), Okoyong, Mamfe. He also took most of the school's official photographs.

In those days, the cameras were mounted on a tall tripod stand, and to take a photograph, Mr. Obians would cover his head and the camera with a piece of cloth which was red on one side and black on the other side, adjust the aperture of the camera, come out, see that the person or persons are well positioned, apply a little talcum powder on their faces if necessary, ask them to smile, and then click to take the picture. To take the photograph of a dead person at a funeral was a whole ceremony. Mr. Obians would perform all kinds of gymnastics, including trying his tripod in several positions, staring intently at the corpse and wiping his face and eyes several times with his hands to give the impression that the powerful wandering spirit of the dead person had to be pacified or forcefully overcome, for the corpse to be photographed. And because he had to 'capture' the spirit of the dead to be able to photograph it, taking the photograph of a corpse attracted a higher fee. Like Mr. Ajagbor, he too had a gramophone.

This gramophone was a center of attraction at the time when Don and David, Mr. Obian's brother were growing up and went to college. During the holidays in Mamfe, David and Egbara (Mr. Ajagbor's wife's teen brother whom they had left behind as an apprentice to Mr. Obians), would operate the gramophone any moment that Mr. Obians was out on assignment. They would play the latest highlife and Congo music of that era and the 'privileged Trio', together with a few of their friends would dance in the small living room ('parlor' as it was called in those days) while the 'ordinary' boys and girls would crowd at the two small windows just to have a glimpse of the gramophone and wonder how such a contrivance could produce such music. They would marvel at the whole 'ceremony' involved in playing a record on the gramophone to make it produce music.

Above photo, **the big house (recently painted) Don's father rented out.**
Built in the 1930s of burnt bricks baked in a kilns he constructed himself.
No iron rods were used.

Another tenant who stayed in the big old house was one Mr. Ako-achare, a tall dark gentleman of the same tribe as Don's father. He was a civil servant. Don remembers him because his wife, Mama Clara, used to bake bread and they had two children—Besong, a boy, and Diana, a girl. Baking bread was quite a novelty in those days so on the days Mrs. Ako-achare did her baking, the small boys often gathered around to watch as she kneaded the bread dough, allowed it to rise after being left to stand for a while, and then baked it in a small 'mud' oven. Three sides of the oven (the left, right and back) sides were made of mud; the top was made of metal on which a small wood fire provides the heat that baked the bread; and the front was the door through which the bread dough was shoved into the oven in small aluminum containers. This 'mud' oven was later replaced by an iron oven which looked like a stove. Quite often Mama Clara would share some small loaves among the boys and occasionally send some to the women.

Coming back to Don's father, a second character which he hated in a child after academic dullness was laziness. Their daily routine left Don and the other children with practically no time for play. In the mornings, they had to go to the stream or river to fetch water, eat, and go to school. After school, they had to follow their mothers to their farms, which were some two miles from town, to weed, harvest cassava or yams or cocoyams and cut and carry home fire wood or any of the harvested crops. Arriving home late in the evenings, they would help their mothers with cooking. On weekends, when the boys did not go to their father's farms, they would go with their mothers to do the weeding,

44

clearing, or the planting or harvesting of crops. When they were on vacation, they would accompany them to their farms to harvest crops and vegetables to be sold in the market on market day, which was usually a Saturday.

However, on most weekends, the boys would go with their father to his farms to tend his cocoa nursery, carry seedlings from the nursery to plant in the field, clear and burn secondary bush, or cut thatches for roofing. Don remembers that on one or two occasions, his father sent his three older brothers (Nathaniel, Amos, Lawrence) and himself, to Ntenako village during the dry season, to assist her other sister, Mama Lydia Agborta by clearing and burning her farmlands and getting them ready for cultivation. Sometimes, when they were free, they would go line fishing for tilapia and mudfish in the Baku stream that straddles Mamfe town and Besongabang village, using a string tied to a small rod and a hook to which they attached an earthworm as bait. The fishing expedition usually lasted the whole day, and they fished along the width and breadth of the stream, often returning home with their small gourds or tin cans full of fish slung over their shoulders.

Their father was a workaholic. After his retirement, he devoted much of his time clearing virgin bush each year. Some of that land he allocated to his wives to burn and cultivate while he established cocoa and coffee farms on the rest. Since in those days, farmers hardly used fertilizers and depended on the bush fallow system as a way of conserving the fertility of the soil, their father had to continuously search for and clear new virgin forests in order to establish new farms while the older farms lay fallow to recuperate.

"Look at him, he traveled with Europeans everywhere serving them and here he is, going to the bush every morning," his illiterate peers would say with a sneer to his hearing, whenever they saw him going to his farms and they were drinking palm wine in a way side bar, which they did often.

Thus, within a decade and half of his retirement, he had acquired much land and established several farms in Baku and Bakarem, near the village of Besongabang and in Enow-anyen and Mile One on the way to Okoyong Village. In fact, many years later, when government wanted to build a federal government bilingual secondary school in Mamfe and needed land for that purpose, their father obliged by ceding several acres of his farmlands for the construction of the school. An account of this is provided in Appendix 2. It is an eyewitness account provided by one of Don's younger brothers, Joseph Ako Oben Jr.[5] named after their father.

By the time they were growing up in the fifties, their father and their mothers had many farms So accompanying their parents to work on the farms and carrying firewood home became a tradition, and they went to the farm almost every day after school and on Saturdays. They never got too big to go to work on the farm or carry firewood for their mothers, not even when they went to university, and not even when they had to pass along main Street in full view of the public!

Don's father's motivation for ceding such a vast area of his farmlands for the building of the school was not just because he had much land. It was because of the importance he accorded to education and his understanding of the relationship between education and the socioeconomic development of the community. Unlike most of his peers, he knew what the town of Mamfe and its people stood to gain by having such a school located there. In fact, the vision which he provided his children and which centered on education, hard work, and honesty provided the underpinnings for their academic excellence and illustrious careers later in life. It made them stand out from the children of their generation. And they have in turn passed this vision and tradition to their own children.

During weekdays, after returning from the farms late in the evenings and helping to prepare and eat dinner, all the children were expected to light their oil lamps and do their homework or read their books outside and on the steps of the big house. Don hated reading after school hours, especially in the evenings. He hated homework too. So he always got angry when he saw his brothers and sisters out there reading because he knew that their father would shortly come around to find out who was not present. Don was hardly there. His father noted it and never found it funny. Don would normally be found, after 7:00 p.m. in front of Royal Bar, dancing to the tune of Ghanaian and Nigerian highlife music with another boy, George Eyong, who also loved to dance.

The Royal Bar was at the time, one of two hottest spots in Mamfe town located just a stone's throw away from their compound in Small Mamfe. It was owned by the Ghanaian businessman, Mr. S.A. Akpey, whom I mentioned earlier in this chapter in connection with the UAC activities at the beach. The other was the West End Bar located at Besongabang Road and owned by Mr. Eyo, a Nigerian businessman from the Cross River State. Royal Bar was run by a young, beautiful Nigerian manageress/waitress from Calabar. It always opened promptly at 7:00 p.m. in the evenings and played some of the latest highlife music of the fifties by Dance Bands of the likes of Black Beats, Broadway, Uhuru, E.T. Mensah (all of Ghana), and Victor Olaiya, the evil genius of highlife music, a Nigerian. The music by those music giants was played on the gramophone.

At such a tender age, Don had developed an intense love for music and dancing, and he would dance until he saw the doors of the bar being shut, which was usually around midnight. Then he would walk back into their sleepy compound, quietly open the door of his mother's house to avoid it making any squeaking noise, and then slip in. He would just fall on his bed with his dusty feet and without changing clothes and fall asleep. He didn't have to change clothes anyway because they didn't have any special clothes for sleeping, and the bed was just a mud bed covered with a mat. So there was no fear of his dusty feet browning the bed!

If Don was not dancing outside Royal Bar, then he would be at Main Street or at the Motor Park, especially on those days when passenger vehicles converged on Mamfe town. He would be jostling with truck pushers, food vendors, and the likes for right of way, as he hawked cigarettes and did portering to earn a few pennies for rice and stew at school, or hawked his mother's koki and plantains or some other foodstuff.

About once a month, Mamfe town was always privileged to host a grand ballroom dance at the Appeal Court Hall animated by a visiting brass band. Don always looked forward to those big ballroom nights. Weeks before the event, advertising notices would go out on public notice boards, on walls of houses, and on tree trunks all over town:

DANCE DANCE DANCE

WHERE:	Appeal Court Hall
DATE:	
TIME:	8:30 p.m. till dawn
GATE FEES:	
Couples:	
Single Ladies:	Free

COME ONE, COME ALL!

Don was always on the lookout for the arrival of the band and therefore, was always at the edge of the town when it arrived. The band would then parade around the town in an open van carrying the musicians and organizers, playing loudly to herald its arrival while he and other young boys and ordinary folks danced ahead of it. That was how the town received confirmation that the long-awaited orchestra had finally arrived, and the ball would take place as advertised.

The ballroom dances were usually for the elite of the town, the top civil servants and university undergraduates, if they happened to be in town. They would arrive at the Appeal Court Hall which had been fenced round with palm fronds, in their tuxedos or long coats and bow ties while the ladies wore long, flowing dresses and jewelry and high heel shoes. Yes, the dress had to be formal, for the music was usually mostly classical, European. Mr. S.E. Takunchung in his bow tie was almost always the master of ceremony. They would dance and swing all night while Don and the ruffians did their dancing outside, closely watched by the police. That did not, however, stop the hooligans from throwing stones on the roof of the building to disrupt the proceedings inside.

Mamfe Town was really cosmopolitan. There were a few Europeans and a large population of Nigerians. There were also many people from other parts of Southern Cameroons and even from French Cameroon (Republique du Cameroun). In fact, certain quarters/neighborhoods in Mamfe town were known by the predominant ethnic groups that lived there. Thus there were, and still are, quarters known as: Banso Quarter, Yaounde Quarter, Hausa Quarter, Mgboko/Ibo Quarter, Banya, etc. where people from Banso, Yaounde, Northern Nigeria, Eastern Nigeria, Banya respectively lived.

The Europeans were mainly British administrators. Some of the Nigerians were senior civil servants. The majority, however, were traders, businessmen, transporters, artisans, and fishermen. Many were also teachers. In standard 1, Don was taught by Ms. Afiong Etta. She was followed by Ms. Angelony. In standard 3, he was taught by Mr. J. A. Akhimien; in standard 6 by Mr. G. O. Braide who was also the Headmaster (HM). And before him as the Headmaster was Mr. S. A. Ekwerre. Don remembers that his headmaster's children, Fubara Braide and Sokari Braide and his wife's teen niece, Shifra Wilcox or Wallcox, were also attending government school.

Shifra was like a gazelle. She could run and jump during the Empire Day sports competitions. There was also the headmaster's eldest son, Victor Braide, who came once or twice to Mamfe on holidays from Nigeria. Don learned he was attending Government Secondary School Owerri, one of the three government secondary schools in Eastern Nigeria.

According to Don, the choir master at the Presbyterian church, Mamfe, who led the English choir was Mr. D.D. Obunge, a Nigerian. He was the postmaster as well. In spite of Don's seemingly rascally demeanor, he was a chorister in this choir. Mr. Obunge brought spectacular changes into the choir. He ordered and introduced the now common uniforms—gowns, hoods, and caps from Nigeria—and taught the choir to chant 'Te Deum Laudamus', 'Benedictus', 'Jubilate Deo', the Psalms, and other chants. They sang anthems, and Don or his friend, Sunday Egozi, were always chosen to sing the duets and descants. But they usually sang the 2nd part or Alto with the other young boys. The girls and some women with high-pitched voices sang the first part or treble. Many of the men and a few women sang the 3rd part or tenor while the older men with deep voices sang the 4th part or Bass.

Don remembers when the new church building was finally completed in 1955 after years of fund-raising and was inaugurated. It was a big feast day. That was when they first wore their new, colorful choir uniforms of gowns, hoods, and caps, and they sang out their lungs! Afterward, they took photographs to mark the occasion and ate rice and stew and lots of meat. A cow had been slaughtered for the occasion.

The District Officer (DO) and the Assistant District Officer (ADO) were British while the doctor at the general hospital at one time was Dr. Budman, a Nigerian married to a white woman. There was a chief magistrate who was most likely a Nigerian; an area engineer, whose nationality Don cannot remember; and a young, handsome chemist and druggist (nowadays called a pharmacist) at the general hospital. His death one Sunday afternoon in a fire accident in his office/laboratory, saw so much outpouring of grief as never before seen in the whole town, especially within the Nigerian community.

The exception was the death of S.A. George, the beloved Mamfe politician who died in London. Those senior civil servants lived in the Government Residential Area (GRA), which was adorned with beautiful flowers and well-tended lawns and was a 'no-go' area for nonresidents. Don remembers how, as little boys, he and his group had been chased away by guards with dogs when they had gone with their small masquerade on Christmas and New Year's Day to dance and solicit for money from the residents there. They were not allowed anywhere near.

As already mentioned, Mamfe had two large commercial companies—the United Africa Company (UAC) and the John Holt Co. Ltd. Mamfe also had a Reading Room (akin to a library), a Magistrate Court, a Customary Appeal Court, a General Hospital, two primary schools (Government School and Roman Catholic Mission, RCM School, and the first girls secondary school in the country—Queen of the Rosary College (QRC), Okoyong, located some four miles away in Okoyong village. The town's layout consisted of one main tarred street (Main Street) about two miles long and a number of feeder roads (some of them tarred), radiating from the main street. Into the Main Street, road traffic came from three axis into the town: from Enugu, Abakaliki, Calabar, and Ikom in Nigeria; from Kumba and Victoria (now Limbe) in the south; and from Widekum, Bali, and Bamenda in the north.

Don was to learn many decades later how important and well known Mamfe Town was, from a Nigerian he met in South Africa and who later became a close family friend. He told Don when he came to know that he was from Mamfe, that in the olden days in his village, Oba, near Onitsha, if a person was seen very much in a hurry, he or she would be asked, "why are you so much in a hurry? Are you going to Mamfe in Cameroon?" Don was amazed.

But there was no electricity or potable water supply. The Cross River was the main source of drinking water for the whole town. It also served as a major commercial sea route between Southern Cameroons, Nigeria, and Europe. It had four main beaches: District Office, John Holt, Ottoborne (behind the Mamfe Government School), and the UAC near Egbekaw village. As already discussed earlier in this chapter, the UAC and the John Holt beaches served as river ports where these two companies had their warehouses, offices and shops.

A remarkable aspect of Mamfe Town which made it quite cosmopolitan even at that time, is that the town had a public cemetery, called a burial ground in those days. It was located on the outskirts of the town, on the left-hand side of Besongabang Road upon exiting the town and opposite the Public Works Department. It was well-tended and fenced with flowers and plants. The cemetery was very quiet and solemn. Everyone in town knew when there was going to be a burial at the cemetery. Each time a funeral procession was to take place from the church to the cemetery, it was an important occasion. Death was not common place in those days as it is now. Several decades later, that burial ground has grown into houses and car and motor bike repair shacks! Mamfe does not have a cemetery anymore.

And there was the Empire Day, the celebration every year, of the Queen of England's birthday throughout the British Empire in the month of June. Mamfe, as the divisional headquarters, always hosted that huge event. During the week, schools from the surrounding villages would converge in Mamfe town. Don particularly remembers the school boys coming for the celebrations from Kunku village across the Cross River, having trekked for miles through the forests, arriving at the UAC beach, and marching along Main Street past the government school to wherever they were to be lodged. They were barefooted and thinly clad, carrying their small bundles of clothes and food on their heads or backs in small baskets made of palm fronds. As they marched along, they announced their presence or rather their arrival with their unique song that 'they were the Kunku boys, who had come, for the Empire Day'.

On Empire Day, all the schools would assemble in the football field of the government school; there would be singing of the British anthem, hoisting of the Union Jack (British flag), reading of the Queen's message by the district officer, and then the march past. It was all so colorful! After that came what seemed to the school children at the time, the main event. That was the sports competition among the schools, consisting of athletics (track and field events) and crowned by the football final. In athletics, the track events which schools were made to compete in included the 100, 220, 440, and 880 yards by both senior and junior boys and girls, and the mile race by senior boys. The field events included the high jump, shot put, discus, pole vault and long jump.

There were certain races which made the competition even more interesting but also sometimes more frustrating to the athletes. These races which are no longer seen these days in athletics championships included the sack race, egg and spoon race, thread and needle race, and the three-legged race. The sack and three-legged races were competed for by both boys and girls but the other two races were for girls. In the athletics competition, the school which scored the highest number of points won the competition and was presented the Athletics Shield. In the football competition, the winning school team lifted the Football Shield, a heart-shaped wooden plaque engraved with the names of the previous winners. It was usually a fiercely fought and emotional football final.

Don particularly recalls the final in 1956. It was like a war between Government School Mamfe and Basel Mission School, Besongabang. In addition to the sports competition, Empire Day was a day all school children looked forward to because it was a day of feasting. A cow was usually slaughtered, and Don remembers that they were reminded in school during the week not to forget to bring their 'small containers' to school on Empire Day, to take their share of rice and beef stew home.

The Empire Day celebrations were a constant reminder that Southern Cameroon was a colony, a colony of Great Britain. And so like in other parts of the country, Mamfe town witnessed some political ferment in the 1950s. Many pre-independent political rallies, conventions, and meetings were held in Mamfe by the Kamerun National Convention (KNC) Party and the Kamerun National Democratic Party (KNDP). Don also remembers a huge rally in Mamfe organized by the National Convention of Nigeria and the Cameroons party (NCNC) led by Dr. Nnamdi Azikiwe. Mbonu Ojike and other political stalwarts were all there, including some KNC politicians.

One of the most budding and admired politicians from Mamfe at the time and a member of the KNC was Samson Adeoye George. His death in 1957 in London was a big shock and a great loss to the people of Mamfe, his constituency. It was a sad page in the town's political history. Don remembers the large crowds and the unending queues of sympathizers that came to view his body in his mother's compound besides the Mamfe Reading Room when it was brought from London.

Don's father was quite cosmopolitan by the standards of those days and almost a jack of all trades too. He had traveled widely in Cameroon and Nigeria and lived among people of different cultures, customs, and ways of life. Don and his siblings often marveled at the different things he did. Early on returning to Mamfe, he built a big house with red bricks, which he baked in a kiln he constructed himself. He established his own cocoa nurseries. He developed ingenious ways of preserving kola nuts, bitter kola, and pork meat in the ground. He had a post office mailbox through which he received mail from abroad. And almost every month, a mailman came by the house to deliver a telegram. In those days, urgent messages were sent via telegrams. They were like the express mail services of today.

Don came to learn about telegrams because he was often there when his father received and read them. The messages were in phrases to make them as short as possible as a telegram was charged according to the number of words. His father had explained this to him. Until a telegram was read and its contents known, the arrival of a mailman with a telegram was always a cause of great anxiety and suspense. Don remembers the day a telegram came from his brother, Tom Njang Ako, in Ibadan in 1956, conveying his Bachelor of Science degree exams results. When his father opened and read it, he sent him immediately with it to his fiancée, Regi, and his sister, Janet, who were washing clothes in the stream a short distance from the house. The news could not wait for them to return from the stream.

And Don's father could entertain. By the time Don was growing up, his first two children, Tom and Janet, were at the University College of Ibadan. His father had already anticipated his son's success and was planning a big dinner for him, his fiancée, and his friends. He always offered a dinner each time he or Janet (Don's eldest sister) came home from the university on holiday. Their sister, Theodosia (Aunty Susanah's first daughter), from Queen's College Ede was always with them and so was Regi. It was a lot of work for Don and his siblings—cleaning the compound; scrubbing, washing, and varnishing the furniture and doors; painting the house; re-ironing the linen and tablecloths; washing new glassware, silverware, crockery, and dishes. A pig or a goat and some chickens would be slaughtered and prepared with rice and stew and yams and a variety of vegetables and sauces. And there was wine too. Don's father was an expert at entertaining. That may have derived from his long experience as a steward for European expatriates.

The large sitting room would be transformed into a dining room with shining silverware, glassware, dishes, and crockery that he had brought from Nigeria, well laid out on the large rectangular table covered with white linen and decorated with flowers. There was no electricity, but their father would light two Tilley lamps. They shone like electric lights. Only very few 'aristocrats' owned Tilley lamps at the time. The feasting and dancing would go on all night and would be the talk of the town for weeks after. They, the little ones would be in attendance, as 'waiters' and 'waitresses'.

Don's Years in the Late 1950s

Don sailed easily through standards 3 in 1953, standard 4 in 1954, and standard 5 in 1955 to standard 6 in 1956. By that time, his eldest brother, Tom, and sister, Janet, were at the University College of Ibadan and his sister,

Theodosia, was at Queen's College, Ede in Western Nigeria (which was later moved to Lagos and became known as Queen's College, Lagos). His two brothers, Nathaniel and Lawrence, were in the Basel Mission College, Bali, later renamed the Cameroon Protestant College, Bali. Their father expected every one of his children, on completing primary school, to gain admission into and proceed to a secondary school.

Don was somehow never interested in the stories his brothers told him about Bali College. But he had always listened with rapt attention to the interesting and fascinating stories his father told them about his travels and work in Nigeria. His father could read and write; he had a post office mailbox; he received letters and telegrams; he owned two Tilley lamps, brought a lot of glassware, silverware, cutlery and furniture from Nigeria; and when occasions demanded, he wore suits and ties and he attended court sessions. He instilled in his children the value of education, self-discipline, and hard work. He was a class apart from his peers.

Don was sure his travels had a great impact on his life, his thinking, attitude, and lifestyle. He wanted to have his experiences too as he grew up. He had begun to nurse a love for travel. He wanted to see other places, see other peoples and their cultures, attend school elsewhere, especially another government school. And so, he wanted to enter one of the three government colleges in Eastern Nigeria. He wanted to see the world, broaden his horizons!

But Don was not thinking about his post-primary school future on that evening early in February 1956 when his father called him to assist him in lighting his Tilley lamp. He had not forgotten how, many years earlier when he was a little boy, his father had given him a terrible slap on the face when he had asked him to come watch him light the Tilley lamp. As Don knelt down beside him that day, his father pointed to the mantle, a small cylindrical white hood inside the glass enclosure and told him how it was a material like silk; it was extremely soft and very brittle once first burned and so must be replaced frequently.

He told him that inside the mantle, the gas burns and causes it to glow with a bright white light. He again repeated that the mantle was very brittle and that the one in the Tilley lamp then had been used many times, and anything touching it, however lightly, would cause it to crumble. And once that happens, it could not be used again and would have to be replaced. He then put paraffin into the lamp and pumped it to send the paraffin up to the mantle. Taking a soft piece of cloth, he began cleaning the lamp meticulously while Don looked on with amazement at his expert handling of this contraption. Then without looking at Don, he asked him to touch the mantle, and he *did*, with his right forefinger. The next thing he knew, there was a loud *slap!* and his left cheek almost went numb. It took him some time to realize that his father had given him a big slap on the face.

"Papa, what did I do that you have given me such a big slap?" Don had managed to ask him after recovering himself.

"You little fool!" he answered back, still angry. "Why did you touch the mantle?"

"But you told me to touch it," Don shot back.

"You don't have any sense. I expected you to think. A bright little boy would have said, 'I will not touch it, Papa, because you told me that the mantle was now weak and would crumble with the slightest touch.' Next time you should use your head," he finally said, looking into Don's eyes and gently rubbing his back as if to say sorry. Don got the message.

Just then, as his father called him to come help him light the lamp, Don wondered what he was up to this time. He knelt beside his father and watched as he held the lamp, raised and shook it to make sure there was enough paraffin in it. Then he soaked the preheater torch in methylated spirit and clipped it around the vaporizer stem. Don handed him a match stick from the match box and he lit the preheater and slid it up just below the mantle. As the methylated spirit was burning, his father turned to him.

"You are completing standard 6 at the end of December, which entrance examinations are you registering for, Sasse or Bali or both?"

These were the two colleges for boys in the country at the time, and they were excellent schools. Don, however, did not reply, which made his father repeat the question after turning to see whether the methylated spirit was about burning down.

"Neither," Don replied, not telling him what he had in mind and afraid that he might not approve.

"What do you mean by neither? You mean you do not want to go to college?" he asked, keeping a close eye on the lamp.

"I want to go to college but not to Sasse or Bali. I want to go to Nigeria, to one of the government colleges, either Government Secondary School Owerri or Government College Umuahia," Don said and held his breath, expecting the worst.

Suddenly, his father turned to the lamp. The methylated spirit had almost burned down, so he pumped it, giving it several strokes. He then turned it on, making the mantle light with a gentle 'pop' sound. It had caught fire and was now burning with a slightly yellow light. He gave the pump some more strokes until the mantle right then burned bright white.

Turning back to Don, he broke into a gentle smile. Don wondered whether he smiled because the mantle had held on well and was burning brightly or he was smiling because of his choice of schools.

"So you think that those are schools where boys like you can just walk into freely. If you don't know, those are schools only for the academically privileged, for boys who have a long history of coming first in their class, not those who come second. And you have to take a very competitive common entrance exam followed by an even more competitive interview," he told Don with much authority.

"Papa, I know all that, I—"

He did not let Don finish before he cut in, "No, you don't know anything. The entrance exam to Sasse or Bali is taken by a few hundred students in Cameroon, but the entrance exam to the government colleges is taken by thousands of students in the whole of Nigeria and the Southern Cameroons. And then, you want to leave Sasse some 180 miles and Bali, just 80 miles away to journey to the unknown?"

Don knew when his father was pleased by just judging from his facial expression and his language. He guessed he was privately pleased with his choice of schools even though he did not say so directly. Don felt that his father identified with the grounds on which he made his choice. He was a man who liked challenges, and Don took it that he was trying to put 'fire in his heart and brimstone in his liver', to use the words of Sir Toby Belch in Shakespeare's *Twelfth Night*. He wanted him to understand the magnitude of the challenge before him. He wanted to get Don 'fired up'.

As he wiped the Tilley lamp and took it to put on the lampstand, he asked Don to find out more information regarding the entrance exam for that year from his headmaster, Mr. G.O. Braide, a Nigerian from the Rivers State. Don did. Unfortunately, the date for registration had long passed and completed applications had already been sent to the principals of the respective colleges.

The entrance exam was coming up in March, just a few weeks away as their school year usually began in September and ended in June, unlike the other schools where the school year began in January and ended in December. He was *late*, very late. It meant that he had to wait and apply for and sit the entrance exam in March 1957 and then enter college in September.

Don consoled himself that that would also allow him to complete standard 6 and take his First School Leaving Certificate examination. He decided that he would wait. His father had no objection to his decision. It made sense to complete primary school, get one certificate before embarking on another, provided, of course, that he would succeed in the competitive entrance examination the following year. To make assurance doubly sure that he got into a school, his father advised him to also sit the entrance exams into Sasse and Bali the following year.

Don completed standard 6 in December 1956. He came 2nd in his class in the First School Leaving Certificate examination. He sat the competitive entrance examination into the government colleges in Eastern Nigeria in early March 1957. He selected Government Secondary School Owerri as his first choice and Government College Umuahia as his second choice. He also sat the entrance examination into Sasse College as his father had advised. His father had a post office mailbox, PO Box 4, through which he received his mail. After Don had taken the entrance exam, it became his weekly routine to go check the mailbox for any mail from Owerri. One afternoon, he found a long brown envelope with a stamp, 'Government Secondary School Owerri' on it. He knew it was his results. He did not open it but rushed home and gave it to his father, who opened it. Don had passed and was being called for interview all the way in Owerri in May. His father gave him a congratulatory pat on his back, and Don immediately remembered his father's words, "And you want to journey to the unknown."[6]

Left: a Tilley lamp. Right: a Gramophone Source: *Wikipedia.*

Part 2
The Journey Without a Known Destination

Chapter 4
Starting the Journey and the Search: The Interview at Owerri, Nigeria

Although Don had always dreamed of studying in Owerri, he had really never looked at the map to see its exact location or find out how far it was from Mamfe. There was, however, a big signboard at the post office roundabout indicating distances to some major towns with arrows pointing to the direction of the towns—to Nigeria: Ikom, 61 miles; Calabar, 80 miles, Abakaliki 155 miles, Enugu 207 miles. Now he went in search of a map and tried to trace where a lorry going to Owerri was likely to go through. The highway from Mamfe enters Eastern Nigeria through Ikom then goes northward and then turns westward through Abakaliki, Enugu, and then on to Onitsha. At Onitsha, it turns southeastward to Owerri. He was fourteen years old and had never journeyed out of Mamfe up to that point. By looking up the distances between Enugu and Onitsha and between Onitsha and Owerri, he estimated that Owerri was about 365 miles from Mamfe. His father was right. He was leaving Bali, just 80 miles away, to travel to the unknown, to Owerri, 365 miles away!

They did not have much time left. A week or two later, his father told him that one of his uncles, Uncle Tom Tabi, would take him to Owerri for the interview. They would take one of the mammy wagons plying the Mamfe-Onitsha route. As luck would have it, one of his nephews, Don's cousin, Mr. Ebai Mbiwan, a chartered electrical engineer, was working with Shell BP in Owerri. His father, Pa Maurice Mbiwan, was going to inform him of their coming. They would stay with him.

They left Mamfe one late morning in May in one of the passenger lorries bound for Onitsha. Don remembers it was 'No Condition Is Permanent'. Although he had always seen that and other similar mammy wagons parked along Main Street, he never thought for a moment that someday, he would be traveling as a passenger in one of them. From the look of things, it was going to be a very difficult journey. Only two benches were left for more than fourteen passengers to sit on as the rest of the vehicle was loaded to the ceiling with cargo and secured by a wooden frame separating the cargo section from the small passenger section consisting of two benches. Even the space underneath the benches where the passengers should put their legs was also loaded with luggage. They sat cramped up with their backs to the driver and their knees almost touching their chins.

The road was dusty and bumpy when the weather was dry, but muddy and slippery when it rained. That did not make it obligatory for the driver to drive more slowly and carefully. In those days, drivers who were considered good were those who drove with speed and got to their destinations earliest, no matter the condition of the road. They often held the steering with one hand while the other hand was outside, often waving at other drivers as they drove past or simply resting by the driver's door.

They reached Yahe, a popular village, about ninety miles from Mamfe and before Abakaliki, late in the afternoon. There, lorries usually stopped for passengers to eat and stretch their legs and, if necessary, release the pressure from their bladders or bowels behind the houses or in the bushes. Don had to be carried down from the lorry and supported for a while before he could stand on his feet. He had cramps and blood was hardly flowing down into his limbs. He was layered all over with brown dust. He couldn't eat and just tried to massage his legs, jumping on one leg then the other to get them ready for the longer stretch of the journey to Onitsha. From Abakaliki, the road was much better; and from Enugu, the road was good. It was tarred. They arrived at Onitsha late at night.

Owerri was another sixty-one miles from Onitsha. Since it was too late to continue to Owerri that night, the driver took them to spend the night in his house. He must have known Don's father and their compound in Mamfe, considering the way he hosted them. Whether or not he did, people in those days were kind and helpful to strangers. They arrived Owerri the next day and asked their way to Shell BP and then to his cousin's house.

Cousin Mbiwan welcomed them warmly to his home. It was not every day that he received a relative far away from home, so he was quite delighted to receive them and hear news from home. Robert, his brother, Manyi, his sister, and Martin, a cousin, were living with him when they made their trip.

Accommodation was arranged for them with the boys in their quarters. They had arrived at Owerri on the eve of the interview.

Don, along with the crowd of boys who came for the interview, were ushered into the school's Assembly Hall on the morning of the interview. Only such a large hall could take in that number of boys. A huge, tall white man who introduced himself as the principal and whom they later learned was a British, addressed them. Some five thousand candidates or so who had selected the school as their first choice had sat for the competitive examination in the Federation of Nigeria and the Southern Cameroons. Out of these, the top 105 successful candidates had been selected for interview. They were the 105 candidates.

The interview would consist of two parts: Part A consisting of a three-hour written paper made up of three sections: Math, English, and General Paper; and part B consisting of a face-to-face oral interview. For the oral interview, candidates will be called, one-by-one, into the staff room. They will be required to come in, mount the small platform, face the panel, and answer the questions that would be put to them. Then, pausing for a moment and looking round the hall as if counting to see if any candidates were missing, he threw the bombshell: out of the 105 candidates called for this interview, only 30 of them will be admitted into form 1. There was dead silence, then some murmurings of dissatisfaction.

As Don and the other candidates left the hall after the written paper, one boy, who introduced himself as Nebuwa, caught up with him and asked the answer he got to question 3 in math. Don told Nebuwa his answer, which he said was also what he had gotten. As the two of them moved along, discussing the catch in that question, a group of boys who had been discussing and comparing answers, as is common among students after an exam, heard them mention the word 'catch' and 'question 3', stopped them and asked what their answers were. When Don and his friend told the boys their common answer, which differed from theirs, it became a problem of 'might is right'. That group not only insisted that their answer was correct and Don's and his friend's was wrong, but became very hostile and aggressive and were trying to start a fight.

"Where are you from?" one of the bigger and more aggressive boys asked Don. Don told him where he came from, wondering what that had to do with the answer to the math question. "Look at the little brat from the Cameroons coming here to tell us what the right answer to such a difficult math question is. How dare you?" he retorted angrily, turning to the other boys as if he was speaking for them too. Don and his friend didn't want a fight; They couldn't have stood a chance with those bullies. So they just sneaked away, disappeared. It emerged later that day, that the two of them had the right answer to that question. That goes to show the state of competitiveness and the high stakes at the interview.

When Don's turn for the oral interview came and he was called in, he climbed and stood on top of a small raised platform facing a panel, which included the principal, who was in the middle, flanked by about six members of staff wearing blank faces. Don was like a Lilliput looking down on some giants. As he stood watching them and waiting for them to speak, his mind went briefly back to the advice his father had given him on the eve of his departure for Owerri. "When you enter the interview room, don't forget to greet the judges with a bow; look straight at their faces when talking, and speak audibly and clearly so they can hear you." And then he had added, "And if you are asked whether your father would be able to pay your fees, say that he is a poor farmer and cannot pay your fees, so they can give you a scholarship."

Among the several questions he was bombarded with were: why he wanted to come all the way to Nigeria to study; were there no secondary schools in Southern Cameroons; what was his motivation for choosing Government Secondary School Owerri out of the three government colleges; why had he attended a government primary school in Cameroon; were there no mission or private schools there; what subjects did he like best; why and how were his grades in school; what extracurricular activities did he enjoy; what do his father and mother do for a living, and etc.

And they finally asked the question his father had anticipated, "Suppose you are admitted, will your father be able to pay your fees?"

Don's reply was almost instantaneous. "Of course!" he said. "My father is a cocoa farmer producing and exporting cocoa. He will be able to pay my fees if I am admitted," he lied. That was *not* what his father had advised him to say.

The journey back to Cameroon was, like before, very tiring, uncomfortable, and uneventful.

"So did they ask you whether your father will be able to pay your fees? What did you tell them?" his father asked him the following morning. They had arrived Mamfe very late the previous night.

"Yes, they did, and I told them that you can and that you are a big cocoa farmer." Don added, "Papa, the interview was very tough. It was even more competitive than the entrance exam we had taken in March. It consisted of a difficult written paper and a face-to-face interview. One hundred and five (105) boys were called for the interview and only thirty (30) were going to be admitted. I could not afford to disqualify myself by telling them I would not be able to pay the school fees. I couldn't take a chance. The stakes were too high," he finished, satisfied with himself that he was able to say what he had planned to say.

"Oh, you have lost a scholarship," his father exclaimed. He had, nevertheless, been unnerved by Don's logic.

But Don was taken aback by his father's presumptiveness. He wondered at his self-assurance. "Papa, why are you so sure that the school would have awarded me a scholarship if I had told them I was a poor student? You should be more concerned about my being among the thirty students that would be admitted. We should pray that I am selected instead of worrying about a scholarship," Don said in a manner almost begging him to be more understanding.

"So when did they say the results would be out?" he finally asked after conceding that Don had a point but still insisting that he had missed a scholarship. Don told him the school had said that candidates would be informed of the results through letters that would be sent to the addresses they had given them. They should receive the letters within the next one month. From that time on, his father would give him the key to the mailbox as soon as they came back from the farm each day to go check the mail for his admission letter, which he was convinced was on the way from G.S.S. Owerri. And each time Don came from the post office without it, his father wondered whether the post office people in Nigeria were on strike.

Weeks passed, but the letter was not among the many Don collected from the mailbox. Then one late afternoon, it came, a thick brown envelope with the stamp of the school on it. Don knew immediately that he was successful. He had been admitted because the envelope was quite thick. He guessed that it must contain his admission letter, some information notes, and a prospectus listing the things he would need to bring to school. Don rushed it to his father. He was right. His father was elated.

"I told you it would come," he said, turning to Don with an air of achievement after opening the letter, as if it was him who had sat for the entrance exam and gone for the interview.

He asked Don to read it. The principal had the pleasure to inform Don that he had passed the competitive exam and the interview, and he had therefore offered him a place in form 1 for the academic year 1957–1958. Congratulations! The school was reopening on 12 September 1957; the tuition fees per term was 12.00 pounds. Don was required to confirm acceptance of the offer by September 1 by sending a deposit equivalent to one term's fees. The school would provide text books, exercise books, and two pairs of uniform per term. The school had a laundry service, and students' clothes would be collected and washed every Saturday morning.

A list of the things Don would need to bring was also provided with a recommendation for the amount of pocket money deemed sufficient for a student in form 1–3 pounds per term. By all indications, it looked like a very privileged school. Don and his father were astonished. It took little time to put together the few things Don was required to bring, including a tin box (not a suitcase as recommended) into which his things were put.

His father told him he had written to his brother Tom to send him twelve pounds to pay his deposit. His brother had graduated from UCI and was then working in Lagos. Then his father asked him to apply for a scholarship from the Mamfe Town and Area Council. He called Mr. Lucas Agbor-atar, who was a member of the Council and who, in those days, Don had thought was his father's younger brother. He asked him to follow up on his application and ensure it went through.

Mr. Agbor-atar returned to see his father some weeks later to inform him that the proceedings were tough because council members thought his father was rich, and his son did not need a council scholarship. He suggested some motivational gesture to the council members, which Don's father reluctantly accepted to offer. His father was not a rich man. He was not a cocoa farmer in the real sense of the word. He planted scattered stems of cocoa and coffee all over the lands he had acquired only as a means of showing effective ownership and occupation of those lands. He had four wives and many children and one was in the university and three were in colleges at the time.

Chapter 5
Broadening His Horizons at Government Secondary School, Owerri, Eastern Nigeria

Don's father arranged for Uncle Tom Tabi to accompany him again to Owerri. They set out for Owerri on August 31, 1957. This time around, Uncle Tom was to leave him in school and return. It is said that a journey of a thousand miles begins with a single step. This journey to Owerri to start secondary school marked the next few steps of his journey to the unknown world; a journey to 'broaden his horizons'. They arrived Owerri on September 1, and like during their previous trip, they were installed with the boys, Robert and Martin. Then the influenza outbreak of 1957 struck almost immediately. Don was so seriously ill that, for two weeks, he did not know where he was. But he remembers seeing cousin Mbiwan one day as he lay in bed, as if he was in a dream, assuring him he would get better soon. Luckily, he recovered just as the school reopened on September 12.

The school campus was packed full with cars by 6:00 p.m. that evening as parents brought their children to school. Many of the buildings were old and lined up round a quadrangle in the middle of which was a field. There was no storied building and only a few buildings were new—the laboratories, dining hall, and assembly hall. For such a great school, the campus looked ordinary and unbefitting. They were later to learn that this campus on which the school was started, was a teacher training college; new and appropriate buildings were to be constructed in due course to accommodate the school. Don was assigned to Pyke-Nott House, one of the five houses in the school. As they waited to go into the dining hall for dinner at 7:00 p.m., they crowded before the big notice board. The list of admission into form 1 was at the top right-hand corner. The first eight students on the list had an asterisk on their names. They had been awarded school scholarships.

Don's name was the eleventh on the list. As he looked at the list, he remembered his father's words when he told him about the interview. "You have lost a scholarship," he had exclaimed. Don wondered whether he would have been awarded one if he had told the interview panel that his father was a poor farmer. They learned later that their names had been listed based on merit.

On the first day of classes, they received textbooks and exercise books for note writing. They had their measurements taken for their uniforms. "You, this Cameroonian, so you were admitted," a voice boomed behind Don. He was the big, aggressive boy who had wanted to fight two of them because of the math question. He was Joseph Okaih, as Don came to know him. Don was pleased to see the other boy who had the same answer with him. He was John Nebuwa. But Don was most surprised to see Fubara Braide, the son of his former Headmaster in Government School Mamfe. He had also been admitted into form 1. He was a class behind Don in Government School Mamfe and he and his parents had left Cameroon at the end of 1956 or early 1957 and returned to Nigeria.

Don was happy to find a compatriot from Cameroon, Santa. He was Christopher Cho Ateh. In effect, two of them had been admitted from Southern Cameroons. In the course of the first week, Don met two Cameroonian students in the school, Shadrack Ndam from Bamenda in form 2 and John Agbor from Mamfe in form 5 (Upper Vth). He also met Fubara's elder brother (Don's former Headmaster's eldest son), Victor Braide, who used to come from Owerri to Mamfe on holidays when their father was a Headmaster there. He was in Form 5 (Upper Vth) with John Agbor.

The school day always started with the assembly in the morning before classes commenced. During the first assembly of the year, the Principal spent much time impressing on them that buildings do not make a good school or any school, as if he had read the disappointment on their faces regarding the school campus and buildings. It is the quality of the teachers and facilities and the students that made an excellent school, he stressed. Yes, the school had quite an impressive staff. Most of the teachers had University of London Bachelor of Science or Bachelor of Arts Degrees. A few had theirs from other universities in the UK and elsewhere. Only two elderly and experienced teachers had higher diplomas from teacher training colleges; one young teacher had just had his higher school certificate and came to teach while waiting to enter the university, and another was also a young undergraduate from Ibadan who had taken time out from school. The principal, Mr. M.C. English, was an Englishman, a huge, former military officer who taught geography.

The principal, in his address during the first assembly, also underscored the need for hard work, for excellence, for scholarship. The school had no patience or tolerance for laziness or academic weakness. Students were required to play hard and study hard. The school would not hesitate to send any student found wanting, packing.

Above, Form 1, Pyke-Nott House 1957. Don standing third from left.

Their first Latin class is reminiscent of the apprehension they felt during those first few weeks. Don recalls that class and Mr. F. Konyeaso, a tall, lanky teacher in white shirt and white shorts with his socks drawn right up to just below his knees. He entered the classroom, greeted them, and introduced himself as their Latin teacher. Then he wrote on the blackboard, 'Latin', and below to the left he wrote, 'A Case'. Then turning and facing them, he asked them, "What is a case?" He was a Nigerian, an Ibo, but he was almost as white as a European, and his eyes were shinning like those of a wild cat. He repeated the question as he paced from left to right in front of the class, staring right into their eyes.

One boy raised his hand. "A case is something for packing things."

"Where are you from?" The teacher asked the boy.

The boy called the name of his village.

"And you will soon find yourself packing your things and going back to your village," he told him.

The class was dead silent. They did not find that funny, given that the principal had warned a few days earlier that the school would not hesitate to send any student who is incapable of learning, packing. Then one boy raised his hand.

"A case is a matter in court, sir," he said with an air of confidence. They all heaved a sigh of relief that one of them had answered the question.

"What is your name and where are you from?"

"I am from Onitsha, sir," the boy replied proudly while still standing.

"I am not surprised. You Onitsha people like court cases, land cases, and all. Sit down," the teacher replied mockingly, repeating the boy's answer, "A case is a matter in court, sir." He asked the question again, "What is a case?" but no boy would raise his hand. Who would want to be sent packing? Tension was rising. The unease heightened. Don shifted nervously on his seat, and in the process, his pen fell, drawing the attention of the teacher.

"Yes, you want to answer the question?" He turned, looking at Don.

The day they were issued their text books, the *First Latin Book*, their prescribed Latin textbook had caught Don's attention as he was going through the books. He was curious to know what Latin was all about. So he flipped through the first few pages on beginning the study of Latin. He tried to remember what he had read.

"A case is like a part of a sentence. A sentence can be divided into parts, e.g., the subject, the direct object, the indirect object, the possessive noun, etc. Each of these parts is a case," He hesitated, not knowing whether he was making sense.

"Yes, continue," the teacher urged him on.

"In Latin, we have the Nominative case, Accusative case, Genitive case, Dative case, and Ablative case. In Latin, the subject of a sentence is in the nominative case, the direct object is in the accusative case, the possessive noun is in the genitive case while the indirect object is in the dative or ablative case," Don managed to explain.

The teacher looked at him for a while and then asked, "What's your name and where are you from?"

"My name is Oben, and I come from the Cameroons," Don replied, not knowing what to expect. The teacher took some time again looking at him. Then rubbing his thin chin and his eyes shining like those of a cat in the dark, he turned and faced the whole class.

"A skinny, hungry-looking, malnourished boy has to come all the way from the mountains of the Cameroons to tell you spoiled, fat, overfed boys what a case is."

Don heaved a sigh of relief. Whether he was skinny or malnourished did not matter. In that case, curiosity, rather than kill the cat, saved it.

That same week, in their geography class, their teacher who was the Principal himself, called a boy who could not answer a question to the front of the class and wrote a capital D on his forehead. Then he asked them what the D stands for. It stands for 'Dunce', he explained. The first few weeks of school were really scary, and Don and his classmates wondered whether they would survive. And they had cause to worry. In the first two years, two of their classmates were sent packing, his compatriot, unfortunately, being one of them and after the very first year.

Apart from the traditional science and arts subjects, they took carpentry in the first two years. They were also allotted small individual plots on the farm (optional) on which each of them made one or two long ridges and planted corn, yams, and tomatoes. They sold the yams to the school and made some money. They harvested a few fresh tomatoes each evening on days they had boiled rice and stew and ate them raw with the rice; the corn they roasted in the evenings, especially during weekends when they wanted to give themselves a treat. They did sports in season—soccer, cricket, hockey, and athletics.

Later in the first term, Don received a letter from the Mamfe Town and Area Council informing him that he had been awarded a partial Council Scholarship. It was eight pounds per term or twenty-four pounds per year. That meant that his father had to make up the balance of his tuition fees per year in the amount of twelve pounds. The Council remittances always came late and were paid only after several reminders by the Principal. During one vacation in the second year, the Principal had to ask Don to go home and resolve the issue of late payment with the Council; otherwise, he was going to send him out of school if the Council continued to delay payment. Don went home and confronted Mr. Ajah, the Administrative Secretary of the Council. Luckily, in his third year, he was awarded a scholarship by the West Cameroon Government with the strong recommendation from the Principal backed up by his academic performance thus far. As that covered all his tuition fees, he had to give up the council scholarship.

They ate well. They had quaker oats, bread, eggs, and tea or akamu or pap (maize meal), and akara (fried bean balls) for breakfast and pounded yam (fufu) or gari and okro, egusi or ogbono soup for lunch and boiled rice with fried ripe plantains (dodo) or rice and beans or boiled or fried yams—all of these with fresh fish, meat, or chicken stew. They were also served a glass of sweet palm wine on most afternoons to improve their eyesight. For the same reason, they were issued a tin of dried yeast at the beginning of each term. But Don cannot forget, and no student will forget the Chenopodium given to each student at the beginning of each term to deworm them. The pungent smell always caused them so much nausea that they would spend a whole day actually vomiting after they took it.

At the end of their first term in school, i.e., December 1957, the school year was changed from September/June to January/December to align it with other schools. So they spent four terms instead of the usual three in form 1. The next admission of students into the school therefore took place in January 1959. One student from Mamfe, Michael Ndip, joined them, bringing the number of Cameroon students in Owerri back to four.

At the end of the first year, Don had changed so much. He had added some eleven inches to his height as well as some flesh to his bones. He was growing into a tall, lanky, nice-looking boy. He only went home during the Christmas holidays like the other Cameroonian students. During the first-term Easter holidays and the second-term holidays in July, the four of them usually remained on campus because traveling to Cameroon was too difficult, hazardous, and expensive. They were usually moved into one dormitory and arrangements were made for their feeding. They would spend their days playing the game or sport that was in season, go to town, read, or occupy themselves in whatever way they deemed fit. Those days were quite lonely, especially for Don as a little boy in his first three or four years in school. Waiting for one whole year each time to see and spend time with his mother, father, and brothers and sisters was quite awful.

The first two years had been different. His cousin, Mr. Mbiwan, now married to Ma Elizabeth Efeti, was still in Owerri. He went home during the Christmas holidays in December 1957 but spent the Easter vacation of 1958 with his cousin and his family. His wife's younger sister, Anne Mojoko, and her friend, Grace Lyonga, had also come to spend their vacation with them from Ibiaku in Ikot Ekpene where they were attending Union Secondary School. Don was, as usual, housed with the boys, Robert and Martin. He also spent the next vacation in July with them. Then they left for the West Indies.

In early 1959, Don was invited by his friend, David Obianime to come spend the Easter holiday with him and his family in Okrika, Rivers State. David was the junior brother of Mr. Obians, the famous photographer who was a tenant in Don's father's big house in the mid-1950s. David was living with him and attending the Roman Catholic Mission (RCM) School, Mamfe. Living together in one compound, he and Don had known themselves and become good friends. Don spent a pleasant Easter holiday in Okrika and traveled to Abonnema and Degema.

After this holiday in 1959, Don stayed on campus with the other Cameroon students during subsequent April/Easter and July/Summer vacations and only traveled home for Christmas in December.

Their experience during one particular journey home provides an insight into the difficulties they faced in trying to travel to Cameroon on vacation in those days. It must have been in December 1958. It took them four days to travel from Owerri to Mamfe. They had arrived Onitsha late from Owerri and, therefore, left Onitsha in the afternoon of the first day. By nightfall of that day, the spring of the left back wheel broke as they were traveling through a small village and the driver had to send the 'motor boy' back to Onitsha to buy a new part. He came back early in the morning of the second day. The part was fitted and they continued the journey by midday. Just after Ikom, they met four vehicles stuck on the road in front of them. Although it was the month of December and the roads were supposed to be dry, that was not so. The rains had continued with an intensity never seen before, and the roads which had not been maintained and had gotten worse, were then at their worst.

Their vehicle also got stuck and sank deep into the muddy sea of water even before getting near the truck in front of them. As if that was not enough, the carburetor took in water. Because there was only one small beaten motorable track, none of the trucks could drive off unless the one before it had been dug out and pushed to dry land. All the drivers and motor boys and able-bodied passengers joined hands in a collective effort to get the trucks out. In three of the cases, including theirs, the vehicles had to be off-loaded to make them lighter and so easier to be pulled out. That was a lot of work. By the time theirs was pulled out of the lake of mud, it was near midnight. Then it would not start. They were on that spot for two days.

Then on the fourth day, midway between Mamfe and Ikom, the vehicle broke down again. The motor boy had to hitch a ride back to Ikom to buy some parts. Meanwhile, all along the way, they survived by roasting yams offered by the yam traders who were also passengers. They arrived Mamfe on the night of the fourth day! That was the worst journey Don ever undertook, and it explained in part why they went home only once a year.

At Government Secondary School Owerri, as in the other two sister schools, boys were allowed to continue in their religious faiths. The Catholic students worshipped in town in the Catholic church while Don and other Protestants went to Christ (Anglican) Church in town every Sunday to worship. But on occasions, the Assembly Hall was converted into a chapel, and they had Sunday service there conducted by Mr. J. A. Garrod, who succeeded Mr. M. C. English as Principal in 1958.

Don had been a Protestant and a member of the choir in the Presbyterian Church in Mamfe before coming to Owerri. The Anglican Church in Owerri, also a Protestant church, was the nearest denomination to the Presbyterian Church. So in 1958, Don decided to be baptized. He attended catechism and was baptized in Christ Church, Owerri by Rev Iwuno in November 1958 as Godfrey Oben. He followed that baptism many years later with his confirmation in 1964 at the same church. That time, he took the name Don Harris and corrected his middle name from Oben to Ebenagborta. He had been named after his paternal grandfather, Ebenagborta. This is how the name is called in their native language, Kenyang. When he was admitted into primary school in 1949 at age six, the teacher, whoever he was, had written his name as Oben instead of Ebenagborta Oben, or Eben Oben, the Eben being the short form of Ebenagborta. So Don decided to correct that error at his confirmation.

That is how he became known as Don Harris Ebenagborta Oben. He dropped the name Godfrey.

Life in OGSS was quite interesting. Don joined many clubs at various times during the years he was in the school. These included the Music Club, Dancing Club, Art Club, Photographic Club, Boys' Scouts, Tennis Club, and the Junior and, later, the Senior Literary and Debating Society. His love for music drew him to the Music Club in his second year where he learned to play the organ. He remembers October 1st 1960, Nigeria's Independence Day. He always remembered that day because after the march past at the stadium, he played the organ all day and he played and sang one of his favorite songs, that sentimental Victorian-era song, 'Won't You Buy My Pretty Flowers' (1874) from *Smallwood's Piano Tutor*. He played and sang so passionately from the depths of his heart and soul that tears flowed down his cheeks.

Won't You Buy My Pretty Flowers

Underneath the gaslight's glitter
Stands the little fragile girl
Heedless of the night winds bitter
As they round about her whirl
While the thousands pass unheeding
In the evening's waning hours
Still she cries with tearful pleading
"Won't you buy my pretty flowers?"

There are many, sad and weary
In this pleasant world of ours.
Crying every night so dreary
"Won't you buy my pretty flowers?"

Ironically, as he got immersed in 'acada' after the third year, the organ and piano and music were the first things that he grew distant from. It is unbelievable that he has not touched an organ or piano in more than five decades. He cannot even read music now; He cannot play the organ or piano either. What a terrible tragedy!

Yes, the competitive spirit in their class demanded an almost undivided loyalty to academic work. Early in forms 1 and 2, they were baffled by some classmates who knew Geometry, Trigonometry, and Algebra and other subjects, which they had hitherto not learned in primary school. They wondered how those boys could master such new subjects so easily and so quickly. These boys were always excelling. Then after form 1, some of them started showing signs of weakness. By the end of form 2, all of them were largely struggling in these subjects. It emerged then that these boys had, in fact, attended private colleges for one to three years with the intention of getting themselves better prepared for the competitive entrance exam to the government colleges.

It was during their years in those private colleges that they learned Algebra, Geometry, Trigonometry, and other subjects, which explained why they did so well in those subjects in their first years at Owerri. By the third year, all of them were on a level playing field. Their real strengths began to show. With the exception of the first term in form 2, when Don came seventeenth, his position in class was always between the fifth and eighth.

As mentioned earlier, life in the school was quite interesting. This was made even more interesting by the mannerism and behavior of some of the teaching staff. There was Mr. J.O.M. (as students called him), who would not want to associate with other staff members because they were 'Bachelors'. He called them 'Bachelors' not because they were not married but because they had only bachelor's degrees while he had a master's degree. He was bespectacled, walked with a dignified gait, and spoke softly and proudly. He would not even sit in the staff room with his colleagues because according to him "Masters and bachelors don't mix." He once refused to act for the principal when the latter was away on duty travel because "he couldn't be holding the fort for a principal who had only a bachelor's degree." Sometime later when the Ministry of Education recruited teachers from India and one of them Dr. Pradesh (not his real name) who had a Ph.D. degree in Math was posted to the school, J.O.M. very soon started to associate with him. When asked one day by someone who thought he could belittle and embarrass him, why he was always in the company of Dr. Pradesh when he knew that the latter had a Ph.D. degree while he had only a master's degree, and if he didn't know that 'masters' and 'doctors' have nothing in common, and therefore don't mix,

J.O.M. responded with a broad and cheeky smile: 'Masters' and 'Doctors' have everything in common. They both went to 'Graduate School'!

Then there was the teacher whom students called 'Ogbons' who was once asked to be the Sports Master. He would wonder aloud why human beings, civilized human beings for that matter, would be running as if a lion was pursuing them. "Why would people be running 100 yards or 200 yards races when no lion or any wild animal is pursuing them?" And he could not understand why people would be kicking a ball as in soccer, or hitting a small ball as in tennis or hockey, when the ball had done them no wrong or committed no offense. And he worried about people struggling to overcome the force of gravity by jumping over a bar as in high jump or pole vault. To him these were some of the most crazy things human beings do even in modern times and the school administration expected him to supervise some of these idiosyncracies. "What a waste of my time but I have to do it," he would sigh.

And there was the teacher Don and his classmates called Mr. Udowood who was the games master. He would be so carried away when he was refereeing a match that whenever there was a tussle at a goal mouth, he would unconsciously start kicking in the air as if trying to kick the ball. Then soon, he would put the whistle in his pocket and join in the tussle and try to score. It would take the crowd a lot of shouting for him to realize that he is the referee and stop playing. Sometimes he would score a goal and it is when he turns around to look for the referee to blow the whistle that he realizes that he is the referee and starts to apologize. There was never a House match that he did not get himself involved as a player.

And there was old Mr. Nwanna who taught carpentry which was a compulsory subject for all students in the first two years of study. Unlike the other teachers, his case was not funny. After working for several years with wood, carpentry tools and machinery, he had sustained serious injuries which had left scars that had thickened and hardened his knuckles. When he disciplined a student for poor wood work which he did quite often by giving him a small knock on his fore-head with those knuckles, the day was over for that student! He suffered from serious headache for the rest of the day!

Finally, there was Mr. Ukaigwe, who taught Latin and tried to dispel the notion which students had that Latin is a 'dead' language and a language only spoken at the Vatican. He would shower praises on the language, its construction of sentences and choice of words as they studied grammar. When they read passages from their Latin text books, he would draw their attention to beautiful flowery expressions in those passages. A short, smallish, bespectacled, loquacious, funny and pleasant man, he had a habit of stretching his neck and standing on his toes as he taught the subject, as if trying to make himself look taller than he really was. In spite of all his efforts, only Don and two other classmates opted to take Latin in the Cambridge West African School Certificate Examination in November 1962.

At the end of the second term in form 5 in 1962, Don came second, and he was surely gunning for a Division 1 in the Cambridge West African School Certificate examination.

As school was about to close in July 1962 for the second term holidays, he received approval to come spend the vacation with his elder sister and her husband in Lagos. He set out for Lagos with Henry Williams, who was in lower sixth and who was also heading for Lagos on vacation. They arrived Benin City late in the evening and decided to spend the night there. Victor Olaiya was performing that night in a big hotel in town. The urge to go watch him, the 'Evil Genius' of Nigerian highlife music, was irresistible. The hotel was full to capacity and overflowing. They watched from outside. Then the heavy rains came. There was nowhere to hide. They had not booked into any hotel, so they just stayed all night, hoping the rain would cease, go away. It rained all night, soaking them to their pants while the cold seeped into them.

By the time they got to Lagos the following day in the afternoon, Don was sneezing, coughing, shivering. He thought it was a small cold, so he stayed mostly in bed, trying to keep warm and hoping it would go away. Instead, it became serious. He was breathing with increasing difficulty. He was taken to the hospital and diagnosed with acute pneumonia. He did not know how the rest of the vacation went, but he remembers he had injections and his sister insisting that he remains in Lagos when school reopened until he recovered.

But he couldn't. It was September, and the West African School Certificate examination was coming up in November, two months away. He had to return to school. He was still very ill, too weak and frail to read, to revise or even to attend the remaining classes. He watched hopelessly as the days went quickly by. The exams came in November, and he managed to sit for them. The results were to be announced in early 1963. He applied for admission into the higher school certificate course to read physics, chemistry, and zoology.

He still had not recovered well by the time he went home in December 1962. His brother, Tom Njang Ako, who was then working with the Cameroons Development Corporation (CDC) as a soil scientist, wanted him to work, so he helped get him a job as a laboratory trainee in the Oil Palms Laboratory located in the oil mill of the Bota Palms Estate of the CDC. He was allocated a small room in one of the long 'German' blocks in the workers' camp overlooking the oil mill in Bota.

Don was also allocated a small kitchen facing the room in a similar block adjacent to the first block. So his room and his kitchen faced each other about seven meters apart. Don furnished the room with a small 'vono' bed and mattress, which served both as his bed and his chair. He placed his carton of books on the floor at the center of the room and used it as his coffee table. He covered it with a small table cloth. The lone window had no blinds.

Don assumed his duties in mid-December as Laboratory Trainee in the Oil Palms Laboratory under Mr. Ferdinand Enow, who was a field assistant in the senior service. His work involved fiber analysis and analysis of free fatty acid in oil palm fruits among others. Every morning, Mr. Enow would bring samples of ripe, newly harvested palm fruits from the field for analysis. But Don had an immediate boss who was an Intermediate Service staff and whose name he cannot remember now. They came to work early in the morning at 7:30 a.m. and went for a half-hour tea break at 9:30 a.m. For Don and many other junior employees, that was their breakfast time since the early time for the assumption of work did not give them much time to cook and eat breakfast. He ate his meals on his small coffee table using the bed as his chair.

It was during one of those break times in mid-January 1963 and when he was crossing the road from the German blocks to enter the oil mill that he heard someone call out, "Scoundrel, Scoundrel." Don knew immediately whom it was that was calling. It was only him and Don who called themselves 'Scoundrel'. But Don wondered what he would be doing in Cameroon at that time of the year. Don stopped and turned round. Surely, there he was, hurrying toward him, Thomas Takor.

"Scoundrel, what are you doing here?" he asked as soon as he got close enough to Don.

"I should ask you what you are doing here. You should be in Ibadan and not in Cameroon," Don replied.

Takor Takor was a friend who studied at Government College Umuahia and was a few years ahead of Don. He was a very brilliant student. He was by then reading medicine at the University of Ibadan. He told Don he just made a snap visit to Cameroon to see to a few issues and was on his way back to Ibadan the next day.

"Scoundrel, you have not told me what you are doing here. I heard you had been given direct admission in your former school to do science in the higher school certificate course and that you were also given direct entry at Umuahia to do arts. So what are you doing here? Schools resumed more than two weeks ago," he pressed seriously.

"I am working in the Oil Palms Lab here as a Laboratory Trainee. I am just from break and returning to work," Don told him.

"You must be joking. With two direct entry admissions into the HSC course in two government colleges, you are here doing what? You really must be joking. To have two direct admissions, that is exceptional! But in case you are really serious that you are working, think twice and hurry up. You're already late. I thought you were a Scoundrel."

Yes, Owerri had offered Don direct admission to do science (Physics, Chemistry, and Zoology). Students who were offered direct admission were those who were exempt from taking the entrance exam because of their exemplary performance in their chosen subjects during the five-year school certificate course. He wanted to read Physics, Chemistry, and Zoology, so he could read Medicine or Veterinary Medicine at the university. At the same time, he loved the arts and Government Secondary School Owerri did not offer arts subjects at the HSC level, so he had also applied to Government College Umuahia to read arts. At the time his school gave him direct admission to do the sciences, Government College Umuahia also offered him direct admission to read the arts—English Literature, History, and Latin. Don loved Latin. Only three of them in their class had offered to take Latin in the West African School Certificate and one of his 'A's was in it. He loved to read Law, and his subject combination of Latin, History, and Literature was just right for the study of Law at the university.

At that time, Don was torn between doing the sciences at Government Secondary School Owerri and reading the arts at Government College Umuahia. It was an agonizing choice, indeed, a choice about his future career. He had to make a decision. Schools closed in December. He decided to go home and hoped that, while at home and by the time schools resumed in January 1963, he would have resolved his dilemma. It was in that state of mind that, while at home, he accepted to work, hoping to resign and return to school as soon as he had made a choice one way or the other. The days went by, and by the time of his meeting with Takor Takor, he still had not made a choice. Now his meeting with him only brought to the fore the urgency in making a decision.

In the end, Don chose to remain in Owerri and study Physics, Chemistry, and Zoology. A major element in that decision was the belief that, if he remained in his present school, it would be easier for the school to get the Cameroon Government to continue his scholarship on the grounds that his studies had not yet ended at the school. It was one of the most difficult decisions he had had to make. Having taken that decision, Don tendered, with much regret and disappointment to some people, especially to his senior brother, his resignation letter to the CDC and returned to Government Secondary School Owerri to undertake the higher school certificate course in Physics, Chemistry, and Zoology. He arrived there one month late. He also wrote to Government College Umuahia, declining their offer on the grounds that he had accepted another offer from his alma mater. Fortunately, the Cameroon government continued his scholarship for the two years of the higher school certificate course.

In April 1963, the results of the West African School Certificate examination, which they had sat for in November/December 1962 were released. Don missed the Division 1 which he was gunning for before he was struck down with acute pneumonia and got a Division 2 (three 'A's, four 'C's, and one 'P'). In those days, they offered a maximum of eight subjects, and they were scored as follows: A (excellent, very good, good), C (pass with credit), P (pass), and F (fail). Although it was a 'strong' Division 2, Don was devastated.

But then, considering the state he was in when he sat for the exam, it was a miracle that he did so well. The HSC course ended in December 1964 and Don returned to Cameroon after seven years studying in Eastern Nigeria. After visiting his parents in Mamfe, he moved to Buea in January 1965 and stayed for a while with another of his brothers, Lawrence Mbi, who was then working in the Treasury Department.

Above, Don in August 1963 wearing the Bay hairstyle of the day.

Above: Pyke-Nott House, 1964. Don sitting first from left.

Chapter 6
A Stint in the West Cameroon Civil Service

Working in Buea in the Mid-1960s

It was the second time that Don was venturing out to any other part of Cameroon by that time. At this time, the country was now called West Cameroon. The first time was when he went to Santa with his classmate in form 1 in December 1957. Don got employed as a 3rd Class Clerk in the Labor Department under an Englishman, Mr. Allen, who was a Senior Labor Officer, and Mr. E. K. Lottin, a Cameroonian, a Labor Inspector. In those days, those who had the West African School Certificate (WASC) or the General Certificate of Education (GCE) 'O' level were employed as 3rd Class Clerks. And employment was quite easy then, just a simple handwritten application attaching copies of one's certificate(s) to the Secretary of the Public Service Commission (PSC). After verification and interview, it was sent to the Establishment Secretary (ES) where it was processed.

The process was quick, and once employed, one's salary started flowing at the end of the same month that one was employed, even if one was employed one week to the end of the month! Don's work description included keeping labor statistics of skilled labor (artisans and technicians), unskilled labor, wages and remunerations, work stoppages, etc., of companies such as Elders and Fiffes, Likomba; Cadbury and Fry, Ikiliwindi; Pamol Ltd., Lobe; the Cameroons Development Corporation (CDC), Bota, etc.

He later moved to the Ministry of Development and Internal Economic Planning (DIEP), where he took charge, among other duties, of incoming and outgoing correspondence. He worked with Mr. V. C. Nchami, the Permanent Secretary; Mr. W. M. Ntuba, the Commercial Officer; Mr. S. K. Ewusi, the

Chief Clerk; and Mrs. Dorothy Abba, the Secretary to the Permanent Secretary. Don was a 3rd class clerk working as a correspondence clerk.

He soon came to know a number of school leavers who were also in town. There was Noah T. Kebulu and Emmanuel Gwan from Government College Umuahia. There was Nyansako ni-nku, who with Kebulu were employed in the Treasury Department and worked under Mr. Henry Agboraw. There were Ndiva Kale and Raph Difang from King's College, Lagos, and Nelson Mbu from Sasse. Kale and Mbu were employed in the Legal Department. There was Sammy Chumbo, who was working at the Scholarship Office under Mrs. Gladys Endeley, and Fondo Sikod, who was at the Radio. Don also remembers William Endeley, George Formundam, and Roy. There were a few others whose names he does not remember. These school leavers and many others were working and waiting for the results of the various exams they had taken at the end of their courses in their various schools namely the Higher School Certificate (HSC), West African School Certificate (WASC) and General Certificate of Education (GCE) examinations.

Buea in those days was quite a small town consisting mainly of Great Soppo, Clerks' Quarters, GRA, and Buea Town (from the old stadium right up to, and beyond, the 'para-para' field). There were no township taxis, so they went everywhere on foot from Buea town to the ministerial block, to Clerks' Quarters, to everywhere. Don had also moved to Buea Town behind the market into a 'karabot' (wooden) house, which he was sharing with his sister Eunice. Most houses at that time were wooden or what were called 'karabot' houses. Clerks' Quarters, where he and other 3rd Class Clerks could have sought accommodation, was taken up by Administrative Officers, Executive Officers, and other senior civil servants who had spilled over from the GRA where senior civil servants were accommodated.

It was cold and rainy in Buea in those days. The rain always fell slantingly, wetting one's shoes and one's trousers even when one was covered with an umbrella. So during the rainy season, they went to work with an extra pair of socks in their pockets and an extra pair of shoes in a plastic bag. As soon as they got to the office, they removed their wet shoes and socks and changed. They were expected to, and they took their office duties very seriously. Every civil servant was expected to study and be very conversant with the General Orders (GO) and Financial Instructions (FI), which carried the administrative and financial guidelines and procedures of the civil service, as well as the rights and obligations of civil servants. They were the civil service 'Bible'.

While life in the office was challenging, the social life appeared dull. There was hardly any extracurricular activity. Some school leavers were taking correspondence courses from institutions in the United Kingdom and elsewhere in preparation for various exams. So they spent their evenings and nights after a hard day's work burning the midnight oil. To make life more interesting, a few of them decided to come together and form a club, the Buea Youths Social and Dramatic Club (BYSDC). They organized debates on a wide range of socioeconomic issues, participated in radio quizzes and competitions, and won small prices such as candies, clothing, small household items and umbrellas, which were their most prized possessions in those rainy days. To add more spice to life, they organized social evenings and dances.

Ndiva Kale, one of the founding members of the BYSDC and now a distinguished law professor, lawyer, political scientist and politician, reminisced fifty years later in 2015 about the club on the occasion of the book launch of Tazoacha Asonganyi's *Cameroon: Difficult Choices in a Failed Democracy*.

Fifty years ago this August, fresh out of college, contemplating our next move, the Reverend (referring to Nyansako ni-nku now the Very Reverend Nyansako-ni-nku, PCC Moderator Emeritus) and I together with many of our college mates were members of the Buea Youths Social and Dramatic Club. We staged plays, organized debates, book reviews and even tea-time dances. There we were, sixteen, seventeen, eighteen-year-old kids, venturing even where grown-ups feared to tread, struggling to read and make sense out of Nkrumah's Consciencism, Nyerere's Ujamaa, Sekou Toure's African Socialism and Senghor's Negritude. This book launch brings back many fond memories of those halcyon days.[7]

A few of the boys left for universities at the beginning of the 1965/1966 academic year. Don missed a scholarship to Canada. His application was late because his HSC results had been sent to PO Box 4 in Mamfe. His father had changed his mailbox from Box 4 to Box 21. He was expecting them at his office address in Buea.

Sometime in 1965, Don ran into one Mr. Mofor in Buea. He was a Cameroonian student at the University of Nigeria, Nsukka (UNN), and a Student Representative in the West Cameroon Scholarship Board at the time.

He told Don that the government was giving priority in the award of scholarships to certain particular areas where the country lacked manpower. One of those areas was Veterinary Medicine. So the following year, Don applied and got admission to read Veterinary Medicine at the University of Nigeria, Nsukka. Mofor was right. Don got a West Cameroon government scholarship to study Veterinary Medicine beginning from the 1966/1967 academic year.

Even though he was on scholarship and was expected to get a passport and an exit visa without any delay or problems, the boys at the immigration front desks always raised issues. After he was told several times to 'go come tomorrow' for his visa by a certain man with a northern name, a friend, Etchu Abunaw, told him what 'go come tomorrow' meant. He too had just experienced the same situation.

The next time Don went, he shook hands with the man and handed him an old newspaper. As the man took the newspaper and put it in his drawer, Don's passport and visa quickly came out from the drawer. The visa had long been issued but it seemed like the man had been waiting for the key—an old newspaper (and its contents!) that would open the drawer for the passport and visa to come out!

Chapter 7
Broadening His Horizons at Nsukka and Ibadan

At the University of Nigeria, Nsukka (UNN)

The Nigeria Airways flight from Tiko landed at Enugu airport after a short stop at Calabar airport. Don couldn't believe he was already in Enugu. It had been less than two hours since he and a few other Cameroon students bound for Nsukka took off from Tiko. As he walked into the airport terminal, he turned back to look at the plane and marveled at how such a giant contraption could soar through the air and get there so fast. He recalled those times in the late 1950s when it took them days to travel on the potholed, muddy road from Mamfe to Enugu and then to Onitsha and Owerri. Just then, he had flown through the skies and had done the same journey in a twinkling of an eye. It was his very first time traveling by air. Little did he know that would be the first of countless numbers of much longer journeys that would take him through the world.

He was assigned to Aja Nwachukwu Hall. He came to meet the other Cameroon students at the university. There was Victor Mukwelle Ngoh in his final year in Law at the Enugu campus; Victor Balinga in his final year in Botany; Ndingsa, also in his final year in Engineering; and Joe Nnoko and Efange, who were doing law. The rest of them were at the main campus in Nsukka. There were also Peter Enyong, John Awemo, and Nkwain Sama in their first year as himself. And there were three civil servants—Mr. Andrew Ndonyi, Mr. Lebga, and Ms. Sarah Thomas, who had come from the Department of Community Development to do a Diploma course in Community Development.

It was not long before Don's passion for dancing drew him to the Victor Sylvester Ballroom Circle (VSBC). He remembered the days in the **mid-1950s,** when as children, they had watched with admiration and wonder, how Tailor Ajagbor taught ballroom dancing to some elites and university undergraduates in Mamfe Town. As it usually happened, associations, societies, and clubs advertised their activities during the orientation week at the beginning of the academic year when new students arrive. When he registered and attended the first practice session of the VSBC and saw the members dance, he was impressed. He knew he had to add ballroom dancing to his arsenal of dancing skills, no matter how much time his lectures and classes demanded from him.

The dancing classes were organized into basic, intermediate, and advanced. Classes were held thrice a week in the evenings after dinner. Don and other new members were put in the Basic Class. After every teaching session, they had a short dancing practice session during which they had the opportunity to engage the women and put into practice what they had learned. They started with basic waltz steps: the right forward change, the left forward change, the right forward change to the reverse turn, the left forward change to the reverse turn, the two respective changes to the natural turn, the whisk, the progressive (side) chasse, the hesitation drag, the backward passing change (reverse and natural), the natural spin-turn, and changing line of dance.

They were shy to engage the women at the beginning, and it was difficult and seemingly awkward. But they were determined and they made it through basic waltz and went on to basic quickstep, comprising the following steps: the walk, the quarter turn, the link chase reverse turn, the natural turn, the (slow) open reverse turn, natural turn to whisk, the progressive side chasse, wing-chasse reverse turn, the natural spin turn, changing line of dance.

From the quickstep, they went on to the basic slow foxtrot and basic tango. The slow foxtrot was a more graceful dance with the following steps: the feather step, the three step, natural turn, the reverse turn, the reverse wave, the open telemark, the whisk with feather finish.

But it was the tango that appeared quite challenging, awkward, and demanding, with the dancing couple assuming an antagonistic demeanor toward each other. With a seriousness of purpose and a burning interest, Don made progress in all the dances—quickstep, waltz, slow foxtrot, tango, rumba, and cha-cha-cha—advancing to the intermediate in some of the dances. By the end of the academic year, they were dancing like small professionals. Dancing at the Victor Sylvester Ballroom Circle became a pleasure he looked forward to every week. Don still fondly remembers some of the melodious tunes they used for their dance practices—'the Tennessee Waltz' for the waltz by Patti Page, 'Mama Teach Me To Dance' by Alma Cogan, for the tango, and many others.

Don also joined the International Students Association (ISA). Most members were from African countries, but a few came from the United States, notably those who came on exchange programs from Michigan State University. There were also some from Canada, India, and a few European countries. The association sought to bring to the attention of the university the welfare of foreign students. It also organized tours to places of interest around the eastern part of the country.

While Don made a determined effort to join the ISA and VSBC, he does not know how he got into this group called 'Saints and Sinners' (S&S). It was a group consisting of some seven to ten 'faceless' students determined to make 'saints' out of perceived sinners in the university community by exposing such sinners and their wrongdoings. He just found himself in the group probably because he identified with its aims, or maybe he enjoyed some of the mischievous ways it used to achieve its objectives. Three of its members were Fine Art students. When they painted a picture of a person or an object, they produced not just a drawing or a painting but a photograph. The rest of them were information gatherers. At its meetings which were held normally around midnight at undisclosed venues, they would identify who was doing what that was not acceptable and agree on what strategy to adopt to expose such bad behavior.

Don remembers the case of a certain professor in the Faculty of Science who was dating one of his female students. S&S got evidence that he was using his office for inappropriate behavior with the girl. That was very unacceptable. S&S decided to investigate and take action. It was not long before he was caught in the act red-handed by some of his students. Days later, a large portrait of the offending couple 'in action' was up at the cafeteria entrance by 4:00 a.m. No words were written except the letters 'S&S' at the bottom right corner of the portrait. It caused a huge commotion on campus. The university sanctioned the professor after an investigation but tried unsuccessfully to identify the S&S members.

Don also remembers the case of a male final year engineering student in love with a young female first year arts student who was supposedly from the same Local Government Area. Being in love was welcome. But what S&S considered unacceptable was the manner in which the engineering student conducted their relationship or consorted with the girl. Each day, he would leave his hall of residence at 7:00 a.m. to meet the girl at Okpara Hall, her hall of residence, hang around the porter's lodge for the girl to get ready and join him and then carry her bag of books together with his heavy engineering books as he walks her to the cafeteria for breakfast. Then on arrival at the cafeteria, while the girl went and chose a seat at a remote corner, he would go queue up; collect a tray, glasses, cutlery and food for two; and they would sit alone by themselves.

After breakfast, he would walk the girl to her department in the Faculty of Arts, still carrying her books, before taking the long walk to his own faculty, the Faculty of Engineering. At lunch time, he would again go meet the girl at her faculty, walk her to the cafeteria, collect the tray etc., queue up, collect the food, and they would again dine alone in a corner. Then he would accompany the girl to her hall before going to his own hall. He would repeat this whole process at dinner time and then hang around her hall till late at night to wish her good night.

S&S considered that labor of love too encumbering, inappropriate and distasteful. As a first year student, the girl needed to feel free, explore her surroundings and express and assert herself. It was S&S's opinion that the girl was being 'caged' and 'regulated'. The boy ought to let the university pass through her as she passed through the university so that she can be found to be 'worthy in character and in learning' when the time comes. And he himself, as a final year student, needed to get down to work, preparing for his degree exams instead of playing Romeo and Juliet. S&S decided to act.

After some hard thinking and several meetings of the group, one early morning a giant poster was positioned in front of the cafeteria. It carried a life-size portrait of a couple walking along a major campus walkway with the woman in front, carrying a small handbag in her left hand and holding one end of a heavy chain in her right hand. The other end of the chain was tied round the long, thin, sagging neck of a tall, lean, tired man heavily weighed down by two big bags of books—one bag of arts books in his left hand and a bag of engineering books in his right hand. Beneath the portrait was written: "And thus, does a man leave his family, friends, countrymen and women, and cling to a woman, and follow her where ever she directs, for better or for worse (S&S)." The couple were never seen together again in public thereafter.

Life at Nsukka was very comfortable and interesting. The Continuing Education Center (CEC) and its ultramodern restaurant had just been opened. The meals were delicious and huge.

Above, Don, third from right. A dinner dance buffet at Nsukka in 1966 in the ultramodern CEC Hall.

The lectures and exams went on very well until the political conflict that had been simmering in Nigeria exploded with the pogrom. Lorry loads and train loads of families of Eastern Nigeria origin particularly the Ibos, arrived each day from the north; some of them had little or no possessions and others had wounds and injuries. The refugees had barely escaped death at the hands of northerners. Lt. Col. Odumegwu Ojukwu, the Governor, came to Nsukka to address the student body about the political situation. He spoke with such eloquence and charisma that even his fiercest critics, if any, couldn't argue against his case for a state of Biafra. The campus was seized by political ferment. Demonstrations were called for by the Students' Union in support of secession from the Federation of Nigeria and the creation of a new and independent state of Biafra.

International students could not remain indifferent. It was difficult for them to remain indifferent or neutral even if they wanted to. As was usually the case when demonstrations were called by the Students' Union, any student seen reading in the library or remaining in his or her hostel was beaten up. And the Biafran propaganda machine was very strong and credible. One only needed to listen to the news on the *Voice of Biafra* and to Okoko Ndem's news talk and commentaries, and one would be in no doubt that the resolution of the Nigerian political crisis lay in the creation of an independent state of Biafra coexisting side by side and in peace and harmony with the Federal Republic of Nigeria.

Don had to join the demonstrations. He remembers one of the worst demonstrations in which he participated in 1967. They had gone to Enugu to demonstrate right in front of Government House. It turned very violent. Police and soldiers chased and teargassed them. Most of them including Don, ran up into the Udi Hills around Enugu. Recounting that terrible experience, he said: "How I found my way back to the campus, is still a mystery. I had bruises on my knees and elbows; my face was 'besmear'd as black as Vulcan in the smoke of war.'[8] My eyes were red, and they hurt. That was my last confrontation with the riot police)."

The East seceded. A new state, Biafra, was born on May 30 1967. There was widespread jubilation. Then war was declared by the Federal Government and fighting broke out. Federal troops started pushing eastward. In spite of the volatile political situation, lectures still went on. June came and with it the end-of-year examinations. The situation had become desperate. Federal troops were advancing fast. Don was determined to sit all his papers. Students hurriedly left the campus as soon as they finished their exams. Some, however, abandoned theirs and left.

Don was among the very last students that stayed on. Before he left for his last paper on July 1, he packed his suitcases and bags and got them ready at the Porter's Lodge. Immediately after the paper, he took off in a hired car to Enugu, where he took another car to the Nigeria-Cameroon border at Mfum. As the car crossed the long bridge over the Cross River into Cameroon, Don could hear the sound of heavy canons and artillery behind them and in the direction of Ikom and Calabar. The federal troops had entered Cross River State.

Later that evening, the radio announced that Nigeria had closed its borders with Cameroon. It was a lucky escape for Don, but it was not so for a few compatriots like Nnoko, and some international students, Don was to learn much later. They were trapped in Biafra and caught in the war.

A Short Stint as a Veterinarian

Don reported in the Ministry of Agriculture and Veterinary Services in Buea on arrival in Cameroon for a vacation job. He was sent to see Dr. Danilo, an Italian and the Director of Veterinary Services. He welcomed Don very warmly and called for a file. His secretary brought it immediately. "Don Harris Oben, Veterinary Officer-in-Training," was written on the front cover. Don was pleasantly surprised. He came to understand that when one was given a government scholarship to study, one became classified as a trainee officer in the relevant ministry. After asking him about his veterinary program at Nsukka and how his studies went, he wrote some notes in Don's file. Then looking up, he announced, "I am sending you to Jakiri, to the Livestock Investigation Center in Jakiri."

"Jakiri, where is that?" Don asked.

Dr. Danilo told him Jakiri was up there after Bamenda, nice climate, lots of animals, the only place to find lots of livestock, and that he will enjoy his time there working with young Veterinary Assistant trainees.

The mention of Bamenda brought back memories of Santa in December 1957, when he was in form 1 in Government Secondary School Owerri—memories of the biting cold. He had secretly arranged with his classmate, Christopher Ateh, to spend the first two weeks of their first term (Christmas) holidays with his family in Santa. Don didn't tell his parents. They arrived Mamfe town from Owerri around 4:00 p.m. From the motor park where the mammy wagon had parked, one could see their compound with the coconut, kola nut, and orange trees spreading out just a hundred yards away. But because he had not informed his parents that he was going to Santa, he didn't want anybody who knew him to see him, so he had to hide inside the back of the vehicle covered by a tarpaulin. He left only a small window through which he could peep outside.

As Don had feared, he saw people he knew passing to and fro, some even hawking foodstuffs close to where the vehicle was parked. Christopher bought food and water and brought these up to him. Don stayed in until nightfall, when it was safe for him to come down and stretch his legs and ease himself. They left for Santa via Widikum and Bamenda early the following morning. Christopher had told Don his village was cold. What Don experienced in Santa was to him like modern-day winter in Canada. They would get up at 6:00 a.m. and spend the whole day in the biting cold, harvesting coffee. On other days, they did drying or dehusking. In the evenings, they sat round a fire. The heat could never be hot enough to keep him warm. After one week, he told Christopher's parents that he couldn't stay two weeks. Santa was too cold for him. They ground some dried coffee and gave him to take to his parents. Don secretly wished they had not given him this present to his parents. It meant he had to tell them where he had been since school closed.

And now Dr. Danilo was sending him to Jakiri, an even colder place than Santa. Don gave all reasons why Dr. Danilo should not send him up North: He had never lived up there; he had never lived in a cold place; Where would he stay? He didn't know anybody in Jakiri.

"Never mind, you will always find a place to stay," was all the director could say.

One of the departmental Land Rovers whisked Don off the next day. He doesn't remember how the journey went. Though his eyes had been on the road, his thoughts were far away, embedded in the memories of the past. Why couldn't Dr. Danilo leave him in Buea? There was the lower farms and the upper farms managed by the Prisons Department, which raised cattle, sheep, goats, and chickens, he recalled. Those farms sold fresh meat and even distributed fresh milk. One could see those animals grazing out there on the hills and valleys. And there was a small veterinary clinic to which small animals and pets were brought for treatment and health care. So why did the Director decide to send him up north?

They stopped in Bamenda for a courtesy call on Dr. Nana Nuketchap who was the only veterinary officer in charge of the North. They arrived at Jakiri and drove straight to the Livestock Investigation Center, often called Livestock Center for short. It was past 9:00 p.m. and the office had closed. Don was taken to see the senior veterinary superintendent, Mr. J. Mobit, in his house. Unfortunately, the latter had gone out. His wife gave Don food and a place to sleep. The following morning, Mr. Mobit told Don he could stay with him and his family—himself, his wife, their little niece, Lilian who was then in form 2, and one or two other relatives. Don could never thank them enough.

He joined the veterinary trainees at the Center in their program activities. Each day's activities always commenced at 6:00 a.m. while it was still dark and the weather was freezing. They would remove the animals from their pens or enclosures to the fields to graze and would bring them late in the evening back to their pens. Sometimes they bathed them; sometimes they drenched them to remove ticks and other parasites, and almost every day, they treated those that were sick. Infestation of ticks, foot-and-mouth disease, pneumonia, and streptotrichosis were some of the main problems they dealt with. They also learned how to milk cows and Mr. Mobit taught them to perform castration, both internal and external.

As they worked together, Don listened to their gossip but also got to know about much of what was going on in the ministry, especially concerning staffing issues. Dr. Protus Atang had recently returned from veterinary studies. Dr. Nana Nuketchap was the only Cameroonian veterinary doctor in the country until then. Mr. Songwe was studying vet medicine in East Africa. There were a few veterinary superintendents-in-training at the Veterinary Institute in Vom, Northern Nigeria. In fact, one of them, Mr. Nfor, returned while Don was just about leaving Jakiri.

Don would have endured working at the Center but for the freezing weather and the fact that he had to get up at 6:00 a.m. Mamfe, where he had spent his childhood, has a hot climate. Owerri, where he had spent the next seven years after leaving Mamfe, was equally hot. His sojourn in Buea after high school had been too short to get him acclimatized to cold weather. So it wasn't long before he started writing to Dr. Danilo, requesting to be brought down to headquarters. He had never experienced the kind of cold as that in Jakiri. It was fierce and relentless, sometimes accompanied by cold winds.

To make matters worse, he was always at the Center after work and at weekends. The town was a kilometer or two away. There was nothing interesting there. For sport, he sometimes played football with the trainees and some office staff. For distraction, he learned to ride a horse, and he occasionally rode it to town to enjoy a long ride. One weekend, Mr. Mobit asked him if he would like to accompany him to Kumbo, a much bigger town some miles away. He was visiting his friend, Mr. John Ngole, the Senior District Officer of Bui Division. Don was quick to oblige. They almost carried the Volkswagen car through half the journey. The road was at its worst.

Don kept sending letters and messages every week through the Superintendent to Dr. Danilo, still requesting to be brought down to Buea. Finally, Dr. Danilo sent the same Land Rover and driver that had brought him up to Jakiri to come take him back to Buea six weeks later, in the third week of August. Don was sent to the small animal clinic located at that time opposite Clerks' Quarters. At the clinic, they received and treated small animals, mainly pets (cats and small dogs), and watch dogs, some chickens and goats and sheep. He also went out to the prison farms with Dr. Danilo to treat cows and other livestock.

Don recalls one particular morning Dr, Danilo had called him. He was coming to pick him to go to Lower Farms with him. He had been informed that a cow was having calving difficulty. They would not know whether that difficulty, technically known as dystocia, was due to improper presentation, position, or posture of the calf during parturition until they get there. They arrived and found the cow had been restrained, using a low head tie secured to a tree. They were told it had been in extended second stage labor and no fetal parts had yet been presented. Its rear areas were covered by light yellow viscous fluids, probably a mixture of urine and fluids from the allantoic and amniotic sacs. The ground around it was a mess of blood, urine, fluid, and feces. Dr. Danilo asked the assistants to cleanse the perineum, vulva and anus area of the dam, which they did by liberally applying mild soap and warm water and rinsing thoroughly the area of the tail head down to somewhere below the vulva.

He then proceeded to examine the dam, passing his hand along the birth canal to determine the position and size of the calf. It would appear that the cow had an abnormally positioned calf, meaning that the calf was not lying in a 'diving' position, that is, with both front legs extended with the head following and facing forward. Rather, it had a normal posterior (backward) presentation in which the hind limbs were extended into the birth canal. Going over to the Land Rover, he got a cotton rope which he knotted into a loop and handed over to Don. He asked him to wash, disinfect, and lubricate his right hand and insert it into the birth canal of the dam. He should search for the hind legs of the calf and insert the loop round the feet, so they could pull out the calf which he had determined, was already dead due to the prolonged birthing process. Although the hind quarters of the cow had just been thoroughly washed, the cow was still exuding smellier, stickier yellowish fluids.

Don had heard Dr. Danilo's instruction clearly. However, he was reluctant to insert his hand into the messy vulva of the cow. So he asked him, "Pardon, what did you say?" hoping Dr. Danilo would change his mind and ask one of the assistants to do it. Dr. Danilo repeated his instruction, explaining that his arms were short and stout and a bit too big to enter and reach the calf's legs. Don's, he had observed, were longer and thinner and so could easily do the job. He was right, but the reality of Don having to insert his hand into the cow left him unimpressed. So he said "Pardon?" a second time.

Dr. Danilo was visibly irritated and commanded Don to get going. Reluctantly, Don pulled the long sleeves of his shirt up his arms and washed his hands and arms with soap, water and an antiseptic solution. Looking up to the skies, he inserted his right hand into the birth canal, searched and found the two hind legs of the calf, knotted them together, after which they pulled the calf out. It was dead as Dr. Danilo had determined. Although Dr. Danilo had commended Don for quickly finding the calf's feet and easily tying them, Don knew Dr. Danilo had noted with much displeasure his reluctance to carry out his instructions.

As they left the lower farms in the Land Rover, Don prayed that no serious emergencies of that nature should ever occur again that would warrant Dr. Danilo taking him to the field to attend to. He was lucky no other serious case happened again, and he continued his routine duties at the small animal clinic for the rest of the vacation. The only incident worth noting was a serious fall Don had one day as he tried to ride a horse at the para-para field in Buea town. Excited to relive a few of the moments he had had in Jakiri, riding to town, he had not taken time to become acquainted with that horse before trying to ride it.

As September approached and the universities were about to reopen their gates for the 1967/1968 academic year, the battlegrounds of the Nigerian civil war were by then deep within Biafra. In view of the war, the Cameroon Government decided to transfer Cameroon students at Nsukka to universities in other parts of the country that were not affected by the war. With the assistance of the Cameroon embassy in Lagos, those students were found admission in universities in their chosen fields. Don was found admission and transferred to the University of Ibadan to continue his studies in veterinary medicine at the Faculty of Agriculture and Veterinary Medicine.

A Soul-Searching Debriefing

Dr. Danilo was reading through Don's file when he knocked and went into his office. He had gone to debrief him on his vacation experience with the Department as he was due to leave for Ibadan the following week. It turned out to be a long heart-to-heart discussion. Dr. Danilo was impressed at the good reports he had received on Don's performance at the Livestock Center in Jakiri and at the small animal clinic in Buea. He was equally amazed at Don's wealth of knowledge concerning the organization and provision of veterinary services in the country. However, he had not forgotten Don's reluctance to go to Jakiri, his incessant complaints about, and dislike for, the cold weather in Jakiri, and his repeated requests to be brought down to Buea.

According to him, it was not the cold in Jakiri that Don disliked. It was because he wanted to stay in Buea. In his view, Don was a city boy. But it was Don's attitude to work, as he had demonstrated during their sojourn to the Lower Farms some weeks earlier, that formed his opinion about his suitability as a future veterinary surgeon.

He told Don that he had watched him right from the day he reported to his office on his arrival from Nsukka. He had noted Don's fancy clothes, his shoes, and his long nails, which, unfortunately, were not suitable for veterinary work. Veterinary services in the country, he explained, were centered on the main livestock—cows, sheep, and goats—which were found only in the Bamenda highlands, and those were the only places which any veterinarian must work. On graduation as a veterinary surgeon, it was to those areas that Don would be posted to work and would spend his working life. But those were the areas characterized by extreme cold winds and weather which he so disliked, and he vehemently refused to live there, he observed. And Don's general attitude at the Lower Farms and his extreme reluctance to assist a cow that was having dystocia showed his unconcealed dislike for work that gets one's hands dirty. And most veterinary work gets one's hands dirty, he repeated emphatically. Then closing Don's file and laying it on the table in front of him, he looked up straight at Don.

"You may be very brilliant academically, but I am convinced you certainly do not have the calling to be a veterinarian. My candid advice to you when you return to the university is to change your course. Otherwise, you will not have a satisfactory and rewarding professional career in the future as a veterinary surgeon, and you will not be happy," he said, getting up and shaking Don's hands and leading him to his Land Rover which he had arranged to take Don home. It was Don's last day at work.

Don secretly welcomed Dr. Danilo's advice. It took a whole load off his back. It came to confirm that the decision he had taken earlier on was right, the decision to change his course of study. His experiences in Jakiri and the lower farms had left him in no doubt that he had chosen the wrong career. (In those days, they had no guidance counselors in secondary schools to guide or advise students on career choices). And as he went to debrief the director of veterinary services, his worry was how he was going to tell him that he wanted to change his course without inviting serious repercussions by the ministry, which could involve his scholarship being withdrawn. But now that the advice had come from the horse's mouth, Don felt very much relieved.

In hindsight however, Don wondered whether the director and himself had not taken a myopic view of veterinary development in Cameroon and his career in veterinary medicine. They did not foresee or envisage that veterinary services could be diversified in future into other products and services and expanded to other regions of the country where the weather was warmer, and he would be more comfortable working there. They did not also anticipate that Don could, with more field exposures, get used to and come to be comfortable with veterinary cases and procedures, which initially seemed nauseating.

After all, cases of first year medical students fainting during their first class in practical human anatomy when they are presented with cadavers are well known. So with time, it is possible that Don would have settled well into a veterinary career and there would have been no need for a career change. Whatever the case, Don made no attempt to benefit from that hindsight. He decided to accept the advice of Dr. Danilo.

Crossing over from Nsukka to Ibadan: At the University of Ibadan, Nigeria

On that September morning in 1967, a week after Don's last meeting with Dr. Danilo, he boarded a Nigeria Airways flight at Tiko Airport for the second time in his life, this time, heading to Ibadan via Lagos. He was on his way to resume his university education at the University of Ibadan. He had no difficulty settling down quickly in Nnamdi Azikiwe Hall, one of the two new halls of residence, the other one being Independence Hall. Unlike the older halls which were close together and close to the central administration, those two halls while close together, were farther away from the old halls and the central administration as well as from the Faculty of Agriculture and Veterinary Medicine.

Come time for registration of courses, Don's headache was how he was going to change his course. He avoided going anywhere near the Department of Veterinary Medicine, as if he would be conscripted into the department if he was found there. His name was on the notice board there, as he was told. He had decided to change his course to General Agriculture with Special Honors in Agricultural Economics. The Head of the Department of Agricultural Economics referred Don to the Dean of the Faculty because he was not admitted into his department. Professor V. A. Oyenuga, the Dean, could not understand why Don would want to change from veterinary medicine to begin a new course in agricultural economics.

After a grueling interview, he asked Don to go sleep over his decision and come again to see him if he still wanted the change. When Don saw him days later, another major issue was raised. Would his government approve the change? The information on Don's admission file was that he was a government scholar admitted to continue his studies in veterinary medicine. After assuring the Dean that the change was by mutual consent and that he would provide him with official confirmation, Don was admitted into the Department of Agricultural Economics.

Above, some Cameroon students at matriculation, November 1967. |
Left to right, Gustav Tabeson, Sama Nkwain, John Awemo,
Ms. Susan Ghogomo, Peter Enyong, and Don.

As a science student, Don had no difficulty dealing with the related subjects, such as soil science, crop science, chemistry, physics, geology, animal science, etc. But he had no notion whatsoever what economics was all about. So it was at the university that he was to have his first lectures in elementary economics.

His hall of residence was quite far from his faculty. In order to get to lectures on time in the mornings and to laboratory practicals in the afternoons, he needed some form of transport that would also facilitate his movements around the campus. So as soon as he had settled down, he went to Lagos and bought a mobylette. In his second year, he sold it and bought a second-hand scooter. He wanted a bigger motorcycle. He also bought a large radiogram, a combination of a radio and record player with loudspeakers all built into a wooden cabinet with a chamber for records. It was the state-of-the-art musical appliance at the time. Don would stack records on it and supply music to the whole hall and beyond free of charge! Zikites and Independites were noted for noise and misdemeanors.

The Victor Sylvester Ballroom Circle at the University of Nigeria, Nsukka, had ignited the flame of ballroom dancing in him. And just when it had started to glow, the war had broken out and caused the university to close, thus putting out the flame. Now the Dancing Club of the University of Ibadan presented another opportunity for him to rekindle it. He joined the club and in the second year, he was to become the Assistant General Secretary and, in the third year, the General Secretary.

Cameroon had quite a large presence at UI at that time. Don remembers Mrs. Nasah and Mrs. Awasum in nursing; Nicholas Songwe, Benedict Fultang, and Augustine Bokwe in forestry; Fred Ngane, Timothy Mbide, and Sam Mbake in the social sciences; Peter Enyong in the pure sciences; John Awemo and Sama Nkwain in agriculture; Anderson Doh, Ben Mengot, Ms. Ghogomu, and Emmanuel Moka Endeley in medicine.

Similarly, the international club, which was actually the International Students Association (ISA) offered Don the opportunity to continue his activities with international students. He joined the Association, and in his second year, Roberts, from the West Indies was elected the President; He, the Vice President; and Nicki Kapula from Namibia, the General Secretary. The treasurer was a girl from the United States. The president was a medical student in his final year at the University College Hospital. As he was very busy with his studies and exams, Don virtually took over the duties of the president.

The ISA sought to cater for the interests of foreign students. It assisted in the welcome and orientation activities organized by the student union for all new students. It provided a forum where foreign students could seek assistance in resolving their peculiar problems. One of the areas where they made a contribution to the welfare of international students was in the cafeteria. Since many foreign students could not eat the purely Nigerian traditional cuisines, such as 'amala and ewedu' or gari, pounded yam and okro or egusi soup or ogbono soup, they made a strong case to the Administration for the cafeterias to provide alternative dishes for foreign students on the days when these traditional meals were served. Not only was their demand met, the university also got the cafeterias to serve a variety of more exotic meals for the benefit of international students.

They also organized sightseeing tours to places of interest, such as cultural sites, important landmarks, etc. In order to implement the Association's program of activities, they needed money. One of the activities which they identified that could bring in money was from profits made by renting movies from the big movie houses and showing them on campus. So Don and the Secretary often went to movie houses in Lagos, such as Odeon, to negotiate and rent films.

Don recalls the first occasion when they screened a movie on campus. On that occasion, Don went to Odeon Cinema in Lagos and negotiated and paid for a film, which he had selected from a long list of movies. It was called *Kiss the Blood Off My Hands* (1948), starring Burt Lancaster and Joan Fontaine. Showing movies was one thing and getting a large audience that would bring in the money was another. So Don had to develop a strategy to attract a crowd that would fill the amphitheater. The role and importance of advertising came immediately to mind. Prior to that time, associations and clubs used typewriters to type their adverts on A4 printing paper. Many adverts were also handwritten. And they were pinned on notice boards in halls of residence where many other notices often made them less visible.

Don had never before seen or heard of the movie he rented from Odeon. Judging only from the title, he conjectured a James Bond-style movie involving espionage, romance, intrigues, shootings, blood, daring escapes, and love and kissing. After composing an advert capturing those images, he went to town and had it printed at a printing press, Jimmy's Press, on giant posters with large red, blue, and yellow letters against a white background. And he signed it "Don Harris Oben, V-President, ISA." Those giant, colorful, and well-mounted posters were awesome. They were mounted in front of cafeterias and other conspicuous places. The advert was captivating. Never before had adverts of that size, color, and poetry been seen on campus. The movie was sold out! The amphitheater was packed to capacity. Even the aisles were packed with students. No student wanted to miss the movie, particularly the lovebirds!

It turned out to be a nice movie but not quite what Don had advertised. He had overdramatized it, and students came looking for him just to see who that Don Harris Oben was. After that, advertisements on campus were never the same again. Don had brought about a revolution in the way clubs, societies, and associations advertised and marketed their fund-raising activities. Small handwritten or typewritten adverts gave way to huge multicolored printed posters!

Apart from fund-raising, ISA organized social evenings and invited guest speakers. As already mentioned, it also organized field trips and excursions to centers of culture, shrines, national monuments, etc.

The third year saw Don more deeply involved with the ISA and the Dancing Club. He went for dancing practices four times a week from 6:00–8:00 p.m., including Saturdays. He would leave laboratory practicals at 6:00 p.m. on Mondays, Wednesdays, and Fridays and head straight to Tedder Hall Common Room where they held their Dancing Club practices. By the third year in the club, Don was dancing an amalgamation of steps for advanced dancers in all the dances. In the Tango, he remembers the walk into progressive side steps, closed promenade, three reverse (top) spins, curved progressive side step into double reverse spin into the walk, promenade into right foot lunge (low), oversway spins into promenade position (or spins into back lock-four step), fallaway lock round to whisk, counter whisk, sharp twist, camelia with right foot lunge, double natural spin turn to back lock. Don remembers with fondness their favorite music/lyrics which they frequently used for dancing the tango: 'Mama Teach Me to Dance' by Alma Cogan.

He remembers in particular the grace with which they danced the advance steps of the slow foxtrot, almost effortlessly: the feather slip, three step; double natural turn to feather finish, open telemark to right hover, reverse pivot to counter whisk box, closed telemark with forward body sway, outside spins to whisk, natural fallaway to quick open reverse, double open telemark, reverse weave to oversway, quick natural spin to back corte ending, forward locks to double reverse spin, three step closed impetus to top spin reverse turn ending, open telemark to telespin.

The waltz too was slow and as graceful as the slow foxtrot. It was one of Don's best dances. And the 'Tennessee Walz' by Patti Page provided the perfect lyrics for this dance.

He cannot forget the rumba too. It is a dance he had enjoyed right from the days of the Mamfe Students Union (MSU) in the late 50s/early 60s when they had organized social evenings during the Christmas vacations in Mamfe town. He had picked up a few basic steps quite easily from the bigger boys and girls. But now at the Club, he was dancing the amalgamated steps for advanced dancers with ease. He remembers those steps in the rumba: the number square, progressive locks to reverse finish, zigzag, check, sideway taps into flicker, the lady's solo, double Cuban top into Alemana ending, eight quick runs into forward locks (broken lock variation), promenade run, check into contra point, rumba square into Alemana top variation, sideway runs into progressive Alemana.

The quickstep was the most exhausting. It was fast-paced and the advanced steps were quite tasking. He recalled to me, such steps as the natural turn to whisk, side chasse, fallaways lock, lady's swivel back lock, running finish, the open impetus turn into forward promenade run to counter whisk skip to unwhisk quick contra chasse to forward lock, the scoop, fishtail to quick locks, hesitating syncopated locks forward check to fishtail, left forward lock, skip to forward lock, check double back lock, double side chasse, the fallaway to right foot lunge, reverse turning to lock to four quick runs check, oversway, natural spins to natural sways, double reverse spins, reverse turning lock.

By the time dancing was over, Don was too tired and hungry to do any academic work. On most days, he got to the hall of residence after dinner had been served and the cafeteria had closed. And there were times when he was so tired that he fell asleep on the chair and never got up until the next morning. As the general secretary, he spent a lot of his time organizing their annual ball to which ballroom circles and dancing clubs around were invited. When he was not dancing, he was organizing ISA activities. To this date, Don cannot forget the much concern his very close friend Anthony often expressed regarding the amount of time and energy he was spending on ISA and DC activities rather than on his academic work.

Don traveled frequently to Lagos by air, using the unused Lagos-Ibadan-Lagos portions of some of his compatriots/friends' air tickets which he got at giveaway prices. In his first and second years at Ibadan, he tried to keep abreast of his academic work. He did his assignments and passed his sessional exams depending mainly on the knowledge he gained from the class lectures and practicals. But in the third year, as he devoted more and more of his time to the Dancing Club and ISA activities, his academic work suffered. By the time the final year sessional (degree) exams arrived, he was unprepared. He had not even started his revision. He was too far behind to even revise together with his two classmates and close friends, Anthony (who had expressed deep concern over his ISA and DC activities), and Nkwain. Don excused himself to study alone. With his back against the wall, he had to fight back. The stakes were too high. He graduated with a second-class Bachelor of Science degree in Agriculture with Special Honors in Agricultural Economics in June 1970.

Above, in Don's room in Azikiwe Hall with the radiogram in the background.

Above, a practice session at the Dancing Club. Don is sitting 1st from Right.

Chapter 8
In the Plantations

Planting Rubber in the CDC Plantations

Back in Cameroon, Don decided to apply to work with the Cameroon Development Corporation (CDC), Bota, Victoria, rather than work with the Ministry of Agriculture. One of his friends, Fred Ngane, who graduated in economics also applied to work with the CDC. While they waited for the outcome of their applications, they dreamed of living in Bota or Tiko and making a career with the CDC. Fred did not have to wait for long. He was appointed Personal Assistant to the Chairman, Nfon V. E. Mukete. Their dreams were coming true. He was given a very cozy office at the Chairman's office in Bota and a big and nice residence in the senior service quarters in Bota. They were very happy, and each time Don visited Fred, he wondered how his own office would be. He knew it would be in a plantation and, therefore, will not be as cozy, but he was0. confident he would be provided a nice house in Bota or Likomba or Tiko.

The CDC, as if on purpose, let him dream for long, long enough to make him feel right in his bones that he was living and working in Bota or Tiko. Then the letter from the CDC Head Office, Bota, arrived.

"...It is with pleasure that the Corporation is appointing you to the position of Graduate Field Assistant in the Senior Service of the Corporation. You have been posted to Mbonge Rubber Plantation..."

As Don read the letter, his heart sank. *Sending him to Mbonge, a pleasure?* he thought to himself. "Why Mbonge?" he asked the Chief Production Manager (CPM), Mr. M. O. Oyebog. He told Don that Mbonge Plantation was where there was a vacant position for a Field Assistant. Since Don had never heard of Mbonge, he knew it must be some small, obscure town somewhere.

As Fred and Don sorrowfully read his letter again, Don remembered how, three years earlier, in July 1967, he had been sent to Jakiri, to the Livestock Investigation Center while he had hoped to remain in Buea. Again, he was being sent to Mbonge! Whom would he blame for always being sent to places he doesn't like? He blamed his stars, of course. Then he remembered Shakespeare's *Julius Caesar*: "The fault is not in our stars but in us, for letting ourselves to be underlings." (8)

Don refused to accept that view. Did he have a choice? However, there was cause to be glad, and thank God for His blessings. He had a good job in the CDC, a government parastatal, which paid more remunerative salaries than the civil service and provided free housing and other fringe benefits. Most importantly and significantly, it was the first time that the CDC was appointing young university graduates into the field assistant category in its senior service, following a major policy shift. That new generation of field assistants would form the pool from which the future managers of the corporation would be drawn.

Prior to 1970, incumbents of posts in that category, as in other categories, worked their way up through the ranks over many years by promotion. That policy change did not sit well with the old staff, who had put in long years of service and were still in the lower ranks. In fact, the old managers with little education had the misguided notion that the new graduate field assistants had been recruited to eventually replace them.

Mbonge Plantation: A Minefield in Waiting

Don's travel to take up duty was delayed for a few weeks because his accommodation in Mbonge Plantation was not ready. The journey to Mbonge was like a journey to the end of the world. They reached Kumba and turned left and went on and on along a brown muddy road, passing through villages and small passenger buses that had gotten stuck in the mud or small lakes of water. Finally, they arrived at the town late on that afternoon of August 28, 1970, and the short-wheelbase Land Rover wheeled to the left at the end of the town and into a dirt road that led through lines of rubber trees to the CDC Mbonge Rubber Plantation. It turned and climbed up a little hill and stopped right in front of the office. The manager, Mr. Gwanpandinga, was in his office with the junior field assistant and the senior overseer. The administration and finance clerk, Mr. Atong, wanted to take Don in, but Don preferred not to interrupt their meeting and, therefore, took a seat near the manager's door and waited quietly and patiently. When eventually he was asked to go in, he knocked and waited until he was asked to come in.

The manager was surprised to learn from Mr. Atong that he had been waiting by the door for a half hour. Then he was introduced to the Junior Field Assistant (JFA) and the Senior Overseer (SO). They probably must have been discussing his impending arrival. They then drove down, crossed the road and up the hill to the guesthouse which was just besides the manager's house. Those two houses were in full view of the plantation office, which was directly opposite, and the workers' camp, situated some one hundred meters away to the right.

The guesthouse, which had consisted of a large living room, one large bedroom, and one bathroom and no kitchen, had been restructured to accommodate Don. The bedroom was divided into two, and a door was fitted to the side facing the manager's house. A small bathroom was fitted inside the bedroom. That then became the guesthouse, a one-room apartment. Don's own apartment then became the former guesthouse that had a living room, a small bedroom, bathroom, and a fitted wooden outdoor kitchen. He was told that was just a temporary arrangement as plans were already afoot to build the field assistant's house. It was never built!

On his first day at work, the manager took him to show him round the plantation. After visiting the fields and the workers' camps, the manager took him to the clinic where they met a woman probably in her early thirties. "This is our doctor," he said, as he introduced the plantation nurse to him.

A welcome was organized in Don's honor the Saturday following his arrival in one of the two prominent bars in town. The bar was packed full, and there were lots of drinks, fried meat and chicken, and sandwiches and snacks. And the loudspeakers were blaring, and the workers were eating and dancing to music from Zaire and sweating. As Don sat between the manager and the junior field assistant sipping only coke and watching the proceedings quietly, he seemed completely out of place.

"Don't worry. That is how they are. Give him two weeks, you will see him drinking like us. He has just come," the junior field assistant said with a quick sneer at Don.

He was responding to the manager, who had asked Don for the umpteenth time to have some beer or something 'hot'. He couldn't be drinking 'water' at his welcome party, the manager opined.

"You will soon find yourself drinking. It is inevitable. That's all we have in Mbonge. After work each day, everyone finds himself in the bars in the evenings, drinking and dancing and socializing," the JFA continued, as if to justify why he had said Don would start drinking soon.

During their conversation, Don was to learn that Mbonge was a small town with a relatively large population of plantation workers and traders and a few big businessmen. There was a small Nigerian population as the town was close to the riverine borders with the Cross River State of Nigeria. The two bars were the center of most social activities, and they came to life every night and especially at the weekends and on paydays, when workers and the town folks came to enjoy themselves.

Then came the time for the welcome address. The Manager spoke and everyone clapped. Don responded. There was more clapping. Then a man got up and asked to speak. He was middle-aged, a bit light complexioned and skinny. Don asked the JFA whether he was one of their staff. He was not. Everybody looked up, surprised.

"I have studied French for a long time," he began. "In fact, I have studied French my whole life. The word which I consider the most important word in the French language is 'attention'. (pronounced 'atang-sion'). I repeat, the most important word in French to me is 'attention'," he continued, seriously frowning. "You are a young man, so the most important advice I can give you is attention. Please, I say it again, 'attention'," he concluded, narrowing his eyes, and sat down. Don couldn't make any meaning out of his speech.

As the JFA and Don walked back to the plantation, Don asked him who the last speaker was and if he understood what he (the speaker) meant in his speech. The JFA just looked at Don and smiled and kept quiet. It was after Don asked the question a second time that he told him.

"Mr. Akpabio (not his real name) is not one of our workers. He is a Nigerian living in the workers' camp with his wife. Both he and his wife are Nigerians from the South-Eastern State of Nigeria who have settled in Cameroon."

"So why did he speak if he is not a staff, and do you know what he was talking about? I hadn't the slightest clue," Don pressed on.

"I think he was warning you about his wife. She is the plantation nurse," the JFA finally got himself to say. Sensing that Don was very upset, he went on to explain that Mr. Akpabio was in the habit of suspecting every young man of having sexual relations with his wife, a reason why they were always fighting at home.

"Seeing that you are not only young and nice looking but you are a university graduate and a field assistant, it is not surprising that he would feel very insecure with your arrival in the plantation, hence, his warning that you should keep off her," he added. Don was very hurt.

With the vacant post of field assistant just filled, it became necessary for the manager to make some reassignments and adjustments in the management of the plantation. A sizable section of the plantation was put under Don's immediate management and supervision with a large labor force headed by the senior overseer. That area consisted of mature and immature rubber and recently planted (1970) fields. A new development, as projects for establishing new plantation areas were called, had been planned to get underway at the beginning of the dry season. A rubber nursery to provide planting material for this new development was being established.

Don settled down quickly to work, supervising operations in the mature and immature areas. Those included the tapping and collection of cup lumps, pests and diseases treatment, weeding, wind damage clearance, etc. The nursery operations, which were carried out by a large group consisting mainly of girls, included filling of polybags with soil, planting of seedlings in the polybags, fertilizing, watering, weeding, and pests and diseases control. Work began at 5:30 a.m. each morning with roll call, then allocation of labor to the tasks/operations that he, in collaboration with the senior overseer, had identified and agreed to.

After the allocation of work, as the laborers left for their respective worksites, Don would go to the office to look into any matters requiring his attention, after which he would dash to his house to have a quick breakfast. By 9:30 a.m. he would be in the field, going round checking on work in progress and ensuring that labor is working on all sites as allocated. He would return from the field around 6:00 p.m. and go to the office to look at any matters requiring his attention and also to prepare the work plan for the next day. It would be about 7:00 p.m. by the time he got home.

Once or twice a month, Don would go spend the weekend in Victoria with his friend, Fred, and he would fill Don in on all the happenings in town and at the CDC Head Office. The driver usually dropped him off in Kumba after work on Friday, and he returned on Sunday evening. He also went occasionally to the Pamol Plantation Ltd., Lobe, Senior Service Staff Club with his friend, Henry Wacka, to play lawn tennis. Henry was a senior customs officer in charge of the area, and he too had just been transferred to Mbonge around the same time as Don. After they met, they found a common ground. They were out of place in Mbonge, like fish out of the water. They loved lawn tennis. During the week, Don spent his time after work at home cooking but, more often, reading or listening to music or the radio from his big radiogram, sometimes sipping some dubonnet or Campari which were his favorite drinks then. Yes, he had brought his large radiogram from Ibadan, which by then became his main companion.

The life Don was living in Mbonge was not the life he had envisaged when he decided to work with the CDC. However, having found himself there, he decided to give his all to his work, at least for that time. He spent most of his time at work and only came home late in the evenings, especially when activities in the New Development started. He also made a commitment to be as nice and fair as possible to all his collaborators and workers, giving honor even to those whom it was not due.

But in spite of this, he noticed that the Senior Overseer always wore an unwelcoming face each time they met. Was Don just imagining it or it was real? Time was to tell. The Junior Field Assistant had seemed quite aloof in the first few months of Don's arrival. He would sometimes make statements in front of the workers, which Don found disrespectful to him, but Don would just disregard or ignore them. It didn't take long, however, for the Junior Field Assistant to start coming closer to Don for whatever reason, and they soon became such close family friends that, when the JFA and his wife had their first child, they asked Don to be his godfather. The Manager too, had also been reserved, cautious, watchful, and very formal in his interactions with Don when Don just came. But he too gradually changed and became more friendly and even invited Don occasionally home to dine with him.

Don particularly tried to show the ordinary workers or field hands a lot of understanding. They were working so hard and yet earning so little. Don could not imagine how they survived on such meager wages with large families crowded into one-room accommodations in the workers' camps. In spite of their small means, some of them often came to visit Don, bringing a little live chicken or a few eggs. The first time that happened was the day a worker from a far-off labor camp knocked on his door. After greeting him, Don asked him who he was and what he wanted.

"Masa, nobi I just come for greet you." (Master, I just came to greet you).

Don asked him in and offered him a seat. Then the man went out and came in with a small chicken in a cylindrical basket made of fresh palm leaves and offered it to Don.

"Masa, I jus wan tank you for the work wei you de do for we," he began.

"Which work?" Don asked him, still very surprised that someone he didn't even know came all the way from a faraway camp, carrying a chicken, to see him.

"Masa, since you come for Mbonge, we money dong go up small; them no deh mark we absent jus any how; them no deh cut we money jus any how; and dem deh calculate we money now well, well," he informed Don.

One of the complaints Don had received as soon as he settled down was that some headmen were marking workers absent for flimsy reasons; the hours worked by some laborers were not accurately kept or calculated by the timekeepers, and unauthorized deductions were often made from their wages. Don had told the workers to report to him any cases of unjustified deductions in their hours or earnings, and he had warned the Headmen and Overseers against any malpractices involving workers' payments.

"And you deh also care for we. You deh ask we how we family deh, weda we deh sick. And when we get palaver with we friends or we woman them, you de come settle am fine, fine," he finished, stretching out his two hands to shake Don's hand.

A Field Assistant was almost everything in a plantation. He was also responsible for ensuring peace and serenity in the camps and settling disputes whenever they arose. Cases brought before him in the camps included theft, fighting, adultery, rape, etc. What struck Don most about his visitor was the fact that, out of his lowly means, he brought Don a chicken. To Don, that was a great sacrifice. Don told him he did not have to bring him anything and that he or any of the workers should never do that again. Don entertained him and when he was leaving, gave him some money to buy some provisions for his family. He did the same thing to a few other workers as a way of helping them whenever they came to see 'masa'.

Don was still puzzled by the unfriendly and sometimes hostile attitude of the senior overseer toward him when the admin and finance clerk, Mr. Atong, dropped by his house just to say hello. He had drawn closer to Don quicker than anyone else, probably because of ethnic links. When Don told him about his concerns with the senior overseer's attitude, Mr. Atong paused for a moment, then said apologetically, "I am sorry to be telling you this only now. The news of your posting to Mbonge plantation as field assistant was not well received here by the manager, the junior field assistant, and the senior overseer. In fact, I hear, but I don't know if it is true, that the manager tried to get his countryman, Mr. Cletus Tita, Area Manager, North, to get head office to reverse the posting but did not succeed. So there has been a lot of resentment by these three to your posting here. It is only the young girls in the nursery that were happy that a young, handsome field assistant was coming." Then he added, "And the husband of our plantation nurse kept asking me whether you had arrived."

"But why this resentment?" Don asked him, quite surprised.

Mr. Atong went on to explain what had been transpiring on the plantation and what the stakes were. The manager's worry had been that the junior field assistant, who only did a two-year GCE 'A' Levels course had been very arrogant, insolent, disrespectful, and had an I-know-it-all attitude. If he was almost standing on his (the manager's) head, then a university graduate would even want to stand on the rooftop when talking to him. The junior field assistant's grievance had been that he had been overdue a promotion to the post of field assistant and had, therefore, been looking forward to being promoted to fill the post, which had been vacant right there in that plantation. Don's appointment to fill the post was, therefore, a serious setback to his career, and Don was the architect. Similarly, the senior overseer had been waiting very impatiently to be promoted to the post of Junior Field Assistant as soon as it became vacant with the promotion of the Junior Field Assistant to Field Assistant. The senior overseer had been the most aggrieved, but all three had assumed an attitude of "let him come, we will see."

Don was dumbfounded. "So I was walking into a minefield," Don concluded.

"Very much so," Mr. Atong agreed.

"You knew all this, and you did not warn me," Don pressed him.

"I am sorry, but you disarmed the manager and the junior field assistant in no time," he replied with a smile.

Mr. Atong then told Don how the Manager had confided in him that he had been quite surprised at his quiet manners and the amount of respect and cooperation he had given him right from the time he entered his office, which was contrary to what he had expected. The Junior Field Assistant too had confided in him that he had been struck by the way Don interacted with him. In spite of his outbursts and aloofness, Don had always maintained a calm disposition and often invited him to his home; that Don had always spoken frankly to him and given him his honest advice. In time, he came to see Don not as a competitor or foe but as a friend he could rely on. That made Don recall the day he made Don so angry that, although he did not completely lose his cool, he had to sit the JFA down and tell him in no uncertain terms that he had to change his conduct toward him and the Manager. As one in a junior management position, he needed to behave more appropriately to his more senior colleagues, especially the Manager.

"I am so glad you are working well with them, and the general labor like you very much. It is only the Senior Overseer who has refused to be impressed," Mr. Atong went on after a while.

"Yes, that is true," Don concurred.

He had often said to Don's hearing, "Head office think say them fit send small boys who no sabi anything for come be big man for inside plantation. Well, we go see."

"By the way, Mr. Akpabio has been asking people whether you are still around," Mr. Atong said as he finished his drink and got up to go.

"Who is Mr. Akpabio?" Don asked.

"The Plantation Nurse's husband," he replied.

Work on the new development started around November with the clearing of virgin and secondary forests close to the Meme River and the felling of trees. That was followed in January and February with the burning of the dry vegetation and stumping (digging of tree stumps) in preparation for lining and holing. Operations in the new development required every worker's energy. They often closed very late in the evenings, even on Saturdays. After a hard day's work on one Saturday evening, Don heard a knock on his door. He opened and found a fairly tall, skinny, fair-complexioned man, standing in

115

front of him. He greeted Don and expecting him (Don) to recognize him, he asked if he could come in.

"Who are you?" Don asked, not recognizing him.

He introduced himself as the husband of the Plantation Nurse and apologized for coming to Don's house and any inconvenience he might be causing him, but he had to come. Don welcomed him in and gave him a seat and poured him a hot drink, a whiskey.

"I had to come to see for myself—"

"See what?" Don interrupted.

"I came to see if you are really still in Mbonge. It is more than five months since you arrived here and we welcomed you at a bar in town. Since then, I have neither seen you in any of the bars or in the workers' camp or anywhere in town."

"Well, you have been looking for me in the wrong places," Don told him.

"So how do you spend your time after work?" he asked.

"Just as I am doing now," Don replied quietly, pouring him another drink. Seeing the way the man was gulping down the whiskey, Don put the bottle away, fearing he would empty it if he left it on the table.

Some days later, Mr. Atong came into Don's office with a file Don had asked for.

"So Mr. Akpabio actually came to visit you," he said.

"How did you know?" Don asked him, quite surprised.

"He told me himself. He had been asking me whether you are still around, and he couldn't believe that you are because he had never seen you in town or in the camp or even in the clinic. He said he has the highest regard for you."

"Why am I of interest to him? He is not one of our staff?" Don asked Mr. Atong.

"Here is the file you asked for," he said, avoiding Don's question.

Don and the Senior Overseer

The operations in the new development were on course. They were ready to start lining, and it was of utmost importance that they start and complete it on schedule in order to go on to holing and planting as the rains were approaching. So on the day lining was to start, Don allocated a team of workers under the supervision of the Senior Overseer to undertake the operation. By 6:00 a.m., all teams had left for the field. As usual, after seeing to a few administrative issues in the office, Don followed them into the field and, eventually, arrived in the new development to see how far the lining operation had progressed. To his surprise, he found all the workers sitting down, including the Senior Overseer himself.

"What is happening? Why are you and all the workers sitting down?" Don asked the Senior Overseer, quite surprised.

"Massa, no bi you we di wait? (Master, are we not waiting for you?)," he responded. Don could read mischief in his smile. "No bi we di wait you make you come show we how for do lining?" he asked, standing up and wiping some dirt from his buttocks.

"Why do I have to come and show you how to do lining? Have you not been doing it before?" Don asked.

"No bi you bi big man? Na you bi fied assistan. Na chain that. Take show we how for do the lining," he finished, picking up the chain and throwing it at Don's feet. (Are you not the boss, the Field Assistant? That is the chain, take and show us how to use it to do lining).

He then turned to the workers with a big grin, as if he had been speaking on their behalf, and sat down. There was dead silence. All eyes were on Don.

As Don stood there, his mind raced back to that last day of their agricultural engineering practical course just before the beginning of their third and final year at the university. During this short course, they had been taught how to use some agricultural machinery and equipment. They had also learned to drive tractors and couple them with rotovators, harvesters and planters. Unfortunately, they had not completed the last topic on the course program. He remembered the words of the Visiting Professor from the United States who offered the course. "Sorry, guys, unfortunately we cannot complete the last topic on the course program, the use of the chain, due to lack of time," he had said, lifting up the chain to show them and putting it down quite quickly.

Many students were already leaving the field and never even saw it. Don happened to have caught just a glimpse of it, and when the senior overseer threw the chain at his feet, he could hardly recognize it. And there he was, being challenged by the Senior Overseer in front of all the workers, to use it to do lining! It was bizarre.

Don could have used his authority and ordered the Senior Overseer to go on with the lining operation, and he would have complied, aware that noncompliance would earn him serious sanctions. But Don didn't. If he did that, it would have given the Senior Overseer and all the workers, grounds to believe that he (Don) was unable to use the chain. The Senior Overseer would have considered himself vindicated that Don knew nothing. The consequences could have been too awesome to contemplate. Bad news, rumors, and gossip travel faster than sound in those environments. The worst news and juiciest gossip don't just travel, they fly. News would have reached the camps and even Mbonge town before Don even left the field, fueled by the Senior Overseer, that the new Field Assistant did "not know anything!" It would be the subject of discussion in bars for several weeks.

"Wuna see, I nobi tell you people say head office just send us young boys wei them no know anything. See now, a whole fied assistan no fit use common chain for do lining which me, senior overseer, I dong do am for so many years." Don could visualize him telling everyone who was willing to listen.

He had unknowingly aimed his arrow at Don's Achilles' heel. But there was more to plantation agriculture than knowing how to use a chain. A good education provides one the ability to apply knowledge to solve problems of the moment.

Don recollected himself very quickly and sprang into action. He went into the thicket behind them and cut a nice straight rod, one meter in length. He always carried a Swiss knife and a 5m pocket tape with him. Then looking around the cleared area and the direction of the sun, he established a convenient base line along the longest straight boundary line with one of the long ropes. Using the rod, a guiding rope, and his knowledge of geometry, he lined and pegged a little area and then asked the team to continue from where he stopped. All the while, the Senior Overseer was moving from one side of Don to the other with his hand on his chin, trying to see what the hell Don was doing as he used the one-meter rod to construct the angles.

"Your task today was to complete the lining of this field, and you must complete it, or else you will be paid pro-rata today," Don told the team in no uncertain terms and turned to leave.

"Sir, but we no fit finish this work when we di just start now for eleven o'clock," one elderly worker protested.

"Yes, you talk true," the others agreed with him.

"That's the price you pay for indiscipline and insubordination. And you, the Senior Overseer, will be sanctioned for orchestrating a sit-down strike." Don hardly spoke pidgin English, and he knew they understood him.

Don wanted to know what the Senior Overseer's reaction would be. So after he left them and turned a corner down the path that led from the field, he entered into the thicket and creeped quietly back. He then hid just behind them inside the thicket. From where he was stooping, he could see and hear them clearly.

"Wetin this small boy wan show me, say him go take small stick measure angle? Bring that chain. Come measure this angle," he commanded one of the workers.

"Exact," the worker reported after using the chain to measure it.

"Measure between this and that row," he instructed him again.

"Exact," the worker replied again. All the workers exclaimed in astonishment, looking at the Senior Overseer.

"Give me the chain; I measure myself," he commanded, almost seizing it from the worker. "What?" he exclaimed after measuring the angles and distances. "Exact," he himself exclaimed in amazement.

"Dis small boy na witch. How him go take small stick do lining wei him no use chain? The boy na witch boy. Make man fear him," he conceded.

"We bin dong tell you since make you leave de fied assistan alone, but you no gree. Now you see, he dong shame you," one young worker sneered at him.

"The fied assistan na young man, but he don learn plenty book. Make you gree say him pass you," another retorted.

"Shut up, you mop!" he shouted at both of them. "Now wuna come make we do dis work. We get for finish am today," he instructed the workers.

"We been beg you since for six o'clock when we come bush say make we no wait for fied assistan, make we do the work, but you no gree. Now he don come teach you lesson. If they pay me pro-rata today, me and you go wear one trosser," one worker swore as he collected a bundle of bamboo sticks for pegging.

"Eta yese (meaning 'Our father' in Kenyang, Don's native language), what have you done this time that they are calling you a witch all over the camp?" Mr. Atong asked Don as soon as he came to the office the following morning.

As Don had expected, the news had spread throughout the camps like wildfire that the Field Assistant was a witch who should be feared. Their interpretation of a witch, in this sense, was that Don had learned so much 'book' that there was nothing he did not know. He was awesome! The Senior Overseer was humbled. Knowing that he was the cause of the late start at work the previous day, he did all he could (including begging the workers) to ensure that the task was completed. Don had returned to the field just before it got dark to check if the work was carried out as instructed. It was.

No other incident occurred, and the operations went as planned. Holing followed lining while at the nurseries, the rubber plants were ready for transportation and planting. As soon as the rains were about to start, they did the planting. They thus, added one more field to the plantation, the 1971 immature rubber consisting of PB and RRIM clones.

As a staff of the plantation, it was inevitable that Don would meet the Plantation Nurse someday, either as a patient or just by chance. However, since the visit to the camps and clinic with the manager on the second day after his arrival in the plantation, he had not entered the camp or gone to the clinic for medical attention, so their paths had never crossed for several months until the day he went to visit Mr. Atong. The latter had come to see Don several times, so Don felt obliged to visit him and his family. He was trying to locate Mr. Atong's house from the directions he had given him when someone greeted him from behind.

"Good evening Mr. Oben." Don turned around to find out who it was.

"It's me your Plantation Nurse. Long time, I have never seen you in the camp before. How are you?"

"I'm fine. Thank you. I'm looking for Mr. Atong's house," Don replied.

"Okay, I will show you, but this is where I live." She was probably just coming out of her house when she saw Don. Before pointing out the house to him, she added, "Mr. Oben, I rear chickens too. Your boy can come here and buy eggs from me instead of going all the way to town."

"Oh, that's nice. I will tell him."

Don was having breakfast some days later when his boy brought a tray of eggs to show him.

"She give you three eggs as dash."

"Who gave you three eggs as dash?" Don asked him.

"The nurse," he answered.

"You mean she gave you three eggs for free?"

"Yes, sir. She just say make I give you," he told Don.

As Don continued his breakfast, his mind went back many years, to the *Iliad* and the *Odyssey* written by Homer in 800 BC on the Trojan War. They had studied the Latin translation as part of their syllabus in Latin for the West

African School Certificate examination. He remembered the Trojan horse and the destruction of the city of Troy. "Quid, quid id est, timeo Danaum et dona ferentes" (Whatever it is, I fear the Greeks and the gifts they bring). King Priam of Troy did not heed the warning believing the horse was a gift from the gods. Calling his boy back, he told him, "Please you will go and thank the Nurse for the eggs. But from now on, continue to buy your eggs from the market in town, okay?" Maybe Don overreacted.

Their paths, Don's and the Plantation Nurse's, never crossed again for a long time after the chance meeting in the camp until that fateful morning Don was struck down by malaria. That was just after they had established the new development. In his adulthood, at least up until that time, he had really not experienced malaria, so he did not really know how one feels the symptoms. But he knew something wasn't right. His boy knew too that Don was not well and asked him, if he was not going to the clinic. When Don went to bed the night before, he was hot and cold at the same time and weak. In the morning, he was so weak, he couldn't get up from bed. He was cold and shivering. He just covered himself up and tried to sleep. He didn't know for how long he had been lying there.

When he opened his eyes, there were people in his bedroom. He was still very weak and just rolled his eyes. He realized shortly after that he was on drip. He recognized the Plantation Nurse. She was sitting by his bed with a cold towel, trying to bring down his temperature. Don was horrified.

"You have malaria, but you will be well soon," she said softly. Don's boy was standing by her side with a bowl of water. Mr. Atong was standing there too, looking down at Don, so was the Manager. Don was to learn later that his boy had gone to report to the Manager when Don couldn't get up in the morning and the latter had called the nurse. Mr. Atong had seen her rushing up to the house with her assistant and had followed, quite alarmed.

The sun was setting when Don was raised up and asked to try and eat some pepper soup or something. The nurse and her assistant left when he felt better, but she came back later in the evening with some medications. She and Don's boy were sitting by his bedside when he dozed off again and didn't wake up till the next morning. He was to learn later that Mr. Akpabio had monitored the proceedings from outside. After his recovery, Don went to the clinic to thank the nurse for her care. It seems they never met again.

The Salesman from Renault Motor Company

During the time they were busy with planting and returning home late in the evenings, Don returned one day to find that he had had a visitor from Victoria. He came again some days later while Don was in the fields and this time around, he left his business card with his houseboy. He was Mr. Niba, a Salesman at Renault Motors Co Ltd, Victoria. Don didn't know him and didn't know why he would come all the way from Victoria to see him. Having missed Don twice, he chose a Saturday to try a third time. He found Don at home that afternoon in late March. After he introduced himself, Don welcomed him and offered him a drink. Then he politely asked Don, "Please, can you come out, let me show you something?"

Outside was a brand-new car. "I have brought this car to show you. It is the latest of the Renault cars, a four-door Renault 12 metallic-gray saloon car," he began.

Don told him that a car was the last thing on his mind. "Okay, just let me show you the features of this car," he suggested. Don obliged. He went in, sat down, moved the driver's seat forward and backward, then reclined the back rest until it lay flat like a bed, then he caressed the dashboard and the instrument panel explaining some of the features. He started the engine and remarked how almost noiseless it sounded. Then coming out, he opened and closed the door gently. Then he caressed the body of the car, pointing out how sleek it was. He then insisted Don go in and do all the things he had done, so as to experience the 'comfort and luxury' of the new Renault 12 saloon car.

Don obliged him. After he had done so and come out of the car, the salesman asked Don how he found the car. The car was great, but because buying a car had never crossed Don's mind up to this point, he pretended not to be impressed. Don told him he was not ready to start making payments for a car at that time.

"Oh, you won't have to pay for the car with your own money. The Corporation has a car loan scheme for senior staff. It gives you a car loan to purchase the car and a monthly car allowance which is enough not only to pay the monthly installments on the car but also to run the car. In effect, it is like the Corporation is giving you a free new car," he told Don.

"Are you serious?" Don asked him, beginning to be really interested.

"Of course! I have been selling cars to CDC staff, so I know what I am talking about. And you don't have to come down to Victoria. All you have to do is sign the papers. I will process and get the loan from the Corporation, pay for the car, collect and have it cleaned, and do the first service free. You will only be called to come collect it when it is ready—in two weeks!"

Don was really now very interested, but he still felt he should give the matter a little more time to sleep over it and then call him later.

"Well, that is fine if you want to think about it. But by the time you decide you want the car, it may not be there anymore. Renault imported only three of these cars. This here is the only one left. The other two were picked up very fast as soon as they arrived by two young smart university graduates, Mr. Fred Ngane of the chairman's office, and Mr. D. N. Fosah, the DO in Victoria—"

"But these are my friends," Don exclaimed in excitement before he could finish.

"There you are! You have been left behind. Those two guys are the guys in town now!" the salesman finished with a broad smile, the kind of smile that reflects a sense of accomplishment and satisfaction. He had clinched the deal! By the time Don was signing the papers, he was already dreaming of the car. What salesmen can do! True to his words, Don was called to come pick up the car from Renault Co. Ltd. sales room exactly two weeks later. When he drove the car into the plantation, it was like he had brought in an airplane. The welcome was tumultuous. The car improved Don's mobility and independence. He could go spend weekends with friends in Bota, Victoria, and Buea more frequently than before if he wanted to. But the poor condition of the Mbonge-Kumba Road would ruin his car in no time if I did so.

By April 1971, eight months after his posting to Mbonge, he was beginning to feel isolated, not from the plantation staff and workers, but from friends and family down the 'coast' (in Victoria, Buea, and Tiko). In the eight months since arriving in Mbonge, he remembers just two occasions when he had visitors from the coast. The first was his sister Eunice, whom he had brought from Buea with her two children, Judith and Brunhilda, at the time to visit him for a few days. The second was the visit of his friend, Santos Agbortabi, whom he had invited to come for a weekend to check his radiogram. They had grilled and enjoyed fresh fish from the Meme River on his verandah facing the camp with that popular Congolese song at the time 'Pont sur le Congo' blaring from the radiogram. Apart from these people, he had no other visitors. Mbonge was too far and the road was too bad for friends to come spend a weekend with him.

But the isolation was not only social. It was also academic and mental. Surrounded by and working with an almost illiterate labor force, Don found his outlook and thinking fast deteriorating. He wrote to the Chief Production Manager, through his Plantation Manager, asking for a transfer down south, to Bota or Tiko. When he handed the letter to his Manager for approval and onward transmission to Head Office, he was alarmed after he read it.

"Mr. Oben, please, sit down. Is there anything I have done to you that has made you angry?"

Don told him no, quite surprised at his question.

"Then, why do you want to leave? Are you not happy with us here?"

Don told him that all was well but that, as a young man who has just left school, there were many issues he needed to resolve and he could not effectively handle them from a distance. He needed to be down south to do so effectively. Since they had completed the new development and all operations in both Immature and Mature Rubber were by then routine, he thought it was the best time to ask for a transfer When the Junior Field Assistant heard of his letter, he too was genuinely upset, and he tried to talk Don out of it, just as the Manager had tried. The reaction of those two was quite a surprise to Don, considering that they had not been happy with his posting to Mbonge in the first place. Even though he had won them over, he still felt that they should have been happy that he was asking to leave, so they could have whatever gains they had envisaged before his posting. Mr. Atong was particularly unhappy. His case was understandable, considering that he always called Don 'Eta yese' (our father).

The Manager was obliged to forward Don's letter to Head Office. Don received no response after one month and everybody in the office was glad that either Don had changed his mind or Head Office had not considered his application favorably. Fortunately, the CPM himself came on a visit to the plantation not long afterward, and Don had the opportunity to put his case to him.

His transfer letter came in June. He had been transferred to Likomba Rubber Estate in Tiko Rubber Plantation under Mr. G. Mesembe as the Plantation Manager with effect from July 1. News of his transfer spread through the camps very fast. The general labor in particular could not believe Don was going to leave. He was accorded a huge send-off. The emotions were high and mixed. Everybody was happy that the Head Office was giving Don the change he wanted, but they were really distraught that he was leaving them after eleven months of working with them so harmoniously. Even the Formidable Four, as Don was later to refer to them—the Manager, Junior Field Assistant, the Senior Overseer, and Mr. Akpabio, who had all been very angry at his posting to Mbonge and had each developed his own strategy for dealing with him—were genuinely unhappy at Don's impending departure.

At the send-off, every worker wanted to speak after the Manager to express their feelings. It was from their speeches that Don learned that he had touched many lives through honest advice, fairness to everyone, motivation and encouragement, interest in the workers' personal welfare, and occasionally, small monetary assistance. Most importantly, however, he had turned out to be what the 'Formidable Four' and the workers had not expected a Graduate Field Assistant to be—humble, caring, and hardworking. As Don drove out of the plantation behind the Land Rover carrying his bags and waved to the crowds of workers who had left work to come and bid him farewell, he realized he would also miss them.

Down at the 'Coast' at Last

Tiko or Bota was where Don had long wanted to be—the coast! The area is so called because it borders the Atlantic Ocean. It was either of these two stations that he had anticipated to be posted in the first place when he was recruited the previous year.

At the Tiko Rubber Plantation, Don was put in charge of Camp 8 and Sonne Moliwe, which were under the Likomba Rubber Estate, with Mr. Don Benton, a European of British extraction as the Estate Manager. As the Field Assistant's house inside the plantation in Camp 8, known as the Camp 8 House, had not yet been vacated by the outgoing Field Assistant, Don was housed in the Likomba senior staff quarters. In earlier days, only Europeans lived there. Since then, both European and African senior CDC staff were accommodated there, including some senior civil servants like the DO. In spite of the passage of time, the quarters still maintained its serenity, cleanliness, well-tended gardens and lawns, and well-maintained and glittering houses. It was also well secured by guards. To Don, it was like he had been moved from a shack in a ghetto to a condominium in a city.

There were, by then, a number of Graduate Field Assistants in the Corporation. There was Noah Kebulu, who was recruited about the same time as Don and posted to Mukonje Rubber Plantation under Mr. Cletus Tita, the Plantation Manager. He was at Umuahia when Don was at Owerri and had come from his studies in Sierra Leone. There was Eboka, who had also been employed in 1970 and posted to Meanja Rubber Estate under Mr. Apollo, the Plantation Manager. And there was William Che and Henry Mimba, CDC trainees who had recently returned from degree courses in Sierra Leone and had been appointed Field Assistants in Tiko Rubber Plantation Camp 6 and Moliwe Palms Estate respectively. They soon got to know one another and before long, they together with Fred Ngane in Bota, were hanging out in the evenings and at weekends.

Don was placed in charge of some 850 hectares of Mature and Immature Rubber in Likomba Rubber Estate. Part of that estate which was also under his supervision, was in Sonne Moliwe, at the top of the Dibanda Hill, on the main road to Buea. Here were two fields of immature rubber, a 1970 Immature Rubber Field and a newly planted 1971 Immature Rubber Field. There were also a few fields of older but still immature rubber. The fields at Camp 8 were mostly of Mature Rubber from which tapping for latex and cuplumps and polybags was being done. So as in Mbonge, Don's duties and responsibilities included planning, directing, and supervising all technical operations in all Mature and Immature Areas. Those included tapping, collection, and transportation of cuplumps, polybags and latex to the Rubber Factory in Tiko; the upkeep, treatment of pests and diseases; and the clearing of Wind Damage.

Other responsibilities included half monthly and monthly payments to labor, the upkeep and cleaning of the camps, and the settlement of disputes. Most of the operations were kind of routine. Nevertheless, they had to be well-planned for, and undertaken, in a timely manner; labor had to be well-allocated, supervised, and well-managed in a way that avoided, or at least minimized, strikes or unauthorized work stoppages and the consequent loss in production. There were also meetings and preparation of reports. One main challenge was managing and supervising two plantation areas—Nsonne Moliwe and Camp 8, which were many miles apart.

Don enjoyed his work at the Likomba Rubber Estate. He had a good working relationship with his Manager, Mr. Benton, and they understood and respected each other well. But that was not until after Don had a brush with him during his first month in Likomba, when he ordered Don to move into Camp 8 House immediately after it became vacant. Don had inspected the house and observed that it was in an utter state of disrepair and needed not just cleaning but renovation, including the replacement of most of the bathroom and kitchen fixtures, some doors and windows, parts of the ceiling, followed by painting of the entire house. Over the years, the house had been rundown by successive Field Assistants with large families, who had been content with the state of the house.

"You should obey before you complain," Mr. Benton had insisted, almost condescendingly.

Don eventually moved out of the Likomba quarters and into Camp 8 House but on his own terms after he made it clear to his Manager that he would not accept his condescending attitude which was reminiscent of colonial administrations in Africa. A few months later, Don was moved back again into the Likomba quarters when the house was to be renovated. He couldn't stay in while major repairs were being done in the house. Moreover, the water catchment, which supplied water to the house, was overrun by floods and damaged at the height of the rainy season and was supplying red muddy water to the house.

Chapter 9
Rockefeller Foundation
Calls Don to Graduate School

A Dilemma: To Leave or Not to Leave

In mid-1972, about twelve months after Don assumed duty in Likomba, he received news that he had been accepted for a Rockefeller Foundation Fellowship to pursue a Master's Degree in Agricultural Economics at the University of Ibadan (UI). This was great news conveying an opportunity he relished. But as he was digesting the news, Don immediately sensed a dilemma he will have to face—a very serious short-term vs long-term dilemma when one takes an appealing job now versus pursuing education or training that may open better opportunities in the long run. In this case, he will be faced with the dilemma of whether to remain in, or leave his job with the CDC.

When he broached the news to his friends and colleagues, inasmuch as they were happy for him, they couldn't understand why he would want to leave such a lucrative job and go back to school. In a way, they were right. Their employment with the Corporation was lucrative. They were earning more than their colleagues in the West Cameroon Civil Service. On top of that, they enjoyed great benefits—their houses were rent-free; they did not pay for electricity, water, and cooking gas; and the Corporation gave them a monthly car allowance that was large enough to pay the monthly installments and run their cars as well. In effect, Don had a high-paying job, a free house, free gas, free electricity, free water, and a free car.

"So why would you leave this job and go back to school when you may not even be sure of a job when you complete your studies and return? What else do you want?" his friends and colleagues questioned.

"And suppose you went, and for any reason, you came back without completing the course?" some even dared to ask.

Don was tempted to admit those concerns as pertinent. But that is, if one took a myopic view of the Cameroon economy. Don believed that the economy was growing and with it, greater employment opportunities. With a Master's Degree, he was also already setting his sights beyond the Corporation to employment in the universities and the world of international development, if he successfully completed the master's program and even went further to do a Ph.D. degree. In spite of this conviction, the concerns raised by his friends introduced some doubt into his mind. Those concerns, as well as some more real personal issues, kept him wavering over whether he should return to school. His indecision took its toll. Time passed. The university had reopened in September, and it was already December and he had not taken up his admission.

Unsure whether his place was still available, Don made a quick and unannounced trip by road to Ibadan in December 1972 and, on his return, wrote to the Chief Production Manager (CPM), requesting for a two-year leave of absence without pay from the Corporation to enable him pursue a Master's Degree course in Agricultural Economics at the University of Ibadan. He had asked for leave of absence and without pay, so that when he returned after his Master's program, he would have a job to return to while looking for a more appropriate employment. The Corporation advised him to resign if he wanted to go for further studies as a Field Assistant's duties and responsibilities were rather routine and did not require a master's degree. Sometime later, when the CPM saw Don during a visit to their estate, he asked him with a sarcastic laugh, "Mr. Doctor, you have not left yet?" Don did not find it funny. He knew that, come what may, he had to leave.

The response of the Corporation only reinforced the questions raised by his friends, and they began to haunt him even more. Should he resign and leave? Will he be able to successfully complete the course, especially as he had been out of school for more than two years? What if he didn't? If he did, would he be able to get another job with benefits as generous as those he was enjoying at the moment? Did he really want to give up the good life now?

Those questions kept haunting Don. But the greatest issues which really worried him concerned the welfare of his little niece Judith and nephew Paul, who were both living with him and going to school. He had taken a personal commitment to bringing them up like his children. They had settled well in school and were happy and were doing well. What was going to happen to them if he leaves? Don agonized so much over that issue, and it was only his sister, Sister Jane, who helped put his fears to rest.

"There will always be someone to take care of them in your absence," she had counseled Don after he sought her advice.

Don finally made up his mind. He tendered his letter of resignation to the Corporation in March 1973 and was paid 'Part A' of his Provident Fund. He lost 'Part B', the Corporation's own contribution which was much greater than his 'Part A', because he had not been in service for the minimum number of years required to be eligible for that part. Don took Judith and Paul to Mamfe and put them in the care of his mother and made arrangements for their fees and upkeep. With the provident fund payment together with his savings which he put into a bank account, he also made arrangements for the payment of his little sister, Becky's, fees at the Queen of the Rosary College, Okoyong.

Finally, Don made the long trip from Tiko to Mamfe in his Renault 12 saloon car to leave some of his personal and household effects. His sister, Eunice, insisted on accompanying him. Thank God she did. That was a trip Don will never forget. Although it was still the month of March, the rains had started to come down, and the Mamfe-Kumba road had begun to deteriorate. That journey to Mamfe saw Brother and Sister often struggling alone to dig a fully loaded car out of the mud and push or even carry it back on to the road as darkness fell.

When all was set for Don's departure, he made a quick trip again to Mamfe to say goodbye to his mother and father, arriving late at night. His father had respected his decision to go for graduate studies when he had broken the news to him some time earlier. He had gone to bed when Don arrived that night, but he woke up because Don had to leave very early the next morning. His father sent for his mother and one of his uncles. Then bringing out a bottle of gin from a small cupboard next to his bed, he poured out a libation and then a toast for a successful journey to Ibadan. Back in Tiko, Don's friends could not believe when he told them he had resigned and was finally leaving.

Graduate Studies at Ibadan on Rockefeller Foundation Fellowship

The master's degree program in Agricultural Economics at UI was a two-year degree program requiring the successful completion of a one-year Coursework and the preparation and presentation of a dissertation on a contemporary problem in agricultural development based on materials collected from a field study. They took some economics courses in the Department of Economics with the master's students of that department and the agricultural courses, including econometrics and quantitative methods, in their Department of Agricultural Economics. After two years out of an academic environment, settling down into student life was difficult for Don. He was alarmed at how much academic stuff he had forgotten during those two years. Even understanding and absorbing the lectures was difficult.

He recalled to me the day he entered the office of the secretary to the Head of Department after the first test they had. Madam Grace had been the secretary to the Head of Department since their undergraduate days, so they both knew each other well. She was gentle, kind, friendly, and motherly, especially to their small circle of friends who were known for their hard work and good behavior. But she was also a no-nonsense lady.

"Don, in case you don't know, Rockefeller fellows don't flunk exams," she told Don, handing him his test papers and a small letter of warning.

"But I didn't flunk," Don protested after looking through the papers.

"Cs are not accepted in graduate school here at Ibadan," she told Don in no uncertain terms.

"But it was just a small test," Don replied, still trying to justify his 'C' grade in the test.

"There is nothing like small tests or big tests here. All are exams," she retorted.

"Madam Grace, don't you think you are making a mountain out of a molehill?" Don replied, trying to make it appear as if the test was of no consequence.

"Well, Mr. Oben, we don't have molehills here. We have mountains." She ended the matter.

Don panicked, more so because Prof. Leonard F. Miller, who was teaching the course and had given the test, was a visiting professor from Oklahoma State

University in the USA and, above all, the Rockefeller Foundation Representative for West Africa. Don had to sit up.

The year 1975 was extraordinary for Don. It was a year marked by milestones. Don was awarded his master's degree; he got married; he won another big fellowship, a Ford Foundation Fellowship to read for a PhD degree, and they had their first child.

Don was awarded the master's degree in Agricultural Economics with specialization in Agricultural Development and Policy in January 1975 after successfully completing his coursework and presenting and successfully defending his dissertation, which was entitled, 'Labor Absorption in Large-Scale Agriculture: The Case of the Cameroon Development Corporation (CDC)'.[9] Having worked in the plantations, it was understandable that he would identify a development problem in that area. He received a lot of cooperation and support from the Corporation during his fieldwork which took him to its head office in Bota and to Tiko Rubber Plantation, Ekona Bananas, Mukonje Rubber Plantation, Tole Tea Estate, Moliwe Palms, and Idenau Palms Plantation.

Don Weds Dorothy

It was in January 1975 that Don got married to his wife, then Ms. Dorothy Ebot Ako. He had met her in early 1972, during a short visit to Mamfe, where she was completing form 5 at the Queen of the Rosary College, Okoyong, Mamfe. Don had known her father when he was a little boy growing up in Mamfe Town. He had settled in Mamfe town from Bakebe village and built his compound besides the Government School Mamfe, which was some two hundred yards from Don's father's compound. But Don had never known anything about his daughter or even heard of her until the day Don saw her in a photograph among his sister, Rosamond's small pack of photos. It was a photo of the cast of a play, *Ali Baba and the Forty Thieves* in which she acted the part of Ali Baba's wife. She wore a long white dress, and her wig fell to her shoulders. She looked elegant and exquisite. Don immediately had a crush on her.

Don's curiosity to see her in person was overwhelming. He could hardly wait. They drove to her school, four miles away, the next day to see her and his little sister Becky, who was in form 1. They were ushered into an anteroom to wait. Then she appeared in her 'naturalness'—in her school uniform (just a simple dress) and a short haircut and flat shoes and no makeup. Don was blown away! So was she too, Don guessed. He knew immediately that she was the one he would marry. She came home for the Easter vacation a few days later, and before Don returned, He proposed, and she accepted—on condition that their marriage would not prevent her from continuing her education. Don had never considered marriage as an impediment to studying, and he told her so. Moreover, the pursuit of education had always been a priority in his family, so even if she did not express it, he was going to encourage her to go for further studies, especially as he himself was, at that time, already contemplating returning to school. She trusted Don that he would keep his word not to let their marriage prevent her from attaining post-secondary education, and that trust Don has always cherished. Don was to learn much later that his fiancée was very much loved by his family and especially by his father. She had, in fact, been like a daughter in the family before Don even met her. That explained why his father arranged with her family and performed the traditional marriage rites so quickly.

But months before she was to take her General Certificate of Education (GCE) 'O' Level Examination, her father fell seriously ill, and she had to leave school at various times to go and attend to him, which seriously affected her concentration at school and preparations for the exam. Very sadly, he passed away in July 1973, just after her exams. She was devastated. She had been very close to him. He had been her father and friend, and she had been his confidante. She joined Don toward the end of 1973 and, as kindly arranged by Don's sister, Janet Arah, and her husband, Mr. Laban Namme, she stayed in Lagos with them while he continued with his degree program in UI.

His sister was then the vice-principal of Queen's College, Lagos, while Mr. Namme was the Deputy Managing Director of the Daily Times of Nigeria Ltd. Because she arrived several months after the colleges in Nigeria had resumed, they could not find her admission into the two-year Higher School Certificate course. So with her consent, she registered for private classes to prepare her to take the Joint Admissions and Matriculation Board (JAMB) examination into Nigerian universities. She settled down quickly and soon became a well-loved member of the family.

On Saturday January 25, 1975, they got married at the Presbyterian Church, Yaba, Lagos, in a solemn ceremony officiated by Rev. Dr. Hall, a Canadian Pastor. As a student of small means, Don pleaded with his sister and her husband for a small wedding. But they, especially her husband, would not want it small. Don provided the bride's and bridesmaids' dresses and the bride's gold ring. Mrs. Josephine Nkwain helped with the sewing of her dress, as well as the dresses of the bridesmaids. She was the wife of Mr. Francis Nkwain, then the Cultural Attaché at the Cameroon Embassy in Lagos, both of them family friends to the Nammes. Their two youngest little girls also served as flower girls.

Don and his best man, Alex Gboyega, then a fellow graduate student in political science, took care of themselves. Don remembers that they both wore their old worn-out black suits and black shoes, and Don picked up his wedding ring from a roadside vendor at Tinubu Square, Lagos, a day before the wedding. His sister and her husband provided the rest—invitations, food, drinks, photographers, etc. The occasion was well-attended, including many Daily Times barons and friends of the Nammes and Cameroonian students and friends from Lagos University and the University of Ibadan. Mr. Namme acted as the bride's father and walked her down the aisle.

It turned out to be a huge, joyful wedding, and the news of their wedding, complete with beautiful photographs, was out in the morning papers by 6:00 a.m. on Sunday, January 26. The only sad thing was that none of the bride's friends and family members were able to come from Cameroon for the wedding.

Top left, Mr. L. N. Namme walking the bride into the church and down the aisle. *Top right*, blessings. *Bottom*, the cutting of the cake.

From Rockefeller to Ford Foundation for the Doctoral Degree Program

After successfully completing his Master's Degree program, Don immediately started to explore the possibility of continuing for the Ph.D. degree. He considered it of utmost importance not to let the momentum die down. His efforts bore fruit when, in March 1975, he was awarded a Ford Foundation Fellowship to continue for the Ph.D. degree at the University of Ibadan.

The Ford Foundation's Fellowship Program at the time was designed for Staff Development in selected African universities. Among the conditions,

Ford Fellows were expected to study in African universities and carry out their research in Africa. Don was, however, given some exception. Considering that he had considerable African academic experiences since he had taken his first and second degrees from an African university, he requested for, and was allowed to spend one calendar year in an American university to do coursework but to return to Ibadan to take his degree. His marital status with its financial implications was also considered in fixing his stipend.

After all arrangements had been firmed up, Don searched for and rented suitable accommodation in Ibadan. It was a small two-room flat with a kitchen at the back on the first floor of a building opposite the university. It was by then April 1975, and Dorothy was five months pregnant. Don went and brought her from Lagos, and they moved into their small flat. They then invited Dorothy's mother to come from Cameroon and spend some time with them, given Dorothy's condition. She arrived a month later.

As soon as Don enrolled in the doctoral program, he decided that he would continue his research in his area of interest, which was labor use in agriculture. Having studied labor absorption in the plantations (agricultural sector) for his master's thesis, he decided he would now examine labor use in the Rural Non-Agricultural or Rural Non-Farm Sector. The Department accepted his research proposal underscoring the importance of the Rural Non-Farm Sector in Nigeria. It acknowledged that though some work had been done in that area in some countries such as Sierra Leone, similar studies in Nigeria were very scanty, hence, the need for his study.

Following that, he and his supervisor discussed and agreed on the methodology and the data collection and analysis procedures to be adopted. It was decided that Don should collect his data before leaving for the United States. With the assistance of a team of research assistants, he spent the three months, May–August 1976, collecting his data in the Kwara State of Nigeria, the agreed research area. It was on his return from one of his data collection missions that he received one of the greatest pleasant surprises of his life.

As he entered the house late that evening, he heard the *cries* of a *little infant*. Dorothy had given birth to a beautiful little baby girl one week earlier, the day following his departure for Kwara State. As he kissed his wife and took the baby and held her in his arms, he could feel the love flowing from his heart into her. He thanked God that his mother-in-law was with them at that time, and Sister Ihidero, a Senior Nursing Sister and family friend, was at the

University College Hospital (UCH) where she gave birth. They named the baby, Lilian Ako Mboti-Ako after his wife's father and Mboti after Mr. Namme's mother, Ma Mboti.

Don was admitted into four universities in the United States with top-ranking Departments of Agricultural Economics at the time: Michigan State University (MSU), East Lansing, Michigan; Purdue University, West Lafayette, Indiana; Oklahoma State University (OSU), Stillwater, Oklahoma; and the University of California, Davis, California. Don chose the University of California, Davis. In addition to its academic excellence, the mild winter climate in northern California was an important consideration in his choice, considering his past experience with cold weather, as already reported in earlier chapters of this Biography. He admits that a long-standing fantasy with San Francisco and the Bay Area was also a pull factor.

August 1976 arrived and Don was bound for the United States. Saying goodbye and hugging his wife and little daughter, Lilian, was painful. He was only consoled by the fact that, while he would be studying in Davis, she too would be studying at the University of Lagos. She had sat for and passed the entrance examination for admission into Nigerian universities administered by the Joint Admission and Matriculation Board. Following her success in the exam, she had been admitted into the University of Lagos to do a three-year diploma course in education, leading to the award of the Nigeria Certificate of Education (NCE). So before leaving, Don arranged for her and her mother and Lilian to move to the Nammes in Ikeja in September and stay in their back quarters.

When the university reopened, she would leave the child with her mother in Ikeja and move into a hall of residence in the campus. But Don was still worried. She was one-month pregnant, and he feared that was going to affect her health, her studies, and her care for Lilian. But he had to go.

Left photo, Dorothy and Don at his graduation (MSc).
Right photo: with their 1st baby, Lilian.

At the University of California, Davis, United States of America

Don arrived San Francisco toward the end of August 1976 and was met at the airport by the Secretary of the International Students' Association, a girl from the West Indies, and a few members of the Orientation Committee of the Students' Union. Joseph Suh from Cameroon was also there. He took Don home. His wife, Nicoline, and their two children were vacationing back in her country, the Netherlands. Don had met Joe in Mamfe way back in 1968, during their long vacation from Ibadan when the Ministry of Agriculture had sent them round its Divisional Services to work as part of their internship. Joe was the Technical Officer in-charge of the Division's Agricultural Extension Services.

Don later learned he had left to study in Davis and was right then a doctoral candidate there. He had, therefore, come to meet Don on receipt of his note that he (Don) would be coming to Davis. He was and still is a well-organized, soft-spoken, and hardworking and kind gentleman whose friendship Don still cherishes. Don stayed with him until early October when he moved into an apartment on University Avenue.

The Fall Quarter was one of the loneliest and most difficult periods of Don's student life. It was a period when he was not only battling with the cold weather, even though the winter in California was considered mild compared to that in states in the Midwest and Northeast United States, he was also being shocked by mannerisms he had never witnessed before. People seemed always in a hurry. No one seemed to have time for anybody. People seemed to be smiling at you as you approached them, but when you smiled back, their smile disappeared and you realize that they were never actually smiling and neither did they intend to smile. You met somebody somewhere and you had a chat, the next time you met him, he behaved like he had never known or met you before.

Most irritating was the habit of American students suggesting that African students didn't speak English well simply because they didn't pronounce words or roll their tongues the way they (Americans) did when they spoke. In one large (elective) class where Don was making a presentation and some students kept repeating 'Pardon' or 'What did you say', he had to stop and tell the whole class in no uncertain terms that he learned to read, write, and speak the Queen's English right from kindergarten. Anybody who did not understand him didn't understand good English. It was like he had thrown a bombshell. That nonsense stopped thereafter.

That fall quarter was also when they took the most difficult courses, courses with a difficult mathematical content: Microeconomics, Quantitative Methods, and Econometrics. The weekly assignments, term papers, and midterm exams kept Don continuously and consistently engaged. The loneliness was awesome. The only time Don had company was during classes. After school, he was alone until the next day when he went to school. But he was invited to spend Thanksgiving Day that November with his graduate adviser, Prof. Alex McCalla and his family.

Don didn't have a car. Although his fellowship was robust enough to get him a fairly new used car, he had a wife and daughter to support and was also sponsoring his wife at the university—tuition, boarding, and all. Don bought an old bicycle, almost the oldest in Davis at the time. Many students had cars, but almost every student had a bicycle. In fact, Davis was estimated at that time to have more than twenty-six miles of bicycle paths and twenty-two thousand bicycles, which gave it the title of 'City of Bicycles'.

Life became a bit more interesting later when he met three Nigerian graduate students—Olusanjo, Jake, and Jaiye. They became good friends, and they would shop for groceries together at the weekends and cook and enjoy

African dishes. On Friday nights, they would attend private house parties to dance and socialize and ease the week's accumulated stress. He remembers with nostalgia how they almost danced their waists off with recently released hits, such as 'I Wish' by Stevie Wonder, 'Rubberband Man' by the Spinners, 'Brick House' by the Commodores, 'Car Wash' by Rose Royce, and many more!

Dorothy and Lilian, his daughter, came to spend Christmas of that year with him in Davis. In preparation for their coming, Don moved to married students housing, taking a two-bedroom furnished apartment at Orchard Park near Joe and Nicoline. Dorothy was already heavy with their second child. She made friends quickly, and soon, they were visiting parks, museums, and other interesting places in Davis, Sacramento, and San Francisco and the Bay Area with family friends. Don remembers, in particular, their breathtaking drive through Lombard Street, a steep, hilly street dubbed 'the crookedest street in the world' with its sharp byzantine curves to switch back down the one-way drive, and the large crowds of tourists in the spring on sightseeing.

Left photo, In San Francisco, December 1976. *Right photo*, at home at Orchard Park.

When Dorothy and Lilian returned to Lagos in February, Don moved from Orchard Park into Graduate Dorm since he was alone. When the dorms closed for summer, he later moved into a two-bedroom apartment on University Avenue with Lehman Walker, an African American guy with whom he was taking a course. Unlike the Fall and Winter Quarters, the Spring Quarter was less stressful. He was then more settled and relaxed, made friends, and was enjoying his classes. Spring had arrived and with it nice and more friendly weather. He had joined the International Students Association and had been elected the Assistant Secretary. In spite of the academic pressure, he managed to find time once a week in the Spring Quarter to attend practices at night in Modern Dance and the martial art, Aikido.

In April, Don received the elating news that Dorothy had given birth to their second child, another cute little girl. She had gone into labor at 2:00 a.m. in Amina Hall, and her roommate had helped get a taxi which had taken them to the Lagos University Teaching Hospital (LUTH) that early morning of April 23. She gave birth just moments later. She named her Lorraine. They had agreed on this name during her visit to Davis. Soon, however, Don began to feel a sense of guilt, guilty that she would soon have to grapple not only with taking care of little Lilian but with a new baby and her studies. How was she going to cope?

Those thoughts began to gnaw at him like a toothache. Dorothy moved temporarily back to Ikeja to be with her mother and the Nammes and began to commute daily to school for classes after she felt well enough to do so. It was a most difficult time for her. What with the sleepless nights caring for the baby or doing her readings and assignments, the commuting and the traffic, her classes, and the fatigue at the end of the day! It was a frustrating time for her mom when she was in school. For the Nammes, it was a trying time too. With her characteristic determination, she successfully passed her sessional examinations and packed and returned to their small apartment in Ibadan in June when the university closed at the end of the 1976/1977 academic year.

Don moved out of graduate dorm after the spring quarter to an apartment at University Avenue and continued his remaining courses. One of those was an elective course on California Agriculture. That course also involved a study tour of the fruit and vegetable producing areas in California and the preparation and submission of a report. During the first summer session, their class of some forty students set off from Davis on a two-week tour of Southern California. From Davis, they went to Napa in the Napa Valley, then southward along the West Coast to Fairfield, Vallejo, Richmond, San Francisco, San Mateo, Hayward, San Jose, Santa Cruz, Salinas, Monterez, San Luis Obispo, Santa Barbara, Ventura, Los Angeles, Irvine, San Diego, and right down to Chula Vista, near the border of Mexico. Their route back took them through El Centro, Indio, San Bernardino, Bakersfield, San Joaquin, and Stockton. They visited large orchards, vineyards, cornfields, wineries, and warehouses and storage depots around those cities and towns. They had lectures and presentations by farm managers or farm owners wherever they visited.

Back in their motels in the evenings, they would have further discussions on the day's visits and get a briefing on the next day's program. Don was also writing his report as they went along, since he knew he would be hard-pressed for time on his return to Davis. So after the evening's discussions, he would stay up late updating his report.

California grew about 80 percent of all fruits and vegetables in the United States: vegetables—asparagus, broccoli, carrots, celery, cucumbers, lettuce, spinach, tomatoes, blueberries; and fruits—citrus (orange, grapefruit, lemon, mandarin), apples, grapes, apricots, berries (blackberries, blue berries, strawberries), pear, avocado, olives, etc. The tour was very enriching and rewarding. Not only did it provide Don with a wonderful opportunity to witness the huge advances made in agriculture but also the rare opportunity to travel round the state at no additional cost to himself.

Don completed his courses in the first summer session. During that session, but especially during part of the second session leading to his departure from Davis, he tried to find time to do some analysis of the data he had collected for his Ph.D. dissertation by working late into the night.

Earning a Ph.D. Degree Back in Ibadan

Don returned to Ibadan at the end of August 1977 to continue his Ph.D. degree program. The reunion with his wife and two kids was exhilarating. Lilian had grown into a beautiful two-year-old little girl and the baby, Lorraine, was so cute and had Lilian's complexion. But their stay together was short-lived. Dorothy returned to Lagos when the university reopened in September for the 1977/1978 academic year, leaving behind little Lilian and infant Lorraine. But she came almost every weekend to be with them and nurse the baby. It was an agonizing time for her too, leaving two little children behind with one only five months old. She endeavored to do all her class assignments during the week, so she could be free to make those trips every weekend. She would leave Lagos after her last class on Friday and return on Sunday afternoon. Only a loving and devoted wife and mother could make such sacrifices. Although she was consoled by the fact that Don was by then around taking charge, Don could see the pain in her eyes on those Sunday afternoons when she had to leave them.

That period was very difficult for Don's mother-in-law and Don too. And little Lilian did not make things any easier for both of them. Because she was hyperactive, Don's mother-in-law found it extremely difficult keeping a close eye on her to prevent her from running all over the place and falling from any of the steep stairs while she did her laundry or cooking and Don was in school. She also needed to keep her from running into traffic on the main road between their apartment and the university. Often, Don would return home to find her standing by the window inside their small living room, clutching on the window protectors and looking outside with her eyes red from hours of crying.

Don would immediately know that her grandmother had put her in her little 'prison' to keep her safe while she carried on with her chores. As soon as he opened the door, she would jump and cling to him and he would almost cry. He would carry her for a while then make her milk and give it to her and wash or iron their nappies. Lorraine, the baby, would often be sleeping quietly or would be on her grandma's back.

While Don was still in Davis, he had received word that his supervisor, Prof. S.M. Essang, had been appointed the Federal Minister of Finance and had moved from the university to Lagos; so Don had to travel to Lagos each time he had to discuss his work with him. Making appointments to meet him was not easy, given the portfolio he held and his responsibilities to his political party which was then the party in power in Nigeria at the time. But he did, as much as he could, make it possible for Don to see him. Once, Don even had to fly to Calabar, the capital of the Cross River State, to meet with him. Working on his data while in Davis paid off.

Don was able to finish, present, and successfully defend his thesis on February 2, 1978. It was titled, 'Labor Absorption in the Rural Non-Farm Sector: Evidence from the Kwara State of Nigeria'. It was presented in partial fulfillment of the requirements for the award of the degree of Doctor of Philosophy (Ph.D.).[10] Some of the findings and conclusions of his research for the Master's and Ph.D. degrees were published respectively in two journals: *Malayan Economic Review,* and *Research for Development (Journal of the Nigerian Institute for Social and Economic Research).*[11]

As mentioned in an earlier chapter, when Don decided to resign from the CDC and leave for further studies, he was already looking beyond the Corporation to the universities, the United Nations, and other international organizations for employment opportunities when he completes his studies.

So, well before he graduated, he sent an application to the Dschang University Center (Centre Universitaire De Dschang) and completed and mailed Personal History Forms (PHFs) with his resumé to the Food and Agriculture Organization of the United Nations (FAO) and the United Nations Economic Commission for Africa (ECA).

By March 1978, he had not received any response from any of these institutions. His stipend from Ford Foundation had ended with his graduation in February, so he was running out of money. Just at that time, the International Institute of Tropical Agriculture (IITA), Ibadan, advertised Post-doctoral Research Fellowship positions. Don submitted his application.

Above, Graduation for his PhD degree in February 1978.

Chapter 10
Joining the Consultative Group on International Agricultural Research (CGIAR)

At the International Institute of Tropical Agriculture (IITA), Ibadan, Nigeria

Don was appointed a Post-doctoral Research Fellow and Agricultural Economist on April 1, 1978, at IITA. It was a great coincidence and also an honor that he, whose graduate studies had been funded by the Rockefeller and Ford foundations would, on completion of his studies, be given an opportunity to make a contribution to a great institution established by both foundations. Those two foundations had, as far back as 1962, held talks on establishing a research center concerned with increasing the production and improving the quality of tropical food crops other than rice. In a December 1963 meeting, the development of a proposal jointly sponsored by the two foundations for locating the institute in Nigeria and at the campus of the University of Ibadan was authorized.

By March 1965, an agreement was reached on the proposal for establishing the International Institute of Tropical Agriculture (IITA) in Nigeria. Construction of the IITA Headquarters began in 1968, and the first building was inaugurated in April 1970. Coincidentally, also, the Director-General of the institute at this time happened to be Dr. William Gamble, who was the Ford Foundation Representative for West Africa when Don won the Ford Fellowship award.

The Accommodation Issue

Don was joined in the course of the year by a few other African Post-doctoral Research Fellows recruited from the United States: Dr. Emmanuel Atayi (Togolese, Agricultural Economist), Dr. Ratemo Michieka (Kenyan, Weed Scientist), Dr. Ndimande (Zimbabwean), Dr. Louis Jackai (Cameroonian, Entomologist), Dr. Braide (Nigerian), There was also Dr. Christine Okali (U.K, Sociologist) and one or two US and Japanese post-doctoral fellows. There were graduate students too: Morris from Liberia, Frank Attere from Benin, Yekini from Sierra Leone, and a few others whose names Don doesn't recall. He and the other post-docs started their tenure with a little 'fight' with one Dr. Reeves who was in charge of housing and who rejected their applications for on-campus housing because he believed that the African post-docs should stay in town.

There were one- and two-bedroom apartments referred to as Dorms in the IITA campus. Although they were initially built for research students and staff coming for short-term training courses and workshops at IITA, their American and Japanese colleagues were accommodated there. The African post-docs made a strong case, arguing that providing them accommodation within the IITA campus would help increase their productivity and efficiency by saving time spent commuting on the Oyo road, notorious for traffic congestion; making it more convenient for colleagues to follow up their field and laboratory experiments more closely if living on campus; giving them access to the library and other facilities in the evenings and night to continue their work; making it easier for them to meet in the evenings after work for discussions and exchange of ideas whenever the need arose, since they would be accommodated in the Dorms; and in general, providing them, like their American and Japanese colleagues and scientists, with a serene, safe, peaceful, and enabling environment in which they could live and perform their duties and responsibilities.

Their case was upheld, and each of them was allocated a one-bedroom apartment in the Dorms. All post-docs were also given small cars—cream-colored Ford Escort Saloons—to facilitate their work.

Dorothy joined Don and the two little girls when the university closed at the end of the 1977/1978 academic year in June. Her mother returned to Cameroon, and they moved from their apartment opposite the university to IITA. The apartments were fully furnished—large living room, large bedroom, kitchen, and bathroom. The IITA campus itself was said to be a 'small America in Nigeria'—large and well-designed buildings; wide asphalted roads with drainage; well-kept, well-watered green lawns with flowers and small shrubs and trees; and uninterrupted sources of electricity and clean water supply. There were the large bungalows for Scientists and other Senior permanent staff, offices, laboratories, and the International House hosting a restaurant, bar, indoor games, entertainment and reception halls, etc. There was also a clinic and a kindergarten and a lake from which fresh fish was harvested periodically and sold to the staff. The campus was enclosed and secured by a high wire fence and a main gate manned by security guards.

Don and his small family started to live comfortably. Dorothy returned to Lagos in September when the university reopened and left the two little girls with Don and his mother, whom they had flown over from Cameroon to relieve Don's mother-in-law who returned before they moved to IITA. But they saw each other almost every weekend—she would come on Friday night after classes and leave on Sunday afternoon. The next weekend, Don would put the girls in the car with drinks and cookies and some homemade food and drive to visit her in Lagos. And so they alternated visits such that the girls did not miss her absence very much.

Working at IITA

IITA was one of the Centers in the then Consultative Group on International Agricultural Research (CGIAR), about thirteen of them at the time. The Center was founded in 1967 and had a mandate to improve food production in the humid tropics. Its mission was to enhance the food security, income, and well-being of resource-poor people in sub-Saharan Africa by increasing agricultural productivity, improving food systems, and sustainably managing the natural resource base. That goal was to be achieved by conducting research (including socioeconomic research) and related activities in partnership with National Agricultural Research Institutions (the NARs) and regional and international stakeholders.

Toward achieving that goal, IITA focused its Crop Improvement Programs (CIP) on roots and tubers (cassava and yams), cereals and legumes (maize, cowpea, soybean), and plantains and bananas, and through international cooperation programs including training, information and germplasm exchange activities, which it conducted in partnership with regional bodies, national agricultural programs, universities, NGOs, and the private sector.

There was a socioeconomic unit that conducted research in support of the work of the Crop Improvement Program. It was to that unit that Don was posted. It was headed by Dr. F.E. Winch, an American and an agricultural economist. Dr. Ken Menz, an agricultural economist from Australia, later joined Dr. Okali and Don, succeeding Dr. Winch as the head of the unit after the latter left. Given the priorities at the time, Don's work was focused on the Root and Tuber Improvement Program and particularly on cassava.

IITA began this program in 1971 with priority given to developing germplasm resistant to cassava mosaic, cassava green mite, cassava bacterial blight, and cassava anthracnose diseases with a view to improving productivity and production. A major expansion of that program was in the pipeline to produce and disseminate improved cultivars of cassava developed from new germplasm in Nigeria and other sub-Saharan countries.

But first, it was important to gain more accurate information about the spread of improved cassava, its possible effects, and the factors that would affect its adoption. What factors were paramount to farmers in their adoption of improved cultivars in Nigeria? What importance did they give to characteristics, such as drought resistance, disease resistance, early maturity, and various other traits such as taste, quality, and root size?

It was also of paramount importance to address issues that were crucial for ensuring that new varieties of cassava developed by IITA were not only acceptable but also beneficial to farmers. One of these was the levels of cyanogenic glucosides in both the cassava roots and leaves.

Research on Cassava and Hydrocyanic Acid

Two types of cassava (*Manihot esculenta Crantz*) were being grown in Nigeria, as in most other SSA countries—bitter and sweet. Bitter cassava was more commonly grown in Nigeria. It is high in cyanide content while sweet cassava is low in cyanide. Some studies attribute sweetness or bitterness to sugars and other chemicals, but the level of cyanide is the key factor. Bitter cassava generally requires processing to reduce the cyanide level before being eaten. Inadequately processed bitter cassava can cause severe health problems. It has been linked to tropical ataxic neuropathy, goiter, and cretinism (F. Nartey[12]).

One possible approach to reducing the health hazard and the resources used in processing that variety of cassava would be to promote the use of sweet cassava. The yields of sweet cassava obtained at the time were generally low, but a plant breeding program could change this. Would a higher-yielding sweet cassava variety be accepted by growers, processors, and consumers who were then using the bitter variety? An even more fundamental question was whether users recognized clearly, the existence of the two types. If so, what factors determined the choice between the two and how did the production and processing characteristics of the two types compare? There were two factors that warranted special attention. One was the potential rodent problem, as many scientists had expressed the belief that rodent damage on sweet cassava was high. The second aspect was the potential effect of a new screw press processing system on the acceptability of higher-yielding sweet cassava.

These were issues which were going to be important determinants of the acceptance of the new and improved varieties of cassava in Nigeria, a major world producer and consumer of cassava, producing about 10.8 million tons per year or 9 percent of total world output (FAO, 1976) and hence the success and prospects of the cassava program. Given the importance of cassava as a major staple food crop in Nigeria and indeed in sub-Saharan Africa, it was important to reduce the likelihood that new germplasm with excellent agronomic traits would not be rejected on the grounds that it was less appropriate for food preparation than the local varieties. More accurate information on these issues was needed to guide the cassava improvement program.

Against this background, Don and Dr. Ken Menz launched a study to explore these issues and to make an overall assessment of the consequences (benefits) of breeding a high-yielding sweet cassava. The study also aimed to make a comparison between these benefits and the costs of breeding a high-yielding sweet cassava within the context of the cassava breeding program at IITA.

The methodology of the study consisted of three components: a survey to elicit information on the growing, processing and consumption of sweet and bitter cassava types; an experiment to gauge the effect of a new processing method on the likely acceptance of high-yielding sweet cassava; and a cost-benefit analysis of the IITA sweet cassava breeding program.

That study provided the underpinnings of much of Don's work at IITA. He conducted a number of studies and collected relevant information from farmers in selected villages in Anambra State in the east, Bendel State in the Midwest, Ogun State in the west, and Kaduna State in northern Nigeria. The results and conclusions of the overall study were presented at periodic research reviews and published in the IITA Discussion Series.[13] Among the conclusions were that the breeding of a low-cyanide cassava variety with yields comparable to improved bitter varieties was a feasible and practically achievable goal at modest cost. The breeding of such varieties would have little or no impact upon growers, processors, and consumers, who were using bitter varieties, except in areas where processing is inadequate in reducing cyanide levels (no such areas were identified in Nigeria). Improved varieties would be readily embraced by farmers that were currently growing sweet types. The potential benefits from the breeding of improved low-cyanide cassava varieties in Nigeria were extremely high relative to the cost. Even after taking into account the pressure on cassava research resources to explore other potentially high payoff areas, continued investment in a high-yielding, low-cyanide cassava was warranted.

Don and Ken Menz also published some of their work in the international journal, *Food Policy* (*Economics, Planning and Politics of Food and Agriculture*), volume 6, no. 3, 1978 ([13b]). Don also published part of the work with Dr. Emmanuel Maduagwu, at the time a Post-doctoral Fellow engaged in a Cassava Apical Meristem Tissue Culture and Acynogenesis Project at IITA, and now, a Covenant University Professor of Biochemistry. Their study was published in the *Journal of Food Technology*.[14]

Don and Ken Menz's work on cassava went a long way in contributing to the expansion and direction of the cassava program in the eighties and beyond—understanding the patterns in the adoption of improved cassava, improving the quality of cassava preparations, processing traits of improved cassava, and developing more rapid and effective technologies for cassava processing (reducing the cyanogenic content and labor requirement), etc. The decades of the seventies and eighties witnessed IITA playing a leading role in developing improved cassava varieties, which are disease- and pest-resistant, low in cyanide content, drought-resistant, early maturing, and high yielding. Disease-resistant varieties have given sustainable yields of about 50 percent more than local varieties. The distribution of cassava mosaic disease (CMD) resistant varieties in response to the CMD outbreak in East and Central Africa resulted in production levels recovering to pre-epidemic levels in less than five years. Improved cassava varieties produced at IITA are now used in most cassava-growing countries in SSA.

Research on Hydromorphic Toposequences

While the Crop Improvement Program was developing improved cassava varieties, work on the design of systems of crop and land management was also going on within the Farming Systems Program. In that connection, another important area of Don's work at IITA involved two research studies on hydromorphic toposequences. Don did that research with his colleague, Dr. Christine Okali, and two other researchers from outside IITA. These were Dr. T. Ojo-Attere and Dr. T. Lawson.

Toposequences are sections of land from hilltops to bottomlands, a succession of sites from crest to valley bottom. That work arose out of discussions within the Farming Systems Program concerning possible improvements in farming systems in areas with hydromorphic toposequences. From those discussions, it became clear that there was no detailed information on how farmers managed such toposequences, and there was, therefore, no information on which to base possible improvements in technology design in relation to the new varieties of cassava and other crops. Thus, it was important to provide this information base, a major objective of that work.

Hydromorphic lands in Nigeria, as in many African countries, vary from those with slightly wetter and fully drained soils to those with flooded or swampy conditions. The development of valley bottomlands for intensified production of rice and other crops is considered to be a high priority by research organizations, especially where such lands represent a substantial proportion of the landscape. In addition, with increasing population pressure, increased use of marginal lands is necessary.

Their studies aimed at providing descriptive information on the present and changing use of these areas; identifying problems encountered in their use; and hence, indicating possible areas for improvement, bearing in mind the work on design of systems of crop and land management.

Three areas were selected for study, one in the Oshun River Basin and two in the Ogun River Basin, both of them in Western Nigeria. In each locality, they obtained soil survey data by conducting soil surveys and had informal and formal interviews with farmers, including farm visits. Together, the three areas reflect the contrasting position of hydromorphic landscapes in the farming system, their classical use for yam and other dry crops, their increasing use for bottomland rice, and their use to meet specialized urban needs for such items as sugarcane. Although their interest lay partly with the integrated use of both upland and lowland areas, they concentrated more on investigating the actual use of lowland areas. The selected sites were, therefore, those where substantial areas of bottomland exist.

Hydromorphic lands can be found in minor valleys and inland swamps. The valleys in the drier forest area, the derived savannah and Guinea Savannah, have less occurrence of prolonged flooding. These are distinguished from hydromorphic soils found in major inland valleys and depressions occurring mainly in major river valleys, such as the valleys of the River Niger, which are prone to periodic flooding. In general, they cover only a small percentage of agricultural land in Nigeria. Their significance, however, varies according to the proportion which they constitute to the total cultivatable lands. Around Abeokuta, in Ogun State, it is estimated that they cover 40 percent of the surface area while some 5,000 acres are said to lie on the Iwo/Oshogbo road near Ede in Oyo State (Moorman et al., 1976) [15]

In the west of Nigeria, the valley bottoms are, in general, little used. Their use near urban markets for vegetable production is highly localized. Lagemann (1977),[16] writing in Eastern Nigeria argues that valley bottoms have been ignored because the farming system is developed from shifting cultivation. Hence, the principle of ameliorating the land by drainage was not part of the cultural heritage. Moorman[17] refers to the lack of adequate rice-growing technology and Sonola (1975),[18] to the lack of adequate equipment for land clearing and preparation and health hazards. It is noted that the classified way of using these landscapes in much of Nigeria is for dryland crops, such as yams and maize, on heaps and mounds. Okigbo (1978)[19] discusses how farmers utilize various parts of large mounds on which different crops are grown on hydromorphic soil in Abakiliki in Eastern Nigeria: crops are located on the mounds according to their root systems and in relation to their tolerance of high water table.

Although currently relatively untapped, hydromorphic lands are considered to have great potential for increasing rice production because the growing season is prolonged by additional soil water, which gives farmers a wider choice of varieties and a longer period for planting operations, continuous cultivation that increases land productivity, and more diversified and intensive cropping. A collateral of the use of hydromorphic land for producing rice is the gradual development of paddies (bunded and leveled fields), which achieves higher and stable yields.

A report from their second study in the Ogun River basin presented information on how hydromorphic toposequences are traditionally used and managed in a humid forest zone where lowland occupies a major proportion of the agricultural land. The objective was also to provide information for designing improved technology suitable for the integrated use of such areas. As in the first study, they collected information from a number of farmers in Ofada, Mowe, Bisodun, Adesan, and Pakuro in Ogun State, Western Nigeria, who cultivated uplands and valley bottoms in 1978.

A land facet analysis indicated that the Ofada area was predominantly colluvio-alluvial terrace, which is gently sloping to fairly flat with *Eupatorium odoratum* forming the dominant foliage canopy. Farmers identified a variety of land types, including those that are flooded throughout the year, those which contain surface water for a few months only, the upland areas with impeded drainage, the dry savannah areas, and the flat areas which are porous.

The lowland areas were used mainly for rice and vegetables, with vegetable following rice in the rotation. The cropping sequences on upland began with first season maize, if grown, upland rice and cassava followed by yam and/or cocoyam. Tree crops such as kola, oil palm, and cocoa were also grown. Bush fallowing was practiced on both lowland and upland with fallow periods ranging from three to five years. Rice and cassava were considered the most important crops followed by maize and cocoyam in terms of consumption, profitability, and suitability to the soils of the area.

Of the constraints faced by farmers, lack of working capital and non-availability and high cost of labor for weeding and clearing were the most important. Hence, famers would rather spend their little capital on herbicides or hired labor than on fertilizer. Also, the limited use of lowland at the time, despite its greater availability, reflected the magnitude of those constraints because tasks on lowland were more arduous and costly than on upland. The apparent preference for upland was also due to the wider variety of crops that could be grown there as against two crops on lowland. On the other hand, the motivation to invest on lowland appeared to rest solely on the benefits from rice production.

Based on those and other findings, a major thrust of improvement in the integrated use of hydromorphic toposequences in that area could be toward utilizing the land which is flooded throughout the year and which was little used for swamp rice. Water control was, at the time, not a problem to farmers, but with the use of flooded land, some means of improved water management and control would be essential in order to reduce the risk of crop loss due to floods and excess water in the valley bottoms. Such water control methods must be reasonably cheap and technologically within the farmers' competence. Other improvements could include the use of disease-resistant, high-yielding rice and cassava varieties. Since upland crops, such as maize, suffer more than lowland crops in dry years, the use of faster maturing varieties in the second season was recommended.

The findings and conclusions of their studies on hydromorphic toposequences in support of the farming system's program were published in the IITA Discussion Papers Series as Discussion Paper no. 4/1979, International Institute of Tropical Agriculture, Ibadan, 1980, 54p and Discussion Paper no. 5/1980, International Institute of Tropical Agriculture, Ibadan, 1980, 54p.[20]

Just as Don's work was supporting the Cassava Improvement Program and the Farming Systems Program, he was also supporting another IITA program through teaching. That program was IITA's Training Program. As would be recalled, a core mandate of the Institute was not only the development but also the transfer of improved technologies developed at IITA and the continual imparting of new knowledge and skills to national programs. Toward achieving that end, IITA organized short-term individual and group training courses which provided one of the most cost-effective means of rapidly disseminating new technologies. Researchers from the National Agricultural Research Centers (NARs), Research Associates or Assistants came to IITA for non-degree training to address their individual needs and the needs of their NARs. To those researchers, Don taught economics-related courses.

Don's tenure at IITA also provided him the opportunity to make a contribution on behalf of IITA to the Department of Agricultural Economics of the University of Ibadan, where he taught courses as a Visiting Lecturer for two years.

A few months after Don and his family moved to IITA, Eyong Charles arrived unannounced at their home from Cameroon. He introduced himself as

Don's nephew. He had just finished, albeit unsuccessfully, his GCE Advanced Level course in the sciences in Cameroon and had come to seek assistance to continue his education. They took him in. Having tried and failed to get him admission into the Petroleum Training Institute at Effurun in Warri, Midwest region where Dr. Egbuna, one of Don's former classmates in the higher school was Head of a Department, Don enrolled him in the evening classes run by the Department of Extra-Mural Studies of the University of Ibadan. These classes were to prepare him for the competitive entrance exam into Nigerian universities administered by the Joint Admissions and Matriculation Board (JAMB). He became Don's responsibility. To his credit, he settled down well into the classes and, in no time, integrated himself into the IITA community and became a friend of their friends.

With Dorothy in Lagos, Don took responsibility for looking after their two children, Lilian and Lorraine, and to an extent, with the assistance of his mom, who was experiencing a few age-related health problems. Don would get up early, bathe them, dress them, give them breakfast, and drive them to school, dropping Lilian at the kindergarten in IITA and Lorraine at a nursery in town before coming back to work. He would pick them up after school and, in the evening, help them with their ABCs, read them stories from their story books and sing nursery rhymes.

Don remembers some of those nice little stories such as Little Red Riding Hood and Cinderella. He also remembers the popular rhymes at that time— Little Bo Peep, Humpty Dumpty, etc. They would sing, dance, and mimic whatever actions were called for in those rhymes. Every second Saturday at least, he would take them to town to have their hair braided, often with beads. On those weekends that their mom visited, she would take care of some of those chores in addition to cooking and stocking the freezer with food that would last several days before Don starts cooking again.

Working at IITA was quite a rewarding experience. Not only was Don enjoying the job, he was also enjoying the few trappings that came with it. That notwithstanding, he was beginning to feel a growing longing to return to Cameroon. It had been six years since he left home. Apart from that, the only time he had really spent in Cameroon was the two years he worked as a 3rd Class Clerk after high school and the two and a half years he worked with the CDC. By early 1979, he still had not received a reply to the application he sent to the Centre Université De Dschang/Dschang University Center in Cameroon in late 1978. So he sent a reminder, and a few months later, he received a reply from the Director-General of the University Center, Mr. Gilbering Bol Alima (he had not received a Ph.D. degree at the time).

After appreciating Don's interest and thanking him for his application, he deeply regretted that there was no vacant teaching position at the École National Supérieure d'Agronomique where Don could be recruited to teach. According to him, the Department of Rural Economy there was full, but that was contrary to the information Don had been given. Friends who wanted Don back home had always cited the paucity of teaching staff at the Center and in that department, in particular.

If Dschang did not need Don's services, he was optimistic that he would find employment elsewhere before his contract with IITA expired. He was even more confident that IITA would renew or extend his contract if he wanted to stay on. So without any regrets, he put Bol Alima's letter behind him and got on with his program at IITA, but it was not to be for long.

The visit to Ibadan in 1979 by Prof. Anomah Ngu, who was then the Vice-Chancellor of the University of Yaounde, rekindled Don's interest in the University Center. Don had known Prof. Ngu when he was a Professor of Surgery at the University College Hospital (UCH), Ibadan, when he was an undergraduate student in the University of Ibadan in the late sixties. He and other students used to visit him and his wife in their home. So when Don was informed of his arrival in Ibadan, he went to visit him.

"Is that Don Oben? You have added a little weight. IITA must be spoiling you guys," he said jokingly in his usual quiet, but warm manner as soon as Don entered the living room.

Don had called to tell him he was coming. Since he was seeing the Professor for the first time since his return home to Cameroon and his appointment as Vice-Chancellor, Don congratulated him. Although he was congratulating him, Don was quite aware of the enormous sacrifice he had made by returning to Cameroon, leaving an illustrious career behind in Nigeria. After welcoming Don and acknowledging his academic progress and his fellowship position at IITA, he told him, "Don, we need people like you back home. You should come and teach at ENSA."

He was taken by surprise when Don told him about Bol Alima's letter to him.

"Did he really say there were no vacancies at ENSA in his letter to you?" he asked in disbelief. But like a seasoned administrator, he was tactful enough not to give the impression that what Bol Alima wrote was not true.

Unfortunately, Don didn't have the letter with him. He had not anticipated that that issue would come up for discussion. Given Prof. Ngu's legendary interest in people, particularly young people with aspirations, Don should have known that he would ask about his future plans.

"Okay, let me have your resumé before I leave," he offered. Don came back days later to give it to him.

Dorothy successfully completed her three-year diploma course at the end of the 1978/1979 academic year and was awarded the Nigeria Certificate of Education (NCE). Thereafter, she was admitted into the two-year degree program leading to the award of the Bachelor of Arts Degree in Education. The two-year program was open only to candidates who had successfully completed the three-year diploma course and awarded the NCE, so she went back to the University of Lagos in October 1979 to begin the BA Degree Program in Education. Don and the girls continued their interchange of visits with her.

Don received a letter from Dschang University Center toward the end of 1979, requesting him to send in a formal application again. Prof. Anomah Ngu had communicated to Don that he had sent his resume to Mr. Bol Alima. Don complied.

In April 1980, Dorothy gave birth to their third child, a boy, at UCH. That was the first child who was born with Don present at the hospital and feeling for the first time, all the anxieties which husbands usually suffer from when their wives are in labor. He remembers that he was so excited on his way back from the hospital to IITA that early morning after the delivery that he lost concentration while speeding at the same time. Before he knew it, he almost drove into the back of a stationary trailer. It would have been a ghastly accident. They named the child Junior after Don.

Don's nephew, Eyong Charles, had continued in the extra-mural classes, and early in 1980, they got him to register for the entrance examination into Nigerian universities organized by the Joint Admissions and Matriculation Board (JAMB). Don suggested he should apply to read Medicine given the courses he had taken. Charles himself chose the University of Calabar as his first choice. In March/April, he sat for the exam.

By April 1980, as Don's tenure at IITA was coming to an end, he received a letter of appointment from Mr. Bol Alima Gilbering, appointing him a Chargé de Cours (Lecturer/Assistant Professor) in the Department of Rural Economy at ENSA. Don accepted the offer and made a trip to Cameroon to take a 'Prise de Service' i.e., to take up the appointment or report for duty. The date was May 20, 1980. He then took a leave of absence and returned to IITA to give notice that he would be leaving the Center and arrange for his separation from service. Lectures had ended for the academic year and students were taking their exams. After the exams, staff would be free to go on leave until September, so the University Center had no problem granting him a leave of absence.

Back at IITA, Don began preparations for the journey back to Cameroon. He bought a used, but still fairly new, long-wheel based Peugeot 504 car from his old friend and classmate, Dr. Anthony Ikpi, then a lecturer in the Department of Agricultural Economics in UI. Dorothy had finished her sessional exams and had joined them at IITA in May 1980. In late June, Don set off early in the morning by road on the journey to Cameroon with his family in a convoy that included a big truck carrying their belongings and the Peugeot car carrying him and his family. They left his nephew behind to await the results of the JAMB exams, which were expected any moment.

It was a long and arduous journey, a journey that took them a whole day, passing through Benin City, Asaba, crossing the River Niger on the Niger Bridge into Onitsha, and then on to Enugu, Abakaliki and Ikom, then crossing into Cameroon. They arrived at the customs post late in the evening. There, customs insisted on keeping his car until he paid duty. However, considering that he and his family could not be put into the big truck to continue their journey, they were allowed to pass through on condition that Don leaves the car at the Customs Divisional Headquarters in Mamfe Town. They then set off on the more jagged road to Mamfe, some forty-five miles away. But their journey did not stop there. They were bound for Kumba, 120 miles farther away, where they would stay with Don's sister Eunice until he had found housing in Yaounde before moving his family and their things to Yaounde. After giving an undertaking to bring back his car to the customs in Mamfe, they set off again to Kumba, arriving near midnight. What a journey for his wife and two little girls and two-month old baby, a journey to Yaounde to join the academia.

A few weeks after their arrival in Cameroon and while his family was still living with Sister Eunice in Kumba, his mother-in-law, who had returned to Cameroon from Ibadan before they moved to IITA, passed away suddenly on 26 August 1980 after a brief illness. Visibly shaken by that unexpected and tremendous loss, Don left Yaounde where he was searching for accommodation to join his grieving wife, Dorothy, and other family members to mourn and give her a fitting burial. She had lived with them in Ibadan for almost three years, taken care of their first two girls, Lilian and Lorraine, so her passing away just soon after their return home was emotionally draining.

Chapter 11
Searching for a Future in Academia: Dschang University Center (CUD), Cameroon

Settling Down in Yaounde: A Frustrating Experience

'Elle est en congé' (She is on leave), 'Il vient de sortir' (He has just stepped out), and 'Il arrive' (He is coming back presently) were three expressions Don soon became very familiar with within the first few weeks of his arrival in Yaounde, as he went from one government office to another trying to get information or request for relevant services. The first weeks were frustrating. He was told wherever he went that the civil servant who would give him the information or service which he needed was either on leave or had just stepped out or would be on seat in a moment. Don would sit down and wait assured that the civil servant would be back soon. He was later to be educated that such civil servants were neither on leave nor had just stepped out nor would be coming in soon. They had simply not come to work! But their colleagues would never tell one the truth.

Don had left his family and stuff in Kumba and arrived in Yaounde with a view to finding accommodation before returning to bring them to Yaounde as soon as possible. This had to be done before the university reopened in September. Naturally, he began to search for accommodation of the standard and quality he was used to at IITA. He was soon disillusioned. The monthly rents of the houses he was looking for in the private sector were twice or three times his monthly salary! After weeks and weeks of exasperation searching private sector housing rentals without success, he was advised to apply for government-owned accommodation. There were government houses which were allocated to civil servants and university staff, he was informed; but he had to see the Minister of Housing, at that time, Mr. Mustapha, if he had to succeed in getting a house.

For three weeks, during which he called at the minister's office almost daily, he could not get an appointment to see him. The Minister was either too busy, or was at a meeting, or was not receiving people that day. But each day Don was there, all kinds of people were streaming in and out of the minister's office. Yet his secretary would not allow Don to see him. One day as he was getting out quite upset, he met a friend, Mr. Mofor, coming in.

"Old boy, you look quite upset. What is the matter?" his friend asked.

When Don told him that he had been trying to see the minister without success for *three weeks*, he laughed. Don was not amused.

"You have been trying for three weeks. I have been trying for *three months*," his friend said. "Here, you just have to be patient or else you will develop high blood pressure," he advised.

One day, one of Don's friends, Nelson Mbu, then a magistrate, and whom Don was temporarily putting up with, suggested they go and see Mr. E. T. Egbe, the Minister of State and Minister of Telecommunications who came from their area, Manyu. The Minister was his friend and he was sure he would put in a word to his colleague, Mr. Mustapha, for Don, Nelson explained. Don was quite apprehensive because he had heard that the Minister, for all his several years in government, and as close to the Head of State as he was, he had hardly helped his Manyu people except for a few girls he had appointed as postal clerks in his Ministry. But there was logic in what Nelson, his friend said.

Moreover, from Don's little experience thus far, it seemed like people got even the entitlements laid down in the law through kinship and personal relations. So, although Don was hesitant and skeptical, he agreed to give his friend's suggestion a try and therefore followed him to see their Minister. They were shown into his office and he welcomed them well. The preliminaries over, Don's friend, Nelson, introduced Don to him as a friend who had just arrived from Nigeria and has been employed in ENSA as a Chargé de Cours and has been trying for the past several weeks without success, to see Minister Mustapha of Housing for a house allocation…

Without letting Don's friend finish, there was a sudden outburst from their minister—so why did he bring Don to him, was he the Minister of Housing, what did they want him to do, to go get a house for Don? If Don didn't get government housing, there were private houses he could rent, etcetera, etcetera. Looking visibly angry, the Minister got up from his chair, opened the door, showed them the way out, and closed the door behind them. They did not speak in the car until they got home. Don was in shock! Nelson, his friend, was embarrassed.

Frustrated by his inability to get government housing, Don had to go back to the private sector and continue his search. Eventually, he came to the painful realization that if he had to rent in the private sector, then he would have to downsize his 'champagne taste' to fit his 'beer budget'. He had to forget the IITA type of housing and face the realities of the housing market in Yaounde. In the end, he had to rent a three-bedroom house in the Biye-masi neighborhood for a monthly rent equivalent to 25 percent of his monthly salary. It was the type of houses that looked elegant, but it didn't require a keen eye to see that it was one of those houses which were built of sticks and mud and finished with a thin coat of concrete and paint, like most 'quartier' houses.

So Don and his family settled in Biye-masi which was within reach of ENSA where he would be teaching. Then September came. They put their two little girls in the nursery at the Government English Primary School while they left little Don Jr., now five months old, in the care of Don's sister, Eunice, in Kumba since Dorothy had to return to Lagos University to complete the final year of her degree program. Don visited Kumba regularly at weekends and whenever possible to see how little Don Jr. was doing. He developed really well as sister Eunice nursed him with such care and love as she would nurse her own baby. Dorothy and Don will forever remain indebted to her.

Don's nephew, Charles passed the JAMB common entrance examination and was admitted to read medicine at the University of Calabar in the Cross River State of Nigeria. Dorothy and Don were elated. They had helped open the door again for him to continue his education. Put another way, they had helped build a bridge for him to cross a ravine and continue his academic journey, which he did. Years later, he graduated as a medical doctor from the University of Calabar.

Teaching and Research at ENSA and ITA

The Dschang University Center was made up of two schools. The main school, the Higher National School of Agriculture (Ecole National Supérieure d'Agronomique, ENSA) located in Yaounde, offered a five-year degree program leading to the degree of Ingenieur d'Agronome. The other was the 'Institut de Technique Agricole' (ITA) located at Dschang. This offered a three-year program leading to the award of a diploma also in the agricultural sciences. Both schools reopened in September and Don commenced teaching and research as a Chargé de Cours in the five-year degree program at the ENSA.

Contrary to the impression he had been given by the Director-General, he discovered on assumption of duty, that there was only one permanent faculty in the Department of Rural Economy. He was also the Head of Department. He probably was being assisted by a few part-time teachers. However, with Don's arrival, the whole teaching load in the Department was shared between him and his colleague. They taught not only at ENSA, but also at ITA, Dschang. Don taught Microeconomics, Agricultural Marketing and Credit, Agricultural Development and Policy, and Farm Management and Accounts at ENSA and Microeconomics and Agricultural Marketing and Credit at ITA.

Since ITA was just being established at the time, most of the courses there were taught by lecturers from ENSA and some part-time teachers. They would usually plan their teaching programs so as to allow them spend two weeks, twice a year, at Dschang giving courses. They would take a twin otter aircraft from Yaounde to Dschang and land at the small airfield with a gravel runway close to the University Center. They would be housed at the 'Centre Climatique' (University Guest House) and would do intensive teaching to complete a course in two weeks. Those teaching missions were quite tasking because they also had to give and grade assignments and tests during their sojourn there.

The other important aspect of their work was supervision of students' fifth and final year theses. Considering that they were just two permanent faculty in the Department, each of them had to supervise quite a large number of students. Don's poor French language skills at the time, meant that he had to work in only one language—English, in which case, he should be supervising students whose working language was English. However, the philosophy at the time was that the teacher should be able to understand the first language of the student and vice-versa. Unfortunately, even though most of the students had taken some English courses at some time, these courses did not give them a working knowledge of English. Those Don had to supervise were 'francophones' who had very poor working knowledge of English. Communicating with them was not too difficult. The difficult part for them was writing their dissertations in English since Don was not able to read and understand highly technical and academic material and texts in French. It was not funny correcting and recorrecting chapter after chapter of their dissertations. Don almost had to literally write them! But they all had very rewarding experiences.

The immediate commitment of the teaching staff to teaching and supervision left little time for research. Their capacity for research was further constrained not only by the paucity of, but also the uncertainty and irregularity in the disbursement of the 'prime de recherche' (Research allowance). In spite of these constraints, they set sights high on research convinced that their career progress depended on the university's popular promotion criterion—'Publish or Perish'. Before coming to ENSA, Don had published in two international journals. Two other publications based on work he did with colleagues at IITA came out in 1981 while he was at ENSA—the first, in the *Journal of Food Technology*, vol. 16; and the second, in *Food Policy*, vol. 6, No. 3.[21] So the research and publishing spirit was still burning in Don when he arrived at ENSA.

A Job Offer—from the UN Food and Agriculture Organization (FAO)

In November 1980, just six months after assuming duty at ENSA, a job offer came from the Food and Agriculture Organization of the United Nations (FAO). Don was being offered a P.4 position of Economic Affairs Officer in the Joint ECA/FAO Agriculture Division at the United Nations Economic Commission for Africa (ECA) in Addis Ababa, Ethiopia. The decision to resign his position in the CDC and go for graduate studies was a milestone in his life. And when he took it, his dream was to eventually seek a career in academia or in international development—find a place in contemporary mass society. In his last years in graduate school, that dream turned into a burning desire to teach in the university but more so to work in a regional or international organization.

Hence, as soon as he got his Ph.D. degree, he sent his resumé and Personal History Forms (PHFs) to a few international organizations including the FAO, ECA, the International Crops Research Institute for the Semi-Arid Tropics (ICRISAT) in Hyderabad, applying for jobs. This job offer was thus a response to the application he had filed just after his graduation and before he got the post-doctoral fellowship at IITA.

The letter spelled out some of the duties and responsibilities, as well as the privileges and benefits of the post. He remembers that some of the responsibilities included providing advisory services to member states, on request. The salary was relatively huge—many times what he was earning on Index 665 in the university. The benefits included Education Grant for all the children, paid home leave once every two years with air tickets for all the family, rental (housing) subsidy, health, dental and life insurance, diplomatic and duty-free privileges including the importation of a motor vehicle duty-free, etcetera, etcetera.

What a great job! It was the kind of career Don had dreamed of. But the timing? Had the offer arrived just a few months earlier, it would have been perfect timing. He would have jumped up for joy. The letter had actually spent several months in transit. It had gone to the Department of Agricultural Economics of the University of Ibadan, then to IITA and still not finding Don, it was left to the United Nations Development Program (UNDP) Lagos, to locate him and deliver the letter. UNDP Lagos, finally convinced that he had returned to Cameroon, tasked UNDP Yaounde to locate him.

One morning, a gentleman in a well-cut blue suit knocked on the door of his office in Nkolbisson, introduced himself as an Assistant Resident Representative from UNDP, Yaounde, and asked if he was Don Oben. Removing a letter from the breast pocket of his jacket, he handed it to Don. And this was how and why a letter that was written in May got to Don, when it did, in November 1980.

No matter how attractive the terms and conditions of the offer were, Don was persuaded to assess the offer within the context of the present situation rather than jump at it. The university had resumed in September and classes had just commenced in October. He really had a desire to serve the university. It had taken him several years and the intervention of Prof. Anomah Ngu to get the teaching position at ENSA. He had just relocated to Cameroon in May after seven years abroad and was just settling down. The children had been placed in school and were also just getting used to their new school environment. No, no matter how tempting the offer was, he was not going to turn his back on ENSA and take off to Addis Ababa. He would serve the university for at least two years.

Don went on the phone to request that the offer be kept open for two years to enable him fulfill his obligations and commitments to the university. The response was quick and as anticipated. The filling of the post was long overdue. Either Don accepts the offer immediately or it would be given to the next most qualified candidate on the long waiting list. He wrote back declining the offer and set about doing the work at hand—teaching. But just as he was trying to put the FAO job offer behind him and get on with his teaching career, he received a letter from ICRISAT responding to an application he had filed in April 1978 and requiring him to come for an interview at its regional hub in Bamako, Mali. ICRISAT is a non-profit, non-political organization that conducts agricultural research for development in the drylands of Asia and sub-Saharan Africa.[22] A round-trip air ticket would be sent immediately after they receive confirmation of Don's availability for the interview. This letter too had taken several months to find him. He did not respond. There was no point responding if he was not going to accept a position if eventually he was to be offered one.

The current academic year came to a close in June 1981. It was a good year in spite of all its challenges. They taught all their courses at ENSA and at Dschang, conducted exams, published the results, final year students graduated while the rest went on vacation. Dorothy also graduated in June with a Bachelor of Arts degree, second class Honors from the University of Lagos and reunited with Don and the children in Yaounde. To keep herself busy, she got a job in a private college in Yaounde to teach English to French-speaking students while waiting for a response to an application for a job she had filed with the Ministry of National Education.

Early during the first academic year, Don had come to meet and make friends with many people from his division of origin, Manyu. He had subsequently learned of, and joined the Manyu Elements Cultural Association (MECA) which aimed ultimately, at fostering the development of Manyu Division. He later became the Assistant Secretary—General, with Dr. Christie Mbi as the Secretary—General and Justice Ekor'Tarh as the President. He remembers that one of their major preoccupations at the time was to build a

'Manyu Hall' for use as the Association's activity center for meetings, cultural manifestations, etc.

The next academic year began normally in September 1981. By early 1982, after someone and a half years at the university, Don had become aware of situations that were troubling. A personality cult was building up around the administration, strengthened by hero-worshipping. Promotions had not taken place for years and seemed to rest at the discretion of the university leadership. And he could never understand the whole issue of 'integration' into the public service. He was informed that he was a 'contractuel'. He was further told that he had to serve at least five years to be eligible to apply for 'integration'. Nobody could tell him exactly what the procedure for integration was and how long it could take to complete it. So it was possible to be over the age limit before he could complete the process or even be eligible. These and many other issues began to open the door to frustration for many colleagues but particularly to Don. Gradually, he found himself beginning to question the wisdom of having declined the offer from FAO one and a half years earlier.

A Second Job Offer—from the UN Economic Commission for Africa (ECA) and the Dilemma and Challenge of Leaving

As it happened, in March 1982, he received a call from UNDP, Yaounde, inviting him for a chat. He was asked to give it priority attention. On arrival there, he was handed a letter from the Economic Commission for Africa (UNECA). It was another job offer—an Economic Affairs Officer position still at the Joint ECA/FAO Agriculture Division in ECA. But this time, it was an offer from ECA. He was informed that UNDP had been charged with arranging an interview for him and a medical examination by a UN approved medical practice as soon as he confirmed his interest in the offer.

This time around, taking a decision as to whether to accept the offer or not, was not going to be difficult. The issues raised above made a compelling case for him to leave the University Center and take up this appointment in Addis Ababa, Ethiopia. He was already being frustrated by the system as reflected in the issues raised above: the uncertainty regarding his integration into the public service, the hero-worshipping, which by his character he was not used to, and the comments about, and attitude toward those who did not do so; the paucity and unreliability of research grants, non-functioning structures, no clear-cut procedures or timelines for promotion, etc. But the case for leaving, while powerful, was not without a counter argument.

Don had been out of the country for seven years and returned just two years earlier. He had settled down well, establishing new friendships and new relationships. His two little daughters were also settling down in school. Did it make sense packing up and moving out again? Was it worth the while? However, the case for leaving was strong and compelling.

A grueling interview was arranged by the UNDP in their offices with a team including a UN Senior Consultant who was on mission to Cameroon. A rigorous medical examination with an UN-designated medical outfit was also arranged. The results of both the interview and the medical were sent to Addis Ababa.

Several months later, Don was to learn by accident, that the Directorate-General at Dschang had received a letter from the ECA informing them of their intention to offer Don a job. In the letter, the Commission had requested a recommendation from the Directorate-General to enable ECA take a decision and complete the process of hiring him. He was later also informed by a source close to the Directorate that no action had been taken. The letter had simply been put away with an attitude of "He wants to get an international job. Let's see how he will go." However, when Dschang couldn't keep the letter secret any longer, it was decided that it was best to convince Don not to take the job. So one day, the Director of ENSA called him to his office and in a short chat tried to do just that. "Okay, I will think about it," was Don's response.

It is important to state that the letter sent to the Directorate-General was only one of several sent to Heads of Department of ministries and institutions where Don had worked during his career. The purpose was just to have some recommendations on file and not that they would influence the recruitment process. So whether the university complied with the request or not, it did not matter, a fact which Dschang was not aware of. Don was later to learn that ECA had even written to Mr. S. K. Ewusi, the Chief Clerk in the Ministry of Development and Internal Economic Planning, Buea, where Don had worked as a 3rd Class Clerk for two years after high school in the mid-1960s.

However, the Directorate-General still had an important, if not a crucial part to play if Don was to succeed in leaving the country. In fact, it had the trump card. At that time, one required an 'exit' visa to leave the country especially if one were a civil servant. This 'exit' visa was meticulously checked at all the country's borders—land, sea, and air. And to get it, one had to obtain a 'mission order'—a letter of authorization from one's employer attesting that the employee has been granted permission to travel out of the country. Such a letter specified the purpose of the journey, the date of travel, the destination country, and the expected date of return. So if Don still insisted on taking the job, he would have to obtain a 'mission order' in order to apply for an exit visa without which it would be impossible for him to leave the country. How was he going to get it from Dschang? Submit a resignation letter to the University Center? If he submitted his resignation and it was accepted, it was most unlikely that the university would issue him a mission order since he would have ceased to be a member of its staff. Based on sources close to Dschang, there was hardly any doubt that the Directorate-General would not send the recommendation asked for by ECA or take any measures that would facilitate his getting the job and leaving the country. Neither the ECA nor the UNDP can assist him in getting an exit visa. However, Don did not resign. He just had to *think*.

Weeks and months passed. Don did not get back to the Director of ENSA. He just let the matter be forgotten. He carried out his work single-mindedly as never before to ensure that he completed his teaching load both at ENSA and at Dschang. With a lot of hard work and determination, he got all the students he was supervising to complete and submit their dissertations. June came and the University Center went on vacation. It was another productive and very enriching year.

Yet, Don kept showing up and working in his office at Nkolbisson almost every day during June, July, and August. He did not take any vacation. He had a lot not only on his mind but on his table. The matter of his 'international job' seemed forgotten to the delight of the university authorities. They had prevailed, probably. But just before midnight on August 25, Don cleared his office at Nkolbisson!

Part 3
Finding a Future in the United Nations Organization (UNO)

Chapter 12
At The UN Economic Commission for Africa (ECA), Addis Ababa, Ethiopia

Arrival in Ethiopia

The Protocol Officers from the UNDP Office in Lagos were standing by waiting to receive Don when his flight from Douala landed at Murtala Mohammed International Airport, Ikeja, Nigeria, at midday on August 26, 1982. Immigration and customs formalities completed, he was whisked to Ikoyi and lodged at the UNDP guesthouse where he was to stay until the following day when he would take his connecting flight by Ethiopian Airlines to Addis Ababa. On August 27, he had a briefing by the resident representative in the morning before being taken to the airport in the evening to take the midnight flight to Addis Ababa arriving there in the early hours of August 28, 1982.

He was welcomed by two Protocol Officers from the ECA who took his ticket and passport and passed him through immigration and customs in no time. As they entered the car and drove out of the Bole International Airport, the Protocol Officer sitting beside him at the back of the car turned to him.

"So you are the Mr. Don from Cameroon?" he asked humorously.

"Yes, I am the Mr. Oben, what's the problem?" Don asked.

"We had come to the airport twice to pick you up but each time you were not on the flight," he explained.

"Well, I am here now," Don replied without getting into a discussion as to why he was not on the flights.

"You are welcome to Ethiopia," he said with a smile.

"Thank you," Don responded and turned to look out through the window at this renowned city.

He was driven to Ghion Hotel, a government-owned hotel which turned out to be just a walking distance to the ECA. There, he had been booked a room; and after he had bathed and had breakfast, he proceeded to report at the ECA.

"Welcome, Mr. Obeng. Finally, we have gotten you to Addis," Mr. Ghansah, a Ghanaian national and the Chief of Personnel, said with a visible sigh of relief as he ushered Don into his office on the eighth floor of the ECA new building.

"Oben, not Obeng," Don corrected him. The Ghanaians have a similar name but with a *g* and pronounced a bit different.

"Okay, Mr. Oben, you are welcome to ECA. How was your flight?" he asked.

"Glad to be here and may I express my sincere appreciation for your understanding and cooperation," Don replied as they sat down.

He understood why Don was thanking him. From the several faxes he had sent to Don, there was no question that he had been under much pressure from the Joint Division to get Don on board ASAP. Don had missed two deadlines Mr. Ghansah had given to him because he really wanted to stay on till the end of the school year so he could finish teaching all his courses at ENSA and Dschang. Besides, he wanted the students he was supervising to complete and submit their final year research projects. In as much as he was eager to leave, the last thing he wanted was to have his departure destabilize or disrupt any of the Center's programs. He had thus pleaded with Mr. Ghansah to give him time to complete the academic year before coming to Addis.

Mr. Ghansah gave Don a short briefing and then proceeded to review some 'housekeeping matters'. He would send a fax to Don's wife informing her of his safe arrival and assumption of duty. He would ask UNDP Yaounde to arrange for packers to collect and ship their household and personal effects to Addis Ababa, and issue Don's family with air tickets when they are ready to join him, etc., etc. In those days, the fastest means of written communication was by fax. Don asked him if his university responded to his letter requesting a recommendation on him.

"No, they didn't. But we received recommendations from some of your past employers. So it didn't matter whether your university wrote or not," was his reply.

He then took Don to the Joint ECA/FAO Agriculture Division on the fourth floor to introduce him to the Division's Director, Mr. Q. B. O. Anthonio, a former Professor of Agricultural Economics at the University of Ibadan. After he left, Don had some lengthy discussions with the Director after which he took Don round to introduce him to his colleagues-to-be in their offices. Finally, he led Don to the office that had been prepared for him in the Agricultural Marketing Services Section. This is how on August 28, 1982, Don assumed service as an Economic Affairs Officer in the Joint ECA/FAO Agriculture Division of the ECA.

Back in Yaounde, his wife went to Nkolbisson and submitted his letter of resignation to the Director-General through the Director of ENSA, the day after Don's departure according to their arrangement. Don had given one month's notice expiring at the end of September. Technically, he was on vacation up to the end of September as all other faculty were. As expected, his resignation was a shock. There was anger at Dschang when it later became known that Don was no longer in the country. "How did he leave?" was the question everyone was asking.

Dorothy got a job at the Ministry of Education and worked as a 'Chef de Bureau' for one month through September but had to join Don in Addis Ababa at the end of September with the children—Lilian, Lorraine, Don Jr., and Gwendoline, his sister's last daughter. Don had found places at Bingham Academy for them and since schools were reopening in September, they had to join him ASAP. They moved into one of the Riviera Chalets in Ghion Hotel after they arrived. They were to remain there for eleven months while in the ECA queue for housing.

At that time, all the embassies, the UN, international and regional organizations had a number of houses allocated to them by the government, which they in turn allocated to their staff on a first-come-first served basis. Any new arrival had to queue up until a house became vacant in his or her own organization's pool of houses. Because demand far outstripped supply, it was common for new arrivals to wait for months before being allocated a house. On seizing power, the socialist military government of Mengistu Haile Mariam had confiscated all houses from the aristocratic class who allegedly had gotten rich by exploiting the masses. It had then established an agency to manage and administer the houses—the Agency for the Administration and Management of Rented Houses. These were the houses which were allocated to the international community and rents were paid in United States dollars. There was no private sector real estate or individual landlords renting houses to foreigners.

Within a few months of her arrival in Addis, Dorothy got a job at the International School (American School) of Addis Ababa) to teach English as a foreign language.

Left to right, the children: Gwen, Don, Lorraine, and Lilian in 1982 in Ethiopian traditional dresses.

The ECA: Its Mandate and Structure

The ECA with headquarters in Addis Ababa, Ethiopia, is one of the five Regional Economic Commissions of the United Nations around the world. The four others are: the Economic Commission for Europe (ECE) with headquarters in Brussels, Belgium; the Economic and Social Commission for Western Asia (ESCWA) in Beirut, Lebanon; the Economic Commission for Latin America and the Caribbean (ECLAC) in Santiago, Chile, and the

Economic and Social Commission for Asia and the Pacific (ESCAP) in Bangkok, Thailand.

The ECA was established in 1958 by the United Nations Economic and Social Council (ECOSOC) following a recommendation of the United Nations General Assembly (UNGA) with a mandate to promote the economic and social development of its member states.[23] At the time Don joined the Commission, it was focusing its programs on the following areas: ensuring increased food production and food self-sufficiency in Africa; promoting regional cooperation and integration in industry, trade and transport and communication; ensuring the efficient exploitation and use of natural resources and the environment; facilitating economic and social policy analysis; strengthening development management; and promoting the development of women.

The Commission therefore structured its programs at that time into the following program divisions: the Joint ECA/FAO Agriculture Division (JEFAD), Natural Resources and Environment (NRD), Socioeconomic Research and Planning (SERPD), Transport and Communication (TCD), Population, Industry, the African Training and Research Center for Women (ATRCW), and the Office of Regional Cooperation. These divisions were supported by the Administration and Conference Services (ACS) Division and the Cabinet Office of the Executive Secretary (COES) which comprised the Executive Secretary, Deputy Executive Secretary, Secretary to the Commission, Special Assistant to the Executive Secretary, the Program Planning and Coordination Office (PPCO), and special advisers and information unit.

ECA also established offices in all the five subregions of the continent. These subregional offices at that time, were known as the Multinational Programming and Operational Centers (MULPOCs) and were designed to bring the Commission nearer to member states and enable it to respond more quickly and efficiently to their needs and demands. These MULPOCs were located in Lusaka, Zambia, for the Eastern and Southern Africa subregion; Yaounde, Cameroon, for the Central Africa subregion; Niamey, Niger, for the West Africa subregion; Tangier, Morocco, for the North Africa subregion; and Gisenyi, Rwanda, for Eastern Africa and the Great Lakes countries.

The Commission is a knowledge-based institution bringing together some of the best minds in the continent. It is thus, a 'think tank' for the region. In this connection, it identifies the major problems plaguing the continent and new issues and opportunities in the region and uses vigorous policy analysis to address them. This is particularly so in the field of macroeconomic policy development and analysis. In pursuit of its mandate to promote the economic development of its member states, ECA's work in the field of macroeconomic policy analysis led by the Socioeconomic Research and Policy Division (SERPD) placed particular emphasis on collecting and analyzing relevant data and synthesizing research results on economic and social policies relevant to Africa. The ECA through the SERPD prepared annual surveys, and produced profiles and reports on the social and economic conditions in Africa.

The Commission reported directly to the UN Economic and Social Council (ECOSOC) through the Conference of African Ministers Responsible for Economic and Social Development and Planning, and convened a number of intergovernmental organs and committees. The conference of Ministers was advised at that time, by the Technical Preparatory Committee of the Whole (TEPCO) whose meeting each year preceded that of the Conference of Ministers. There were sectoral ministerial conferences, advised by appropriate committees of officials, to assist the functioning of the Commission. All member states were also expected to be represented by their experts at these meetings. Over the years, the member states of the Commission have used the forum of the conference to adopt various regional plans of action and programs, develop common positions for global conferences, and share experiences on follow-up, including implementation of various regional and global programs.

The Conference of Ministers usually considered several reports prepared by the ECA secretariat concerning Africa's preparations for various global conferences/summits scheduled in the immediate future as well as international programs of action related to Africa's development. It usually urged member countries to participate actively in these global conferences/summits and at the same time, underlined the need for accelerated implementation of the regional and international programs of action on Africa's development. It also always requested progress reports on these global conferences and on programs related to Africa's development. Three reports that were always on the agenda of each conference were: A Review of Socioeconomic Development in Africa, the Situation of Food and Agriculture in Africa, and ECA's Program of Work and Budget for the biennium.

Settling Down to Work

The Joint ECA/FAO Agriculture Division to which Don was assigned on recruitment was established by ECA and FAO within ECA and under the administrative control of ECA in order to pool their resources (both staff and financial) to jointly implement programs in the agriculture sector. With FAO as the sole UN Agency with a global mandate in agriculture and ECA with a regional mandate for ensuring the socioeconomic development of Africa, both FAO and ECA had a mandate to promote agricultural development in Africa. The division was thus established to pool resources together and avoid duplication of programs, efforts, and resources. The division's work program was developed by ECA in consultation with FAO.

At the time Don joined the Joint Division, it was implementing a program on food and agriculture as reflected in the policy for food and agricultural development in Africa in the Lagos Plan of Action (LPA, discussed later). This policy focused on the promotion of increased food and agricultural production through agricultural intensification and area expansion, adoption of new and available technologies, and provision of agricultural marketing and distribution facilities and services. The Division was therefore organized into the following three sections: (A) Agricultural Policy and Planning (APPS), (B) Agricultural Marketing (AMS), and (C) Agricultural Production, Institutions and Services (APISS).

It was hoped that with this organizational structure, the Division was well placed to respond to the needs of ECA member states and assist in addressing the issues of agricultural development facing them such as agricultural policy development and analysis, agricultural production, institutions and services, and agricultural marketing, infrastructure and services as embodied in the LPA.

The program of work of the Division was structured into biennia within ECA's Program of Work and Priorities. The Division's work also included identifying burning issues in the agricultural sector of African economies and preparing relevant technical reports and publications for dissemination to member states. It also contributed agriculture-related chapters or sections of reports prepared by the Commission and mandated by various conferences and meetings. Thus, in the early 1980s, the Joint Division's work program included among others: 'The Report on the Situation of Food and Agriculture in Africa'; 'Contribution to The Report on The African Economy: An Overview of

Developments in Major Production Sectors' (agriculture, mining, and manufacturing) prepared by SERPD; reports requested by the Conference of Ministers of Economic and Social Development and other sectoral conferences and meetings for presentation at their respective conferences and meetings; advisory services on request, to member states on agricultural policy and planning, agricultural marketing, institutions and services, and agricultural production, institutions and services.

In fact, one of Don's early assignments at ECA was when he and a statistician colleague, Godfrey Coker from Sierra Leone, were assigned to prepare the 'Report on the Situation of Food and Agriculture in Africa' in 1984. This report was to be presented to the Fourth Meeting of TEPCO and Ninth meeting of the Conference of Ministers due to take place in April 1984. So it was a very important assignment. They were to go to FAO Headquarters in Rome and make use of the most up-to-date data in FAO's database to prepare the report. At that time, FAO's agricultural data was published in FAO's Statistical Yearbook. As there were no computers at the time, one could not access this data directly from the organization's database. Also, the data published in the Yearbook was not always current. It was for these reasons that Don and his colleague had to go to FAO headquarters, Rome, to get the data they needed in situ.

Before leaving for Rome, they had prepared an annotated outline of the report and discussed it and agreed on the data requirements at two meetings of the Division. The need for them to go to Rome was not only to obtain and use the most current data but also to have inputs from FAO by way of comments on the drafts and final report.

At FAO, they were provided with office space and a secretary to type their drafts since at that time, there were no laptops which they could use to draft the report themselves. They had hardly settled down on the assignment when Don received the sad news that his father had passed away at the CDC Cottage Hospital in Tiko, back in Cameroon. It took quite some time for the news to get to him as no one back in Addis Ababa knew his contact address. On arrival in Rome, they had been too preoccupied with trying to get started that Don had not yet communicated his contact details to his wife or the Joint Division.

So, when his wife received the sad news from home, she didn't know how to get in touch with him. She had to call a family friend, Dr. Frank Attere, in Nairobi who then called their mutual friend Dr. Namanga Ngongi in Rome.

Failing to get him as he was on mission himself, Dr. Atterehe gave the news to his brother with a request that he break the news to Don as 'tactfully' as possible. It was he who came to Don's hotel late that evening when he was sure he would meet Don in the hotel to inform him that his father had passed away. He knew where to find Don because, fortunately, Don had called their home immediately on arrival in Rome to let them know he was in town.

Don had known that his father's health was failing. He was eighty-two. During one of his missions to West Africa, Don had made a determined effort to fly to Cameroon and visit him in the hospital. His first wife, Ma Alice, and his dear sister and confidante, Aunty Susanah, were at his bedside. His condition was not too serious at the time of Don's visit. So Don was jolted by the news of his death. The funeral was to take place in the next few days. At that time, it was not the practice, as it is now, to preserve the dead in mortuaries for months while planning for an elaborate funeral. It wasn't just the tradition, but the facilities for preservation were not there either. Don reported the news to his Division.

Considering the importance of the report to the Commission and the need for it to be ready several weeks before the conference in April, Don had to continue with the assignment. He would leave for Cameroon after their return to Addis Ababa even though the funeral would have been held. He traveled home and attended the after-burial ceremonies during which he and some of his brothers and young nephews were initiated into their esteemed traditional Ekpe Society.

Back to the assignment, he and Godfrey spent the first week after their arrival in Rome collecting, collating, analyzing, and discussing the data together. Godfrey, however, did much of the statistical analyses and Don wrote most of the chapters of the report. They met with relevant FAO Divisions to discuss the various drafts and receive their comments and suggestions. After the third draft, they finalized the report, integrating to the extent possible, the comments from their FAO colleagues. The assignment was grueling. The report was sound and thorough.

At this point, it is important to recall an incident concerning this report which remains green in Don's memory. Based on the analysis of the food situation and outlook, they had warned in the report of an impending food crisis in Africa and urged African member states and the international community to take all necessary actions to avert it. For this timely warning supported by concrete analyses, they were berated by the then Acting Chief of the Assistance Planning Service at FAO, an Ethiopian national probably, when he read through the third draft. He called Don and his colleague 'alarmists'.

"Food crisis, food crisis, food crisis, where is the food crisis?" he asked. "It's true there are pockets of crop failure here and there and areas of food shortages. But that does not mean that there is a food crisis," he asserted, advising strongly that they delete all reference to a food crisis in the report.

Don and his colleague refused to back down and took responsibility for whatever was in the report. Well, as it is now well known, it was not long before Africa was engulfed in one of the most devastating food crisis in the continent. Never before, except perhaps in the early 1970s before the World Food Conference, had the attention of the entire world been so captured as by the famine and starvation in Africa. This momentarily took central stage in the agenda of the UNGA, and numerous international and regional conferences and meetings, as the world sought to find immediate and long-term solutions to the African food crisis. The famine, hunger, and starvation spreading across Ethiopia in particular, aroused so much sympathy and indignation around the world that humanitarian aid groups and even music pop stars ('Band Aid', 'We Are the World') also jumped into the fray to raise money to save lives.

Don and Godfrey Coker returned to ECA and presented their report to the Joint Division. They had another Divisional meeting to critique it. It was accepted and then sent to PPCO for vetting and printing.[24]

This report was presented to the Fourth Meeting of TEPCO and Ninth Meeting of the Conference of Ministers which took place from April 14–23, 1984. This was the first Conference of Ministers which Don attended and served as a member of the secretariat team and a resource person. This meeting considered quite a large number of agenda items among which were: A Review of Socioeconomic Developments in Africa, 1956–83; Implementation of the Lagos Plan of Action and the Final Act of Lagos: (a) Joint Progress Report by the OAU Secretary-General and the ECA Executive Secretary, (b) Contributions by ECA-sponsored Institutions to the Implementation of the Lagos Plan of Action and the Final Act of Lagos, (c) Situation of Food and Agriculture in Africa.[25]

As per the agenda above, one of the important agenda items also considered during the meeting was a Joint Progress Report by the OAU Secretary-General and the ECA Executive Secretary on the Implementation of the Lagos Plan of Action and the Final Act of Lagos and another progress report on the Contributions by ECA-sponsored institutions to the Implementation of the Lagos Plan of Action and the Final Act of Lagos.

In order to see these agenda items in their proper context, it is important to dwell momentarily on (a) the Lagos Plan of Action (LPA) and (b) the ECA-sponsored institutions, both in light of some of the major contributions which the ECA had made or was making to Africa's economic and social development.

The Regional Programs and Plans of Action

The Lagos Plan of Action (LPA)

One of ECA's major contributions to the continent's economic advancement in the 1980s was in trying to chart a development path for its member states through developing a number of regional plans and frameworks which were adopted by African member states under the political aegis of the OAU. One of these was the Lagos Plan of Action (LPA) for the economic development of Africa, 1980–2000, and the Final Act of Lagos (FAL), 1980. The LPA was the culmination of a four-year-long effort initiated and led by the ECA to undertake an agonizing review of the development paradigms and strategies that Africa had pursued since independence in 1960. This was in an effort to craft Africa's own indigenous development strategies and policies that would best address the intractable development problems that had continued to challenge the continent since independence.

The Lagos Plan of Action[26] was a plan in which African leaders resolved to adopt a regional approach based primarily on collective self-reliance by undertaking measures that would restructure the economic base of their economies. These economies had remained almost stagnant or witnessed no significant growth in the general well-being of their populations in the past twenty years from 1960 to 1980.

Drafted in Lagos in April 1980, it was a big departure from, and a collective response by African states to the World Bank's 1981 Berg report[27] which had intended to analyze the development problems facing African countries. This report had claimed that development in Africa could be achieved through industrialization, global equality in trade relations, a decreased reliance on raw material extraction, and an increase in development aid from the international community.

While the Lagos Plan endorsed inward-looking policies of African self-reliance, the Berg report advocated for outward-looking policies of increased international trade; the LPA blamed Africa's economic crisis on the structural adjustment programs of the World Bank and International Monetary Fund and the vulnerability of African economies to worldwide economic shocks, such as the 1973 oil crisis.

The Plan as well as the Act were adopted by African Heads of State and Government meeting in Lagos at the Second Extraordinary Session in 1980 devoted to Africa's economic problems. The Plan and Act were, in fact, concrete measures for the implementation of the Monrovia Declaration. This Declaration was adopted at the Sixteenth Ordinary Session held in Monrovia, Liberia, in July 1979 as the "Monrovia Declaration of Commitment of the Heads of State and Government of the OAU on the guidelines and measures for national and collective self-reliance in economic and social development for the establishment of a new international economic order."

In adopting the Declaration, they recognized the need to take urgent action to provide the necessary political support to promote the economic and social development and integration of their economies based on self-reliance and to reduce Africa's almost total reliance on the export of raw materials. Through the LPA, African Leaders sought to achieve the goals of rapid self-reliance and self-sustaining development and economic growth, promote the economic integration of the African region, and establish the necessary national, subregional, and regional institutions which would facilitate the attainment of the objectives of self-reliance and self-sustainment. More specifically, they recognized the need to give an important place to the field of human resource development, put science and technology in the service of development, achieve self-sufficiency in food production and supply, implement completely the programs for the United Nations Transport and Communications Decade for Africa, and cooperate in the preservation, protection, and improvement of the natural environment, etc.

These commitments, they firmly believed, would lead to the creation at the national, subregional and regional levels, of a dynamic and interdependent African economy and will thereby pave the way for the eventual establishment of an African Common Market leading to an African Economic Community.

They also resolved to give special attention to the discussion of economic issues at each annual session of their assembly; and in this connection, called on the OAU Secretary-General, in collaboration with the Executive Secretary of the ECA to draw up annually, specific programs and measures for economic cooperation on subregional, regional, and continental bases in Africa.[28]

As concerns the area of agriculture, the Plan recognized that the root of the food problem in Africa was the fact that member states had not usually accorded the necessary priority to agriculture, both in the allocation of resources and in giving sufficient attention to policies for the promotion of productivity and improvement of rural life. For an improvement in the food situation in Africa, the fundamental requisite was a strong political will to channel a greatly increased volume of resources to agriculture, to carry through essential reorientations of social systems, to apply policies that will induce small farmers and members of agricultural cooperatives to achieve higher levels of productivity with increased real incomes.

In the short term, 1980–1985, the objective should be for member states to take measures to bring about immediate improvements in the food situation and to lay a strong foundation for the achievement of self-sufficiency in widely consumed food commodities such as cereals and livestock and fish products. The Plan also called for priority action to be directed to substantially reducing food waste and losses, attaining a markedly higher degree of food security, and bringing about a large and sustained increase in the production of food, especially of tropical cereals, with due emphasis on the diversification of agricultural production.[29]

As seen in the LPA, the Heads of State and Government resolved to give special attention to the discussion of economic issues at each annual session of their assembly; and therefore called on the OAU Secretary-General and the ECA Executive Secretary to draw up specific annual programs and measures for economic cooperation on subregional, regional, and continental basis in Africa.

The specific annual programs and measures for economic cooperation mentioned above refer to efforts which the ECA and OAU were making toward the establishment of regional economic communities considered as the building blocks of an eventual African Economic Community. These Regional Economic Communities (RECs) in Africa were economic entities in which individual countries in subregions were grouped together for the purpose of achieving greater economic integration. They are described as the 'building blocks' of a future African Union (at that time in the 1980s, it was still the OAU) and included in the 1980s: the Economic Community of West African States (ECOWAS, 1975); the Southern African Development Community (SADC 1980); the Preferential Trade Area for Eastern and Southern Africa (PTA, 1981) replaced in 1994 by the Common Market for Eastern and Southern Africa (COMESA); Economic Community of Central African States (ECCAS, 1983); and the Arab Maghreb Union (UMA, 1989).

In fact, the first ECA-sponsored meeting of one of these institutions which Don attended as a staff member of ECA was the First Meeting of the Technical Committee on Agricultural Cooperation of the Preferential Trade Area for Eastern and Southern African States (PTA) which was held in Mulungushi Hall in Lusaka, Zambia, October 26–29, 1982. This meeting was organized and serviced by the Joint Division as the Interim Secretariat of the committee and Don was among the professional staff selected to attend and serve as resource persons. The meeting was convened to initiate the implementation process of the PTA in compliance with the decision of the first meeting of the PTA Council of Ministers held in Lusaka in June 1982 which called for a meeting of the Technical Committee of the PTA to initiate the implementation process.

At the inaugural meeting of the Committee, it elected its officers, reviewed and adopted its terms of reference and rules of procedure before going on to the consideration of the substantive issues. Among these issues were the establishment and management of national and subregional food security facilities, harmonization of agricultural policies for increased food and agricultural production in the countries of the subregion, and progress report on the establishment of a subregional maize research and distribution center. Other issues brought up for consideration were harmonization of research in the fields of crop production, livestock, fisheries, and forestry; training, research, and technology development in post-harvest food losses; and appraisal of existing intergovernmental organizations in agriculture.[30]

The PTA and the First Meeting of its Technical Committee on Agricultural Cooperation have been given much attention here for two reasons. First, regarding the meeting, it was the first ECA meeting which Don attended and serviced. It thus gave him his first experience and insights into intergovernmental meetings—the strict protocol, the meeting procedures, negotiations and compromises, the politicking, etc. Second, as one of the regional economic entities being established by the ECA and OAU at the time, the trade area provided some insights into how those entities were going about achieving the goals for which they were created—to be the 'building blocks' of a future African economic community.

The treaty establishing the Preferential Trade Area for Eastern and Southern Africa was signed in December 1981, as a first step toward higher forms of regional economic cooperation and integration to bring about sustainable growth and development of member states. The treaty came into force in September 1992 following ratification by nine member states. As mentioned earlier in this chapter, the ECA, following the recommendation of the Lagos Plan of Action to expand intra-Africa trade, set up five subregional Multinational Programming and Operational Centers (MULPOC's) for Eastern and Southern Africa, West Africa, Central Africa, North Africa, and the Great Lakes Community.

The LPA further recommended that preferential trade areas with similar arrangements be established within each MULPOC area not later than December 1984. It was within this context that the MULPOC for Eastern and Southern Africa, based in Lusaka, Zambia, successfully negotiated the treaty for the establishment of the Preferential Trade Area for Eastern and Southern Africa in 1981.[31] It is also within this context that the other regional economic communities mentioned above and many others were established by ECA and the OAU.

As mentioned earlier above, the Assembly of Heads of State and Government in adopting the LPA and the Final Act of Lagos had called on the OAU Secretary-General and ECA Executive Secretary to report on progress in the implementation of the Plan as well as progress in the establishment of subregional economic communities at the Conference of Ministers and the meeting of Heads of State and Government.

By the time Don arrived at the ECA in 1982, the Lagos Plan of Action and Final Act of Lagos were being implemented by many African countries as a blueprint to guide their socioeconomic development efforts. In compliance with the call by the Heads of State and Government, the OAU Secretary-General and the ECA Executive Secretary, presented a joint progress report on the implementation of the Lagos Plan of Action and the Final Act of Lagos as an important agenda item at the Fourth Meeting of TEPCO and Ninth Meeting of the Conference of Ministers in April 1983—meetings which ended with the meeting of the Assembly of Heads of State and Government. Under the same agenda item, the two chief executives presented another progress report on the contributions of ECA-sponsored institutions to the implementation of the Plan and Act.

In effect, they reported on the progress which member countries were making in implementing the Plan and Act and the assistance which the regional institutions had provided these countries in this regard. Their report also contained the activities undertaken by the two secretariats to assist member states and their intergovernmental organizations in implementing the Plan and the Act. After discussing that report in 1983, the Heads of State and Government adopted resolution AHG/115(XIX) in which they requested the two secretariats to prepare the second progress report on the implementation of the Plan and the Act for submission to the assembly in 1985 highlighting implementation by the following: (a) member states, (b) African and international organizations, and (c) OAU and ECA secretariats.[32]

After the adoption of the LPA and the FAL in 1980, the African continent continued to face new and emerging challenges as well as recurrent problems of poverty and food insecurity. The ECA therefore continued the search for indigenous and appropriate strategies, frameworks, and plans that would get the continent from this socioeconomic quagmire. It is in the light of these developments that the ECA carried out intensive studies to develop a number of new plans and frameworks in the 1980s and early 1990s in order to address these recurrent problems and challenges. Three of these include: Africa's Priority Program for Economic Recovery (APPER) 1986–1990 which was later converted into the United Nations Program of Action for Africa's Economic Recovery and Development (UNPAAERD) and the Alternative Framework for the Socioeconomic Development of Africa (AAF-SAP) 1986.

Africa's Priority Program for Economic Recovery (APPER) 1986–1990

Africa's Priority Program for Economic Recovery 1986–1990 was adopted by the Assembly of Heads of State and Government of the Organization of African Unity at its Twenty-first Ordinary Session held at Addis Ababa from July 18 to 20, 1985. In adopting this program, African governments reaffirmed their primary responsibility for the economic and social development of their countries, identified areas for priority action, and undertook to mobilize and utilize domestic resources for the achievement of these priorities. They further committed themselves fully to the implementation of the sharply focused, practical, and operational set of activities, priorities, and policies elaborated in the priority program. It was their conviction that if they successfully implemented the program, they would be laying the foundation for durable structural changes, improving the levels of productivity and ensuring the rapid recovery of the African economies while at the same time enhancing long-term development prospects.

It was envisaged that the implementation of the priority program would also contribute to the realization of the Lagos Plan of Action for the implementation of the Monrovia Strategy for the Economic Development of Africa as well as the two 'Decade' Programs: the Industrial Development Decade for Africa, proclaimed by the General Assembly in its resolution 35/66B of December 5, 1980,[33] and the Transport and Communications Decade in Africa, proclaimed by the Assembly in its Resolution 32/160 of December 19, 1977.[34] The implementation of the Priority Program was also to contribute to the realization of the Harare Declaration on the food crisis in Africa adopted on July 25, 1984 by the thirteenth FAO Regional Conference for Africa.[35]

With respect to agricultural development at the national level where the Joint Division provided the major inputs, the Priority Program laid considerable emphasis on the food and agricultural sector. It put primary focus on women farmers who contribute significantly to agricultural production. The measures to be carried out for the development of the agricultural sector were delineated into immediate, short-term, and long-term measures.

The immediate measures which were aimed at combating food emergencies and catastrophes included the creation of sustainable emergency preparedness and establishment of effective early warning systems, flexible and efficient regional networks of crop protection agencies and national food security arrangements.

In the medium term, the Priority Program aimed at increasing the levels of productivity and production through raising substantially the level of investment in agriculture; increasing food production, restoring, protecting, and developing arable land and rendering it more productive; and establishing remunerative producer pricing policies, incentive schemes, and agricultural credit programs. Still in the medium term, the program envisaged the development of livestock and livestock products through the utilization of agricultural by-products, improved management, and attention to animal diseases. Focus was also on the development of mechanization and the use of modern farm and processing machinery, increased use of fertilizers, improved seeds and pesticides, and expanding the storage capacity, and the distribution and marketing system. The program also gave emphasis to the development of agricultural research and extension through the creation of a network of agronomic research stations and extension for the design and diffusion of appropriate agricultural technologies.

Considering the preponderance and importance of small farmers and women in African agriculture, the program considered it of vital importance to place at the disposal of small farmers necessary inputs for increased yields; establishment of assistance programs for small farmers, especially women food producers and rural youths and establishment of low-cost irrigation schemes; and better utilization and improvement in the management of water resources. Action was also required on reafforestation, drought and desertification control programs including firewood schemes, and improvement of agricultural implement maintenance capacity.[36]

The Priority Program emphasized that the manner in which the above actions were to be used and suitably combined together to achieve the expected result should take account of the particular situation in each country. It also recognized the need for national efforts to be complemented by other measures at the subregional and regional levels as well as the support which other sectors in the national economy would have to provide to the agricultural sector for it to achieve the objectives stated above. In this connection, the program called for relevant actions in agro-related industries, the development of transport and communications, and trade and finance, the objective of the latter being to improve the distribution channels for domestic trade.

The Priority Programs also identified areas where actions should be taken in the long-term. Prominent among these are drought and desertification; human resources development, planning, and utilization; and policy reforms. With regards to drought and desertification, it stated that although drought and desertification require a long-term approach, there was need for immediate action by African countries at national, subregional, and regional levels to implement a comprehensive program for drought and desertification and to stem and control the effects of drought and desertification on both the ecological environment and the development process. Actions which African governments were committed to undertake in this regard included the full implementation of the Plan of Action to Combat Desertification approved by the General Assembly in its resolution 32/172 of December 19, 1977.

Considering that the effective participation of the people in development and the efficient development, planning, and utilization of Africa's human resources is central to the successful implementation of the proposed actions in the Priority Program, the program contains some comprehensive policies for human resource planning, development, and utilization which should be adopted and integrated in the overall national development policies and plans.

Finally, the Priority Program underscored the need for African governments to undertake, individually or collectively, all measures and policy reforms that were necessary for the recovery of their economies and the revitalization of genuine development particularly in the following areas: improving management of the economy, undertaking appropriate adjustment measures such as exchange rate adjustment, debt-relief arrangements, wage and salary reduction, and public employment freeze. It also accorded special importance to a population policy that would, inter alia, address issues of high fertility and mortality, rapid urbanization, rural-urban and rural-rural migration, the problems of children and youths and the protection of the environment.[37]

United Nations Program of Action for African Economic Recovery and Development (UNPAAERD) 1986–1990

The UN General Assembly that met in its eighth plenary meeting on June 1, 1986[38] analyzed the critical economic situation in Africa noting that the crisis had not only jeopardized the development process of the African economies, but had also threatened the very survival of millions of Africans. This persistent economic crisis which had been exacerbated by drought and desertification and the more recent tragic famine and hunger had, nevertheless, strengthened the resolve of the African countries, individually and collectively, to take immediate and concerted actions to achieve sustained economic and social development of their countries in the medium- and long-term.

It noted that urgent, far-reaching, and imaginative economic policies were required to avert further deterioration in the economic conditions in Africa and to launch the continent on the path of dynamic self-reliant and self-sustained economic development in a favorable external environment. One immediate task of such efforts was to increase substantially productivity in all sectors, particularly in the central sectors of food and agriculture. In this connection, it noted that African leaders had taken the main responsibility for their own development by resolving to undertake the necessary measures to overcome the current economic crisis through the adoption of Africa's Priority Program for Economic Recovery 1986–1990 (which has been presented above), by the Assembly of Heads of State and Government of the Organization of African Unity at its twenty-first ordinary session, held at Addis Ababa from July 18 to 20, 1985.

However, given the dimensions of the internal and external problems facing the continent, the assembly noted that it was obvious that in order to accomplish this complex task, Africa must receive the full support of the international community because the African development crisis was not an exclusive African problem. The African economic crisis was one that concerned mankind as a whole considering that the world was an interdependent, global community. It was therefore essentially urgent to develop and implement an international strategy to complement the exceptional efforts that the African countries had themselves initiated to put their economies on course. In developing such a strategy, it was necessary to take full cognizance of the special problems and needs, not only those common to Africa as a whole, but also those of subregions and individual African countries in order to ensure balanced and equitable development.

Against the background above, the UN General Assembly meeting at its Eighth Plenary Meeting on 1 June 1986 adopted the United Nations Program of Action for African Economic Recovery and Development, 1986–1990, in its resolution A/RES.13/2.[39] This program was based on mutual commitment and cooperation and consisted of two central elements:

(a) The determination and commitment of the African countries to launch both national and regional programs of economic development as reflected in Africa's Priority Program for Economic Recovery, 1986–1990, adopted by the African Heads of State and Government in July 1985.

(b) The response of the international community and its commitment to support and complement the African development effort.

Thus, the UNPAAERD was essentially Africa's Priority Program for Economic Recovery but with a renewed call for the increased support of the international community in terms of substantially increased financial resources to Africa and a new era of cooperation based on a spirit of genuine and equal partnership. This genuine and equal partnership was deemed an essential element for harmonious and mutually beneficial economic cooperation in an interdependent world.

In fact, the UNPAAERD emphasized the need to intensify economic and technical cooperation with African countries during and beyond the period of the program of action and urged all governments to take effective action for the rapid and full implementation of the program of action. The general assembly that adopted the plan of action had the conviction that, given the necessary support from the international community, Africa would be capable in the not too distant future of establishing national, subregional, and regional structures which would ensure self-reliant, sustainable, economic development in the 1990s and beyond.

The African Alternative Framework to Structural Adjustment Program for Socioeconomic Recovery and Transformation (AAF-SAP)

The African Alternative Framework to Structural Adjustment Programs for Socioeconomic Recovery and Transformation (AAF-SAP) was adopted by the Joint Meeting of African Ministers of Economic Planning and Development and the Ministers of Finance held in Addis Ababa, Ethiopia on April 10, 1989. It was the result of Africa's search for an African alternative framework to structural adjustment programs that sought to address simultaneously both adjustment and structural transformation problems of the African economies in the face of a dismal economic performance by many African countries in the 1980s. **By 1988, over thirty African countries had adopted and were implementing Stabilization and structural adjustment programs with the support of the International Monetary Fund (IMF) and the World Bank. These programs had failed to bring about the desired adjustment and structural transformation of the economies of these countries.**

The search for an African alternative followed increasing concerns with these stabilization and structural adjustment programs. These concerns were with respect to their relevance to Africa's long-term development objectives and their social, economic, and financial impacts in the countries.

From their economic point of view, the orthodox structural adjustment programs by their very design assume that the classical instruments of control of money supply, credit squeeze, exchange rate and interest rate adjustments, trade liberalization etc., which may be valid in well-structured economies, could bring about positive results to African economies characterized by weak, disarticulate structures. Sadly, however, the expected sustained economic growth did not materialize in many countries. The social impact even raised more doubts and questions. The implementation of these programs called for significant reductions in expenditures in the social sectors especially education and primary health care as well as in the size of the public sector and parastatals with negative consequences on employment.

The overall assessment of the orthodox adjustment programs led to the conclusion that although these programs aim at restoring growth generally through the achievement of fiscal and external balances and the free play of market forces, these objectives cannot be achieved without addressing the fundamental structural bottlenecks of African economies. For these reasons, at the beginning of 1988, the ECA with the financial support of the UNDP, embarked on a search for an African alternative framework.

The main thrust of AAF-SAP[40] is its holistic nature; it puts great emphasis on the full mobilization and efficient utilization of domestic resources and the need to establish an enabling environment for sustainable development and to adopt a pragmatic approach between the public and private sectors. At the center of the alternative framework is the human dimension—the fact that development must be inclusive and human-centered—both at the planning and implementation levels as well as in the equitable distribution of income. Only then can development take place on a sustainable basis.

The other major characteristics of AAF-SAP that also need to be stressed are the following. First, the alternative framework is country-specific, used for designing specific country programs, selecting appropriate policy instruments and measures, and adopting the relevant implementation strategy depending on the peculiar characteristics of each individual country. Second, as mentioned above, it is a human-centered framework. It thus implies full

194

democratization of all aspects of economic and social activities and in all stages from decision-making to implementation. Third, the alternative framework calls for intensified intercountry cooperation in the designing, implementation, and monitoring of national programs for adjustment with transformation. And fourth, AAF-SAP should constitute a basis for constructive dialogue between African countries and their development partners in the implementation and financing of country programs. It was in this context and on the basis of this mutual understanding that it was hoped that the resources provided by the international community, which must be significantly augmented, would lead to sustainable development through the process of adjustment with transformation, thus ensuring that the 1990s would witness the socioeconomic revival of Africa.[41]

ECA-Sponsored Institutions

It is recalled that during the meeting of TEPCO and Conference of Ministers of 1983, which has been discussed earlier above, the OAU Secretary-General and ECA Executive Secretary also presented another joint progress report on the contributions of ECA-sponsored institutions to the implementation of the LPA and the FAL. Pari passu with the establishment of Subregional Economic Communities, the Commission had encouraged member states to create several multinational institutions as centers for stimulating socioeconomic development in Africa. Many of such institutions were established from the 1960s to the 1980s covering most of the sectors of social and economic development and intended to serve different groups of countries at subregional or regional levels.

Since the ECA initiated and was closely involved in the preparatory work for their establishment, these institutions became known as 'ECA-Sponsored Institutions'[42] even though they were established by the member states who were themselves the owners and were responsible for their existence and functioning. In the formative years, these institutions were supported by the United Nations, especially UNDP and UNFPA, through projects which were mostly executed by ECA. However, member contributions were supposed to form the bulk of the required resources for their operations. The first institutions established in this framework were the African Institute for Economic Development and Planning (IDEP), 1962, and the African Development Bank (ADB), 1963.

By the 1990s, a total of thirty-three such institutions had been established and were at different states of health. Some were very healthy and independent (e.g. ADB, ESAMI). Others were functional with some support from outside Africa (e.g., IDEP), while others were barely functional. In all cases, several changes had occurred over the years which called for a reconsideration of the relevance of the objectives for which these institutions were established, as well as their track record in achieving those objectives. Among these changes was the coming into force of the Abuja Treaty establishing the African Economic Community (AEC), the implementation of which was to be mainly incumbent on the different subregional groupings of countries. Other changes include the creation of new institutions (RECs) and the development of national institutions that were now capable of undertaking some of the functions previously envisaged for these ECA-sponsored institutions. Others were the changed development cooperation environment which in part had resulted in reduced emphasis on institutional support especially at the regional level, and the changed development paradigm from government-run and centralized economies to free market-orientation which demanded a reorientation of partnerships with new economic actors.

Because of these changes in the development environment, and at the request of the African countries themselves, these ECA-sponsored institutions were rationalized and harmonized after long and careful studies. Those institutions that were doing well were strengthened, those with similar objectives were consolidated or merged together to avoid duplication of functions; others were integrated as institutions of the regional economic communities while a few others were abolished.

A list of some of these institutions is provided in Appendix 2 in the fields of cartography, mapping, and remote sensing; engineering and industrial technology; economic and social development; finance and trade; and minerals and transport.

Back to the Joint Division

As mentioned earlier in this chapter, the Joint Division was implementing a work program, which included the preparation of technical publications on contemporary issues concerning Africa's food and agricultural development for dissemination to member states. It was also contributing the agriculture-related chapters or sections of ECA's flagship publications and reports prepared by the Commission and mandated by various conferences and meetings in addition to, of course, the provision of Advisory Services to member states on food and agricultural production, policies, marketing and institutions and services.

In this connection, every report or paper prepared in the Division by any professional was circulated for comments by all other professionals. The report or paper was then revised in the light of those comments and meetings were also often convened, whenever necessary, to examine and discuss these reports before they were finalized to ensure that the quality was of the highest standard. These discussions were sometimes characterized by heated arguments as the paper or report or document tried to pass the test of scrutiny. Sometimes, however, the discussions were punctuated by incredible humor which would revitalize the meeting and the discussion.

Don remembers one such meeting where Prof. Odero-Ogwel, the Director, Ephata Pallangyo, Chief of Agriculture Policy and Planning, George Abalu, Regional Adviser, and Don convened to scrutinize a certain report. They examined it page by page, paragraph by paragraph, line by line. It was painstaking and tiring. Halfway through the report, they came to a line and George remarked: "This phrase doesn't seem to fit in this line. It is hanging!"

They all were dead silent, staring at the phrase. Then Ephata Pallangyo, removing his pipe from his mouth and flicking it in the manner of an accustomed pipe-smoker, looked at each of them and then asked: "Gentlemen, if this phrase is hanging, so what do we do, to make it *come down*?"

They all had a hearty laugh. The laughter was really contagious. They were invigorated. Perhaps that was what they needed at that point to be able to continue the examination of the report. That was the spirit in JEFAD!

Still on reports, one of the important and significant assignments Don undertook during his early years at ECA was that to the University of East Anglia at Norwich, UK, in 1985 to coordinate the preparation of a report requested by the UN General Assembly (UNGA).

The UNGA which met on 20 December 1983, states in its resolution A/RES/38/198: "Noting with great alarm that, since the adoption of its resolutions 35/69 of 5 December 1980, 36/186 of 17 December 1981 and 37/246 of 21 December 1982, the situation of food and agriculture in Africa has worsened, as evidenced by a drastic decline in self-reliance in food; Recognizing the critical financial gap which seriously hinders the growth of the agricultural sector in African countries; Recognizing also that the technological gap in Africa has a direct relationship with declining agricultural productivity which is aggravated by natural factors such as drought and desertification... Notes that the year 1991 might be designated international year for the mobilization of financial and technological resources to increase food and agricultural production in Africa, bearing in mind the relevant criteria set forth in the annex to Economic and Social Council resolution 1980/67 of 25 July 1980: requests the Secretary-General, in consultation with the relevant organs, organizations and bodies of the United Nations system, to elaborate action-oriented proposals in respect of the international year for the mobilization of financial and technological resources to increase food and agricultural production in Africa and to report on the implementation of the present resolution to the General Assembly at its fortieth session, through the Economic and Social Council."[43]

Responsibility for the elaboration of the action-oriented proposals in respect of the international year for the mobilization of financial and technological resources to increase food and agricultural production in Africa fell on the ECA as the UN Regional Economic Commission mandated to promote socioeconomic development in Africa. Given that this resolution was in the domain of food and agriculture, the Joint Division was assigned the task of preparing the report given its central role in food and agriculture in the Commission. This was a huge and important assignment, which unfortunately, could not be handled entirely by the Division considering its heavy workload and other commitments at the time.

Reports to the General Assembly had to be of the highest quality. The Division therefore contracted the assignment, like most UN agencies do, to a consultancy group or institution. In this case, the Division contracted it to the Overseas Development Group (ODG) of the University of East Anglia, Norwich, UK, which had done a lot of work in Africa on agriculture and food security issues. Don was assigned the task of coordinating the preparation of the report at the University of East Anglia at Norwich. The group was to be joined by Carl Eicher, an eminent Professor of Agricultural Economics at Michigan State University, East Lansing, Michigan, with vast experience in food security and agricultural research and technology development issues in Africa. Prof. Eicher was to fly to Norwich and Don was to join him and members of the ODG there.

Before embarking on the assignment, the Division had devoted much time to brainstorming on the resolution and had prepared, discussed, and approved a draft annotated outline of the report which Don was again to discuss with FAO, Rome en route to East Anglia, and get its input and finalize the outline on arrival at East Anglia. Given the importance of the report and their relationship with FAO, it was important to also involve the latter in the assignment.

At the first meeting of the team, Don made a formal presentation of the UNGA resolution—its background and the issues involved. He also presented the annotated outline which they were to follow in preparing the report. After discussions and agreement on procedural matters, they divided the work among the team members who now consisted of Don himself, Prof. Eicher, and the ODG members headed by Prof. Deryke Belshaw. Don had responsibility for drafting the introductory and concluding chapters, putting the report together and getting FAO's input at various stages of the report. So for the next seven weeks, he was to shuttle between Norwich in East Anglia and Rome, arranging and convening meetings of relevant Divisions of FAO to discuss and comment on the various drafts. He also had some other assignments to accomplish in between the work on the report. It was one of the most engaging assignments Don had to carry out, but he managed to spend a few weekends in London to break the monotony of reading and writing.

He had brought some documentation relevant to the report from Addis. Carl Eicher had also brought some of his material from East Lansing. They still had to search for more data from the ODG database and library. The first two weeks were spent sourcing for more material, researching, collecting and analyzing the data so collected before they settled down to the real business of drafting the report. As there were no laptops at the time, John, their ODG coordinator would collect their drafts at the end of each day and give to the secretary to put together using a word processor.

It was here that Don saw a secretary using word processing for the first time. He marveled as he stood behind her on the first day they gave their drafts to her and watched her work noiselessly, making texts disappear entirely or disappear and reappear elsewhere or move along a line. Then once a while, she would press some keys and the small machine next to her computer would click, and sheets of paper containing what she had typed would start rolling out. It was like he was watching a magician. As he was to learn later when they started using word processing, what the secretary was doing was simply deleting, cutting and pasting, transferring texts, and finally printing the drafts.

Back at ECA, their secretaries were still using mainly manual but also electric typewriters. They were also still using stencils and ink (a very messy operation) to produce or reproduce their documents by the cyclostyle duplicating process. Computer technology was still some years away. Once when John 'caught' Don curiously looking at what the secretary was doing, he was too embarrassed to admit that he did not know word processing. "Oh, I am just checking on some of the drafts," he replied with the air of an anxious supervisor.

"Never mind, Don, she is one of the best," John assured him.

Don kept in touch with ECA on a regular basis to apprise them of the team's progress. He also was on to Rome, as and when necessary. The group met at the end of each day, or as agreed, to review the day's progress and plan the next days' work as well as collect their various drafts from the secretary to review and correct them at home at night. They allowed themselves free at the weekends to rest. After seven weeks in Norwich and three trips to Rome for meetings with FAO on the draft report, Don returned to ECA with a final copy of the report titled: 'The International Mobilization of Financial and Technological Resources for Food and Agricultural Production in Africa: An Analysis and Action Proposals for the International Year for Africa.'

This report was presented to the Eighth Meeting of the Technical Preparatory Committee of the Whole held on April 13–20, 1987, and the Twenty-second Session of the Commission and Thirteenth ECA Conference of Ministers held on April 23–27, 1987, in Addis Ababa before eventually being presented later to the General Assembly through the Economic and Social Council at its Forty-Second Session in 1987.[44] At this session in July 1987, the Council "reaffirmed the individual and collective commitment of African governments and the international community to the UN Program of Action for African Economic Recovery and Development 1986–1990, with its focus on food and agriculture, as envisaged in Africa's Priority Program for Economic Recovery, 1986–1990; requested the ECA to take all necessary measures to facilitate and ensure effective cooperation among national and subregional research institutions in Africa; called upon the international community to give high priority to the agricultural sector in Africa, in particular to agricultural research and the development of technology;

requested the secretary-general to consider making concrete proposals to the General Assembly that would be relevant to the international year for the mobilization of financial and technological resources to increase food and agricultural production in Africa."[45] It was adopted without a vote.

Two memorable incidences connected to this assignment in East Anglia are reported in chapter 18: In Search of a Future: Fascinating Stories and Reminiscences from the Journey. The incidences are #14: 'It's a Small, Small World' and #15: 'Working With Appetite'.

The Eighth Meeting of the Technical Preparatory Committee of the Whole in April 1987 and the Thirteenth ECA Conference of Ministers in 1987 in Addis Ababa were significant because their report on the International Year was presented to these meetings. The two similar meetings held the previous year in 1986 were also significant and memorable to Don for two reasons. First, the meetings were hosted with much extravagance by Cameroon, Don's country; and second, it was at the Seventh Meeting of the Technical Preparatory Committee of the Whole and the Twelfth Meeting of the Conference of Ministers, held in Yaounde, Cameroon in April 1986, that Don himself presented for the first time, a report that he had prepared.

This report was on "Measures for the Improvement of Cooperatives and Small Farmers' Organizations/Associations in the Marketing of Food and Livestock Products in Africa."[46] At that time, the presentation of reports and documents by the secretariat was done by Division Directors or Directors of the MULPOCS. On this occasion, Don's Director decided that he should present his report.

Cameroon had opted to host these sessions of TEPCO and the Conference of Ministers in 1986 and had followed subsequently with an invitation to ECA to hold the meeting in Yaounde. In April of that year, the government sent a Cameroon Airlines Boeing 707 jet airliner to Addis Ababa to convey the staff of the secretariat from Addis to Yaounde for the meeting. Don was one of the staff members, going not only to service the meeting but also to present his report. The plane was more than half-full.

As the Bole International Airport runways at that time were a bit too short for the 707 jet airliner to conveniently take off with the plane's fuel tanks full with fuel that would last the entire flight from Addis to Yaounde, the pilots decided to fly via Djibouti. There they would take enough fuel for the flight to Yaounde. In Djibouti, while the plane was taking fuel and other supplies, its passengers were taken to the VIP lounge. It was the first time Don had been to Djibouti. The country was as hot as an oven. Soon after take-off, the flight crew began to entertain them with snacks, water, beer, wine, hot drinks, and champagne. It soon turned into a 'party in the air' as staff members, ate, drank, and moved around chatting, joking, laughing, and 'letting off steam' from stress from weeks of preparation for this meeting. Less than halfway through the flight and before lunch was served, water got finished. But wine and champagne continued to flow.

By the time they arrived Douala, champagne had remained inexhaustible and a number of staff were visibly tipsy. One very senior staff member was so drunk that he missed the stairs as he was descending from the plane in Douala and fell in full view of the television cameras. As if the entertainment during the flight was not enough, a welcome 'cocktail' was waiting for them in the VIP lounge where they were ushered into by a government delegation from Yaounde on arrival at the Douala airport. It was another party—a welcome party! After an elaborate welcome, they boarded the flight for Yaounde.

The Cameroon government went to great lengths to make the Conference of Ministers in Yaounde, one of the most lavished ECA ministers' meetings Don ever attended. The country bore the full cost of hosting the meeting including the provision of conference halls, facilities and services, and transportation of country delegations during the meetings. All country delegations and ECA directors were allocated expensive cars and drivers for their use during the meeting. For the ECA, it provided a 707 jet to convey the secretariat from Addis Ababa to Cameroon for the conference and back to Addis after the conference, buses to ferry ECA staff to and from meetings and paid all staff members full daily subsistence allowance at UN rate for the duration of the conference.

The conference was huge and well organized by the government. Most, if not all of ECA member states attended. As usual, the Twelfth Meeting of the Conference of Ministers was preceded by the Seventh Meeting of TEPCO. Don presented his report as scheduled. It was well-received as reflected by the clapping of hands and nodding of heads. It was such a big relief. The atmosphere had been very intimidating.

Don remembers on the third or fourth day after the conference started, ECA staff were paid about half a million CFA francs each as the first installment of their DSA which at that time was quite high for the city of Yaounde. They all became half-millionaires, and at the weekend following this payment, ECA staff especially the secretaries who had never had the opportunity of traveling out of Ethiopia, 'invaded' Mokolo and other markets and carted away bulging suitcases of assorted goods—clothes, shoes, handbags, etc. It was almost scandalous the way these staff were shopping. Before the conference ended, they were paid almost half a million CFA francs again. Another shopping spree!

Then a bombshell fell that changed the mood within the secretariat in Yaounde. News came from Addis Ababa that, as a result of the worsening financial situation of the United Nations, the General Assembly had adopted a resolution calling for the restructuring of the UN Secretariat and its organs that would entail the downsizing of its structures and programs. The Secretary-General had been called upon to take immediate action to implement this resolution.

For some years, the financial situation of the organization had been worsening. The United States, the main contributor to the UN budget had not only been in arrears with its dues, it was threatening to make no further payments to the organization unless it undertook major reforms that would not only cut down costs but also reduce the power of the smaller member states. The US always had a habit of flexing this financial muscle whenever it failed to get its way on any issue involving a majority vote. In the view of the US, "he who pays the piper must dictate the tune." The resolution of the GA did not therefore come as a surprise. What was surprising and what caused the most unease in Yaounde was the news that New York had asked the regional economic commissions to take immediate action to separate short-term and temporary staff, as well as staff without contracts from the commissions.

For some staff members to suddenly lose their jobs was agonizing and many staff were in the categories listed for separation. The uncertainty as to how the ECA would deal with the situation was very worrying. It was in this situation that the Executive Secretary took a decision for those staff who had finished their assignments at the conference to return to Addis before the end of the conference. Don was among the first group to leave Yaounde. Back at ECA in Addis Ababa, the mood was equally gloomy. The rest of the secretariat including the Executive Secretary and the remaining Directors returned to Addis at the end of the conference.

Toward Getting a Permanent Contract

Don's progress at ECA was relatively slow even though he worked hard and long right from his first day at work. In addition to his regular work program, he did assignments on behalf of the ECA. At the end of the first year, his Division put him up for promotion. Personnel failed to support the recommendation arguing that Don had not met the minimum period of three years required for a staff to be on a post before being eligible for promotion as stipulated by the staff rules. After he had served three years on the post, the Division now convinced that he had met all the requirements for promotion including excellent Performance Evaluation Reports, again put him up for promotion. This time, the personnel asked the Division to make their recommendation against a vacant post, that is, identify a vacant post at the requested level in the Division to which he should be promoted. He could not be promoted in a vacuum, they insisted.

There was no such post in the Joint ECA/FAO Agriculture Division and even though there were a few such posts in other divisions, the Personnel argued that they could not transfer a vacant post from another division to the Joint Division for the purpose of promoting Don. They rested their case. It was final. The Joint Division and the Personnel Services Section were to have this argument again and again in subsequent years each time the promotion exercise came around as no such post became vacant in the Joint ECA/FAO Division.

The conversion of Don's appointment from 'fixed term' to 'continuing' or 'permanent' was also not without roadblocks. At the time the Division put him up for promotion after three years of service, it also made a strong recommendation for his fixed-term appointment to be converted to 'continuing' or 'permanent'. Don still remembers as if it was yesterday, the response of the executive secretary, albeit, based on the advice of personnel, to the Division's recommendation. "The staff member has not served the mandatory five years required for his fixed-term appointment to be converted to a continuing or permanent appointment." Two years later after Don had served the mandatory five years, his case was resubmitted for consideration.

At this time, the UN was facing a series of financial crises due to the nonpayment or withholding of dues by some big powers notably the United States which had been calling for structural reforms and the elimination of certain organs and programs. In fact, some agencies were already implementing cost-saving measures that involved a cutback on staff. In such cases, the first to go were the temporary staff, then the fixed term. At the ECA, the executive secretary was resisting pressure to take such draconic measures. But there was much unease among the staff all the same. Getting a permanent appointment at that time, while 'compensating' Don for the loss of promotion, would kind of insulate him from any possible layoffs in case it had to happen at ECA.

The response from the executive secretary was unexpectedly disappointing. But it bore some hope. "The conversion of the staff member's fixed-term appointment to a permanent appointment cannot be considered at this time when he is in the middle of his present contract. His case can be brought up when his current contract expires." Don got his continuing or permanent appointment as soon as his contract expired. It had taken him seven instead of five years. Well, many staffers never got it. Getting a permanent contract even after serving the mandatory five years was not a 'given'.

During this time, as mentioned earlier, Don not only implemented outputs in his work program, he also undertook some assignments on behalf of the Joint Division and ECA in the area of food and agriculture. He remember two of several of these assignments. The first of these was a Macroeconomic Review of the Ethiopian Highlands requested by the Ethiopian government in March 1984 as part of the Ethiopian Highlands Reclamation Study. Don was part of a three-man team consisting of himself from ECA, Phil Packard, an FAO Consultant, and E. Zerai, an Ethiopian government Economist.[47] The second which Don remembers was an invitation to the Commission by the African Association for Public Administration and Management (AAPAM) to attend and present a paper at its Seventh Roundtable in Accra, Ghana, Dec. 2–7, 1985.

The invitation was sent to the Joint Division which accepted it and nominated Don and another colleague, Halidou Ouedraogo, to participate at the Roundtable. They prepared and presented a paper entitled 'The Formulation, Administration and Management of Prices as an Incentive to Increased Food Production in Africa.'[48] Don recalls that after their presentation, the women's discussion group 'conscripted' him into their group so as to help them with the economic issues.

During these seven years too, there were a few developments in Don's family. They had moved out of Ghion Hotel in July 1983 after eleven months occupancy to a four-bedroom house with a large compound at the Old Airport area. The children had settled in and were doing well at the Bingham Academy. Gwendoline left them to join her parents in South Carolina in the summer of 1983, and in October of that year, they were blessed with their fourth child, Vanessa Enowma, a beautiful girl born in Zauditu Hospital in Addis Ababa. They named her Enowma after Dorothy's mother.

Left photo, With Dorothy, Lorraine, Don, and Lilian in late 1983.
Right photo, Dorothy with Vanessa, Valentina, and Don in 1988.

They experienced some of their busiest years as parents during this period. Bingham Academy kept them and other parents very engaged with the school. They would attend the children's many school evening performances each term as well as their sporting events and field days. Fortunately, Bingham had a school bus which picked up the children to school and dropped them home after school each day, thus saving them, the parents, from this inconvenient and time-consuming task. But there was the daily home work to help the children with. While Dorothy took care of the arts subjects, Don helped them with the sciences. As Bingham Academy only ended with the primary school, they, like other parents, had to find secondary schools abroad for Lilian and Lorraine after they reached sixth grade.

They sent them to Wadhurst in East Sussex, England, and later to Tigoni Academy for Girls (TAG), a British secondary school in Kenya. In early 1987, the International School of Addis Ababa where Dorothy was teaching, sent her on a three-month assignment to teach ESL at the newly established International School of Asmara. At the time, Eritrea was a region of Ethiopia, and Asmara was its capital. Don took Don Jr. and Vanessa to visit her twice in Asmara. The most remarkable thing that stuck in Don's memory about Asmara apart from the clean and picturesque streets and attractive palm trees, is the steep and scary descent of the highway into the city. Situated on the eastern edge of Eritrea's highland plateau at a height of about 2,250 meters, the highway into the city descends steeply in a series of z-bends over several miles, with deep ravines on one side and rocky hills on the other side; and these ravines and rocky hills alternate with each other with the turning of the highway at each z-bend. On their second visit, they all went on a weekend trip to the port city of Masawa on the Red Sea coast where they swam in the Red Sea during the day and ate roasted fresh Nile perch in the evenings at seaside resort restaurants.

On Valentine's Day 1988, they welcomed another lovely daughter, their fifth and last child also born at Zauditu Hospital, Addis Ababa. As she was born on Valentine's Day, they gave her the name Valentina and also Don's mother's name, Ayuk.

Looking Outside the ECA

Don's promotion was not as easy as should have been expected either. Given the lack of a vacant post at ECA to which he could be promoted, he began to feel it was time to find a position elsewhere in the UN system and leave ECA. In March 1989, the kind of position which he had been looking for was vacant and advertised at the UN World Food Council (WFC), Rome, Italy. The requirements of the post, i.e., academic qualifications, experience, and duties and responsibilities, were as if they had been intentionally drafted to fit Don's profile. He guessed there might have been many other prospective candidates who felt the same way. Most vacancies advertised at that time were open for competition only to internal candidates (staff in the UN system). But the vacancy at the WFC was open to both internal and external (non-UN system) candidates. This was quite disappointing to Don because it expanded greatly the field and increased the competition.

Don filed his candidacy. His application was acknowledged. Normally at that time, the selection of internal candidates for a vacant post was done by asking for and reviewing and assessing their personnel records which included their academic qualifications, experience, their duties and responsibilities, their seniority at their grade, their Performance Evaluation Reports, etc. It was straightforward. The candidate assessed to be the best based on these records generally got the post, although at times, some other considerations could override this. Don was quite confident.

However, his first surprise came when after some months had elapsed, the Council wrote and asked him to send a sample of his publications and writings. This was quite strange as he had never heard it done before in the UN system. Don saw this as a warning sign that the competition would be stiff. He packaged and sent by pouch seven articles—three articles published in international journals before he joined the UN, one project report published at UC, Davis, and three technical reports prepared at ECA. A greater surprise was still to come. In January 1990, some nine months after the vacancy was announced and Don applied, he got a call one afternoon from Mr. Giuliano Comba, the Executive Officer at the World Food Council, informing him that after a review of his articles and writings, he was being invited for an interview at the WFC secretariat in Rome. A round-trip air ticket (Addis/Rome/Addis) would be sent to him as soon as possible. Calling an internal candidate for an interview? This was becoming bizarre. But Don thought may be, this is how God wanted the process to proceed. So be it.

It was winter in Italy. Friday was Don's last working day before his departure to Rome on Sunday morning. As he went to say bye to his Director in his office after closing hours, he asked Don if he had a winter coat. Don had gone on mission to Rome several times but not in the winter. So he never had a need for a winter coat. His Director offered him his which he kept in his office. Later, Don's friend, Abdoulaye came to see him just as he was about to leave his office around 7:00 p.m.

"Well, Don, bonne chance (Good luck)!" he said. "During the interview, just keep talking, do not stop even if you are talking nonsense. They will not know you are talking nonsense if you don't stop. If you stop, they will think, oh, this guy perhaps does not know what to say," he advised.

"Abdoulaye, I will not stop talking but I will talk *sense*, not *nonsense*," Don replied and they both laughed.

Don arrived Rome on that cold Sunday evening and checked himself into his favorite hotel—the International Hotel Pension on Via Carpo D'Africa, quite close to the Colosseum and not far from FAO. He had tried many hotels in the FAO area and eventually found he liked this one best. It was a beautiful, clean, comfortable, not-too-expensive hotel, just a ten-minute walk to FAO, past the Colosseum. Don remembers with nostalgia dinnertime when the guests returned from their various engagements for the day. They would dine together like a family, with discussions, arguments, lots of laughter, and wine. And the hotel provided lots of free Italian wine which it 'brewed' itself. So they drank 'ad lib'. Most of the guests were usually FAO consultants, booked there by FAO. In fact, FAO had booked Don in this hotel some two years back. That's how he got to know it.

The following day, Monday, was the day of the interview. Considering that it was the first time Don was experiencing winter in Rome, he put on all that was necessary to protect himself from the cold and to keep warm—winter coat, winter hat, and leather gloves in addition to a well-cut dark suit and tie, thick socks, and black leather shoes. As he walked past the Colosseum to the FAO, he couldn't resist looking up as he had done numerous times before, at the huge structure, marveling at the ancient Romans who built such an architectural edifice and the gladiatorial fights that had been held there several centuries ago. In fact, on his first mission to Rome years earlier, he had been part of a guided tour which brought them here and to the Vatican City, St. Peter's Basilica, Foro Romano, Spanish Steps, Sistine Chapel, the Pantheon, and other tourist sites in Rome.

The World Food Council secretariat was located at FAO Headquarters on Viale delle Terme di Caracalla. Don found his way to the premises of the Council on the second floor of Building A and was directed to the Office of the Executive Director. The time was 9:45 a.m. The interview was to start at 10:00 a.m. He would have some fifteen minutes to catch his breath and collect himself. He was going to meet the Executive Director himself, an Under-secretary-General. Don had made a few inquiries about him as soon as it was certain he would be coming to Rome. He was Gerald Ion Trant, a former Professor of Agricultural Economics, University of Guelph, Canada, and a Senior Assistant Deputy Minister, Department of Agriculture, Canada, before being appointed to the World Food Council. Don knocked and entered his office hoping his secretary would give him a place to sit down and wait until the time for the interview. Meanwhile, he would be able to rest for 15 minutes and collect himself before being taken to see the executive director at 10:00 a.m.

"Good morning. My name is Don Oben from the ECA and I—"

Before Don could finish introducing himself to the executive director's secretary, a voice said softly behind him: "Yes, Don, we have been expecting you all morning. Welcome to Rome. Let me help you with your coat."

Don wanted to say, "No, no, don't worry, I will take it off myself." But before he could utter those words, whoever was behind him had taken off the coat and was hanging it on the coat hanger in the secretary's office. Don turned round to face whoever he was.

"My name is Gerald Ion Trant, the Executive Director. You can call me Ion or Gerry," he said, leading him into his office with his right hand over Don's left shoulder. "Jacqueline, one coffee for me please. Don, tea or coffee?" he asked Don.

"Coffee, please," Don replied.

"Jacqueline, two coffees then."

"How was your trip? Hope you don't find the weather here too cold. Well, *if* you ever come to work and live in Rome, this is how you will find the weather at this time of the year," he said as they sat by his conference table facing each other.

Jacqueline came in with his coffee, and as he took the cup off the tray and was stirring it, he turned and asked Don, "What is your experience with quantitative techniques commonly used in studying agricultural and economic phenomena? I mean in particular, your experience with the application of these techniques to address common problems in agricultural economics research."

"Well, we studied econometrics, linear programming, regression analysis, operations research, and simulation in graduate school. I think I have applied a few of these techniques in research projects," Don replied, and turning to Jacqueline who had asked whether he needed sugar and milk in his coffee, he answered, "Yes, please, coffee with milk."

"Oh yes, I remember reading that article of yours in which you used linear programming techniques to formulate a least-cost ration for California mature turkeys. How applicable is this technique in commercial feed production?"

"Linear programming is a special case of mathematical programming where the objective function is linear as are the restrictions on the decision variables. I was trying to explore the extent to which this technique is applicable to commercial feed production with a view to recommending the technique to commercial turkey growers."

"And what did you find?"

"Well, I set up the LP model using fourteen commonly used feed ingredients which contain fifteen nutrients considered essential for optimal turkey growth. The costs per ton of the ingredients were used as the coefficients of the objective function while the nutrient levels in the feeds were taken to represent the coefficients of the activity matrix. The minimum requirements of each nutrient in the entire ration represented the restrictions. With this model, the objective function was then to minimize the cost per ton of a ration compounded from fourteen ingredients containing fifteen essential nutrients. Of the fourteen ingredients, only four were used in compounding the ration: blood meal, cottonseed meal, fish meal, and milo. I cannot remember the proportions in percentage terms. The amounts of each nutrient in the ration was greater than the minimum requirements except for two nutrients."

"And did you recommend the use of LP to turkey growers?"

"Yes, I did of course. However, in doing so, it was important for them to understand that the optimal solution is obtained only so long as the specified costs of feeds and the levels of the essential nutrients remain unchanged. As soon as changes occur in these variables, the LP solution ceases to be optimum."

Don stretched his hand to pick up his cup of coffee which was now almost getting cold.

"How is the food security situation in Africa?" the executive director asked before Don could take the first sip of his coffee.

Don put down the cup of coffee. The issue of food security, he told him, was not just an issue of food and agricultural production. It was also an issue of quality, nutrition, distribution, physical, and economic access and affordability. A long discussion of Africa's food security situation led to another major question and another long discussion.

"How familiar are you with the work of the international agricultural research centers in the Consultative Group on International Agricultural Research (CGIAR) with respect to their role in ensuring food security around the world?"

Don brought his experience at IITA and knowledge of the international research centers which he gained while there, to bear on this question. He went into a long discussion on the role of the CGIAR centers in agricultural research, technology development, and transfer and application including their mandates, activities, and breakthroughs. They were about thirteen centers at the time, hubs of scientific expertise across the world, dedicated to sustainable food security through scientific research. They worked together informally within the CGIAR system to reduce rural poverty, increase food security, improve human health and nutrition, and ensure sustainable management of natural resources.

He discussed IITA's crop improvement program in roots and tuber crops (cassava and yams), particularly in Nigeria and Zaire; legumes and cereals (maize, cowpea, soybean); and plantains and bananas in the context of its mandate for improving food production and food security, income, and well-being of resource-poor people in the humid tropics of Africa; the development and introduction of high-yielding, disease- and pest-resistant varieties particularly of cassava but also of yams and cowpea and plantains. Of course he did not fail to mention its international cooperation programs which included training, information, and germplasm exchange activities which were important in technology transfer and adoption.

The International Maize and Wheat Improvement Center (CIMMYT for Centro Internacional de Mejoramiento de Maíz y Trigo) located in Mexico, was another of the non-profit, research and training centers affiliated with the Consultative Group on International Agricultural Research and dedicated to developing improved varieties of *wheat* and *maize*, and introducing improved agricultural practices to farmers with a view to improving their livelihoods. He dwelled at length on CIMMYT's two main programs—the Global Wheat Program and the Global Maize Program which form the core of its work. Both programs specialize in breeding varieties of wheat and maize respectively that are high yielding and adapted to withstand specific environmental constraints such as infertile soils, drought, insects, and diseases. Of course, one could not discuss the breakthroughs at CIMMYT without underscoring the work of Norman Borlaug which led to the Green Revolution in Asia and which won him the Nobel Peace Prize in 1970.

The discussion then shifted to another CGIAR Center in Latin America, the International Potato Center in Lima, Peru, known by its Spanish acronym CIP founded in 1971 to seek sustainable solutions to the pressing world problems of hunger, poverty, and the degradation of natural environment. This, it was expected to do, through root and tuber research, principally on the potato. Produced in over one hundred countries, the potato is the world's third most important food crop after rice and wheat. And roots and tubers play a critical role in the global food system, especially in the developing world and are among the top ten most commonly consumed food staples and grow in marginal conditions with relatively few inputs and simple techniques. Core in the discussion was the center's global priorities which included sustaining root and tuber biodiversity; breeding more nutritious, adaptable, pest-and-disease-resistant varieties; and building resilient agro-economic-social systems for marginal populations in developing countries in Latin America and the Caribbean, South Saharan Africa, Southwest Central Asia, East and South-east Asian Pacific.

From CIP, Don moved on to the International Rice Research Institute in Manila, Philippines, the oldest and largest international agricultural research institute in Asia and the development of the IR-8 rice variety dubbed the 'miracle rice'.

As he was proceeding to another center, Mr. Trant called Jacqueline to bring Don another cup of coffee. The first cup had gone cold without him having taken it. As if to give Don some respite, he asked about his family status. They had been talking close to two hours at that point.

"Don, you may want to check out some international schools here in Rome that may be suitable for your children, *in case* there is a possibility that you do come to live in Rome," he advised after Don told him that his last three children were ten, seven, and two years old.

"Jacqueline, there are some very good British and American schools. Please, check the names of these schools," he called out to his secretary and turned to Don.

At this point, Don decided to turn to another group of research institutes—those which although working toward reducing food insecurity and poverty in the world, were not working directly on food crops. ICIPE, the International Center of Insect Physiology and Ecology located in Nairobi, Kenya, was one of these. Established in 1970 as an international scientific research institute in direct response to the need for alternative and environmentally friendly pest and vector management strategies, the center works toward improving lives and livelihoods of people in Africa by conducting research and developing methods that are effective, selective, nonpolluting, and nonresistance inducing in combating pests and diseases in crop production. These methods are affordable to resource-limited rural and urban communities.

Don did not, of course, fail to mention the central role played by Professor Thomas Odhiambo, a renowned Entomologist, in founding the institution. Worthy of mention was also the collaboration which Don's Division at ECA, the Joint Agriculture Division, had established with ICIPE and the pest management project which they were jointly implementing at Mbita Point in Kenya. Professor Odhiambo was still the Director of the institute at the time and they had several meetings with him.

The International Livestock Center for Africa (ILCA) established in 1974 with Headquarters in Addis Ababa, Ethiopia, was another institution. Unlike the food crop-based research centers, ILCA's mandate was to improve livestock and food production throughout sub-Saharan Africa. Don discussed ILCA's research based on a multidisciplinary farming systems approach, the small ruminant research network, the draught animal power systems, pastoral research systems, and its collaboration with national agricultural research systems (NARS) in developing their research capacities through the provision of specialized training programs and a range of information services.

His survey of the CGIAR centers continued to the International Crops Research Institute for the Semi-Arid Tropics (ICRISAT) which as mentioned earlier in this book, had invited Don for an interview for a position while he was at the Dschang University Center. It's mission is to help empower millions of poor people to overcome hunger, poverty, and a degraded environment in the dry tropics through better agriculture; then to the International Center for Tropical Agriculture (CIAT) which conducts socially and environmentally progressive research aimed at reducing hunger and poverty and preserving natural resources in developing countries.

Just as Don started to discuss the role of the International Food Policy Research Institute (IFPRI) in policy research, which is fundamental to achieving poverty alleviation, food security, and sustainable management of natural resources, Mr. Trant cut in.

"Don, in defining food security, you did mention the ability of an individual (or country) to have physical and economic access to sufficient and nutritious food for an active and healthy life, as important elements of food security. What potential is there in the rural sector in sub-Saharan Africa for governments to generate employment that would provide rural people with incomes to have this economic access to food?"

This was a big question but it was in an area in which Don was quite comfortable having done considerable work on labor absorption in the rural farm and non-farm sectors in Africa. So, taking a sip of coffee and adjusting himself well, he began, "First of all, the problem of urban unemployment in the developing countries has arisen principally because of the failure of the industrial sector which had hitherto been relied upon to create enough job opportunities for the rapidly growing population. In these countries, an almost exclusive emphasis had, until recently, been placed on the development of the industrial sector as a prerequisite of economic growth. As a result of the failure of the industrialization policies, many developing countries were now turning to the agricultural sector as the labor absorber of the last resort. In fact, the 'go back to the land' plea which characterized many political speeches in the 1960s and 1970s in Nigeria and many African countries was evidence of a realization of the fact that the agricultural subsector can serve as a potential source of employment and income generation. In Cameroon, this realization received practical expression in the form of the 'green revolution' which was formally launched by the Head of State in March 1973."

"The rural sector in developing countries consists of two subsectors—the agricultural subsector and the rural non-farm subsector. Each has a potential for generating employment that would provide rural people with incomes and enable them have economic access to food. Agriculture is practiced by millions of small farmers cultivating small areas mostly three to five acres and producing mainly for subsistence and marketing a small marketable surplus. In the same subsector are found large agro-industrial plantations growing tea, bananas, coffee, rubber, oil palm, cocoa, cotton, etc., for export."

"There are many considerations which make the agricultural sector attractive as well as a potential source for labor employment. In most developing countries, land is still 'surplus', i.e., arable, uncultivated. A fuller use of such land inevitably involves the use of more labor since agriculture is labor intensive in these countries. In fact, in the 1960s and 1970s, some countries such as Nigeria had taken advantage of this abundant resource among others, to set up young farmers' and cooperative schemes as a means of providing employment to school leavers. Large-scale plantation agriculture provides year-round employment to large numbers of people in the same manner, and at wages comparable to those in the urban industrial sector. The Cameroon Development Corporation, an agro-industrial establishment employed 12,151 workers in 1972/73. In addition, large farms use mechanical power, which by reducing the drudgery of labor, makes agricultural production more attractive to school leavers who would otherwise migrate to urban areas."

Turning to the rural non-farm subsector, the other subsector in the rural economy, Don discussed the great potential in the non-farm sector of the rural economy in sub-Saharan Africa. There were grounds for this assertion. Policy makers argue that small-scale industries which proliferate the rural non-farm sector are characterized by greater labor intensity. A program of rural industrialization would thus help provide employment for the majority of the people. Besides, it is cheaper to create the same amount of employment in the rural non-farm sector than in other sectors of the economy owing to the higher labor intensity of small-scale rural industries and the generally lower capital investments required. The creation of jobs in the rural non-farm sector through the expansion of rural, small-scale industries not only has potential for raising rural incomes by providing jobs and increasing rural purchasing power but could also broaden the income distribution base in rural areas and narrow the rural-urban income differential in sub-Saharan African countries.

Further, by providing jobs in rural areas, the expansion of the non-farm rural subsector can be seen as an instrument for inducing rural people to remain in rural areas instead of migrating to urban centers in search of jobs. Also important is the potential contribution which this sector also makes to agricultural development, employment, and income growth in the farming sector through forward and backward linkages which exist between agriculture and small-scale rural industries. These include the processing of agricultural products and the supply of farm inputs and simple machine tools.

"Governments in sub-Saharan Africa recognize and acknowledge the potential of the rural sector to generate employment. Some have, in fact, evolved policies which can effectively achieve industrial development, provide employment opportunities in rural areas and increase the incomes of rural people as can be seen in their development plans. In Nigeria for example, the Second and Third National Development Plans had among other objectives, the equitable distribution of income and the provision of employment in rural areas through the expansion of rural small-scale industries."

Just as Don finished, Mr. Trant came back to the issue of schools for his children.

"Don, I *will advise* you to try and visit one or two of the schools to get more information before you leave Rome. Marymount International School is an excellent American school."

"I see from your personal history form that you were an assistant professor in Cameroon before coming to ECA. Tell me about your tenure."

"And how do you find your work at ECA? Why do you want to come to the World Food Council? What contribution do you think you will make to our work here?" he asked after Don finished talking about his work and experience at the Dschang University Center.

These were well-loaded questions. Well, for some unexplained reasons at the time, Don had been quite interested in the Council. So he often tried to acquaint himself with its work especially as it centered around food policy issues, an area which was to become of profound interest to him. He had known about its establishment after the World Food Conference in 1974, and its Mandate. He had read much about the Council meetings and some of its Resolutions, and he had taken much interest in, and read widely about the Council's 'Initiatives' and 'Food Strategies'.

Don took his time as he responded to these questions. He was at his best. He talked about the Cyprus Initiative against hunger adopted in Nicosia and the Program of Cooperative Action with its four main goals, then the Beijing Declaration, the National Food Strategies for addressing world food problems and the Cairo Declaration. He also gave much importance to the most recent call by the Council for a New Green Revolution and the need for interregional consultations on the food production challenges in various developing regions in the 1990s to address crucial policy issues in the development and effective transfer of agricultural productivity-enhancing technologies. After Don had finished talking about the work and achievements of the Council, he then told him how his past experiences especially the knowledge he had gained working at IITA on agricultural research and technology development and transfer, and at ECA on issues of food security, would be an asset to the Council.

Don could sense that Mr. Trant was blown away! Apparently, he seemed quite surprised that Don was so familiar with the Council's work. He came back to the issue of schools for Don's children and *reminded* him not to leave Rome without visiting the schools Jacqueline had recommended especially Marymount International School.

At the end of the interview with Mr. Trant, he told Don he still had three other candidates to interview and Don would hear from the Council in a few weeks. Then he asked:

"Have you been to your embassy in Rome? If not, it would be nice to go see your ambassador while you are here. The embassy can help you with admission formalities and other information about schools—in case it becomes necessary."

Don thought the interview process was over. No, it wasn't. As he took leave of the executive director and came out of his office, Jacqueline told him he had to talk with one senior economist (a Dutch) and two senior economic affairs officers (a Chinese guy and an American woman). They had been waiting for him 'all day'.

When Don met each of them separately in their offices, the discussion was short and just a formality.

"Well, Mr. Oben, what else can I talk to you about? If Mr. Trant kept you in his office for more than three hours, what can I say? Maybe you can just tell me about yourself," was just about what each of them said.

Don was later to understand the context in which those statements were made. James, one of two Africans in the Council secretariat met Don as he was about to leave. He had come twice to see Jacqueline while Don was with Mr. Trant and was very surprised that the interview was taking so long. Two of the Senior Economists who had been waiting had also come to check when it was time for them to take their lunch breaks and Jacqueline had told them that this candidate seemed quite awesome. Since the door leading from her office into Mr. Trant's was half-closed, she could hear their exchanges. Jacqueline was Australian.

"Bobo (meaning my friend in Sierra Leon Pidgin English), I was quite surprised but very happy you stayed so long with Mr. Trant. It means you are very good. Mr. Trant doesn't have any patience for mediocrity or nonsense. One candidate who came some weeks ago lasted twenty minutes. The one who came last week lasted just fifteen minutes. He kept you for three hours plus! What were you talking about?"

Mr. Trant had encouraged Don to go check out some schools for his children before leaving Rome. This gave him some hope. What James had just told him now strengthened this hope further. But Mr. Trant had also said that he still had three other candidates to interview in the coming weeks. This kind of dampened Don's spirit. He neither went to Marymount International School to inquire about admissions nor to the Cameroon embassy to see the ambassador as Mr. Trant had advised. He would take one day at a time.

The following day, Don took a flight to Cameroon to spend a few days there before returning to Addis Ababa. He had asked for three days leave of absence before leaving for Rome. The few days he spent in Cameroon were some of his happiest. He was basking in the warm sunshine of possible success.

Don did not, however, have time to relish in this envisaged success. He still had some work to do. If he was selected for the post and had to leave the Joint Division and the ECA, he wanted to leave knowing that he had met all his commitments to the Division vis-à-vis his work program and any other issues. He had implemented many of his outputs in the previous two years—1988 and 1989. One of such significant 'outputs' was a 'Technical Publication on Measures for the Improvement of Women's Land Holdings and Land Rights in Africa',[49] which he completed in December 1989 just before he was called for the interview in Rome.

This report examined the role of African women in agriculture and the extent to which land tenurial systems including land holdings and land rights affected women's productivity, production, and household food security. It recalled the Plan of Action adopted by the World Conference on Agrarian Reform and Rural Development (WCARRD) in 1979 which stated that "rural development based on growth with equity requires full integration of women, including equitable access to land, water and other natural resources, inputs and services and equal opportunities to develop and employ their skills."

It also recalled that the philosophy, principles, and objectives of the Lagos Plan of Action (LPA) and Africa's Priority Program for Economic Recovery (APPER) similarly reflect the WCARRD ideals. In both the LPA and APPER, African member states are urged to facilitate access to land, credit, and other inputs to small farmers especially women. The Arusha Forward Looking Strategies for the Advancement of Women in Development beyond the UN Decade for Women likewise recommend that the pivotal role of women in development must be taken seriously into account in development planning and in the disbursement of resources both as contributors to and beneficiaries of development efforts.

It was within this context, and in pursuance of its role in promoting the socioeconomic development of the continent that ECA was preparing this report. The data used in its preparation was collected during a mission Don undertook to a number of countries including Mozambique, Lesotho, Ghana, Sierra Leone, and Liberia, supplemented with information presented at the ILO Regional African Workshop on Women's Access to Land as a Strategy for Employment Promotion, Poverty Alleviation, and Household Food Security.

The study essentially attempted to identify the constraints in land tenure systems in Africa which affect women's access to land and their activities in food and agricultural production. It reviewed the crucial role which women play in agriculture, examined the land tenure systems in Africa and the laws, traditions, policies and other factors governing women's access to land. Following this the report examined the implications which women's limited access to land have for food and agricultural production and the strategies which they have usually adopted to enable them to cope with some of the problems posed by inadequate access to land. The report also assessed, on the other hand, the impacts which some of the major rural development and agrarian reform policies, programs and schemes which have been, or were being implemented have had or could have on women's access to land. On the basis of this examination and assessments, the report made some proposals for improving women's land holdings and land rights and the ultimate long-term goal of increasing their productivity, output, incomes, and household food security.

In the last months in ECA, Don had also made a commitment to contribute an article to the Division's new Staff Paper Series—'Food and Agriculture in Africa'—based on data from his data bank on food production, consumption, and trade in Africa. He completed this paper and finalized it in May after the usual vetting process. The article entitled: 'Ensuring Food Supply and Availability in Africa through Efficient Marketing and Distribution' was published in April 1991.[50]

The paper was premised on the importance which the African regional development plans of the 1980s accord to agricultural marketing and distribution infrastructure in Africa. The AFPLAN in 1978, LPA in 1980, and Africa's Priority Program for Economic Recovery (APPER) in 1986, had successively called on African countries to establish and develop efficient marketing and distribution systems as a sine qua non for increasing food production, supply, and availability in Africa. Underlying the importance of such systems is the fact that marketing is regarded not only as a precursor, but also as an extension of the agricultural production process. It is through the market that inputs used in production are procured. Likewise, the market provides the medium whereby commodities so produced are exchanged and farmers earn cash returns for their labor. The degree of efficiency of the marketing system is therefore a major determinant of the availability, structure, and profitability of input use and the costs, returns, opportunities, and income levels in food and agricultural production and marketing.

This notwithstanding development policies, strategies, and programs adopted by many African countries to increase food production and supply have mainly focused on improvements in science and agricultural technology, manpower development, research and extension and the conservation of the natural resource base. Very little attention had been given to the mechanism whereby various utilities are added to the increased production and subsequently distributed. Apparently, the assumption among most policymakers had been that an efficient food marketing and distribution system automatically puts itself in place once production has occurred. Unfortunately, African and other experiences have shown that this had not been the case. As a result, there exists in many African countries, a wide and unbridged gap between food producers and consumers and thus what is produced often times does not reach consumers. The result is lack of access by consumers to food supplies and loss of incomes to producers. In some countries where rudimentary, traditional, or inefficient marketing systems exist, a large proportion of the food produced is lost through poor handling, storage, processing, and transportation. Inefficient marketing systems also give rise to high food prices and to situations where regions of food scarcities coexist with areas of food surpluses.

This paper examined the case of food marketing and distribution in the Yaounde-based MULPOC countries with a view to identifying areas where improvements were needed as called for in the LPA, APPER and the UN Program of Action for African Economic Recovery and Development (UNPAAERD), 1986. The paper hoped, and rightly too, that policies and adjustments called for in the paper would, to a large extent, be applicable to many countries in sub-Saharan Africa. The data used for the paper were collected during a survey of selected countries of the subregion supplemented with relevant information collected from reports on those countries which were not surveyed.

A few of the other publications and reports which Don had produced alone or in collaboration with other colleagues of the Joint Division or with some consultants can be found after the References at the end of the book.

Returning to the WFC Matter

Coming back to the WFC matter, the waiting after the interview was surprisingly quite long. But deep in Don's heart, he knew that he had nailed the interview. This confidence sustained him during this long period of waiting. Finally, in April 1990, three long agonizing months after the interview, Don received a long faxed message from the Executive Officer with copy to personnel, informing and congratulating him for his selection to fill the vacant position at the WFC secretariat which he had applied and had been interviewed for. It also requested the ECA to release him ASAP to take up his appointment. After consultation with the Director of the Division, it was decided that Don couldn't be released before June 5, 1990.

A few weeks later, the Deputy Executive Director of the WFC, Alain Vidal-Naquet, visited Addis and Don met him at the Addis Ababa Hilton Hotel at the former's request. Among the issues they discussed was whether the ECA could release Don earlier than June 5 and if not, at least allow him one week to attend the WFC Ministerial Meeting to be held in Bangkok, Thailand, in May as part of the WFC secretariat. The ECA still was **not willing** to do this so Don could not attend this meeting. He had a lot of work to complete before leaving the Division and the ECA. Since he was leaving the ECA for the WFC which was also within the UN secretariat, Don decided to apply for a transfer (of service) from ECA to WFC rather than resign. This way, he would carry his eight years' service with the ECA to the WFC which would make his service with the UN continuous.

Don started his 'clearances' as early as possible. In those days, staffers leaving Ethiopia finally after their term, had to obtain clearance from the Administration for Rented Houses showing that they owed no unpaid bills (electricity, water, and telephone) in the house and that the condition of the house was exactly as it was when it was rented out to them no matter how long ago it had been rented. To get this clearance, they had first to get clearances from the state utility companies (electricity, water, and telephone). They also had to be cleared by the Duty-Free Shop and the Victory Shop (for foreigners). It was after obtaining all these clearances that they would be given an exit visa without which they could not leave Ethiopia. But the most feared clearance among male staffers was the 'baby' clearance. For the departing staffer, his prayer always was that no woman should show up at the foreign ministry and claim (rightly or falsely) that he had a baby with her. Don got all his clearances and his exit visa and news spread that he was leaving the ECA for the World Food Council in Rome.

The Joint ECA/FAO Agriculture Division gave him and his family a very rousing send-off. Colleagues and friends from other Divisions were invited. They were loaded with gifts. Deep emotions were expressed. And during the last two weeks before they left, friends from ECA, other international organizations, and the OAU tried desperately to find a window in Don's calendar to invite them for a send-off lunch or dinner. The dinners always ended up as parties. If eating and drinking and dancing could kill, then Don would say that they would have died during this period. By the time they left Addis, they were really tired and exhausted. Yes, 'goodbye' can be the loneliest word when one parts from close friends.

Chapter 13
At the United Nations World Food Council (WFC), Rome, Italy

Its Mandate and Initiatives

The World Food Council (WFC), headquartered in Rome, Italy, was a *United Nations* organization established by the General Assembly in December 1974 upon the recommendation of the World Food Conference that took place in that same year.[51] At that time, the world was experiencing a food situation that was marked by extreme food shortages in many developing countries in Africa and parts of Southeast Asia, and by a general lack of progress in the world in fighting hunger and malnutrition. This situation was compounded by very slow progress in creating a system of internationally coordinated cereal reserves to meet shortfalls and other abnormal situations.

It was against this background that the General Assembly decided in 1973, to convene a conference to deal with global food problems. The UN World Food Conference, held in Rome in November 1974, called for the creation of a thirty-six-member ministerial-level World Food Council which should have a mandate to review annually, major problems and policy issues affecting the world food situation and to bring its political influence to bear on governments and UN bodies and agencies alike.[52] The Council was thus to serve as a coordinating body for national ministries of agriculture in order to help reduce malnutrition and hunger. It was also to serve as the food policy arm of the United Nations that sought to end world hunger and draw attention to famine. In this connection, it was to exercise leadership in sensitizing the international community as to the nature, extent, causes, and consequences of hunger and malnutrition and in recommending appropriate practical policies for remedial action.

The council was expected at its ministerial level to (a) review periodically major problems and policy issues affecting the world food situation, and (2) make recommendations to the UN system, regional organizations, and governments on appropriate measures that they might take toward resolving world food problems.

The Council was established as a subsidiary body of the UN General Assembly to which it was to report annually through the Economic and Social Council. From its creation in 1974 up through 1992, it met each year in plenary session at the invitation of one of its member states.

Since its inception, the WFC had adopted several approaches to solving world food problems. Its first approach was to encourage and promote the adoption of National Food Strategies by developing countries within national development efforts in order to emphasize and better coordinate country actions and international assistance in the progressive eradication of hunger and malnutrition. Under this plan, each country would assess its present food situation including its needs, supply, potential for increasing food production, storage, processing, transport, distribution, marketing, and the ability to meet food emergencies. In this regard, the Council organized a series of consultations between 1979 and 1983 among African governments that focused on the need for developing countries to establish National Food Strategies.

These consultations also identified a number of areas where priority action was required by African countries and international agencies. The food strategy approach to solving world food problems was generally supported by most countries as well as by major funding institutions and the donor community as a whole. However, it is important to stress that the design of food strategies was specific to individual countries; hence there was no single food strategy blue print, as food problems, resource endowments, and development priorities vary from country to country throughout the continent.[53]

In 1987, the World Food Council meeting in Beijing gave extensive consideration to the WFC secretariat study, 'The African Food Problem and the Role of International Agencies' (February 1982). This study concluded that "the economic future of Africa was with the African farmer" and proposed a strategy whereby the World Food Council could assist in the fulfillment of this proposal by effectively coordinating the activities of some thirty organizations which are involved in assisting in developments in African agriculture.

The WFC member states unanimously approved this declaration at this Beijing meeting. It became known as the Beijing Declaration. However, this was a declaration of good intentions, weakly supported by statements, which indicated a clear lack of political will to act. But it concluded with the statement, "We proclaim our intention to join together, and in our united strength and interest, to eliminate the scourge of hunger forever."

Meeting in Nicosia, Cyprus, from May 23–26, 1988, at its fourteenth session, the WFC presented a report titled: 'Ending Hunger: The Cyprus Initiative'.[54] It called for the combined efforts of member and nonmember countries to eliminate world hunger and requested an action-oriented report. The final report, 'The Cyprus Initiative Against Hunger in the World' emphasized why certain policies had failed to halt growing hunger and endeavored to identify those which had been effective in ending it. It proposed a program of cooperative action, which at the national and regional level, would, if implemented, alleviate the severe problems of hunger and malnutrition which prevailed in most developing countries.

The report was presented to the Ministers and Plenipotentiaries of the World Food Council meeting at its Fifteenth Ministerial Meeting in Cairo, Egypt, in May 1989. The Council discussed the report and adopted a set of conclusions and recommendations which formally became the Cairo Declaration. In adopting this Declaration, the Council delineated a Program of Cooperative Action with four main goals for UN member countries within the next decade: the elimination of starvation and death caused by famine; a substantial reduction of malnutrition and mortality among young children; a tangible reduction in chronic hunger; and the elimination of major nutritional-deficiency diseases. The Program of Cooperative Action contained proposals for immediate action to be taken on food-for-work programs in rural areas where employment opportunities were not available and measures to make specific food items affordable to the poor.

Over the longer term, the WFC recommended projects to create production and employment opportunities in rural and urban areas; community initiative projects designed to enable the communities themselves to identify and implement projects; vocational training schemes; retraining schemes; food stamp schemes. In the area of nutrition, the WFC recommended the implementation on an emergency basis of supplementary feeding programs for children; primary health care programs including programs to improve sanitation and drinking water; family planning programs; nutritional education programs; and support to food and nutrition programs undertaken by WHO, UNICEF, and other international agencies.

At its Sixteenth Session in 1990, held in Bangkok, Thailand, the Council observed that most countries had not yet set specific goals and targets to implement its call to action. However, by 1991, those goals had been adopted by all UN member states as part of the International Development Strategy for the Fourth United Nations Development Decade.

Arrival and Work at the WFC

Don arrived at the World Food Council secretariat in Rome on 5 June 1990, to take up his appointment. This was shortly after the Council had held its Sixteenth Ministerial Meeting in Bangkok, Thailand, the meeting which WFC had wanted the ECA to release him to participate in as a member of the WFC secretariat even though he had not formally left the ECA. The WFC secretariat was a small secretariat which serviced the thirty-six-member ministerial-level World Food Council. It was headed by an Executive Director with the rank of an Undersecretary-General. He was assisted by a Deputy Executive Director, a French national. It had a Policy Development and Analysis Unit which was at the core of the secretariat's work as the food policy arm of the United Nations on issues of world hunger, malnutrition, and famine.

This core group consisted of a director (German), a senior economist (a Dutch), two senior economic affairs officers (American and Chinese), an economic affairs officer (Canadian) and two assistant economic affairs officers (German and Chinese), all of various specializations. It was to this core group that Don was assigned on recruitment. They were serviced by secretaries who were all women of various nationalities. The other parts of the secretariat included the public relations unit headed by a director (a Kenyan), the administration headed by an executive officer (Italian), and the office of the executive director. The WFC also had a small liaison office at the UN headquarters in New York.

The secretariat in Rome was provided office space by the FAO at its headquarters in Rome—on the second floor of building A. Agreements were made between the two organizations for the secretariat and its staff to have access to the facilities and services available in the FAO compound. These included the FAO library, the commissary (duty-free shop), security, utilities, restaurants and coffee shops, the banks, staff union services, etc.

On the Monday morning he assumed duty, he had a briefing session with the executive director on the work of the Council; then he was shown round and introduced to other staff members after which he was shown his office and introduced to his secretary.

Top photo, With a colleague and their secretaries, 1992. *Bottom photo,* Don in his office at the WFC, 1990.

These preliminaries over, Don sat down to make a note of some of the urgent matters he had to see to before he got busy with the Council's work program. He needed to meet and discuss pressing personnel issues with the Executive Officer, open an account with a bank, rush to Marymount

International School to settle his children's admission there, search for housing and move out of the expensive hotel he was staying, call the packers in Addis Ababa to find out the situation with their personal and household effects, and take other actions necessary to facilitate their settling down in Rome.

One would have thought that Don would be given the first week or a few days, at least, to settle down. He had not even finished the note when his secretary came in and said the deputy executive director wanted to see him.

"Welcome once again to the WFC and to Rome," Mr. Vidal-Naquet began as soon as he shook Don's hands and ushered him into the chair directly opposite him. "It's nice having you here and I hope you will find the secretariat a nice and enriching place to work, of course, if you work hard. I will be going on mission in three days' time and will be visiting and discussing with regional and international agricultural research institutions, WFC's planned interregional consultation on meeting the food production challenges of the 1990s and beyond. I would like you to prepare for me an 'Issues Note on Africa' which I can use as my speaking notes, on some of the burning issues in international agricultural research and technology development and transfer."

"That's fine with me," Don lied, knowing the urgent issues on his mind which he wanted to address first before settling down to the Council's work.

"When would you want this paper?" he asked.

"I am leaving on Friday morning, so any time before Friday. Good luck," Mr. Vidal-Naquet replied with a smile.

Don was back in his office thinking about the things he had to do first before turning to the assignment when James knocked at his door and came in. Don had met him when he came for the interview in January and now it seemed as if they have been old friends.

"Bobo, we don't close our doors here. We work with the doors open so people can see that we are working but also that there is no 'hanky-panky' going on inside our offices."

"Yes, I know from my several missions to FAO. I have to get used to leaving my door open. At ECA, we worked often with our doors closed—for concentration and privacy," Don answered.

"I heard Alain called you a short while ago. What was it about? I know he is leaving for a mission this weekend to Africa and, may be, to Latin America also."

"James, he wants me to prepare an 'Issues Note on Africa' on agricultural research and technology development, transfer, and application by Thursday for him to take along and use as 'speaking notes' at research institutions during his mission. I have not even settled down. I have so many urgent personal things I have to do."

"Bobo, here at the Council, we work—really hard. If you don't work hard, everyone knows. You know we are relatively very few, so everyone knows what everyone else is doing. If you are lazy or not professionally good, everyone knows. Even our secretaries know. They type our reports," James confided.

"Oh really?" Don looked at him surprised which prompted him to go on.

"Well, you better get going with the paper. This cannot wait until you settle down. Your urgent personal matters can wait," he advised rather frankly.

"I know. It's just that it is difficult writing such a paper when one has such urgent matters on one's mind. It is difficult to concentrate. Whatever is the case, it's not a big deal. Okay, I will not wait to settle down before I start working; I will start working while I settle down," Don joked.

"Bobo, I am sure Alain will be looking forward to an excellent paper, considering the much praise Mr. Trant has showered on you and the extent to which he fought to recruit you," James confided in Don.

"Did he have to fight?" Don asked. "Fight who?"

"Bobo, you should know the system very well. When your post was advertised, you will not believe the number of ambassadors in Rome and in New York who were bombarding him with faxes and telexes sending names of their nationals and pressurizing him to select them for the post. Mr. Trant stood his grounds, stressing that the post must be filled by the most qualified candidate and the selection process must be very transparent. And he made it clear that he would personally also interview the short-listed candidates and ensure that only the candidate meeting the requirements of the post both in terms of academic qualifications and experience would be selected. And even after the interview results were made known some 'powerful' ambassadors were still persistent and even tried to arm twist him," James revealed.

"But Mr. Trant did not bulge. He stood by his choice. Did you not notice that the selection process took such a very long time?" James asked.

"Yes, I was surprised that it took nearly four months after the interview," Don agreed.

"That's why. I will show you a big confidential file containing faxes and telexes from some of these ambassadors and even some big guys at headquarters later when you have settled down," he told Don in confidence. He was the information officer in the public relations unit and he had come into the Council from IFAD. He was a journalist by profession, and being the information officer and in the public relations unit, Don was not surprised he had access to this information.

Casting his mind back at the process Don went through, he could not but totally agree with James that the rigorous procedure which the Council had adopted in filling the post was in line with Mr. Trant's determination and commitment to selecting the most qualified candidate. As noted in the last chapter, the normal procedure for filling an internal post such as this one, was to call for, obtain, review, and assess the candidates' personnel records which included their academic qualifications, experience, their duties and responsibilities, their seniority at their grade, and their annual performance evaluation reports. It was as straight forward and easy as that. The candidate assessed to be the best got the post. But perhaps the Council recognized the flaws in this procedure. Some personnel records especially the performance evaluation reports did not always reflect performance or the capability of the staff member.

With this post, the procedure adopted had been very different and quite strange. First, the position was opened to candidates both within and outside the UN system thus widening the competition. Second, candidates were asked to submit samples of their publications or writings (a requirement which had hitherto been unheard of) for assessment. Third, the short-listed candidates were called for a face-to-face interview by the executive director himself and his senior professionals.

Don finished and submitted his paper to Alain on schedule, and he embarked on his mission. On his return, he was gracious enough to call Don and acknowledge and appreciate his 'Issues Note'.[55] It had enabled him to raise just the right issues on international agricultural research and technology development and transfer. They were the burning issues of the day, and the note had enabled him to stimulate intense discussions wherever he went.

James showed Don the 'big file' some weeks later after he had settled in, and on a Saturday afternoon, when there was hardly any other colleague around. Don was stunned at the sheer number of letters and telexes that he saw and the CVs of the candidates these ambassadors and some high officials at headquarters were proposing. Some of Mr. Trant's replies to these letters were also on file. But what struck Don most was that one of these ambassadors was very forcefully pushing the candidature of one of Don's female colleagues back at ECA. Even though she knew Don had applied for the post, she never once mentioned that she had applied too. Several scores of these candidates did not have the qualifications and experience advertised in the post. Yet they were being pushed in. Many were qualified, but why were their mentors not willing to let them pass through the recruitment process? Why were these candidates being forced on Mr. Trant? Given what Don saw, it could only take a man of Mr. Trant's character, resolve, and belief in justice and fairness to withstand the barrage of these letters.

While they were going through the file, James remarked humorously, "These candidates were being supported by their home countries. There was nobody here fighting for you. Bobo, I didn't know you are an orphan."

In reply to his remark, Don told him that his credentials were his own godfather. Then he reminded him of the African saying, "For a cow that has no tail, it's only God that drives the flies away." Only God had been his godfather and mentor throughout his career.

For Mr. Trant to have not succumbed to the pressure from such powerful forces, heightened Don's respect for him. But above all, it made him resolve to work with even greater dedication and excellence at the Council. He would not disappoint him.

Don's family—spouse, Dorothy, and three children (Don Jr., ten, Vanessa, seven, and Valentina, two) joined him in July, before schools were to start. Getting them well settled was not straightforward and easy. With their arrival, Don had to move from the hotel in which he had been staying to one which was self-catering and therefore more economic for a family. Eventually, they found a flat in a rental property but on the day and hour they were to move in, the contract fell through and they had to be accommodated by a great friend, Namanga Ngongi of the World Food Program in Rome for some three weeks before they found a house in Casal Palocco. This is a residential neighborhood some fifteen kilometers from the city center, near Via Cristoforo Colombo and Via Otiense and halfway between the city and the sea.

By now, their household and personal effects shipped from Addis Ababa had arrived and had been in storage waiting for delivery. Winter had also set in. Problems began to surface in the newly rented property—doubtful source of water, power malfunctioning and insufficient heating, etc., etc. Once again they had to move. Luckily this time, they found a reasonably big flat with car packing on Via Cechov located in a residential area near Roma Settanta (Roma 70) some two or three kilometers from FAO's building F where they were to remain until the end of their stay in Rome.

As mentioned earlier in this chapter, Don joined the Council secretariat on June 5, 1990. The Council had just held its Sixteenth Ministerial Session in Bangkok, Thailand, in May of that year. That meeting called for a 'Renewal of the Green Revolution'. The need for such a revolution had been first raised within the UN system by the World Food Council Regional Consultation on Food Security in Asia and the Pacific held in February 1990. The consultation had noted that Asia's Green Revolution was beginning to show signs of strain as yield gains achieved in the 1960s and early 1970s either stagnated or declined in most parts of the region. Given that Asia was approaching the limits of its potential for agricultural area expansion, it therefore underscored the need to continue to push the technological frontier outward making such technology accessible to small and marginal farmers, as well as the landless.

In calling for a renewal of the Green Revolution, the Sixteenth WFC Ministerial Session in Bangkok was therefore mindful of these considerations and also the fact that the first Green Revolution had only limited impact in Latin America and largely bypassed Africa. The new Green Revolution being called for was seen as one which would bring about a new food production breakthrough through many advances in the development, transfer and application of productivity-enhancing agricultural technology in the developing regions to meet the food needs of their growing population in the 1990s and beyond. In this connection, the Council endorsed a proposal by its President, Dr. Youssef Amin Wally, Deputy Prime Minister and Minister of Agriculture and Land Reclamation of Egypt, to call an Interregional Consultation on the Food Production Challenges in various developing regions in the 1990s to address crucial policy issues in the development and effective transfer of productivity-enhancing technologies.[56]

Against this background, the secretariat spent the second half of 1990 and the first half of 1991 laying the groundwork for an Interregional Expert Consultation on the Food Production Challenges in the Developing Countries scheduled for Cairo, Egypt, in 1991. Don was given the task of synthesizing into one concise report, the big reports of the three regional studies on Asia, Latin America, and Africa on the food production challenges in the 1990s in the respective regions prepared by IFPRI and the International Service for National Agricultural Research (ISNAR) for this consultation. He also followed this synthesis with an executive summary of the synthesis report. The synthesis report and the executive summary report, as was the practice, had to pass through the critical eyes of the executive director after comments from colleagues had been received and integrated into the final reports. These two reports as well as the original regional reports constituted the substantive documents for the consultation.

In early 1991, Don and his family had an accident at home that caused them a lot of anguish and sadness. While busy in his office one morning, he received a distressed call from his wife, Dorothy that their youngest daughter, Valentina now three, had fallen from the top of the high table on the terrace. She had placed her big toy car on the table, climbed into it, and was trying to ride in it when it fell off the edge to the ground with her inside. According to Dorothy, it seemed the right upper arm bone, the humerus, had cut because her hand was just drooping and she would not let her touch it. Don rushed home and found her in intense pain.

Fortunately, a renowned orthopedic hospital was not too far away. They rushed her there. She was immediately admitted and her arm x-rayed. Truly, her humerus had cut midway into two and the two bone pieces were now lying almost aside each other thus contracting the arm. They were all in shock, including the nurses. She was immediately taken to the theater. The bones were realigned and other orthopedic procedures done. She was in hospital for weeks lying on her back with her chest and right hand in a plaster cast and the right hand hung up. They wept inwardly as they watched her trying to hide and bear her pain with fortitude. After discharge from the hospital, she carried the plaster cast for some months before she fully recovered. They can never forget the kindness and care the doctors and nurses showed them during their daughter's admission and treatment at the hospital and they thank the Lord Almighty for taking them there.

While she was recovering, Don was asked to represent the Council at the Twenty-Sixth Session of the Commission and the Seventeenth Meeting of the ECA Conference of Ministers of Economy and Planning held in Addis Ababa from May 9–13, 1991. He was visiting Addis and Ethiopia after one whole year. So it was a sort of 'home coming' to him. However now, he was wearing a WFC conference badge and sitting in the WFC seat in the conference hall. During one of the cocktails, he met the Executive Secretary, Prof. Adebayo Adedeji, and he joked, "I see we prepared you very well to be on the other side," apparently referring to Don's interventions and critical comments on some of the issues brought on the floor by the ECA during the conference.

Don replied, "Well, it is said that a prophet is never respected in his own country or by his own people," a subtle reminder to him of Don's promotion 'saga' at ECA.

While in Addis, information was circulating that the Ethiopian People's Revolutionary Democratic Front (EPRDF) forces were advancing on Addis Ababa from all sides and that the city could fall any time. And it came to pass that just a week after Don left Addis and Ethiopia, the EPRDF captured Addis Ababa and overthrew the Marxist-Leninist regime of Mengistu Haile Mariam on May 21, 1991. He fled to Zimbabwe where he sought asylum from his long-time friend, Robert Mugabe.

The WFC/UNDP Interregional Consultation on 'Meeting the Food Production Challenges of the 1990s and Beyond' was convened in Cairo, Egypt, in April 1991 by the WFC and the UNDP. Selected professional and administrative staff went for the meeting as well as a good number of secretaries to serve as the secretariat. Don and his professional colleagues served as resource persons. It was a large meeting that brought together senior researchers from national, international, and regional research institutions, high government officials involved with agricultural research policy formulation, and administration as well as donors and finance institutions.

The Consultation had before it four substantive documents to facilitate its deliberations: the three Regional Overviews of the Food Security-focused Agricultural Research, Technology Development and Transfer, and the synthesis report. It focused particularly on the future direction of technology development and transfer in the broader context of ensuring food security and development with equity in the developing countries. The meeting came to a broad agreement which recognized that the First Green Revolution had serious limitations and had not reached sub-Saharan Africa and many developing countries in Latin America and elsewhere. It however, concluded that a New Green Revolution was needed which could be based on agricultural productivity increases achieved through technologically, socioeconomically, and environmentally sustainable research, technology development and application, covering a wider range of plant and animal foods of importance to the world's hungry people.[57]

The Consultation also suggested some directions for agricultural research and technology development which could help usher in a new green revolution which would be different from the first. These were: a better coverage of plant- and animal-based foods important for the food security of low income groups; a shift in emphasis from single-commodity research toward research cutting across commodities and focusing on approaches such as farming systems research and research on natural resource management in different agro-ecological zones; recognition of the importance of ecological sustainability in future technology development and application; better integration of socioeconomic and policy research with technology focused research; use of new tools provided by biotechnology as a complement to conventional approaches to technology development; the need to build genetic databases ('genome mapping') and to ensure the access of developing countries to advanced biotechnology; utilization of technologies which are 'on the shelf'—especially in Africa and Latin America; effectively addressing problems common to the NARS—seeking cooperative arrangements with universities, the private sector and regional and international research institutions and networks, human resource development for more effective NARs, and greater attention to the sustainability of research and development institutions, and long-term commitment by developing countries and donors alike.

Other directions were to strengthen subregional cooperation through the development of research programs on common commodities in similar agro-ecological zones or through a division of work in research on complementary commodities.

The consultation also endorsed the need for developing countries to renew their political commitment to their food security efforts in terms of developing an overall policy framework that is conducive to creating a domestic economic environment favorable to sustained agricultural development.[58]

Pari passu with preparations for this interregional consultation, the secretariat was also preparing for the Seventeenth Session of its Council of Ministers due that same year in Helsingør, Denmark, to which the Conclusions and Recommendations of the Cairo meeting would be presented. This was the first meeting of the Council of Ministers that Don would be attending. They flew into Copenhagen, the capital of Denmark and from there were taken by a conference bus to Helsingør. This is a very historical town with richly colored, well preserved architecture and cobblestone streets, castles, museums, churches, woods and golden, clean beaches.

The Council's Ministerial Meetings were WFC's equivalent of ECA's Conference of Ministers of Planning and Economic Development. So every staff member of the secretariat had to be very productive and efficient and be ready to put in extra hours. There was no room for errors or lateness in submitting draft reports for typing by secretaries. In fact, the secretariat had to work all night before the third and final day of the meeting to ensure that the Report of the Seventeenth Session was ready for consideration and adoption by the ministers.

The meeting was a huge success. Council ministers considered the Conclusions and Recommendations of the Cairo Consultation in the report which had called for the need for a New Green Revolution. Based on these conclusions, council ministers made a number of recommendations aimed at strengthening agricultural research especially in the developing countries and requested the secretariat to follow up on the other suggestions and recommendations made by the consultation, many of which have been mentioned above.

As usually happens after big meetings, a few visits were arranged for the secretariat staff to see some museums, churches and most importantly, Kronborg Castle, often referred to as King Hamlet's castle, one of northern Europe's most significant Renaissance castles. The secretariat staff left Helsingør a day after the meeting back to Copenhagen where a day's guided tour had been arranged for them to see some of the most interesting attractions of this fascinating city. They visited landmarks such as Copenhagen's most famous attraction—the Little Mermaid sitting on a rock, the famous Tivoli amusement park and pleasure gardens and the Copenhagen Zoo in Frederiksberg.

Following the conclusions reached at the consultation in Cairo and endorsed by the Seventeenth Session of the Council Ministers Meeting in Helsingør, Denmark, that a new Green Revolution was needed which should be different from the first, the WFC secretariat spent the second half of 1991 and the first half of 1992 preparing for the Eighteenth Session of the Council scheduled in Nairobi, Kenya, in June 1992. For this meeting, it prepared substantive documents for consideration by the ministers. One of these was "Toward a New Green Revolution: Perspective for Future Food Production Increase in the Developing Countries with Priority to Africa."

Considering the major developments that were unfolding in Eastern Europe after the break-up of the Union of Soviet Socialist Republics (USSR) and given the council's mandate to exercise leadership in sensitizing the international community on the nature, extent, causes, and consequences of hunger and malnutrition in the world, the secretariat also prepared another substantive document drawing attention to the food security challenges that the people of Eastern Europe and the Commonwealth of independent states were facing or likely to face following the disruption of their economies and the migration of large populations to western Europe. The secretariat also undertook a series of follow-up consultations with international organizations including the FAO, UNDP and the CGIAR, ISNAR, IFPRI to name a few, on the need for, and directions of, a New Green Revolution.

The Council met at its Eighteenth Session from June 23–26, 1992, in Nairobi, Kenya. It considered the documents placed before it and called for a 'New Green Revolution', noting that although most developing regions made some progress during the 1980s in reducing hunger and malnutrition, the peoples of Africa had not experienced a similar head way because of disastrous droughts and civil disturbances which had caused widespread starvation in recent years. In order to accomplish this new green revolution, the Council emphasized the need to intensify the transfer of technology as well as the need for substantial increases in investments in research, extension, and training particularly in Africa. It also acknowledged and praised the IFAD Special Program for Sub-Saharan African Countries Affected by Drought and Desertification which had gone a long way to alleviate the problems of food shortages, etc., caused by drought and desertification. Finally, the ministers noted the problems of millions of people in Eastern Europe and the Commonwealth of Independent States (formerly the USSR) in gaining access to adequate food as a result of the dislocation of their economies.[59]

In August 1991, Dorothy had left for the United Kingdom to study for a master's degree in Women and Development. Don had suggested and insisted that she seizes the opportunity of their being in Rome to continue her education especially as she did not have a paid job. He had also suggested that given the increasing importance of women and development as an emerging development paradigm at that time, she should do a master's degree in that area. He would make all the sacrifices possible to meet the costs—tuition, board, books and supplies, travels, research, etc. To assist him with the children now only Don, Vanessa, and Valentina, after she leaves, they brought one of Don's nieces, Hannah, from Cameroon to live with them during the time she would be away in the UK. Just like Don did when she was studying in Lagos University, he took the two younger children—Valentina, three; and Vanessa, eight—to visit her at Christmas in 1991 and Easter in 1992. Once or twice, he also sent them alone in the care of the airlines to visit her.

In early 1991, he took them with Don Jr. on a week's visit to Sister Elizabeth Bovier and her family in Sion, Switzerland. They took the night train from Rome in the late hours of the evening across the Alps and through several tunnels into Switzerland arriving in Sion early the next morning. Dorothy earned her Master's degree in Women and Development from the Institute of Development Studies of the University of Sussex, Falmer, Brighton, in August 1992 and joined them again in Rome.

Above, Dorothy's Graduation at the University of Sussex, Falmer, Brighton, 1992.

Shortly after her return, she was asked by the International Alliance of Women (IAW) to serve on a voluntary basis as its Representative to the food agencies in Rome—the FAO, WFP, and WFC.

Above, Dorothy attending one of FAO's meetings at headquarters in Rome in 1992 as IAW's representative.

The WFC and the UN Financial Crisis

About this time, there was growing awareness of the increasing financial crisis that the UN had been facing particularly in the last few years. This as usual, was primarily due to the nonpayment or withholding of contributions by some big powers notably the United States. In this regard, the US had made it abundantly clear that as a precondition for the payment of its arrears and subsequent contributions, the UN had to undergo a restructuring process which should involve downsizing—abolishing some of its institutions and programs to avoid duplication of functions and waste. By 1992, calls for the UN General Assembly to take action to avert its financial collapse by undertaking this restructuring exercise had grown louder and louder.

As the WFC secretariat staff were leaving for Nairobi in June for the 18th Session of the Council, rumors were rife that the streamlining process would soon be underway and that the World Food Council was likely to fall victim in the exercise. Don had been told, on joining the Council secretariat that calls for the WFC to be abolished had been made in the past notably by the FAO which, since the creation of the Council in 1974, had seen it as a usurper of some of its functions.

As part of its mandate, the WFC was designed as a coordinating body for national ministries of agriculture to help alleviate malnutrition and hunger and to facilitate the development of new agricultural techniques to increase food production. It was also created in part to check the power of developed countries in the FAO. For these and other reasons, Don had been told, the FAO under Edouard Victor Saouma, had 'fought' relentlessly for the abolition of the Council. But in spite of FAO's efforts in previous years, the Council had survived. That was then. Now, with the envisaged reorganization and streamlining of the activities of the United Nations, Council members had to discuss the future of the Council at this 18th Session in Nairobi. In particular, it considered its future role within the framework of the restructuring process.

There was much unease and disquiet among the WFC staff especially the secretaries as Council members agreed that the Council had fallen short of achieving the political leadership and coordination role expected from its founders at the 1974 World Food Conference. It concluded that, in a rapidly changing world, the continuation of the status quo for the World Food Council and the United Nations as a whole was not possible. Unable to decide on the future role of the Council at the meeting, the session established an Ad hoc Committee to review the mandate and future role of the WFC.

The period from the Nairobi meeting to early 1993 was a period of much uncertainty as the Council secretariat waited for the report of the Ad hoc Committee on the future role of the Council. The secretariat was hoping that the Committee would strongly reiterate the political leadership and coordination role of the Council and propose measures to strengthen it to play that role. The Committee met in New York on 14–15 September 1992 and submitted its report to the 47th Session of the General Assembly in 1992. Unfortunately, however, it could not reach agreement on what the Council's future role should be with views ranging from abolishing it, to strengthening it, and integrating its mandate with another intergovernmental body.

The General Assembly to which the Committee referred the matter, requested the Council members to continue informal consultations with its members in efforts to agree on appropriate measures to be taken. After informal meetings from January to May 1993, the Council reported to the General Assembly that "Council members are agreed on a set of principles to guide the United Nations' response to global food and hunger problems, but disagreements continue to exist concerning the most effective institutional response to these principles."[60]

Closure, Redeployments, and Separations

By early 1993, the continued existence of the Council was very much in doubt. Yet there was no communication neither from Headquarters nor from the Office of the Executive Director to clarify the rumors circulating that the Council was about to be abolished. Finally, sometime in mid-1993, an Assistant Secretary-general for Human Resources, Ambassador Cisse who was then holding brief for the President of IFAD was asked to come and address Council staff on the situation of the WFC in the context of the restructuring exercise. He confirmed their fears. There were plans to abolish the Council.

A new Department for Policy Coordination and Sustainable Development (DPCSD) was being established at Headquarters in New York which would take over responsibility for servicing any future meetings of the WFC. Efforts would be made, to the extent possible, to find positions within the system to place staff on fixed-term appointments but there was no guarantee that this would be possible. Secretarial staff would be laid off. They were therefore advised to look for positions elsewhere. On the other hand, permanent staff, i.e., staff with continuing appointments were given the option either to be absorbed in the new department, i.e., DPCSD in New York or to return to the former organizations from which they were seconded to the WFC.

This was one of the saddest moments at the secretariat. Secretaries and other general service staff who were mainly locally recruited, wept openly especially those who were nearing retirement. To be laid off especially without much notice after putting so many years of hard work into the Council was unbearable. Some European countries later tried, albeit unsuccessfully, to intervene on behalf of their nationals on fixed-term contracts. The staff all felt for one another. They had become like a small hardworking family. Now they were being torn apart and forced to go their different ways with many uncertain about their prospects for the future.

They received their individual letters from the same assistant secretary-general sometime later. In Don's own letter, he was asked inter alia, to indicate as soon as possible, whether he would like to move to New York or return to ECA. Although his position was intact, the axing of the World Food Council was a big blow to him. After three years at the secretariat, he was enjoying the

242

work and was optimistic that within the next year or two, he would get another promotion in the secretariat considering his performance so far and the very high regard which the secretariat had for him. Now all that hope was gone.

The decision as to whether to join the new department in New York or return to Addis Ababa was quite agonizing. This again was one of those times Don had to make a difficult decision in his life. Although he and his wife, Dorothy, liked Rome, the cost of living there had been very high. Rents, school fees in international schools, medical and dental charges, etc., were unsustainable. For international staff with children, their monthly incomes could hardly keep up with their expenditures.

As a result, the bank accounts of most staff including even those at the director level were always overdrawn. In order to ensure that staff had money in their accounts to survive until the payment of salaries, the Banca Commerciale Italiana (BCI) at the FAO kept increasing its overdraft to staff to a level which, at some point, equaled the monthly salary of some staff members. As the overdraft increased, so also did the overdraft charges, thus putting these accounts deeper and deeper in the red.

With three children in international schools in Rome and two in schools in the UK, the financial burden Don was carrying was unsustainable especially at a time when the pound sterling was exceedingly strong against the US dollar. And Dorothy had completed just a year earlier, her master's degree program in women and development at the Institute of Development Studies at the University of Sussex, Brighton, under Don's sponsorship.

In deciding where to go, it was therefore foremost in Don's mind to go to a duty station where he could save, build up some reserves and thus lift the financial yoke off his shoulders. Colleagues who had worked at UN headquarters before coming to Rome had unending complaints about life in New York—the high rents, high medical and dental fees, the time, inconvenience and cost of commuting to and from work, the insecurity, the racism especially in schools, the culture, etc. Indeed, based on their accounts, Don concluded that going to New York would only compound his financial problem. On the other hand, the situation in Addis Ababa, which he knew very well, was the exact opposite of that in New York. Therefore, in consultation with Dorothy, he replied to the letter stating that he would choose to return to ECA. He then waited.

Given the situation in the Council in 1993, the secretariat did little substantive work neither did it prepare any documents as the activities of the WFC were suspended in 1993. No formal WFC session was held either. Instead, 1993 witnessed the redeployment of secretariat staff, that is, those with permanent contracts.

Redeployment to the ECA

While Don waited for directives regarding his own redeployment to ECA, he found himself anxious about his impending relocation to Addis Ababa and reintegration into ECA Headquarters there. He did not have to wait long after he replied indicating his preference to return to ECA. He received a surprise phone call from the Office of Human Resources and Management (OHRM) at headquarters.

"Is that Don Oben? I am calling from OHRM, New York. It is in connection with the redeployments and your decision to return to the ECA. Congratulations! After consultations with the Commission, I am pleased to inform you that the latter has decided to post you to its subregional office for North Africa in Tangier, Morocco," a female voice announced delightfully.

Posted to Morocco? Don couldn't believe it. All the while he had been focusing on life in Addis Ababa after Rome. It never once crossed his mind that he could be sent anywhere else apart from Headquarters. He was too stunned and shocked to respond except to say "Okay."

"OHRM will be finalizing arrangements for your redeployment after which ECA will get directly in touch with you to arrange for your movement to Tangier. If you have any questions, please feel free to call me. Once again congratulations," the lady finished and hung up.

Don thought about this posting the whole of that day particularly how it could affect his future progress. He was thinking about the disadvantages of working away from headquarters, of being kind of tucked away at some remote and obscure corner of the continent far from Addis Ababa, where one can easily be forgotten. He wanted to be at Headquarters, at the center of all the happenings at ECA, where one gets information as soon as it is available, where one knows about decisions that are to be taken and when they are taken, where one can take advantage of opportunities quickly, where one is always seen and one's presence is felt. He couldn't think of any advantage working in a subregional office except if one was being sent there on a promotion, which was not the case now.

Dorothy's views on this were similar to Don's. So the following day, he called OHRM and spoke to the lady who had called him the previous day. But it was not to advance arguments about how his posting to Tangier could lead to his isolation and impair his progress. Those arguments were baseless and therefore inadmissible. He had thought of more convincing propositions. After appreciating OHRM's efforts at redeploying him so quickly (he was about the first or second WFC staff member to be so redeployed), he tried to make a strong case as to why his posting to Morocco was not in the best interest of the ECA or himself and why he thought that being posted to ECA Headquarters would be more beneficial to the organization.

First, the subregional office for North Africa covers six countries which are all Arab countries. The official language in these countries is Arabic. French is also spoken in Morocco, Tunisia, and Algeria, and English in Sudan. He has no knowledge whatsoever of Arabic and although he comes from Cameroon, he does not have a working knowledge of French. He would also guess, and rightly so, that most of the books, publications, and reference materials that are available at the Subregional Office and in the countries would be in French or Arabic. Given this North African subregional environment, he will be greatly handicapped in performing his duties and responsibilities which will involve meetings and discussions with high officials of member states, studies and publications, organization of conferences, meetings and workshops, provision of advisory services, on request, to member states, promotion of cooperation and collaboration among member states, etc.

After he had finished, she agreed with him that he had a very strong case. His arguments were very valid. But she told Don that the position to which he was being sent to fill had been vacant for more than three years, and the 'outputs' that were supposed to be produced on that post have been transferred from one biennium to another; and this cannot continue. So it was important to have this position filled and when his name came up in the context of the redeployment, it didn't take ECA time to consider his posting there. The position needed a development economist who also had a strong agronomy background. He was the ultimate choice. The decision had been made and the OHRM and the ECA were confident that in spite of the arguments Don had advanced on the language issue, he would deliver the 'outputs' and fulfill the other duties and responsibilities of the post in a timely and very efficient manner. (An output is the final product of a work program activity such as a policy paper, a technical publication, a report of a research study, a conference, a workshop, training, or an advisory service to a member state, on request, produced by a staff member during the course of program implementation.)

On a more personal note, the lady advised, urged, and encouraged Don to take his posting to the North Africa subregion as a personal challenge and an opportunity for him to learn the French language, reminding him that if he became proficient in French and passed the UN language proficiency examination, he would be entitled to a language allowance and other career growth benefits. Don could discern the sincerity in her voice. He took her advice in good faith, and they kept in close touch over the phone for much of his early months in Tangier. Apparently, she was trying to get feedback on how Don was facing the language challenge.

The ECA eventually sent Don a long fax message detailing his relocation to Tangiers—packing, freighting, and shipment of their household and personal effects, air tickets direct to Morocco from Rome, installation in Tangier, etc. But nowhere was there any mention of his going to Headquarters for a 'briefing' before taking up his new posting in Tangier. Don considered this an oversight and called the Acting Chief of Personnel Section who, surprisingly, turned out to be one of his old friends, Wilfred Asombang. He requested for a visit to Addis for briefing as is usually the case, but Mr. Asombang bluntly refused explaining that as a former staff member of ECA for many years, Don knew everything about the Commission, and so there was nothing to be briefed about. He should therefore just proceed straight to Tangier from Rome.

Don felt Mr. Asombang was right but only to a limited degree. It had been three years since he left ECA, and there would have definitely been a lot of changes there that he needed to know. And most important of all, Don had never been to the subregional office in Tangier and not even to the Kingdom of Morocco. So he needed some briefing especially from the director of the Regional Cooperation and Integration Division under whose supervision the subregional offices were placed, on the situation there and what to expect. He was disappointed but had to accept the decision and prepare to travel as authorized. But Don suspected that his friend, the Acting Chief of Personnel thought he just wanted a mission to Addis to socialize with old friends and colleagues at the expense of the organization.

Don was about the first reassigned staff member to leave the secretariat. The mood in the secretariat was somber as he said his goodbyes to Mr. Trant, Mr. Alain Vidal-Naquet, and colleagues and secretaries and especially to his good 'Bobo', James Kanu. He left Rome in June 1993 to take up his assignment in Tangier and get accommodation before returning two months later to arrange for their shipments and take his family.

The secretariat in Rome was eventually abolished in December. Responsibility for servicing any future meetings of the WFC was given to the newly established Department for Policy Coordination and Sustainable Development in New York. WFC's functions were absorbed by the United Nations Food and Agriculture Organization (FAO) and the World Food Program (WFP).

Don was later to learn that the other staff members on continuing contracts had been reassigned. Peter Temu, the Director of Public Relations who had also opted to return to ECA had been posted by ECA to Zambia as the Director of its Subregional Office for Eastern and Southern Africa in Lusaka, Zambia. His friend, James, returned to IFAD from where he had been seconded. Two staff members were reassigned to DPCSD in New York. Sadly, those on fixed-term contracts including many secretaries were separated from the organization. Don's friend, Jan returned to his university in the Netherlands. He joined the International Cocoa Organization in London some years later and eventually became its executive director. Don visited him during one of his trips to London after his retirement, and he took Don out to an Italian restaurant for lunch.

Chapter 14
Redeployment to the UN Economic Commission for Africa

At the ECA Subregional Office for North Africa, Tangier, Morocco

When it became known within the food agencies in Rome that Don was to leave for Morocco, he received an unexpected call from a senior staff member of IFAD, a Moroccan. He had heard that Don was going to take up a position in Tangier and wanted them to meet anytime and have a discussion before Don leaves. He had a proposal which he wanted to make and was sure it would interest Don. They met and he told Don he had a three-bedroom unfurnished apartment in Tangier. It was large, located on the fourth floor of a new 8-story residential block, 'Residence Omnia', quite close to and facing the sea and only some five-minute walk from their Subregional Office.

He would be delighted if Don could rent it. He would give Don access to have a look at it on arrival in Tangier and if Don wants it, he would make arrangements for it to be cleaned up and redecorated if need be and Don could move in any time he wanted or when his family joined him in Tangier. Don found it to be a beautiful apartment, great location and safe. As it turned out, it became their residence during their entire stay in Tangier.

One of the sad issues Don and his wife had to deal with again when it became evident that the Council was going to be abolished and they would have to move from Rome, was the children—Valentina now five, Vanessa, ten, and Don Jr., thirteen. Valentina had been put in the Italian kindergarten, 'Garden Bimbo' at two years old when they got to Rome, had settled in very well, was now speaking Italian fluently, and just when she was to start primary school, they would have to move. Vanessa and Don Jr. were in Marymount

International School (American School) where they were doing very well and had made nice friends. Don Jr. was an all-rounder but especially in games, sports, and athletics (both field and track). During the school competitions, he would collect all the gold ribbons and his chest would be so covered with them that there would hardly be anywhere left to pin them. He also had the respect of his peers and they began to look up to him as an emerging leader. Don Jr. loved the school and his friends so much he didn't want to leave; he wanted to be left to continue schooling in Rome. Sadly, his parents couldn't grant his wish. Where would they leave him?

Considering that they were moving to Tangier where they would have difficulty placing Don Jr. in a suitable school, they got him admission into Christ's College, Blackheath, London, where he was to start his secondary school studies in September. They took Don Jr. with them to Tangier with sadness in his heart from where he left for London in September 1993 while they settled Vanessa and Valentina in the American School of Tangier. Thus, once again they had moved, and once again, they were destabilizing the children.

Don Jr. and Vanessa who had started bonding very well both in school and at home in spite of their few small disagreements had been separated. Once again too, Dorothy was dislocated. Since her return to Rome from her studies in Sussex in 1992, she had been serving as the Representative of the International Alliance of Women (IAW) to the food agencies in Rome. Now she had to give that up and follow Don to Morocco for the sake of keeping the family together.

No 'Welcome Aboard' in Tangier

Don arrived in Tangier from Rome by air in June 1993 to take up duty. He was to learn that the city of Tangier had for centuries been Africa's gateway from Europe located on the Maghreb coast at the western entrance to the Strait of Gibraltar, where the Mediterranean Sea meets the Atlantic Ocean off Cape Spartel. It is just a few miles across the Mediterranean Sea from Spain. It was an international zone from 1912 to 1956 and only joined with the rest of Morocco following the restoration of full sovereignty in 1956. It is probably because of its historical international status that many international and some diplomatic missions were located there instead of in Rabat, the capital of Morocco.

Apart from the ECA subregional office, there were two other ECA-sponsored institutions located there—'Center Africain de Formation et de Recherche Administratives pour le Développement/the African Training and Research Center in Administration for Development (CAFRAD/ATRCAD)' and the 'Association of African Trade Promotion Organizations (AATPO)'. The city looked impressive with lots of tourists.

Don's first day at work in Tangier was a bit bizarre. The driver from the regional office who had met Don at the airport on arrival in Tangier the previous day, came to take him from his hotel to the office the day he was to assume duty. Their offices were on the fourth floor of a new 8-story building built by the Moroccan Government for international organizations located in Tangier. Don was told on arrival there that it also housed CAFRAD/ATRCAD on the seventh floor and AATPO on the third floor. They were to go up by the staircase. Everyone uses the staircase, even those on the eighth floor! Don was struck.

"Doesn't this building have lifts?" he asked, quite surprised. To this question, he was told that the contractor who built the complex was not paid fully after he completed the contract so he locked up all the lifts and went away.

"And the government has not done anything to resolve this?" Don pressed on.

"If it had done so, we would not be using the staircase," was the answer. "Wow, Africa!" Don could already imagine what this means for commuting daily to the office. How many times would one have to climb those stairs each day when one is at work?

"Well, we have a bonus here—a daily compulsory physical exercise to keep us fit," Don remarked, not finding it funny.

So they took the staircase. At least it was easier climbing to the fourth floor than to the eighth floor.

Up at the offices, Don was told that the director, Mr. Ben Saoud, was on a short duty travel to Rabat, the capital city. His secretary called to inform him of Don's arrival and he asked to speak to Don. The conversation was quite weird to Don.

"Mr. Oben, I hear you arrived in Tangier yesterday. What is your mission about and how long will you be staying?" he had asked.

Don was taken by surprise at these questions. How can he ask a senior staff member who has just been posted to his office these kinds of questions? Don was expecting the director to say he was sorry that Don had arrived in his absence and that he would be back soon. Don should make himself comfortable in the meantime.

"I am not so sure how long I will be staying, and if and when, I will be returning," Don replied, ignoring the first question. The director tried to get more information from Don about his 'mission' to Tangier but Don couldn't give him any because he expected the director to have known why he had come to Tangier.

When the director couldn't get any information out of Don, he asked Don to pass him back to his secretary. It was at this point that his secretary went and took a file and read a long fax that had come in his absence concerning Don's posting to the subregional office. The secretary later told Don the fax came on the day the director left for his mission and so he had not seen it and had therefore no knowledge that Don was coming on a permanent posting. Don could hear him raising his voice at the other end, and since they were speaking in Arabic, Don couldn't understand what they were talking about.

Don was to learn later from Addis Ababa that his posting had been done without consultation with the director or his involvement. And it was done on purpose to present him with a fait accompli. As mentioned earlier, the position which Don was filling had remained vacant for many years and the reason is that each time a candidate was proposed to him, he found reasons to turn the candidate down. Even the few who had successfully been selected and sent to work with him had been frustrated by him and each had left. So this time it was decided not to consult him.

He rushed back to Tangier the following day and met with Don in his office for the first time. He welcomed Don and they had a chat with him trying to learn more about Don—his professional background, his service at ECA, his experience, etc. Finally when Don would not tell him much about himself, he decided to ask Don bluntly to provide him with his CV. To Don, this was unprecedented. Don told him he had no CV to give him but if he wanted his personnel records, he was free to go to personnel at Headquarters in Addis Ababa. At this point, Don had had enough. So he excused himself and walked out of the meeting quietly. The director was furious. He made frantic calls all through that week to headquarters trying to get the posting canceled.

Finally, when he got the supervising division, he was told in no uncertain terms that Don's posting had been done in consultation with OHRM in New

York and had been approved and signed by the Undersecretary-General and Executive Secretary of the ECA and it was final. And they added, "We have sent you one of the best. He will be an asset to you and you will like working with him." As Don came to learn later, the director was not a technocrat. He was more of a political appointee. He spoke Arabic and English fluently.

Serving Countries of the North African Subregion

ECA's five subregional offices including that for North Africa in Tangier to which Don was redeployed, were originally conceived as Multinational Programming and Operational Centers (MULPOCs) and mandated to act as operational arms of ECA at the country and subregional levels. They were to be instruments for ensuring improved coordination between subregional and regional program orientation and those defined in ECA's Strategic Directions; provide advisory services to member states, regional economic communities, and subregional development operators; and facilitate subregional economic cooperation, integration, and development. They were also to promote gender issues, act as centers for policy dialogue and collect and disseminate information. They had still another role and that is to act as coordinators of UN system activities for regional integration within the framework on the ground, such as the UN coordinator system.[61]

Since the regional economic communities had been designated as the building blocks for the African Economic Community, ECA, along with the Organization of African Unity (OAU) and the African Development Bank (ADB), within the framework of the joint secretariat, had undertaken the responsibility for strengthening the regional communities. Among the activities to be carried out in this respect was institutional support to the regional economic communities for capacity building and rationalization of IGOs in the subregions. Consequently, the country coverage of the MULPOCs should correspond, to the extent possible, to those of the regional economic communities. This constituted the principal criterion for grouping countries under each MULPOC region.

However, while the regional economic communities form the anchor for MULPOC activities in the subregions, other factors were considered as well in determining the most effective configuration of MULPOC membership and location. These included similarities of problems/priorities among countries in a given subregion; historical and cultural background of the countries and organizations in a particular subregion, which may have a bearing on integration activities (e.g., language affinity and organizations); the number of countries to be served by each MULPOC; and proximity of the MULPOC office to countries and regional economic communities. In consideration of these guiding criteria for grouping countries under each MULPOCs, the six countries of North Africa that were grouped under the Tangier MULPOC were Algeria, Egypt, Libyan Arab Jamahiriya, Morocco, Sudan, and Tunisia with the MULPOC to provide institutional support to the Arab Maghreb Union (AMU).[62] Thus, the Subregional Office for North Africa supports the six countries in North Africa mentioned above.

Eventually, Don had a meeting with the director during which he gave him a short briefing on the situation at the subregional office. The subregional offices usually had a core team of professionals and a multidisciplinary expertise responsible for developing, promoting, overseeing, and implementing agreed strategies for addressing subregional food security, nutrition, agriculture, forestry, fisheries, and rural development priorities.

But in Tangier, apart from the director, there were two regional advisers and only one associate economic affairs officer. The two regional advisers had been redeployed to the subregional office from the ECA Multidisciplinary Regional Advisory Team at headquarters. They were under his administrative but not supervisory authority and had their individual work programs which were concerned mainly with regional integration and development issues. There was an administrative and finance assistant, secretaries, and a number of other general service staff.

At the end of the briefing, the director provided Don with a newly prepared copy of the work program with his name clearly marked against the 'outputs' which he was to take responsibility for implementing. But he provided no guidance. Don could see that many of these outputs had been carried from one biennium to another because they had not been implemented when they were due. Many were technical publications to be produced from studies; some were advisory services to member states while some were reports to the Committee of Experts of the North African MULPOC.

Don had surveyed the library during the first few days of his arrival anxious to see what information and material was available and in what languages. There were publications on a variety of subjects on the region. The country boxes also had information and statistics on the individual countries but this information was quite outdated. As suspected, many of the publications were either in French or Arabic. However, most of the information on Egypt and Sudan was also in English. Having taken stock of the information available in the Regional office, he prepared his Program Implementation Plan (PIP), travel plans and work schedule and he settled down to work.

The first output in the PIP was the preparation of a technical publication on 'A Strategy for Sustainable Land Development in North Africa Maritime Areas' which had been carried over from the previous biennium. For countries of North Africa faced with the immense challenge of providing food security for their rapidly expanding population, increases in domestic food production would have to come from lands in their maritime area. These are their coastal zones—coastal regions extending seaward and landward along the Atlantic Ocean, the Mediterranean Sea, the Red Sea, and the River Nile including their continental shelves. These regions have the best arable and fertile lands and their vast resource potential offers significant opportunities for agricultural production, shipping and fishing, mining, petroleum, and manufacturing.

In the absence of consistent policies and strategies designed and implemented specifically to fight land degradation and conserve the natural resource base, these multiple uses of land for agriculture and other purposes which are not always compatible, have facilitated natural degradation processes, soil erosion, etc., leading to the partial or total loss of the productivity of land in many of the maritime areas. Some 170 million ha of land in the maritime and other areas of North Africa were already affected by desertification hence the urgency for conservation efforts to save these lands from further degradation.

Don spent the early months of his arrival at the Subregional Office working mainly on this publication with the data he collected from official government records, publications of relevant national, regional, and international organizations and from discussions with concerned divisions at FAO headquarters in Rome in December 1993.

The objective of this report was to provide a suitable strategy or framework within which member countries of the subregion could formulate and implement conservation programs and projects and thus slow down and reverse the degradation processes in the maritime areas of North Africa. It attempted to examine within the limits of available data, the agricultural and other natural resources of the maritime areas, their utilization and susceptibility to environmental degradation, assess the agricultural policies and strategies adopted by member states of the subregion to combat degradation, and propose a suitable and appropriate strategy or framework which could enable countries of the subregion individually or collectively to promote optimum land conservation and sound land use management [63].

In writing this report, Don was handicapped by the lack of colleagues in Tangier who could critique his drafts. He thus had to send them by pouch to relevant divisions at ECA for their comments. This was a painstaking and time-consuming exercise but it had to be done and it paid off. The divisions were very cooperative and supportive and provided very incisive and objective comments. Don's preoccupation with quality was such that they would sometimes have long telephone conversations to try to iron out some sticky, unsettled or controversial issues.

The report suggested a framework which focused on three main priority areas: the improvement of land use which involved a thorough evaluation of the natural resources, identification of the causes of land misuse and mismanagement, and land use planning; increased government advocacy in land conservation and encouragement of popular participation in land conservation; and the establishment and strengthening of national and subregional institutions for promoting land and environmental conservation. This framework offered a challenge for member states to start seriously addressing environmental degradation in their maritime regions and a great opportunity to reap the benefits of sustainable agriculture and food security both for present and future generations.

When the final draft was ready for printing, Don went to the library and searched and chose a photograph for the cover page which reflected most appropriately, the subject of the report. Then he personally supervised the printing in town, making sure all the statistical data (tables, graphs, maps, etc.) and annexes were clear and neatly done and the cover page was printed in color.

He remembers the day he placed two copies of this publication on the director's table. It was a Thursday and he was not in office. He was to travel to Addis Ababa at the weekend to attend a meeting at ECA the following Monday but Don had learned that he was not sure whether he would attend the meeting. Don never saw him during the rest of the week. On the following Monday, Don received a call from a former colleague at headquarters telling him that they had seen a new publication from their regional office with his director. The director of the Economic Cooperation Office (ECO), the supervisory division called Don later to say how elated his director was with the publication he had prepared, a copy of which he had left with him. He had commended his director for the publication but did not fail to remind him that it was just one publication from his regional office in many years. Don's director's secretary was later to tell Don how the director had spent much of Friday going over and over the publication and marveling at it when he saw the two copies on his table.

After he returned to Tangier from Addis Ababa, his view of, and attitude toward, Don marked a dramatic change—from being aloof and reserved, to being more friendly and respectful. Don was not impressed and continued single-mindedly with his program implementation plan.

The next two outputs on his implementation plan were two reports on: (1) "Follow-up and Monitoring of the Locust and Grasshopper Situation in the North Africa Subregion and on the Establishment of an Early Warning System," and (2) "The Role of Financial Institutions in the Mobilization of Resources for the Implementation of Multinational Core Projects Within the Framework of the Industrial Development Decade for Africa (IDDA) in North Africa." Both of these reports were for presentation to the Committee of Experts of the North African MULPOC at its Twelfth Meeting in March 1995.

The objective of the first report was to examine the situation of locusts and grasshoppers in North Africa and the progress made including improvements in the early warning systems, to ensure the long-term sustainable management of the locust plague in the subregion as well as suggest other actions that need to be taken in this regard.

The threat posed by locusts and grasshoppers to food security in the semi-arid environments of North Africa and the repercussions on health and the environment, of current chemical techniques of locust control had continued to generate considerable concern in countries of the subregion and the international community. The havoc inflicted by these voracious insects during the major invasions of 1987, 1988, and 1989 underlined the need to seek a permanent solution to this menace to ensure the sustainability of the agropastoral systems in the arid areas.

Several national, subregional, and regional meetings, workshops, and conferences aimed at formulating a strategy for combating this scourge had followed in the wake of these attacks. Among these was the subregional meeting for North Africa held in Tangier in 1990. Like some similar meetings held earlier it was convened to exchange knowledge and information on locusts and grasshoppers and to develop a long-term strategy of preventive control in the subregion. Among others, the meeting examined the use of meteorological information and remote sensing in monitoring locust activities as well as the impacts of pesticides and other chemical methods of locust control on the environment. The meeting also examined the role of research in the development of biological methods as potential alternatives to the use of pesticides and possible strategies for the preventive control of locusts.

The role and importance of cooperation among member states in the campaign against locusts and grasshoppers in the subregion was also examined. Among the conclusions and recommendations, the meeting called on member states to intensify the collection and sharing of information on locust activities, to strengthen their meteorological systems, extend the use of remote sensing especially in the areas of aggregation and ensure the training of relevant manpower as well as the mobilization of institutional and other infrastructure for the campaign against locusts and grasshoppers in the subregion. It also underscored the need for research to develop biological methods of locust control that pose minimum risks to health and are environmentally friendly. Underscoring the importance of strengthening and enlarging the existing cooperation among countries of North Africa, the workshop urged the ECA, in collaboration with FAO, WHO, IDB, and relevant subregional, regional, and international organizations to assist in reinforcing this cooperation in the subregion by organizing frequent workshops so as to permit the exchange of information and data on locusts among countries of the subregion.

The report of this workshop was considered and adopted by the Tenth Meeting of Experts of the Tangier MULPOC in April 1991. In view of the importance of the issue and the need to keep the locust and grasshopper situation under constant review and monitoring, the MULPOC prepared and submitted to the Eleventh Meeting of the Committee of Experts of the Tangier MULPOC in 1993, a report on preventive measures against the invasion of agricultural land by desert locusts and grasshoppers. It is in continuation of the monitoring process that this report on the "Follow-up and Monitoring of the Locust and Grasshopper Situation in the North Africa Subregion and on the

Establishment of an Early Warning System" was prepared and submitted to the Twelfth Meeting of the Committee of Experts of the North African MULPOC in March 1995.[64]

The second report on the Role of Financial Institutions in the Mobilization of Resources for the Implementation of Multinational Core Projects within the Framework of the IDDA in North Africa, had as objective, to examine the extent to which the first decade program for North Africa was implemented and the major constraints that affected its full implementation. It also examined the role which the member states of the subregion and the subregional, regional and international financial institutions and agencies were playing in the mobilization of relevant resources for the implementation of the second decade program in North Africa.

The period 1980–1990 was proclaimed the First Industrial Development Decade for Africa (IDDA 1) by the United Nations General Assembly (UNGA) by its Resolution 35/66B of 5 December 1980 in order to focus world attention to the need to give greater priority to the development of the industrial sector in Africa. The first decade integrated industrial promotion programs for the North Africa subregion comprising Algeria, Egypt, Libya, Morocco, Sudan, and Tunisia, contained a series of identified projects in 'core' industries for implementation during the decade. These were industries which provide essential and strategic inputs to other industries and economic activities particularly in agriculture, mining, transport, building and construction, and energy, and thus contribute to the creation of a self-sustaining industrial base in the subregion. The industries identified included metallurgical, engineering, and chemical industries. Because these industries are capital intensive, require complex technologies and have high energy content, member states were to implement the 'core' at the multinational level using their pooled resources and assisted by the relevant financial institutions and organizations.

The second decade covering the period 1991–2000 was declared by the UNGA in its Resolution 44/237 of 22 December 1989 as the Second Industrial Development Decade for Africa (IDDA 2), after an agonizing appraisal of the first decade revealed that most of the ambitious plans for industrial development in the First Decade had not been realized due mainly to lack of resources for investment. A major effort to stimulate domestic private investment and attract foreign capital was therefore particularly viewed as an intrinsic part of the preparation of the industrial development plan for the Second Decade.

In this connection, the international community, particularly the bilateral and multilateral funding institutions were urged to increase significantly their contribution to the industrial sector in African countries and give full support to the second decade program. It is against this background that this report was prepared in October 1994 with the aforementioned objectives and submitted to the meeting of the committee of experts of the North African MULPOC in March 1995.[65]

Don's fourth assignment in the long list of outputs waiting for implementation was a 'Study on Experiences, Techniques, and Know-how of Date Production in the North Africa Subregion'. This output had been put in the work program in order to respond to the request by countries such as Libya which had expressed interest in developing and expanding their date industry. These countries wanted to benefit from the experiences, techniques, and know-how of the major date producing countries. The major objective of the study was to examine the production and marketing of dates in countries of the subregion, the main diseases and pests that have plagued date production and the major advances or breakthroughs made in agronomic research and the development of technologies for cultivation, processing, and marketing in the subregion. The study was also to assess the future prospects of the date industry in the subregion by placing past and current trends in consumption, production, productivity, and prices within the subregion against similar trends in the global economy in order to guide relevant policies in countries interested in expanding their date industry.

The data needed to prepare the report was collected during a mission Don fielded to Cairo (Egypt), Tripoli (Libya), Rabat (Morocco), Khartoum (Sudan), and Tunis (Tunisia) to discuss with high officials of concerned government ministries, research institutions and other national as well as subregional and international organizations which had the information and data he needed. Owing, however, to time and financial constraints, the duration of the mission in each country was very short. Algeria, one of the major producers of dates was, unfortunately, not visited because of safety concerns due to the political situation at the time.

Data and other information relevant to Algeria was obtained from secondary sources. Concerning the data in general, the database particularly on date marketing and processing in some of the countries Don visited was little developed. Thus, while there was a large volume of information on agronomic research, there was a great dearth of data on such aspects as techniques of cultivation and processing, marketing channels, marketing costs and margins, export promotion activities, etc. Also worthy of note is that the production and trade data obtained from many member states during the mission were either not continuous over time or did not fall within the same time frame which would allow an examination and comparison of production and trade trends. Luckily, relevant FAO trade data came to the rescue.

This study was needed because of the importance of dates in the economies of some of the countries of the subregion and the many challenges confronting these countries. Regarding its importance, not only are dates an important and highly nutritive food in urban and rural households particularly during traditional ceremonies and religious festivities, the dried morphological parts supply various materials for traditional home construction, energy, and production of artisanal products. To some countries such as Algeria and Tunisia, date production is a significant source of foreign exchange earnings amounting on average to about fifty-three million dinars per annum in the case of Tunisia. As concerns the challenges, the scourge of bayoud has been the major concern. In Morocco, the disease destroyed more than two-thirds of the date palm trees, reducing the area under date cultivation from 150,000 ha at the turn of the century to only 44,000 ha at the time of this study while date production per annum has fallen by more than 27,000 tons in the last fifteen years. In Tunisia, annual production has fallen by 7,200 tons in the last five years.[66]

In the face of these challenges, farmers wanted improved date varieties that are high yielding, resistant to bayoud and other diseases and pests, and tolerant to drought and salinity. They also wanted improved methods of irrigation and drainage, improved tools, equipment and machinery for pruning, pollination, spraying and harvesting and new techniques for storage and preservation of fresh dates. Consumers on their part, wanted clean, wholesome, fresh, or dry dates and well-processed, high-quality date products. The small but emerging agro-industrial date sector was interested in technologies for the production of sound industrial date products that would enable it to diversify its production and enhance the value added to dates. If the date industry in the subregion was to attain its full potential, public sector policies had to effectively address these concerns. New methods for improving packing, handling, transportation, preservation, and product presentation to meet the standards of both the local and export markets and promote the consumption of dates and date products were essential.

This study which was undertaken in 1995, hopefully provided some useful experiences from several decades of cultivating and marketing dates in the subregion which these countries could draw upon in their efforts to further develop the industry and expand the considerable opportunities offered for increased employment, food production, and foreign exchange earnings [67].

"A Prefeasibility Study on Efficient and Rational Exploitation of Natural Resources within the North African Subregion (Energy, Water, etc.) to Support Industrial Development and Industrial Cooperation in the Subregion" was the next study Don undertook after the publication on dates. This study was intended to examine how the six countries of North Africa which are so endowed with vast reserves of natural resources (land, water, energy, flora, and fauna) could achieve industrial development and industrial self-reliance through cooperation—moving away from dependence on the production and export of primary commodities and raw materials to a stage where they combine agricultural and food production with industrial processing and manufacturing. The study thus attempted to examine the potential natural resource wealth of the subregion, explore the opportunities that exist for cooperation among member states in exploiting this wealth for industrial development and propose some actions that could assist member states in achieving this goal.

The data used for the preparation of this report was collected from Egypt, Libya, Morocco, Sudan, and Tunisia in May/June 1995 as well as from relevant documentation of regional and international organizations. The report was prepared and submitted in September 1995.[68]

After this technical publication, Don subsequently prepared two reports intended for submission to the Intergovernmental Committee of Experts of the Tangier MULPOC. The first of these two reports was entitled 'The Coordination and Harmonization of Food and Agricultural Policies, Strategies, and Production in North Africa'. This report attempted to identify key food and agricultural policy areas where harmonization and coordination of policies and strategies could significantly increase food production and supply and improve nutrition in the subregion. To this effect, the report examined the status of food production, analyzed the food and agricultural policies and strategies adopted by countries of the subregion to promote food production growth and identified some areas of cooperative advantage of countries of the subregion in food production and supply.

Based on the foregoing some strategies and effective mechanisms for coordination and harmonization of policies and strategies at the subregional level were proposed. Don collected the data and information used in preparing this report during a mission he undertook to Egypt and Sudan and supplemented this data with information he obtained from FAO food and nutrition profiles on Algeria, Egypt, Libya, Morocco, Sudan, and Tunisia. This report was submitted to the Thirteenth Meeting of the Intergovernmental Committee of Experts which was held in Tangier from April 1–4, 1997.[69]

The second report was on 'Monitoring and Follow-up of Progress in Desertification Control in North Africa'. The grounds for preparing this report for the consideration of the Intergovernmental Committee of Expert stems from the severe impacts which the twin problems of drought and desertification have had on these countries as reflected in the loss of arable lands, pastures, forests, and water resources. Algeria, Egypt, Libya, Mauritania, and Tunisia which border the Sahara Desert had lost an estimated 0.6 million square kilometer of fertile land during the last fifty years. Tunisia is estimated to have lost eleven thousand hectares of land yearly from wind and water erosion.[70] In the five Arab Maghreb Union (AMU) countries, seventy million hectares are in desertification prone areas. In Sudan, it is estimated that sand dunes cover over one-third of its total land area. And in Darfur, one of the driest regions of Sudan, deserts are advancing at about seven to ten kilometers per year.[71]

The problem of desertification and the urgency to address it had generated serious concerns not only in the North African subregion, but also within the international community. The International Conference on Desertification convened by the United Nations in Nairobi, Kenya, in 1977 was a landmark aimed at putting together international efforts toward desertification control. The United Nations Conference on Environment and Sustainable Development (UNCED)[72] held in Rio de Janeiro, Brazil, in 1992 was a second milestone. Chapter 12 of Agenda 21 devoted to drought and desertification control reflected the importance given to these two problems. The ECA Conference of Ministers of Economic Planning and Development in May 1993 in its

Resolution 744(XXVI) underscored the need for preventing and reversing desertification.[73]

Within the subregion itself, concern among the Arab Maghreb Union countries regarding the serious consequences of desert advancement and the associated environmental deterioration led them to draw up in 1992, a Maghrebine Charter on Environment and Sustainable Development[74] that would serve among others, as a basis for regional cooperation in desertification control. Among other initiatives by the AMU, the International Meeting on Desertification Control in the Maghreb convened in Rabat, from October 5–6, 1994, provided an opportunity to shed further light on the problem of desertification in the subregion, identify future AMU collaboration in addressing this problem and discuss possibilities for international collaboration. The non-AMU countries (Egypt and Sudan) on their part had, following Agenda 21, striven to combat desertification and therefore had during the past three decades, designed specific policies and tools on desertification control in prone areas and integrated them in their development programs and projects.

In spite of all the policies, programs, and projects implemented by member states within the framework of the Nairobi Plan of Action, Agenda 21, the Maghrebine Charter, etc., drought and desertification had remained a veritable scourge in the subregion, the reason why it was necessary to keep these twin intractable problems under constant examination with a view to galvanizing cooperative and sustained action to combat the roots of both phenomena. This called for constant monitoring, follow-up and exchange of information on progress made in desertification control in the subregion. It was in this context that this report was prepared for presentation to the Thirteenth Meeting of the Intergovernmental Committee of Experts of the Tangier MULPOC to be held in April 1997. The report briefly reviewed the problem of desertification, its nature, causes, and extent in the North African subregion and assessed the progress achieved so far to combat it as well as some of the major problems that had constrained progress in this regard. It then identified opportunities for collaborative action in the fight against desertification in the subregion[75].

Six months down the line, Don had become the Director's right hand man, his de facto assistant since the two regional advisers at the Regional Office were staff of the ECA Multidisciplinary Regional Advisory Team *at ECA Headquarters deployed to the Regional Office*. In addition to his work program, the Director was now giving him more and more administrative assignments and even his mission and other reports to 'polish up'.

But one area in which Don was to play a frequent role was as Officer-in-Charge (OIC) of the Regional Office. In this capacity, he acted in the Director's place any time the latter was away either on duty travel or on home leave or sick leave. The first of these occasions was in March 1994 when the ECA organized a subregional workshop in Tangier. This was one of the subregional workshops in Africa in preparation for the World Conference on Women due the following year in Beijing. So it was a very important event and it was expected that the Director would be present to host the workshop. However, a few days before the workshop was due to take place, he made Don officer-in-charge and took a short leave. The workshop (known as the Subregional Workshop for the North African Subregion on the Preparation of National Reports for the Regional and World Conferences on Women), and organized by the African Training and Research Center for Women convened from March 28–30, 1994, in Tangier. These African regional preparatory meetings were organized by the ECA to articulate an African Common Position for the Fourth World Conference on Women in 1995.

The aim of the Tangier Workshop was to sensitize and inform member states of the objectives of the regional and world conferences, to clarify the issues related to the overall preparation of the two conferences, to assist member states in the preparation of national reports, and to further ensure the maximum understanding of the guidelines for the preparation of the national reports as provided by the conference secretariat at the UN headquarters in New York.[76]

It was well attended with almost full representation (five out of the six North African countries attended). The ECA was very honored with the presence of Princess Lalla Fatima Zohra, elder sister of King Hassan II of Morocco and Patroness of the National Union of Moroccan Women (UNFM). A representative of the Governor of Tangier was also present.

Ms. Mebo Mwaniki of the African Training and Research Center for Women, presided over the opening session. As the officer-in-charge of the subregional office, Don read the executive secretary's message on his behalf. The message focused on the importance of the preparatory process for the national reports on the assessment of the implementation of the Nairobi forward looking strategies leading to the regional and global conferences. Princess Lalla Fatima Zohra also addressed the workshop.

Top Left: Don as officer-in-charge, welcoming Princess Fatima Zohra to the ECA-SRDC; Top Right: opening session of the workshop; Don and Ms. Mebo Waniki sitting right, Princess Fatima Zohra sitting extreme left. Below: A short discussion with the Princess. On her right is Ms. Waniki and on her left is Don.

As office-in-charge, Don also frequently represented the regional office at official state ceremonies and receptions when the director was out of town or took leave or was not feeling well. These were occasions where all heads of international and diplomatic missions were expected to be present. During each of those occasions, the director would designate Don to represent the regional office and he would use the official car and fly the UN flag to the ceremonial grounds or event.

The governor of Tangier as the representative of the king presided over those ceremonies/receptions. As each car drove along a long drive way lined by the military and police and pulled up at the entrance of the reception hall, the diplomat or representative came out, was saluted by protocol and led into a hall where he/she joined other guests for a cocktail before being taken and presented to the governor in the ceremonial hall. Most of the diplomats and representatives spoke fluent French or Arabic. Very few spoke English and even if they did, they were reluctant to do so. Don was handicapped in French and Arabic and so he found it a bit uncomfortable mixing and starting or sustaining a conversation with guests during his first few attendances. But as time went on and he came to learn French, he began to enjoy those receptions.

Those occasions provided Don with an opportunity to know high government officials and other diplomats. In fact, most of them believed that Don was the director of the regional office since it was him who was always representing the regional office. They had never met the director. In his second year in Tangier, Don was made Deputy Warden for the City of Tangier within the UN Security Plan for Morocco for the period 1994–1996.

In August 1993, Don had returned to Rome to arrange for the shipment of their household goods and personal effects and bring his family to Tangier. Vanessa and Valentina were placed in the American school in Tangier come September when schools reopened. Don Jr. left for Christ's College, Blackheath, London, to begin secondary school. They had moved into the apartment on the fourth floor in 'Residence Omnia' close to the sea and just five-minute walk from the office.

Don had not forgotten the challenge he had accepted when he agreed to take up the assignment in Tangier which was to achieve fluency in French. His stay in Tangier and his travels so far in the region convinced him more than ever before that achieving fluency in French was an absolute necessity if he was to accomplish his duties and responsibilities efficiently and live and interact comfortably in the subregion. Now he thought the time was right to register for evening classes in French. He and Dorothy both registered with Alliance Francais for the French language classes offered by the French Ministry of Cooperation in cooperation with the Moroccan Ministry of Education.

For two years, they attended these classes religiously (except when Don was on mission), sat in the same class, did their assignments and prepared successively for the respective examinations in Levels I, II, III, IV, V, and VI. In addition to the evening classes, they practiced their French in their daily interactions in the shops, restaurants, parties, etc. As time went on, their French language skills kept improving and within six to nine months, they were communicating fairly fluently in French.

During the period January 1995 to January 1996, they sat for and passed the examinations set by the Center d'Examen du Maroc, Commission Nationale du DELF et du DALF, Ministere de l'Education Nationale, Republique Francaise as follows[77]:

1. DELF, Unités A1 (Expression générale), A2 (Expression des idées et des sentiments), and A3 (Expression écrite), January 1995
2. DELF, Unités A4 (Pratique du fonctionnement de la langue), May 1995
3. DELF, Unités A5 (Culture et civilization) and A6 (Expression spécialisée); January 1996.

They were thus awarded the Diplome d'Etudes en Langue Francaise (DELF), Unités A1, A2, A3, A4, A5, and A6, by the Ministere de l'Education Nationale, Republique Francaise (French Ministry of Education, France).

Don traveled quite extensively within the region but mostly to the capital cities since the government ministries and regional and international organizations were located there. But he did travel to other towns, as and when, necessary. He found Tunis, capital of Tunisia a very lively, western city, apparently peaceful, with beautiful hotels, full of tourists, and lots of shopping. The ministry and other officials he often met were quite friendly and spoke mainly French or Arabic. But many were quite understanding when they came to know he was English speaking and they tried to speak in English. In fact, most high officials spoke some English and just as Don felt shy speaking French for fear of making mistakes, they also often felt the same way. On the surface, the city and indeed the country was enjoying much calm, peace, and serenity, but private discussions with ordinary people suggested that underneath this calm and serenity was a lot of discontent with the ruling party and regime (a dictatorial president, accumulation of wealth and power by the president and his family, friends and a small elite group, lack of free speech and press freedom, lots of poverty among the lower classes in society, etc.) that had been in power for many years. So the upheavals and the revolution that engulfed the country and gave birth to the 'Arab Spring' and the overthrow of President Zine El Abidine Ben Alion on 14 January 2011 came as no surprise to Don.

Cairo was a city Don had traveled to before while he was at the World Food Council, Rome. He and other members of the WFC Secretariat had gone there to service the WFC/UNDP Interregional Consultation on 'Meeting the Food Production Challenges of the 1990s and Beyond' convened in Cairo in April 1991 by the WFC and the UNDP. So he was already familiar with Cairo by the time he was undertaking missions to Egypt from Tangier. Cairo was at that time noted for its hot climate, huge urban population, traffic quagmire and housing congestion in the inner city. Don came to like the Zamalek neighborhood where he always stayed at the Diplomat Hotel. This neighborhood was relatively calm and quiet, clean and orderly, kind of middle-to-upper class. English was the most commonly used foreign language and most of the street plates were bilingual in Arabic and English.

Most of the officials Don held meetings with were fluent in English so he was always very comfortable in Cairo as he had no communication problem. The main problem in Cairo was getting to his appointments and meetings from Zamalek especially to the old and crowded area of the city where the Ministry of Agriculture and its Department of International Cooperation were located. It was always a nightmare getting through the traffic.

It is worth recalling his mission to Cairo from Tangier in connection with the report he was preparing on the implementation of multinational core projects within the framework of the IDDA in North Africa. A meeting had been convened for him to meet and discuss the Decade with high officials from the Ministry of Industry and related services. By the time Don found his way to the meeting room, the officials were all seated around a large table—all white Egyptians. The meeting began, not with Don introducing himself and stating the purpose of his mission as is usually the case. Instead, one of the officials, probably the most senior of them began to introduce his colleagues. They were mostly specialist engineers and they were all Ph.Ds. The introduction completed, he turned to Don and demanded that he tells them who he is and what he is. Don found this weird. However, he just told them his name was Don Oben and he was from the Subregional Office for North Africa of the Economic Commission for Africa.

"So what are your academic qualifications?" the official pressed on. Instead of answering his question, Don just took out one of his business cards and passed it over to him and asked if they could get down to business.

"You did not tell us you had a Ph. D.," he said looking up in amazement after scrutinizing the card. "The letter we received from your office addressed you as Mr. Don Oben."

Don now knew what the objective of this interrogation was all about—to show that he was less qualified than they were and that he should get that quite clear before they started the meeting. The issue of whether he had a doctorate degree or not should not have been raised at this meeting because it was quite irrelevant. And the way in which it was done left no doubt that it was done to embarrass Don, a black man from sub-Saharan Africa. Returning to his question about the letter from Don's office which addressed him as Mr. Don Oben, Don said simply, "That is the way of the UN."

Don had meanwhile looked at them individually and come to the conclusion that most of them were younger than he was. So he went on the offensive. He asked each of them where they were in their careers in 1978. Many of them were still studying for their bachelor's degree. A few were just completing high school. None of them had had his doctorate degree.

"You know what, 1978 was the year I earned my Ph.D., February 2, 1978 to be exact." Don rubbed it in looking straight at each white face in the room. "Now can we start the meeting?" he asked. He saw their egos visibly deflated.

"But you don't look it," one of them stammered.

"Well, I don't know how a man who received his doctorate degree in 1978 should look like," Don responded.

The meeting turned out to be one of the most interesting and productive meetings Don has had. It was a meeting in which he was tested. It was a meeting in which he had total control.

Ironically, it is also in Egypt that Don ever received a gift from a very high government official during a mission. He had gone to debrief the official, Dr. Mamdouh Riad, Undersecretary of State for Afforestation, Ministry of Agriculture and Land Reclamation, of his mission to Egypt. As a tradition, whenever ECA staff go on mission to a member state, after the mission is completed, the staff member meets with the ministry or office which arranged and coordinated the mission in the country. The purpose of the meeting is to apprise the concerned coordinating ministry or office of how things had gone during the mission—the meetings held, the discussions had, the data collected, the problems encountered and most of all, to express appreciation to the host government for the welcome accorded the staff member and the assistance provided to make the mission a success.

It was quite a long debriefing during which the Undersecretary of State listened very attentively. This was followed by a long discussion on the subject of his mission and frankly, Don was quite surprised at his keen interest in and deep knowledge of the subject. At the end of the debriefing, he opened one of the drawers of his large desk and brought out a small packet wrapped in beautiful blue and red wrapping paper and handed to Don saying: "Mr. Oben, this is a small gift from me to remind you of your visit to Egypt." When Don opened the gift, he found it was one of Egypt's historical artifacts.

Don was delighted by this gift because Egypt is a country whose history he has found fascinating. Most of this history is reflected in the monuments and tourist attractions for which Cairo and its environs is famous for. So it is not surprising and unexpected that Don would, to the extent possible, use the opportunity of his missions to Cairo to explore some of her historical monuments and landmarks. However, no matter how much he tried, the free time he always had in Cairo to participate in tours was always very limited as he had meetings throughout the week and by the weekend he was taking his flight out of Cairo to the next country in his itinerary. He was, nevertheless, able to take part in a few tours to the pyramids of Giza, Sphinx, Memphis, and Sakkara. At Giza, he rode a camel for the first time; He often wandered around Tahrir Square either shopping or window shopping. Once he made a tour to the Egyptian museum.

Another fascinating tour he once undertook was a two-hour dinner cruise on the Nile during which they were entertained to Egyptian cuisine, music, and belly dancing. And during his last mission to Cairo, an Egyptian friend and a senior official of the Department of International Cooperation took him on a rare tour of the Palace of King Farouk, the tenth ruler of Egypt from the Muhammad Ali Dynasty and the penultimate King of Egypt and the Sudan. He was forced into abdication and exile on 26 July 1952 following a military coup led by Abdel Nasser. The tour took Don into the innermost recesses of the palace. It was awesome. Given Egypt's long history, one is not surprised at the amount and variety of artifacts found in the museums, at tourist sites, large shops and street vendors. And in fact, Cairo is the city from where Don has had the largest collection of artifacts among which include the pyramids, the sphinx, Cleopatra, and 'The Judgement' on papyrus, a material made from papyrus reeds, used as writing and painting material in ancient Egypt.

Khartoum, the capital of Sudan was, to Don, very unique. It was one of the hottest places on earth that he has visited. His flights always left Khartoum at 0200 hours so he was always picked up from the hotel to the airport and checked into the flight before midnight and he would wait almost alone in the VIP lounge for hours for the flight. Khartoum was the only city where he scarcely had any urge to go out shopping because of the sun and heat. He doesn't know if the city is this hot all the year round or that he happened always to be there in the hot season. Because of the heat, water pots, and drinking points were positioned in convenient places in the city for thirsty or dehydrated commuters to stop and have a drink. And in the ministries and other offices, a visitor was welcomed first with a large cup of water.

Don, like most foreign visitors, always carried a bottle of mineral water from the hotel with him or her wherever he or she went since one couldn't be sure of the quality of water that one was offered at the offices where one went. It had only been once and that was during Don's first mission to Khartoum that he had gone, out of curiosity, to 'survey' the city. Since that first mission, Don's itinerary in Khartoum had always been thus: from the airport-hotel-ministries/institutions/organizations-hotel-airport/departure.

Don's mission to Tripoli, capital of the Libyan Arab Jamahiriya, was perhaps his most memorable mission in the region. It was part of a three-country mission. It was the third country he was to visit after Sudan and Egypt. At that time, Libya was under UN sanctions which included the ban on international flights to Tripoli. To travel to Libya, most foreign travelers had to route their travel through the city of Djerba in Tunisia on the Mediterranean coast. From there, they would travel by road into Libya. This was therefore the route Don took from Cairo.

He arrived at Djerba airport, passed through immigration and customs and was met at the arrival hall by a driver and protocol officer from the government of the Libyan Arab Jamahiriya. They then sped in a huge black Mercedes Benz toward the Tunisian/Libyan border with Don tired and slumped in the back seats and the protocol officer seated in front with the driver. At the border, the protocol officer took Don's UN laissez passer and processed his exit from Tunisia and entry into the Libyan Arab Jamahiriya. On arrival in Tripoli, Don was driven to and lodged in a five-star hotel without asking him what type of hotel his preference was. Obviously, he could not have chosen to lodge himself in a five-star hotel given the level of the daily subsistence allowance for Tripoli. It would not be enough to support his stay. He watched with unease, as the protocol officer checked him into the hotel, told him to feel at home and that he would be coming for him at 8:00 a.m. in the morning. Don decided he had to be very economical in the use of the hotel's services. It was first class! It offered every type and quality service a five-star hotel could offer. The dinners were huge—barbecues, vegetables, fruits, wines, all exotic.

At 8:00 a.m. the following morning, the protocol officer came for Don with the same driver and two other officials from the Ministry of Agriculture. During their drive through the city, it was clear that Arabic was the official and perhaps the only language spoken in the Jamahiriya. The street names, the road signs, shop names, and everything else were in Arabic. In the ministries too, the officials spoke only Arabic. The objective of his mission to the country had been communicated to the government well in advance of his arrival. So a detailed program of meetings and visits had been arranged with two officials who were fluent in English assigned to accompany Don and serve as interpreters.

Don was to learn two days later that the driver and the man from protocol who had picked him from the airport and lodged him at the hotel had been assigned to him for the duration of his stay. The huge Mercedes Benz was for his use also. Two days into the mission, Don was having diner in a quiet corner of one of the restaurants when the driver and the protocol man appeared from nowhere and joined him at his table. They expressed surprise that they had not seen Don in the restaurants or bars or anywhere in the hotel. They were also surprised that he was having an 'a la carte' dinner, and a small bottle of water when huge buffets, barbecues and wines were being served and guests were wining and dining noisily. "Didn't I like the food and wine?"

Before Don could respond to any of their questions, the protocol man told him: "Mr. Oben, please, eat as much as you want and whatever you like. Order whatever drinks and wines you want any time of the day. The hotel also has a laundry, a swimming pool, a sauna and massage, a gym, etc. Please feel free to make use of these services. Your stay in this hotel is at government's expense. You are a guest of the government."

"Wow, what a blank check," Don said to himself. And then he added: "And by the way, we are in the room next to yours." Wow! Don had never had such lavish reception in any country. But did they have to be lodged also in the hotel, and next to his room?

Well, in spite of this generous hospitality, it did not change the way Don made use of the hotel facilities. He hardly had lunch at the hotel as he was often busy with his itineraries all afternoons. He often returned late in the evenings from his meetings and visits very tired and barely just able to eat dinner and retire to his room. Alcoholic drinks don't go well with him, neither is he a big eater. He also didn't use the gym, the sauna and massage, the swimming pool nor the laundry. Because of the language barrier, he never had the inclination to go out into town for shopping or sightseeing even if he had had the time to do so. Even then, he would have had to take along an interpreter with him. All street names, road signs, shop names were in Arabic and the man in the street spoke only Arabic.

His mission was well prepared and his itineraries, visits to ministries and meetings and discussions with concerned officials were well coordinated and productive. He had a long debriefing meeting with the coordinating ministry at the end of the mission which lasted four days. During the meeting, he also expressed not only his appreciation, but that of the director of the regional office, their national, for the very warm welcome and hospitality characteristic of the Libyan Arab Jamahiriya extended to him which made his mission a huge success.

The following morning, he was whisked off by the same driver in the same large black Mercedes car and accompanied by the same protocol officer to the Tunisian city of Djerba through which he had traveled to Tripoli and checked into his flight to Tangier. Back at the subregional office, Don briefed his director of his mission to Libya and the warm reception and extraordinary hospitality accorded to him by his government. Whether the director had arranged it or not, Don did not know and would never know. It's quite unlikely that he did. He was visibly very pleased but never made any statement.

Don did also undertake several missions to Rabat, capital of Morocco. In fact, Morocco was almost always included in each mission. The headquarters of the Arab Maghreb Union (AMU) was located in Rabat. As an institution promoting regional integration in North Africa, it had vital economic integration information of immense value in much of Don's work which made it an important port of call during most of his missions. French and Arabic were the dominant languages spoken in the ministries, the AMU and other institutions and agencies but many officials also spoke English. As Don's French language skills improved with time and he became more fluent in French, he felt more at ease at meetings.

With Spain and Gibraltar just fifteen miles across the sea facing Tangiers, and daily boat cruises and ferry crosses from Tangiers and Ceuta to the European Mediterranean coast, it was only a matter of time before Don started to take his family on weekends to Spain and Gibraltar. In fact, Ceuta was an 18.5 square kilometer (7.1 square miles) highly-populated Spanish autonomous territory on mainland Africa sharing a western border with Morocco. It was one of two Spanish port cities on the North African coast and part of a special low tax zone in Spain. Before long, Don and his family started driving to Ceuta at weekends for sightseeing and shopping. A single road border checkpoint allowed for cars to travel between Morocco and Ceuta, the driving distance between Tangier and Ceuta being about seventy-three kilometers and a travel time of forty-five minutes.

Don remembers in particular, two memorable trips they made—one to Gibraltar and one to the southern coast of Spain. The children had looked forward very much to these trips especially that to Gibraltar. They had heard and read so much about the Rock of Gibraltar. In fact, on some very bright days, they could see it in the distance from the terrace of their eight-story residential building.

Gibraltar is a British overseas territory located on the southern end of the Iberian Peninsula covering some 6.8 square kilometers (2.6 square miles) and sharing a 1.2 kilometer (0.75 mile) land border with Spain. They left for Gibraltar via Ceuta by road in their Mercedes Benz car on a Friday afternoon after work. In Ceuta, they took a ferry to Algeciras, a port city in the south of Spain in a time of about one hour. From there, they drove to the coastal town of La Línea de la Concepción, more commonly known simply as 'La Línea' and often referred to as 'The Gateway to Gibraltar' because it forms the boundary between the British territory of Gibraltar and Spain. They took up lodgings in a hotel and spent the evening of that first day savoring Spanish cuisine, wines, and juices (for the children) in a nearby restaurant.

The following morning they left to spend the day in Gibraltar. They passed through identity checks required to cross the Gibraltar-Spain border which is the international boundary between the British overseas territory of Gibraltar and Spain. This border runs east-west for a total of 1.2 kilometers (0.75 mile) and separates Gibraltar from the neighboring Spanish municipality of La Linea de la Concepción. On entering Gibraltar, they came face to face with the Rock of Gibraltar, the iconic landmark of the region. At the foot of the rock was the densely populated city area, home to over thirty thousand Gibraltarians and other nationalities.

Within the city, the Gibraltar Airport was in full view. Its location seemed quite unusual and dangerous for an airport—unusual because of its proximity to the city center resulting in the airport terminal being within walking distance of much of Gibraltar. One end of the runway also juts out to the sea. They were later to learn that Gibraltar Airport had been consistently listed as one of the world's scariest for air passengers. It was exposed to strong crosswinds around the rock and across the Bay of Algeciras, making landing and take-off in winter particularly uncomfortable.

They took a guided tour of the city. The tour was enlightening, revealing, entertaining, and as anticipated, long and tiring. They were shown around some of the city's landmarks, cultural heritage and other popular tourist attractions. It was like a walk through history.

The tour's itinerary included a ten-minute ride in a cable car up the rock. As the major landmark of the region, no visit to Gibraltar was complete without a ride in the cable car to the top of the rock. The panoramic views were spectacular, taking in the straits of Gibraltar and Southern Spain. They could also see the northern coast of Africa. They saw the Barbary Apes, one of the rock's oldest inhabitants and the only wild monkey population in the European continent in the upper rock area of the Gibraltar Nature Reserve. They were cute, playful, energetic, and, as they were told, were often good pickpockets whenever they had the opportunity.

Within the rock was a network of tunnels, the tunnels of Gibraltar, constructed over the course of nearly two hundred years principally by the British Army, which have made the Rock of Gibraltar 'a veritable warren of tunnels that housed guns, hangars, ammunition stores, barracks, and hospitals'. Within a land area of only 2.6 square miles, Gibraltar has around thirty-four miles of tunnels, nearly twice the length of its entire road network. At the beginning of the second world war, Don and his family were told, a pair of tunnels—the Great North Road and the Fosse Way, were excavated running nearly the full length of the rock to interconnect the bulk of the wartime tunnels. The tunnels accommodated what amounted to an underground city.

The entire sixteen-thousand-strong garrison in Gibraltar could be housed there along with enough food to last them for sixteen months. Within the tunnels, there were also an underground telephone exchange, a power generating station, a water distillation plant, a hospital, a bakery, ammunition magazines, and a vehicle maintenance workshop. Inside the rock was also a network of caves among which was one of the hidden attractions of the rock— St. Michael's Cave, a large, natural cavern filled with large, beautiful stalactites and stalagmites. They were told that it had once been believed that this cave was linked to Africa by a fifteen-mile passage under the sea! They visited many other landmarks including the museum before the tour ended and they did their own tour of the city center—visiting city hall, Gibraltar parliament, the supreme court, library, Pizza Hut and McDonalds, King's Wharf, etc.

Gibraltar, they had also been told, was a cocktail of Spanish and British influences and this was reflected in the culture and traditions—languages, cuisine, music and dance, etc. They had seen this during the tour. They spent time at Casemates Square which boasted lots of little bars and restaurants and then past the Elliot O'Callaghan Hotel nearby surrounded by well-known UK high street stores.

As they walked along Main Street from the Grand Casemates Square to the Southport Gate, they saw shops of all kinds, pubs, open-air restaurants, and street entertainers, as well as Bobbies, British mailboxes, and telephone booths. Apart from the several small shops and restaurants, what is unique about Main Street is that it is pedestrianized and reflects to some extent, it's Moorish and Spanish history. There were also shops selling duty-free cigarettes, alcohol, and a broad range of other merchandise.

As the sun began to set, Don and his family did a little shopping from one of the shops and made their way back to La Linea for dinner before retiring to their hotel for the night. Due to exhaustion from the previous day's trip to Gibraltar, they embarked on the return journey home after lunch as planned but could not go window shopping in the morning as they had envisaged. At Ceuta, they drove out of the ferry and off to Tangier with the children happily recounting some of the memorable moments of the trip.

The other memorable journey which they undertook outside Morocco was that to the Southeastern coast of Spain a few months after their travel to Gibraltar. They had an elderly family friend, a Palestinian called Zaki, married to a French lady who was very helpful in enabling them to settle down quickly in Tangiers. He had suggested that Don needed to take a break from work and take the family on a vacation to Spain or Gibraltar.

"There are so many ferry crosses every day to Spain. Take a break after you settle down. The children will love it for a change," he had argued.

He was a much older man and Don always found his advice very sound and rewarding. He always seemed to Don an 'old wise man'. It was partly at his suggestion that Don and his family had taken the weekend trip to Gibraltar.

"You will find a weekend trip to the southeastern coast of Spain a very interesting experience," Zaki said bringing up the issue again when Don and Dorothy were visiting him and his wife.

Then he brought out a map and laid it on the dining table. Using a pencil, he showed Don the places they could visit—La Linea, Torremolinos, Marbella, and Malaga—all along the Mediterranean coast. They had often taken vacations and enjoyed the seacoast, the hotel environment and the city tours. Dorothy loves exploring new destinations and she had, in fact, also suggested several times the need to take a weekend, if not a short vacation, in Spain. So this proposition by their friend was welcomed by her. They decided to spend the Christmas Day of 1995 wherever it met them during the trip. The children were excited when they told them the plan to spend a weekend in Spain.

They left on December 22 to Ceuta and, as with the previous trip, took the ferry with their car to Algeciras from where they drove to La Linea. They lodged at the same hotel as during their previous trip and spent the day in La Linea. The next day, December 23, they drove to Torremolinos and then to Marbella, stopping at interesting places to snack and take in the scenic view of the sea and coastline. They spent the rest of the day in Marbella and took a hotel for the night. On December 24, they drove to Malaga. Don remembers it was on this leg of the journey that he was pulled aside by the police for speeding but cautioned on presentation of his identity papers. He had been caught on radar. They spent much of the day touring the city, sometimes by car, at other times on foot.

Toward the evening, they set out on their return journey to Mabella where a huge Christmas Eve party had been arranged in their hotel. They joined in the Christmas Eve celebrations and it was a big surprise when the hotel and those present treated them as special guests. May be, because they were the only black people around. There was lots of food, wine, and juices (for the children) and dancing. They also won prizes in the big raffle organized that night—wine and champagne. This was the first time they had ever won a prize in a raffle and it was undoubtedly, the high point of their trip. The next day, December 25, 1995, they spent Christmas Day quietly in Mabella touring the city and the following day December 26, set off for Torremolinos and La Linea and across the Mediterranean to Ceuta and Tangier. Their friend, Mr. Zaki had been right. Not only the children, but Dorothy and Don also enjoyed the trip.

Incidentally, they did not travel much as a family within Morocco except for an occasional trip to Rabat and once or twice to Casablanca. They did, however, go on picnics with family friends to some touristic sites in Tangier. Their visit to Marrakech in May 1996 was quite memorable. Marrakech is the third largest city after Casablanca and Fez in the Kingdom of Morocco. Like many Moroccan cities, Marrakesh comprises an old fortified city packed with vendors and their stalls (*medina*), bordered by modern neighborhoods, the most prominent of which is *Gueliz*. Today, it is one of the busiest cities in Africa and serves as a major economic center and tourist destination.

The first and most interesting place they visited after checking into Hotel Marrakech was the Jamaa el Fna, the main square and market place in Marrakech's medina quarter (old city). This is the center of city activity and trade. During the day it was predominantly occupied by orange juice stalls, water sellers with traditional leather water bags and brass cups, youths with chained Barbary apes, and snake charmers. As the day progressed, the snake charmers departed, and late in the day, the square became more crowded, with Chleuh dancing-boys, storytellers, magicians, and peddlers of traditional medicines.

As darkness fell, the square filled with dozens of food stalls as the number of people on the square peaked. Bordering the square along one side was the Marrakech souk, the largest traditional market, the principal shopping attraction in Morocco catering to both the common daily needs of the locals, as well as those of tourists, especially with crafts such as carpets and textiles, ceramics, wood work, metal work, and *zelij*. On the other sides were hotels, gardens, cafe terraces, and narrow streets leading into the alleys of the medina quarter.

The city walls or ramparts of Marrakech which stretch for some nineteen kilometers around the medina part of the city, and stand up to about nineteen feet high with twenty gates and two hundred towers along them, Don and his family were told, were just awesome. The other important place they visited was the Koutoubia Mosque. This is the largest mosque in the city, located in the southwest medina quarter of Marrakech alongside the square. Their guide wanted to take them to other landmarks but because they had spent so much time at the square and the children were tired, they could not visit these other landmarks. These included the two gardens (The Agdal and Menara Gardens), the palaces (El Badi and Royal Palaces), the Marrakech Museum and the Ben Youssef Mosque.

One of the things Don had enjoyed most at the Joint Division at ECA and the World Food Council was the professional environment—an environment in which professional staff met and discussed their colleagues' writings, made objective comments and suggestions for improvement, shared information and data, brainstormed on contemporary regional and global issues of relevance to their work programs, and generally demonstrated a spirit of camaraderie in spite of individual differences.

This environment was missing at the subregional office in Tangier and Don was missing it very much. He had been working virtually alone. The regional advisers were almost perpetually on mission. And once when Don tried to get feedback on a report from one of them, he told him he was not conversant with the subject of the report. Don had to write or call Addis Ababa for any important information he needed. Similarly, news of any happenings or changes at headquarters took time to get to Tangier. Increasingly, Don began to feel isolated, like he was tucked away in a tiny corner of the African continent. By late 1995, this situation had started to weigh heavily on his mind and he felt the need to do something about it. He began to feel an increasing desire to move to Headquarters.

It was at this time in 1995, that the then UN Secretary-General Boutros Boutros-Ghali appointed Mr. Kingsley Y. Amoako as the Executive Secretary of ECA with the rank of Undersecretary-general with a mandate to transform the institution into an influential voice for Africa and an effective player in global development. Mr. Amoako began to hold town hall meetings at headquarters with ECA staff for soul searching as to how to move ECA forward to better respond to the needs of its African member states in the face of economic stagnation, civil unrest, and political turmoil. The deliberations at these meetings and the conclusions and decisions taken were to lead to a process of reform and renewal of the Commission. These town hall meetings generated a lot of fervor and Don longed to be there. Representatives of some regional offices attended some of the meetings. Don was not aware of any participation by Tangier.

Don made a decision to write to the new executive secretary. In his letter, he welcomed him to ECA and hoped he would have a productive, rewarding, and successful tenure. He then asked for a transfer to his former Division at Headquarters with strong arguments to support his transfer request. Although in the letter he asked for a transfer, he made it look like a personal letter so he did not have to channel it through the Director or copy him.

As expected, the executive secretary acknowledged his letter with thanks but told him he had passed on his request to the Economic Cooperation Office (ECO), the supervisory division to look into and advise him. The director of ECO called Don later and confirmed that he had been asked to look into his request by the executive secretary. Unfortunately, his transfer to headquarters would diminish the staff strength in Tangier which already was far below requirements as he himself was aware. However, he would keep Don's request in view. He very much appreciated Don's immense contribution to the work program in Tangiers and wished that he exercise patience. He would seize any opportunity that came his way to propose the transfer.

Mr. Jose De Pedro was a Forestry Expert and former colleague in the Joint Division when Don was there in the 80s. He was a Spanish national and was due retirement the next year. When he learned of Don's interest to return to the Division, he saw this as an opportunity for him to move to Tangier where he would be near his country, Spain from where he could more conveniently arrange for his retirement and relocation back home. So he contacted Don and they discussed the idea of a possible swap, with him coming to Tangier and Don going to Addis Ababa.

Having thus agreed, the idea was mooted to the two divisions concerned, i.e., the Agriculture Division and ECO. Since both of them were at the same professional level, the swap was agreed to. The Director of ECO in a recommendation to the Executive Secretary informed him that after consultation with the Acting Director of the Agriculture Division, it had been agreed that Don should be transferred to the Agriculture Division and Jose De Pedro transferred to Tangier.

The news of Don's transfer reached his Director before the letter of transfer. It was like a bolt from the blue and it jolted him more than the news of Don's transfer to his office nearly three years earlier. Thinking that the transfer was probably a request Don had made and was still under consideration, he called Headquarters to discuss the matter. When he was told that the decision had been taken, he was furious and took a flight to Addis Ababa. He questioned why he had not been consulted before the decision was taken to transfer a staff who was the pillar of the regional office. Making a strong case for the reversal of the decision, he asked that it be rescinded.

To this, he was reminded that he had not wanted Don in Tangier in the first place and had made a similar trip to Addis Ababa asking that his transfer to Tangier be canceled. He was further reminded of what he had been told 3 years earlier: "We have sent you one of the best. He will be an asset to you and you will like working with him." This has proved to be true. In any case, he was told that the Executive Secretary had already signed the letter and the matter was closed. But he was also informed that an equally experienced staff at the same level was being transferred to replace Don so the staff strength at the subregional office remained the same.

Back in Tangier, he called Don and asked why he hated him so much as to ask for a transfer from Tangier and without discussing the matter with him. Don was doing an excellent job in Tangier and he had relied on him more than anyone else in the regional office. Of course, Don told him his request for a transfer had nothing to do with him as a person. He had a good working relationship with him and he had enjoyed working with him. He just wanted a change after three years in Tangiers.

The regional office gave Don and his family a rousing send-off. His colleagues were heartbroken to see Don go. And once again, he and his wife were leaving behind families and friends whose friendships they had treasured and enjoyed during their stay in Tangier. Their daughter Valentina also was leaving a school she had just settled in and was breaking friendships she had established. She was now looking forward to a new school in Addis Ababa, a city where she had left at the age of two years. Her sister, Vanessa, whom they had brought to Tangier in 1993 had left for college in Croydon, UK, the previous year having finished primary school at the American school of Tangier.

Packers came and packed, crated and carted away their personal effects and household goods for shipment to Addis Ababa. They shipped their car too. It was the third time they were shipping it—first from Addis to Rome, then from Rome to Tangier and now from Tangier back to Addis. They moved out of their flat into a hotel and then flew out of Tangier via Rabat to Addis Ababa.

Top: Left photo, some staff posing with Don on his last day. Right photo, Touring the Pyramids at Giza.

Chapter 15
At the ECA Headquarters, Addis Ababa, Ethiopia: A 'Homecoming'

Ethiopia: New Changes

While waiting for their departure to Ethiopia, Don's mind often flashed back to the situation in Ethiopia in the 80s during his first tour at ECA. Inasmuch as he was looking forward with enthusiasm to returning to Ethiopia, he could not help thinking about some of the experiences they had with the socialist policies of the Derg government of Mengistu Haile Mariam. Back then, the economy had been subjected to central planning that had suffocated the factors of economic growth and the potential of the forces of production and exchange.

As a result, the scarcity of important food items like rice, vegetable oil, flour etc., was common place. These items and many others including luxuries could be found in the Victory Shop and the duty-free shops, where diplomats and other foreigners shopped—they were required to pay in foreign currency. Don remembers the long queues of ordinary people waiting so long for bread to receive so little.

Foreign currency was also stringently managed. Don remembers the problems ECA and other international staff faced with getting foreign currency even from their foreign currency accounts when they had to travel out of Ethiopia. They were required to provide to the Ethiopian Commercial Bank evidence of their impending travel: i) their valid passport, ii) an exit visa issued by the foreign ministry, iii) air ticket with, iv) the flight confirmed. Even then there were limits to the amount they could take out at any one time. Rented houses were also in short supply. Letting out houses on rent by private landlords was prohibited or nonexistent.

Foreigners had to rent their accommodation from the Administration of Rented Houses which was a government agency set up to manage all houses seized from landlords by the socialist government and put into a pool for renting to the OAU, UN, and other international organizations. No new houses were being built. Don and two other ECA staff members and their families who arrived in Addis in August 1982 had to stay in a hotel apartment for eleven months before being allocated houses. Don wondered what the situation in Addis Ababa was now. He knew many changes had taken place in Ethiopia, but how far had the situation changed?

They arrived in Addis Ababa in June 1996. Ethiopia had undergone profound political and economic changes since 1990 when Don left ECA for the World Food Council in Rome. The socialist government of Mengistu Haile Mariam had been overthrown in 1991 by the Ethiopian People's Revolutionary Democratic Front (EPRDF), a coalition of Tigray People's Liberation Front (TPLF) and Eritrean People's Liberation Front (EPLF) led by the TPLF. A transitional government, the Transitional Government of Ethiopia (TGE) had been formed with Meles Zenawi as President from 1991 to 1995. He was later to become the Prime Minister. The new government had ushered in a new era of radical transformation involving both political and economic reforms.

In the political sphere, Mengistu's unitary state had been transformed into a federal system with the attendant devolution of power to component regions and their communities, replacing the command economy with a market economy, and instituting human rights buttressed up by an independent judiciary. Also of significance was the launching by the new government of an economic policy involving the rehabilitation and transformation of the socialist command economy inherited from the Mengistu regime into a functioning and vibrant market-based economy.

Under a Supported Adjustment Program undertaken from 1992/93 to 1994/95 to promote growth, a number of measures had been taken aimed among others at eliminating direct price controls and letting the free market determine prices; liberalizing the distribution of almost all commodities; and largely devaluating the local currency. These measures were aimed at enhancing the export possibilities of domestic products and introducing a foreign exchange auction market to involve the market in determining the exchange rate of the local currency. It also aimed at expanding the list of commodities for which foreign exchange may be purchased, thus providing importers the opportunity to obtain hard currency to import any commodity that is in demand in the domestic market.[78]

The impact of some of these changes was quite evident to Don and his family on arrival in Addis Ababa in June 1996. Many private enterprises—shops, restaurants, hotels, supermarkets, grocery stores, etc., were almost everywhere. So was a private sector house-renting market. In fact, whereas they had waited for eleven months to be allocated a house in the 80s, this time they rented a house from a private landlord within two weeks.

But an incident which happened on the first day Don assumed duty at ECA suggested that all was still not well. As he approached the new building that morning, a staff member who was coming out of the building and apparently had known him in the 80s, stopped him and, rubbing his eyes as if he wanted to be certain that it was Don he was seeing, asked: "Are you not Mr. Don?"

"Yes, I am," Don answered, surprised that the staff member did not even say good morning before asking the question.

"But you left Ethiopia some years ago," he asked, still looking astonished.

"That's right," Don replied, wondering where this was leading to.

"And you came back with your eyes open?" he continued.

"Of course, with my eyes open." Don assured him he didn't move around with his eyes closed.

"And in your right mind?" When Don told him he was not crazy, he simply said, "Okay, if you say so." And shrugging his shoulders, he wished Don welcome and went away.

They ran into each other again some days later, and he told Don he did not believe that somebody in his right mind would return to the country after successfully clearing himself out into the wide world.

ECA: The New Strategic Directions

ECA had undergone quite a number of changes too. Adebayo Adedeji's term as Undersecretary-general and Executive Secretary of ECA ended in 1991, and he was succeeded by Issa Diallo (1991–1992), and Layashi Yaker (1992–1995). In 1995, Boutros Boutros Ghali appointed Kingsley Amoako to succeed Mr. Yaker as Executive Secretary. As mentioned earlier, following several town hall meetings with ECA staff as well as a series of consultations within the African region, the new Executive Secretary initiated a process of reform and renewal of the Commission which brought about new orientations of the Commission, as outlined in the document "Serving Africa better: Strategic Directions for the Economic Commission for Africa."[79]

With the new orientations, the Commission was to focus on policy analysis and advocacy, enhancing partnerships, technical assistance, communication and knowledge sharing, and supporting subregional activities and regional economic communities. Subsequently, effective January 1996, ECA was restructured into six programs which were expected to enhance the Commission's capacity to serve its African member states better, in line with the new orientations. These programs were: Development Policy and Management, Economic and Social Policy, Gender and Development, Information for Development, Sustainable Development, and Trade and Regional Integration. The in-house discussions on the new strategic vision of the Commission confirmed the relevance of the Subregional Offices (MULPOCs). So they maintained their mandates but were to work closely with the Regional Economic Communities (RECs), UN agencies, and member states.[80]

Thus, based on the new strategic vision, the new Executive Secretary Mr. Amoako made far-reaching changes to ECA's organizational chart effective 1997. The Cabinet Office now comprised the Executive Secretary's and Deputy Executive Secretary's Offices, Program Planning and Coordination Office (PPCO), and the subregional offices (SROs). The new Divisions were Human Resources Management and Finance, Conference and General Services, Economic and Social Policy, Food Security and Sustainable Development, Development Policy and Management, Development Information Services, Trade and Regional Integration, and the African Center for Gender and Development. And most importantly, he introduced a flat management structure into the ECA in which all the sections that existed in the Divisions, within the 1978–1996 structure were abolished together with the positions of 'Head' or 'Chief' of those sections.

Following the withdrawal of FAO some years earlier from the Joint ECA/FAO Agriculture Division at ECA, the Joint Division had been renamed the Agriculture Division. It was in this Agriculture Division that Don assumed duties as the Chief of the Food and Agriculture Policy and Planning Section (FAPPS) in June 1996.

The Division was then focusing on food security sectorally and implementing the outputs due in 1996/97 biennium. Among the issues Don had to work on was the issue of non-conventional food resources that are important for food security. In March 1997, he participated in a symposium on Food Security: A Recipe for Survival, organized by the Lusaka MULPOC in Pretoria, South Africa, from March 18 to 21, 1997. At this meeting, he presented a paper on 'Diversification of Food-Based Sectors: The Contribution of Non-Conventional Food Resources'[81] based on the work he had begun in the work program on arrival back in the Division.

Since the division was now focusing on food security issues, the work aimed at exploring sources of food other than the conventional food commodities, such as food crops, domesticated livestock, and fishery products that would improve the food security especially of rural households. The main economic importance of African forests lies in earnings from the exports of timber. But apart from timber, there are certain forest products that are increasingly being used in certain rural communities in Africa as important sources of food. These nontimber forest products include forest leafy vegetables, spices, fruits, nuts, roots, and forest fauna. The paper examined the contributions that these forest products make to household food security and discussed how their development could enhance food security in those communities.

A Study Tour of New Zealand

Shortly after participating in this meeting and while still serving as Chief of the Food and Agriculture Policy and Planning Section (FAPPS), i.e., before the flat structure was introduced, Don was nominated by the Executive Secretary to represent the ECA in a study tour of New Zealand for West African senior policy and decision makers sponsored by the World Bank on New Zealand's macroeconomic and agriculture sector policy reforms. Following his nomination, ECA sent his passport to Headquarters in New York which sent it to the Australian embassy with a request for the issuance of a visa into Australia and New Zealand to him.

Don arrived at Wellington via Johannesburg, Perth and Melbourne on the afternoon of Saturday, April 12. After clearance by Customs, he and other delegates whom he had met in Johannesburg, were met by the tour leaders, Dr. Veit Burger and Dr. Malcom Bale from the World Bank, and AGRITOUR tour escort Graham Taverner and interpreters Ruth Bourchier and Elaine Bouhyer.

The tour took off with an orientation meeting that evening followed by a dinner that brought together twenty-six senior policy and decision makers from Senegal, Togo, Cote d'Ivoire, Mauritania, Niger, as well as the World Bank and Don himself from ECA. According to the Economic Development Institute (EDI), the goal of the study tour was to support selected West African countries in designing and implementing policies and institutions that are conducive to strong and sustainable rural development. Within this context, the objectives of the tour therefore, were to allow leading 'opinion makers' from participating countries to learn from best practices, and to contemplate the suitability of adopting and adapting New Zealand's reforms for their own countries, the rationale being that first-hand examination of successful reforms and their impacts was more convincing than merely discussing from afar. Furthermore, policy and institutional reforms must be looked at holistically to view how changes in one sector were necessary for, and conditional upon, changes in other sectors.[82]

Among the African countries represented in the tour, only three (Cote d'Ivoire, Senegal, and Togo) had been selected by the program based on the willingness and readiness of their governments to contemplate reform. Participants were senior policy makers from both government and civil society. Participants from Niger, Ethiopia, and Mauritania were observers.[83]

New Zealand's bold experiment with economic policy and public sector management in the 80s had increasingly attracted international attention. The country had faced an economic crisis and decided to adopt a deep and comprehensive economic program of macroeconomic adjustment policy revision and institutional reform. The reform program radically redefined the state's role in economic and social spheres especially in the agriculture sector, where most subsidies were withdrawn overnight and the state quickly took a back seat to the private sector.

The country's 'Big Bang' reform was highly successful particularly in the agriculture sector. This sector emerged as one of the most competitive in the world. The reforms were also said to have increased competitiveness of New Zealand's businesses, brought about low and stable rates of inflation, and led to fiscal surpluses. They also brought about a reduction of the public debt burden and an improvement in public sector performance.

However, not all the effects were beneficial. It has been noted that there was clearly greater income inequality as a result of the reforms as the unemployment rate rose rapidly in the 80s to over 10 percent, a problem which was particularly serious among the Māori and Pacific Islanders whose unemployment rate exceeded 20 percent. A widespread sense of insecurity also emerged regarding social benefits that were thought cast in stone, in particular, old age security, health care, and children's education.[84]

The tour consisted of lectures and discussions on the reforms and a long road trip along the west coast of North Island from Wellington in the south to Auckland in the north during which the participants visited selected farms and orchards.

Beginning with lectures and presentations, they had high-level public and private sector officials and university dons who gave lectures on various aspects of the reform process. These included lectures on the principles and framework of public sector reforms, the importance of public information in managing reforms, and the role of federated farmers in representing farmers' interests and in advising government on agricultural policy. Other lectures were on the structure of agriculture in New Zealand, the reforms in agriculture, and the newly defined role of the Ministry of Agriculture, knowing the market and developing market expertise, and the origin, principles, and design of economic reforms.

But perhaps one of, if not the most, engaging and memorable lecture/presentation was that made by Hon Ruth Richardson, former Minister of Finance on 'Economic Reforms: New Zealand Style'. Her presentation was aimed at inspiring participants to champion for change in their countries. Beginning by arguing that in the face of economic crises in both the developed and developing world, doing nothing was not an option, it was more critical for African governments to do something to accelerate the pace of economic reform or risk missing out on the globalization process as it was a time of both danger and opportunity for Africa.

The lessons from the New Zealand experience were that firstly, leadership was best exercised from the front not from the crowd. Secondly, economic and political responsibility must be institutionalized and thirdly, government must focus on the factors over which it has sovereignty such as the quality of governance. Her final message was her belief that there were no gains from doing reforms slowly. 'Bold is best' and that progress required i) a clear vision, ii) a comprehensive and clear vision for getting there, iii) a shared feeling that it is worth making the effort.[85]

Among the highlights of the visits to the private sector during the road tour were visits to the farm (sheep, pasture, and agroforestry) of Phillipa and Hon John Fallon, former Minister of Agriculture, in Bideford in the Wairapa where the participants had a tour of the farm and had discussions on management and grazing problems as well as on changes in agricultural policy and farming; Pukemarama Farm, a cropping and pasture operation involving mixed sheep-cattle-cropping-forestry-dairy farming in Bulls, Wellington; the farm of Mr. Paul Geurjens, a 120-ha small livestock farm on the Manawatu Plains near Palmerston North where they had a talk on the effects of reforms on small farmers; Te Kouka Farm, an 840-ha farm with sheep, beef cattle and agroforestry owned by Bibby and Tony Plummer; the Red Apple in Hastings, an orchard where they visited the apple packing house. The Participants also visited Diane and Graham Johnstone's 2,000-ha sheep and beef cattle farm with agroforestry in Waikoha Station where the owners discussed the management and financial aspects of sheep and beef farming.

Apart from the farms, the tour also included visits to some of NZ's landmarks on their way. Most remarkable and fascinating were the Huka Falls and the Wairakei geothermal area in Taupo where they had a brief stop. In Rotorua, they had a guided tour of the trout pools, native bush, native fauna, and a tour of the New Zealand Institute of Māori Arts followed by a Māori concert and a Māori 'hangi' dinner.[86]

At the end of the tour, they had two plenary discussions. The first which took place on April 22, was devoted to articulating the key lessons of the New Zealand experience. This session was used to articulate, summarize and prioritize the lessons the participants had learned from the study tour. According to the participants, the most important lessons appear to be the realization that there is a crisis, political will, strong leadership, and government action that is transparent, equitably applied, and credible. The second and final plenary session held on April 23 aimed to develop plans for disseminating and using the knowledge and ideas that had accumulated during the tour. For this exercise, four groups were formed, and each group developed its own ideas. The elements that were common in each plan were then identified.[87]

The tour ended in Auckland on April 23. On April 24, participants took flight QF40 at 06:45 a.m. to Sidney, where they spent the day at Sidney Harbor. As night fell and the rest of the participants took their flight to West Africa via

Perth and Johannesburg, Don boarded a Qantas airline flight to Bangkok (Thailand) en route to Mumbai (Bombay, India) and Addis Ababa.

Left photo, slaughtering a sheep to celebrate Ramadan during the tour.
Right photo, on a cruise at Sydney Harbor.

The Program on Agriculture: A New Orientation
The Nexus of Population, Agriculture, and Environment

The consensus that had emerged during the open space sessions in 1995 and from the consultations regarding the issues of population, agriculture, and environment was that ECA should encourage its African member states to conceptualize them as nexus issues (i.e., holistically) even though their ministries were structured along sectoral lines, in order to optimize the exploitation of each of the three sectors. Addressing the issues of population, agriculture, and environment in a holistic manner, it was believed, would ensure the transition from low- to high-performing agriculture and sustainable food production in the countries. The strategy with regards to population was to encourage the countries to formulate and implement policies and strategies that would accelerate the onset and pace of the demographic transition from larger to smaller family sizes.

In the environment sector, the strategy was to raise awareness among policy makers so they can integrate environmental concerns into their development plans including the reform of the management of the environment. The overall strategy was to assist the various countries of the region to address these issues holistically, i.e., as nexus issues.

With this new orientation in view, the ECA merged its former sectoral programs in agriculture, population, environment, science and technology, human settlements, and water into one program called Food Security and Sustainable Development (FSSD). The mandate of the FSSD Division (FSSDD) was to address, in a holistic and integrated manner, Africa's urgent nexus of population, environment, and agriculture. Population was the center of the nexus, given the profound impact of population on agriculture and the environment.

In order to achieve its mandate, it was suggested that the FSSD Division should concentrate on six issues as guidelines: enhancing national capacity to manage the nexus issues, strengthening population policies, increasing water supply for food production, supporting regional efforts to enhance food security, furthering the advancement of women and keeping an overview of science and technology development as it relates to nexus issues. However, there were many uncertainties as regards how to address the nexus. Principal among them was how to define the nexus or bring its three components together in a manner that they could be subjected to analysis so as to be able to determine quantitatively, how changes in one of the components affect the others and in particular, the incidence of poverty. Also, how was the Division to be organized to deal with the nexus?

With the abolition of sections and section chiefs in the Divisions as indicated above, FSSDD constituted three teams to work collectively in drafting an issues paper on the interlinkages between agriculture, environment, and population. Mr. Ousmane Laye was Team Leader of the Environment Team, Mr. Oben was Team Leader of the Agriculture Team, and Mr. Ita Ekanem headed the Population Team. Mrs. Paulina Adebusoye was recruited later in 1997 by Mr. Amoako to head the new division and in that capacity had the responsibility of coordinating the work of the division.

The issues paper was aimed at laying a new foundation or basic framework on which to base FSSDD's nexus programs. The Division sought to enrich this paper as well as its comprehension of the nexus issues by engaging in consultations and exchange of views with ECA development partners at nexus-related conferences, meetings, and workshops. Among the major partners was the World Bank which was noted for its earlier activities in food security. Eminent individuals in selected member states were brought into the conversation. The ideas which emanated from the consultations with the World

Bank and the other partners were quite useful in enabling the FSSDD to better conceptualize the nexus approach. It was also important for the division to know the extent to which the interlinkages between population, environment and agriculture were understood and utilized by African member countries as a basis for formulating and implementing action plans being put in place toward fostering food security and sustainable development.

The division thus undertook missions to eleven countries in Africa namely Cameroon, Chad, and Gabon in Central Africa; Tanzania and Uganda in East Africa; Namibia, Zimbabwe, and Zambia in Southern Africa; and Cote d'Ivoire, Gambia, and Senegal in West Africa. From the findings of the missions, virtually all the countries visited acknowledged the existence of the interlinkages between the population, environment, and agriculture sectors and the interlinked nature of the problems between these sectors. However, the national action plans that were put in place at the time by the governments were conceptualized sectorally and therefore had not taken into consideration their interlinked nature.

The PEDA Model

The issues paper which had been prepared by the Division provided the framework for building human and institutional capacities to develop programs for managing the transition from extensive to intensive land use (agricultural transition), large to smaller family sizes (demographic transition) and degradation to conservation of the environment (environmental transition). Such knowledge was used in developing a powerful advocacy tool in the form of a computer simulation model for comprehending the interlinkages between population change (P), environmental factors (E), socioeconomic development (D) and agriculture (A), or simply PEDA. (See the theoretical underpinning of the PEDA below). This computer model could serve to raise policy makers' awareness in the countries about the urgency to achieve poverty reduction.

The Division followed the issues paper with a study and prepared two reports in December 1997 on 'Facilitating the Demographic Transition in Africa: Issues and Challenges'; Vol. I: Main Report and Vol II: Case Studies of Selected Anglophone Countries: Botswana, Egypt, Mauritius, and Nigeria.

With the assistance of a consultant from the International Institute for Applied Systems Analysis (IIASA), FSSDD successfully developed the PEDA model for about twelve African countries. This model was based on the theoretical construction, often labeled the 'vicious circle model', and became an influential paradigm in the discussion around population, poverty, food security, and sustainable development. It essentially assumes that high fertility, poverty, low education, and status of women are bound up in a web. An illustration of this mechanism is the parable of firewood (Nerlove, 1991). In many countries, the collection of firewood takes a lot of time, and more children can help to collect more firewood. But this leads to less firewood near the villages, increasing degradation of the natural resource and the desire for more children to go help in collecting firewood from greater distances, thereby also depriving children of educational opportunities.

The PEDA Model[88] was an interactive computer simulation model (developed for Microsoft Windows) demonstrating the medium- to long-term impacts of alternative national policies on the food security status of the population. Through the manipulation of scenario variables, the model enables the user to project the proportion of the population that will be food secure and food insecure for a chosen point in time. As food security is a factor of development in the field of population, agriculture, environment and socioeconomic development, the model demonstrates the relationships between these fields as well.[89]

With the development of the PEDA Model, the immediate goal of the Division was to raise the awareness of policy makers in member states about the urgency of the need to conceptualize in an integrated manner, food, population, and environment concerns into their development plans. In addition, it was important for the Division to offer them, to the extent possible, feasible solutions drawn from best practices in this regard within and outside the region. The Division now began to use the model as an advocacy tool by practically demonstrating the possible impacts of population, agriculture, and environment on each other. The member states were thus empowered to estimate the incidence of their poverty level as a prelude to formulating policies to address the nexus issues and their impacts on poverty.

In many conferences, workshops, and meetings of ECA's intergovernmental bodies, that followed the development of the model, FSSDD staff presented the PEDA model. For example, Don presented it as a new approach in ensuring food security and sustainable development in Southern Africa at the Fifth Meeting of the Intergovernmental Committee of the SRDC-SA held in Lusaka, Zambia from October 5 to 8.[90]

In his presentation, he introduced the PEDA model to the participants emphasizing that 'food security status' must be considered when discussing sustainable development indicators. The PEDA model clearly illustrates that the food security status of the population is dependent on evolutions in the different development related sectors, i.e., population, the environment, agriculture, and education. He stressed the potential of PEDA as an advocacy tool with the major objective of the model being to illustrate the magnitude of the relationships between the different variables in the model and the kind of interactions at hand between the different sectors covered by it.

It was therefore not to be conceived as a short-term econometric planning tool, the reason why a number of variables had been left out to keep the model simple and comprehensible for a broad public, including policy makers. Following this introduction, he carried out some projections and discussed the outputs of the simulation exercise. This was followed by long and enriching discussions during which participants sought clarifications, and he provided the answers.

While still focusing attention on awareness-raising on the nexus issues using the PEDA Model, the Division was also responding to invitations from relevant organizations and partners to contribute to their activities in the area of food security and sustainable development. It was in this connection that Don undertook a mission to Bamako, Mali, to attend and represent the ECA at Workshop 99: The Food Chain in Sub-Saharan Africa: Linking Farmers to Markets held from October 14 to 19, 1999. This huge workshop was organized by the Center for Applied Studies in International Negotiations, Geneva, and sponsored by the Sasakawa Global 2000.

Its aims were firstly, to identify ways and means to overcome some of the bottlenecks and constraints (scarcity of infrastructure, especially in transport and travel systems, telecommunications, rural energy and electric power, lack of sufficient modern processing facilities, incompletely developed input and output markets systems, etc.) which constituted major obstacles in the transformation of small holder African farmers into commercial food producers. Secondly, it aimed to examine the required public policies, sources of funding including private investments, the role of farmers' associations and communities in the overall process of rural development, with focus on rural transport, access to inputs, food processing, and marketing.[91]

The workshop was attended by eminent personalities from Africa and other parts of the world associated with Sasakawa 2000 activities. They included former President Jimmy Carter and Rosalyn Carter, President Oumar Koumare of Mali, former President Amadou Toumani Toure of Mali and former President Neciphore Soglo of the Republic of Benin. The President of Nippon Foundation, Tokyo, and Chairperson of Sasakawa Foundation, Ms. Ayako Sono also attended the meeting as well as the Ministers of Agriculture of Mali, Ethiopia, and Uganda, and the former Minister of Agriculture of Ghana and the Deputy Minister of Agriculture of Malawi. The Special Adviser on food security to the president of Nigeria represented the president. Many representatives from the World Bank, African Development Bank, Club du Sahel, World Food Program, the Intergovernmental Committee for Combating Drought in the Sahel (CILLS), the International Fertilizer Development Center (IFDC), Lome, the Carter Foundation, Sasakawa Peace Foundation and representatives from the ministries of agriculture and Sasakawa country offices in some African countries also attended the meeting.

The workshop was organized into seven plenary sessions and six task forces. Field trips were also organized in five groups during the weekend to enable participants see some of the advances achieved in agricultural production by farmers assisted by the Sasakawa Global 2000, the Ministry of Agriculture, and the national research institutions in sorghum and millet, sugar cane, rice and maize, and cotton.

The Task Forces were devoted to in-depth discussions, analyses, and recommendations in the following areas: the sustainability of food production; policies to be implemented; strengthening rural transports and travel systems: lessons, institutions and policies; improving the functioning of input and output markets; and developing and investing in modern food processing systems. Recommendations were also made in the areas of rural transport and travel systems, improvement of the functioning of input and output markets, and development and investment in modern food processing systems.

Edward Schuh, Regents Professor, University of Minnesota provided a summary of the workshop proceedings. While acknowledging and thanking participants for the intensive work done and the meaningful discussions and exchange of experiences during the exhausting five days of the meeting, he addressed the big question of 'where to go after Bamako'. Placing the workshop in the context of Adam Smith's work on the Wealth of Nations in

296

1776, he expounded on the benefits of international trade, the specialization of labor, and the raising of productivity in the process of economic development. These benefits underscored the market and the role of transportation in linking farmers to the markets which was the subject of the workshop, stressing the revolutions occurring in modern transportation. Also drawing attention to the fact that communications and information systems have drastically reduced the cost of global trade, he identified the main implications of the discussions and recommendations of the workshop for transportation and the linking of farmers to markets.

In conclusion, Prof. Schuh underlined the fact that Africa must take control and the lead in bringing the implementation of the recommendation made and decisions taken at the meeting. Its partners such as Sasakawa Global 2000 and the World Bank and others can only act in a supporting role.

The benefits of the workshop to Don and the ECA were several: the workshop provided an important opportunity for Don to revisit and experience Sahelian agricultural production and research and to better understand the activities of Sasakawa Global 2000 in increasing agricultural productivity and providing the missing link between farmers and markets. Don provided a subregional and regional perspective to most of the discussions which tended to be national-oriented, and it enabled him to meet and discuss with participants and provide ECA's perspective and approach in addressing the issue of food security in Africa. He was also able to collect important documentation on the crucial issues discussed at the workshop. These and the knowledge gained from the discussions and field trips were to him invaluable for a better analysis of Sahelian agricultural development issues in the future.

As emphasized earlier, the use of the PEDA in raising awareness continued to take center stage in the work of the Division. In meetings and workshops at which the model was presented, participants raised almost similar concerns or asked for further clarifications. For instance in one workshop, they asked for further clarifications on the treatment of the different variables in the model (e.g., on the treatment of water, fertilizer and machinery use, and education) and the level of analysis; the availability of reliable data and aspects that were not taken into account by the model such as livestock and fisheries, land tenure systems, international migration and remittances, international trade, the effect of climate changes and population-land dynamics in urban areas.

Regarding the data, it was pointed out that in its present format, the PEDA model used internationally available data and further relied on some estimations because some of the needed data were simply not available. The ECA intended to support initiatives that would collect relevant and adequate data at the national level for its application. The structure of the model was, however, flexible enough to allow for a customization of the model to similar situations or specific countries. This had, in fact, been done for Ethiopia, Cameroon, and Botswana.[92]

Don was the team leader of the Agriculture Transition Team and afterward, head of the Advocacy and Awareness Raising Team within the FSSDD during the in-house brainstorming and the meetings and consultations with partners in the search for a conceptual framework on which to build the synergies between population, environment, and agriculture interactions. He provided professional and technical leadership and guided the contribution of the two teams during the period when the new division was grappling with the huge problem of developing PEDA. And he continued in this capacity afterward when it was being disseminated as an advocacy tool to demonstrate the new integrated approach to tackling the problems of food security, i.e., the medium- to long-term impacts of alternative national policies on the food security status of the population. And at each meeting or workshop where he or other colleagues presented PEDA, they noted issues raised by participants with a view to further enabling the Division to improve on the model.

In 2000, two years after presenting the PEDA Model in Lusaka, Zambia, he attended, on behalf of the ECA Secretariat, the 6th Meeting of the Intergovernmental Committee of the SRDC-SA in Windhoek, Namibia, which was held from April 11 to 12, 2000 where he again presented the model under Agenda Item 7a: Impact of Population, Environment and Agriculture (PEDA) Model on Different Policy Options in Relation to Food Security. In his preliminary remarks, he underlined the mission of ECA which was to ensure food security and promote sustainable development in Africa which was why FSSDD had planned a critical program to raise policymakers' awareness of the urgency of food, population, and environment concerns in development planning and the need for integrated planning.

The negative synergy arising from high and rapid population growth, food insecurity, and environmental degradation posed immense challenges which needed to be addressed in order to achieve these objectives. It was in this context that the ECA with the assistance of the International Institute For Applied Systems Analysis (IISA) had developed the PEDA Model, a user friendly, interactive computer model for the analysis of population, environment, and agriculture interactions. The model which he was now to present, focused on the vicious cycle of poverty, illiteracy, high fertility, land degradation, and food insecurity and quantitatively operationalizes the vicious cycle and possible ways to break out of it.

After explaining the data requirements of the model which included demographic, agricultural production, land and water, food losses, food exports and imports as well as food distribution data, he used a prototype model developed for Burkina Faso to demonstrate the long-term implications of alternative policy scenarios for the food security status of eight population subgroups defined according to age, sex, education, and place of residence. At this stage, only a prototype of PEDA had been developed. However, it had been initialized for six countries and for real applications, local experts needed to fill the model with the best empirical information available for their countries.

During the discussions on the presentation, the Committee commended the ECA secretariat for the excellent presentation of the model and ECA for developing the model as an advocacy tool. It was suggested that the model should be able to accommodate differences among countries with respect to drought conditions, soils, prices of agricultural inputs and outputs, rural-urban migration and the over- or under-use of technological innovations which can affect food security.

To this suggestion, Don explained that rural-urban and external and internal migration had been incorporated in the model because the demographic and transition intensities estimated for the starting period as well as the assumed trends over the projection period took into account changes in migration and other demographic variables. He also emphasized the flexible nature of the model that enabled the user to put in data and make assumptions which reflect the situation in the country he/she is dealing with. In fact, this was the purpose of initializing the model for different countries.[93]

This meeting was dove-tailed into a subregional workshop on National Information and Communication Infrastructure in Southern Africa (NICI) from April 13 to 14, 2000.

ECA and FSSDD: The Last Years

In the years that followed the building of PEDA, the various teams individually or collectively prepared papers and reports on food security and poverty, based on the nexus of population, agriculture, and environment, for presentation at meetings and workshops to raise awareness on these issues. Among the papers Don prepared included two that were entitled, 'Poverty, Food Security, and Environmental Linkages: Policy Challenges in Selected Environmentally Fragile Areas in Africa'[94] and 'Sustainable Food Production and Food Security in the Sahelian Countries: Some Key Issues And Policy Challenges'.[95]

Another important development in FSSDD was the constitution of two Advisory Boards for the Division in 1999. These were the Advisory Board on Population, Agriculture, and Environment and the Advisory Board on Science and Technology. These boards were made up of eminent persons and experts appointed in their personal capacities with a mandate to bring their expertise to bear on the work of ECA. They were to assist the FSSD Division in ensuring that its work program remained relevant to the needs of member states by identifying burning issues in food security in Africa and making recommendations as to how they could best be integrated into the work program of the Division. They also provided inputs into ways and means whereby the Division could enhance the quality and delivery of its outputs.

At the first meeting of the advisory boards, for example, among other preoccupations, some of these developmental issues were tabled and the Board reviewed some of FSSDD's programs as well as PEDA, its advocacy tool created to promote holistic development planning. At the second meeting, the Boards were invited to make suggestions on critical emerging issues pertaining to food security and sustainable development in Africa in the twenty-first century and what implications these may have on FSSDD's proposed work program for the biennium, 2002–2003. They also reviewed draft documents prepared by the Division which constituted the Division's outputs for 2000 and 2001 so that the Division could receive suggestions for their improvement.

Don was appointed the Coordinator of the Advisory Board on Population, Agriculture and Environment. In this capacity, he convened annual meetings of the Board. These included the first meeting held on September 20–21, 1999, the second one held from October 24 to 26, 2000, and right up to 2003.

He also organized and coordinated ad hoc expert group meetings. These meetings were attended by high-level experts and practitioners in the field of food security invited in their personal capacities as well as experts from relevant United Nations agencies and subregional and regional institutions to examine food security issues affecting the region. The meetings were usually formally opened by the director of the division after brief welcome remarks by Don as the coordinator of the meetings.

The division's collaboration with two of ECA's partners is worth mentioning. With the World Bank, the Division collaborated in its Institute's Distance Learning Program on Poverty. Don served as a facilitator for the World Bank Institute (WBI) Distance Learning Rural Development Courses on, a) Attacking Rural Poverty for Anglophone Africa from May 16 to June 27, 2001 and b) Rural Poverty Reduction through Food Security and Agricultural Growth for Anglophone Africa from November 14 to December 19, 2001.

The other collaboration was with the FAO in its Forestry Outlook Study for Africa (FOSA). FOSA aimed to provide a long-term perspective for the development of the forestry sector in African countries within the context of wider economic, social, institutional and technological changes to the year 2020 by analyzing the trends and emerging economic, social and political forces that will shape the sector during the next two decades. Based on this analysis, it was to identify the policy, program, and investment options necessary to enhance its contribution to sustainable socioeconomic development.

FOSA was designed to complement African countries' other forestry-related strategic planning initiatives including national forest programs. In cognizance of the fact that some of the previous strategic planning frameworks had not been successful because they had been donor-driven and implemented within Overseas Development Assistance packages, FOSA was designed to be participatory, owned and driven by the African countries themselves. It promoted the participation of the private sector and communities in African forestry. In this way, the expectation was that FOSA would reinvigorate the interest by donors and other stakeholders including policy makers in the further development of the African forestry sector anchored around the domains of poverty reduction and environmental management. The forestry outlook study for Africa also recognized and lay stress on the potential of African forests as sources of livelihoods for the poor in the continent.[96]

Don served as ECA's focal point for this study. During the study, a number of reports were produced, the most important being five Subregional Outlook Reports and a Regional Overview. It was considered that the assessment of options for future development and defining a vision for African forestry should be an inclusive process evolving from the country level. It was also considered that the subregional and regional overview reports needed to be scrutinized to ensure that all relevant issues were taken into account. For these reasons, a Final Technical Review Meeting was hosted by ECA in Addis Ababa, Ethiopia from September 17 to 19, 2001. This final technical review meeting was organized by FSSDD and coordinated by Don as the FOSA focal point at ECA.

The objective of the meeting was to i) undertake an in-depth technical review of the five subregional and regional FOSA outlook reports specifically ensuring that all critical issues relevant to the future development of the sector were fully taken into account, and ii) exchange ideas concerning the long-term prospects of forestry development in Africa and to articulate a shared vision of the various options available for positive changes. This meeting was the final technical meeting in the FOSA process before presenting the reports for endorsement at the 15th Session of the Near East Forestry Commission and the 13th Session of the African Forestry and Wildlife Commission held in January and March 2002, respectively.

As the FOSA focal point at ECA, Don also participated at the 13th Session of the African Forestry and Wildlife Commission convened in Libreville, Gabon, from March 25 to 29, 2002 at which the reports were presented for endorsement. The reports provided a good overview of the situation prevailing in the forestry sector at the regional and subregional levels. They elaborated on the main driving forces, the possible scenarios, their implications for key aspects of forestry and wildlife and the priorities and strategies for enhancing the contribution of forestry to sustainable development in Africa. Specifically, the reports took note of the opportunities emerging in the context of the New Partnership for Africa's Development (NEPAD) and indicated the nature of interventions required for forestry to contribute significantly to the objectives of poverty alleviation and environmental protection.

In endorsing the reports, the Commission highlighted aspects that needed to be given added attention in the reports. These included mechanisms for enhancing funding for sustainable forest management; cultural dimension of forests and their implications for the future use of forests; the need for strengthening regional and subregional cooperation and collaboration especially as regards improving human resources; the potential for intra-African trade in forest products particularly in view of the enormous demand from the subregion; the potential for eco-tourism; and the processing of non-wood forest products. The reports also needed to emphasize some of the recent positive developments in African forestry and provide an indication of the opportunities for moving into a positive scenario.

Beside the in-session seminar held on the Forestry Outlook Study for Africa, three side meetings were also held during the 13th Session. These were on i) Sustainable forest management and reduced impact forest logging in Africa, ii) Wood energy and forest conservation, and iii) The contribution of wildlife resources to poverty alleviation. The African Development Bank was called to chair the FOSA In-Session Seminar while the ECA represented by Don, was called upon to chair the meeting on energy and forest conservation.[97]

Aside from the developments in the Division's work program, Don and other ECA staffers had the privilege of welcoming Kofi Annan to ECA in the last years at the ECA during his visit to Ethiopia.

Above, Secretary-General Kofi Annan's visit to ECA: Don first from right.

Outside of FSSDD's work program, Don and Dorothy continued their quest to attain proficiency in the French language. Before their arrival in Addis, their plan was to sit for the placement test as soon as possible on arrival and get enrolled in a class appropriate to their knowledge of the language in the language training program at ECA. In the second week of their arrival, Don went to see the coordinator of the French language courses in his office. He greeted him, introduced himself and narrated their experiences in the language training program in Tangier as well as life generally in Morocco. Don did not realize that they had been conversing in French until the coordinator told him at the end of their conversation that his language skills were such that he would exempt him from the placement test and just register him in the proficiency class. That was how Don was enrolled to continue his French language training on his return to ECA.

In 1999, the French government gave about eight scholarships to ECA for a one-month intensive French language course in France. These scholarships were managed by the French language coordinator's office on behalf of ECA in collaboration with the French embassy in Addis Ababa. Only candidates in the proficiency class were deemed qualified to compete for these eight scholarships. Those in the proficiency class were numerically far more than the number of scholarships hence competition was intense. As had been the case in previous years, selection was through an examination—both written and oral, with the first eight candidates in order of merit being the successful candidates. Don did well and was selected to participate in the one-month intensive French language course at the 'Center Audio-visuel de Royan pour l'Etudes de Langues' (CAREL), Royan, France, in August 1999. After fulfilling all the visa requirements, they left for Paris and thence to Royan in the southwest of France.

CAREL was a huge audiovisual language center of the University of Poitiers, Royan, France. There they met hundreds of other students and people who had come from various parts of the world for French language courses. They were to learn that the Audiovisual Center of Royan for Language Study was founded in 1966 by the Town of Royan and the University of Poitiers. It offered intensive language programs and immersion courses in German, English, Spanish, French as a foreign language and French as a native language both for French and foreign students. It also offered a multitude of programs and courses of instruction including intensive, immersive, evening classes, summer holiday courses, etc.

They arrived at CAREL on a Friday and spent the weekend sorting out their accommodation, collecting information packages, and taking part in small guided tours to acquaint themselves with the facilities and services of the center. The 'preliminaries' over, the center organized a large placement test on the Monday following the weekend. They must have been nearly a thousand students. Based on the results of the test, they were placed in different module levels. Don with many other ECA staff members were placed in the Advanced Level class which was the fifth out of seven levels of language study at the center in ascending order.

The program was really intensive and was divided into two sessions, the first from August 2 to 13, 1999, and the second from August 16 to 27, 1999. They had lessons on a wide range of French subjects especially French culture and civilization. They would watch television news and afterward recall and discuss all the news items they had seen and listened to. They were exposed to, and they discussed, French cuisine and restaurants, French literature and newspapers, travel, and they watched clips on various aspects of French life especially life in Paris through the years. They wrote essays and often made oral and video presentations in class. From the moment they arrived in Royan, all their conversations, even among themselves from Addis Ababa, were in French.

During the inter-sessional break, a guided tour was arranged for them and other participants to interesting sites in and around Royan from August 14 to 15. This was the only period when they had time to relax and really feel free because throughout the session, they had classes during the day and home work/assignments on most nights. They visited sightseeing and tourist attractions including wineries, Marché Central de Royan, an aquarium, museums, and churches.

They had two examinations, one at the end of the first session and a second examination at the end of the second session. In each examination, they were examined in the following competences: Expression Orale, Expression écrite, Compréhension orale, Compréhension écrite, and Orthographe Grammaire. At the end of the course on August 27, 1999, Don was issued an 'Attestation de Stage' by the University of Poitiers, Royan, France. His 'Rapport Pedagogique' shows that he scored 'Bien' or B in Expression orale and 'Très Bien' or A in all the other four areas of competence.

Don making a short video project presentation at CAREL, Royan, France.

The Cameroon Community in Ethiopia

Outside of ECA, Don's activities in Addis Ababa cannot be complete without mentioning his role within the Cameroon community in Ethiopia. At that time, apart from the Cameroon embassy staff, all the Cameroonians living in Ethiopia were professionals and experts working either with the OAU, ECA, UN agencies or in subregional and nongovernmental organizations. Almost all these people got into these organizations through their own efforts and were therefore in Ethiopia in their own right. Although they attended embassy functions and maintained a good relationship with the Cameroon embassy in Ethiopia, they did so not out of any political obligation but out of love for country. Members of the community maintained good friendships with one another.

However, sometime in 1998, the idea of Cameroonians in Ethiopia coming together formally to form an association was mooted by H.E. Mbea Mbea, the Ambassador. This suggestion seemed to go well within the Cameroon community in Addis Ababa which seemed also to feel the need to strengthen solidarity among all its members and to promote the image of Cameroon. Thus, on October 24, 1998, the community decided to form an association referred to as the Cameroon Community in Ethiopia herein after referred to as the

'Community'. Membership was open to all Cameroonian nationals living in Ethiopia who agreed to abide by the guidelines of the association.

The Community comprised the following organs: the General Assembly (GA), the Executive Bureau, and the Advisory Committee. The GA, which was the supreme organ, was composed of all members of the association. The Bureau which was the executive organ of the Community was to be elected by the GA for a two-year renewable term and comprised the President, Vice President, Secretary-general with an Assistant, Social Affairs Officer with an Assistant, Cultural Affairs Officer, Public Relations Officer, Treasurer with an Assistant, and an Auditor. The Advisory Committee (committee of 'Wise Men and Women'), on the other hand, comprised three members elected by the GA for a two-year term. Its function was to advise the Executive Bureau and act as a mediator between members of the association in case of dispute or misunderstanding. There was also an Honorary President, a position reserved for the head of the Cameroon diplomatic mission in Ethiopia.[98]

The election of the first Bureau in October 1998 was hotly contested. The Ambassador who had first mooted the idea of the Community was nursing the hope of the Community being under the strong control of the Embassy. Hence, he seriously supported and campaigned for the embassy presidential candidate. Unfortunately, Don was elected instead of his candidate, with a landslide. But the Secretary-general came from the embassy with an assistant from the OAU. Members of the Executive Bureau and the Advisory Committee were to carry out their duties on a voluntary basis.

At the time of the establishment of the association, there were about thirty-five families in the community. After the elections, Don convened several meetings of the Bureau at which they brainstormed and developed guidelines which they put forward to the GA for discussion and adoption. It similarly established the functions of the various positions in the Bureau which were also approved by the GA. He convened and presided over all GA meetings. The enormity of the duties of the President was not obvious to Don until he took office. Bringing together Cameroonians for a common purpose, which was not central to their existence in Ethiopia, was not easy especially as some of them were big bosses in their organizations.

The Terms of Reference of the President which included drawing up the agenda of the GA meetings, convening and presiding over all such meetings, implementing the policies and decisions of the GA, and submitting proposals on issues considered important to the growth of the association, did not reflect this enormity.

In reality, the President was like a servant to the Community—everybody's keeper. The Presidency was voluntary and hence his work was unremunerated. It was common for him to be called even at the unholy hours of the morning to attend to a sick member taken to the hospital or a dead member in a mortuary or to intervene in a misunderstanding between two members or even between couples. And it was even more common for the president to be called in times of crisis even before the ambassador. Don would also often stop by or visit members in their homes just to see how they were doing. In fact, he made it a point to know where each family lived and to visit community members as regularly as possible.

In all this, he was assisted by a dedicated Bureau which worked silently, circulating information about members like when they were sick or bereaved, sending delegations to visit members on such occasions, extending financial support to members as required by the association's guidelines, mobilizing the community for various activities and expressing solidarity as was the case with the Late King Ondoua, an interpreter/translator based in Kenya but who died in Addis Ababa. The solidarity shown by the Community in this case right from the time he was admitted into hospital in Addis to the time of his death was exemplary. The association also organized receptions for visiting Cameroonian teams and met visiting Ministers and officials from Cameroon whenever possible. Thus, by the end of the first two years when Don's term of office was ending, there was increased solidarity, cohesiveness, understanding and love among members of the Community.

Although the term of office of the first Executive Bureau expired on October 2000, elections were not held until June 2001 in spite of efforts made in this connection. After two and half years in office, the GA finally met on June 17, 2001 for elections into the organs of the association. In remarks after the presentation of his report, Don thanked the Community for the excellent cooperation he had enjoyed, and the 'Committee of Wise Men' and the Bureau, for their hard work and dedication. Many Bureau members had worked long and hard. He very much urged these members to accept to serve in the next Executive if they were nominated. Don also mentioned that a few Bureau members had fallen far short of expectation and he hoped that, for the good of the Community, they would not accept nomination to serve again. He told the General Assembly:

"The work of the Bureau requires a lot of personal sacrifice. As you elect the next Bureau to carry on the work of the Community, I enjoin you to elect only those whom you know are committed because service in the Bureau involves commitment and self-sacrifice. Let me say that I have devoted these last two and a half years trying to ensure that the association is built on a strong foundation. I am confident that with the cooperation and support of the Bureau and all of you, we have succeeded. I will not seek re-election for a second term as I strongly believe that every member should have the opportunity of serving the Community..."

It was not just because others needed to be given the opportunity to serve. Combining his work at ECA which often involved lots of missions, and his family life, with the work of the Community was unsustainable.

Surprisingly, when the post of President came up for consideration, not even one member had presented his or her candidacy for the post. Members of the GA were therefore asked to make nominations for the presidency. Still surprising, each member nominated declined. Then a member stood up and proposed that Don be re-elected for a second term and he implored that he (Don) should please accept the nomination. Don honestly did not see it coming. Instantaneously, the GA rose to their feet clapping and shouting his name. In such an atmosphere and with the urging of members, Don couldn't decline. Thus, he was re-elected by acclamation for a second two-year term which began in June 2001. Most of his former Bureau members—those who had served with devotion—were re-elected. Members of the Advisory Committee were also elected.

During the second term, they built on the experience they had gained during the first term. By November 2003, when the term of the Bureau came to an end, the list of their accomplishments was long. The number of activities which the Bureau had undertaken included organizing meetings, special events, condolence visits to members, dissemination of information on Cameroon, widening and deepening the association's revenue base and making amendments to the constitution.

Concerning the dissemination of information on Cameroon, while the association served to disseminate information on developments in the country from the embassy, for example, the laws creating the National Election

Observatory in Cameroon, the role of the association was not to substitute the Embassy neither was it to be seen as an arm of the Embassy. Consequently, the Bureau later thought it wise that the Embassy should communicate such information directly to Cameroonians resident in Ethiopia, some of whom were not members of the association. The Bureau also held a joint working meeting with the Ambassador and his staff to prepare for the expected visit of the President of the Republic and his wife to Ethiopia that had been scheduled for January 2003. The visit did not materialize.

The Bureau widened and deepened the revenue base by pursuing an aggressive membership enrollment policy and revenue collection measures. As a result of their aggressive revenue collection measures, the funds in the account of the association by November 2003 was three times what it was at the beginning of the second term. During the period, they welcomed many new members including Madam Elizabeth Tankeu, a former Assistant Minister of Economy and Plan who joined the African Union Commission as Commissioner for Trade and Industry.

The special events which included end-of-year parties and a number of send-off parties for departing members and to which Leaders of other communities in Addis Ababa such as the Nigerian and Ghanaian Communities were invited, gave the association a lot of visibility. They also served as tools to foster their good relations with these other communities. Some of the events were held at the Embassy Residence but many others were hosted at the residences of the President and some members.

The account of the successes registered by the Association should not be misconstrued to mean that it was all smooth sailing. The Association experienced some difficulties which impeded to some extent, it's functioning. These included the departure of the Secretary-general, and difficulties of holding GA meetings regularly due to a lack of quorum since most members were always on the move and many had to be reminded constantly. These difficulties notwithstanding, the President and his Bureau discharged their mandate honorably. They helped in keeping the Cameroon Community spirit alive and promoting the spirit of a great Cameroonian family, made up of brothers and sisters who shared their joys and sorrows together. The number of events organized, the number of visits made to members and the financial record of the association were proof of the dedication with which members of the Bureau took their roles which, as has been repeatedly mentioned, were essentially voluntary. In fact, the Community was doing so well that other Communities in Addis Ababa often contacted it to study how the Cameroon Community functioned with a view to organizing theirs along its lines.

On November 23, 2003, Don stepped down as President of the Cameroon Community in Ethiopia after serving a second term of two years. In fact, he had been President since the Association was founded and from the look of things if he was not retiring from the ECA and therefore preparing to leave Addis Ababa and Ethiopia, he might have been forced to remain in office by acclamation. It would have been difficult for him to accept such a proposition as he is not an advocate of 'presidencies for life'. Serving such a community of diverse, highly educated, highly placed, and well-respected personalities as President for five and a half years, was an honor and a privilege. He will always treasure the enriching experience he gained from his tenure, the enormous demands made on him notwithstanding.

Preparing for Retirement

Don turned sixty on May 16, 2003. Retirement is mandatory at the age of sixty for staff members within the UN Secretariat appointed before January 1, 1990 and sixty-two for those appointed on or after January 1, 1990. They retire at the end of the month in which they turn sixty or sixty-two whichever is the case. Thus, Don was due retirement on May 31, 2003 when he turned sixty. In January 2003, he received a letter[99] from the Human Resources Section notifying him of his upcoming retirement and thanking him, on behalf of the Executive Secretary, for the services he had rendered to the United Nations and more specifically, to the Commission since August 29, 1982. To assist him in making preparations for final clearance, he was provided the necessary information for his guidance as they affect his emoluments and entitlements.

However, not long afterward, at the recommendation of the new Director of the Division and supported by the Executive Secretary, his contract was extended by UN Headquarters for six months up to November 30, 2003 due to exigencies of duty. This was at a time when very few contracts were extended. He still had some important unfinished assignments to complete including the convening of the Annual Meeting of the Advisory Board on Population, Agriculture, and Environment, in the latter part of the year.

When Don turned sixty, his dear wife, Dorothy, and his children decided to give him a surprise birthday party. Lorraine, their second daughter, flew in from the US and Vanessa, the fourth arrived from London just about that time. Don's understanding was that they had both come to visit. These two and their mother and Valentina, the last daughter who was still with them in Addis, arranged a huge party with music and all, silently and craftily under his very nose and he did not know it. Invitations were sent out to their foreign and Ethiopian friends and they were asked to keep the information secret from Don.

Once when Don suspected something was happening, Dorothy told him that she was arranging just a small meeting for their church group at their home and she was going to let Don know. Keeping the party a secret nearly backfired. On that day, since Don did not want to get in the way of the 'small meeting' of her church group, he decided to remain in their bedroom upstairs all day after breakfast working on the computer and occasionally watching TV. His lunch was brought up to him there. Just before the party was to start, Dorothy came up to him and said she would like him to join the group as the meeting was over. Don didn't see the need so he did not go down. The problem came when guests started arriving and the celebrant was nowhere to be seen.

To cut a long story short, when Don came down wearing the birthday outfit Dorothy had made for him, some of his friends including his director were climbing up the staircase to come get him. As soon as they saw Don, the 'Happy Birthday' song rose from the guests. It was a huge party, almost ethereal. Don will never forget the element of surprise that ushered it. It was astonishing!

Cutting the Cake: left to right: Lorraine, Don, Dorothy, Valentina, and Vanessa.

Three years earlier in 2000, they had celebrated their twenty-fifth (silver) wedding anniversary. Again, it was Dorothy who initiated it and made most of the arrangements. Initially intended to be hosted in the banquet hall of the Addis Ababa Hilton, they later changed the venue to the garden and grounds of a reserved restaurant on Bole Road. It was organized as an open-air party with canopies set up on the grounds to accommodate the more than two hundred guests they had invited. Small woodfires which kept burning throughout the night and kept the guests warm in the cool night breeze, gave the party a uniqueness, an allure.

The large hall was reserved for dancing. A big banquet followed the speeches and dancing followed the banquet. The party went on all night and guests almost danced their legs off. On this occasion, only Valentina was with them to celebrate the anniversary. Although they threw many parties during those days, these two parties, the silver wedding anniversary party and Don's sixtieth birthday party were their greatest and most memorable, both in significance and scope.

They hosted a lot of luncheons and dinners too especially for friends and fellow compatriots who came to Addis Ababa for meetings and conferences. But the dinner Don and his wife organized early in his UN career in late 1983 needs particular mention. It was a dinner they hosted for three eminent personalities who had each played a prominent role during Don's journey. They were Prof. Q.B.O Anthonio, Prof. Alex McCalla, and Dr. William Gamble. Prof. Q.B.O. Anthonio was Don's professor and head of department at the University of Ibadan in the late 60s and was at this time, the director of his division at ECA—the Joint ECA/FAO Agriculture Division. Alex McCalla, a professor of Agricultural Economics was Don's academic adviser when he was a graduate student at the University of California at Davis and was at this time, the chairman of CGIAR's Technical Advisory Committee (TAC).

Dr. William Gamble was the Ford Foundation Representative for West Africa when Don was awarded a Ford Fellowship to study for his Ph. D. degree. He later became the Director-general of the International Institute of Tropical Agriculture, Ibadan, Nigeria, at the time Don got a position at the Institute as a Post-doctoral Fellow/Agricultural Economist after his graduate study. He was at this time, the Director-general of the International Service for National Agricultural Research (ISNAR) in the Hague, Netherlands. Both

Alex McCalla and William Gamble were in Addis Ababa to attend the CGIAR International Centers Week hosted by the International Livestock Center for Africa (ILCA). Also attending the meeting was Dr. Hartman who became the Director-general of IITA just as Don was leaving the Institute, Dr. Eugene Terry, a scientist and an old friend at IITA, and Dr. Jacques Eckebil, the Director of National Agricultural Research in Cameroon.

It was such a pleasant coincidence to have all six gentlemen in one place at the same time that Don and his wife could not miss this rare opportunity to host a dinner for them. It was an opportunity to show Prof. Anthonio, Prof. McCalla, and Dr. Gamble their appreciation for the contribution which each of them had made to Don's academic journey. They were greatly humbled and honored when they all accepted the dinner invitation in spite of prior commitments.

Don was to learn later that Prof. McCalla and Dr. Gamble had to turn down some important invitations for that evening so they could honor theirs which had come to them quite late because Don and his wife learned of their arrival in Addis Ababa quite late too. Their gesture showed the high regard they had for Don as one of their successful students. They arrived strictly on time; the dinner which was a buffet, was sumptuous; the atmosphere was very informal and relaxed; and the discussions were enriching. Their hostess, Dorothy, Don's wife, was as usual, just wonderful. What was most memorable was how their guests felt so much at home. Don remembers, for instance, Dr. Gamble sitting on the soft, red carpet with legs outstretched and very relaxed, enjoying every moment. The dinner provided an opportunity for them all not only to unwind after days of hard work, but also to establish new relationships and contacts.

The six months extension of Don's contract was due to end on 30 November 2003. On 23 October, Don received another letter from the Chief of the Human Resources Services Section again notifying him of his upcoming retirement. In the letter, the Chief took the opportunity, as Don prepared to separate from the ECA, to thank him for the service he had rendered to the United Nations and more specifically to the Commission for twenty-one years. She also availed herself of the opportunity to give him some guidance on clearances and departure formalities at UN offices, some of which were contained in ST/AI/155/Rev2 on personnel payroll clearance action, which was attached to her letter. This included information on: (1) after-service health and life insurance, (2) United Nations Joint Staff Pension Fund, (3) administrative clearances (consisting of forms for completion and return before separation), (4) host-country clearances, and (5) repatriation grant.

In Don's experience, when staff members receive such letters, it brings home the reality that they are really about to separate from the organization which they had served and which had been part of their lives; that they are going to leave colleagues with whom they had worked and lived together; that they were now about to start a new life back in their home countries or some other countries where they would choose to relocate. Don has seen uncertainty, sadness, disillusionment, and pessimism creep into the lives of staff members who had not prepared for this moment.

The Preretirement Arrangements and Workshops

To prepare retiring staff members to cope with the transition into life in retirement, the ECA organizes preretirement briefings and seminars for retiring staff. While in Rome, Don attended one of the preretirement workshops organized by FAO for interested retiring staff. He did so out of curiosity as at that time, he still had up to ten years to his own retirement. He wanted to know what retirement was all about and the kinds of topics that were discussed at such workshops. During discussions at lunch breaks, the outlook and pronouncements of some of his older friends who were attending the workshop seemed to portray retirement as a very unwelcome stage in life. They complained that retirement had come too soon. If only they could be given a few months extension! Being proactive in preparing for retirement was an important lesson Don learned from this FAO workshop.

The preretirement briefing and seminar organized for them had on its agenda topics on major issues of paramount importance to retiring staff. They had presentations from experts from the Human Resources Services, the Joint Staff Pension Fund in the Geneva office and from the ECA Health Center as well as from some ECA Divisions. There were also presentations on life after retirement, health and aging (staying fit while you age), the writing of wills, second careers (after the UN), etc.

For the After-Service Health and Life Insurance coverage, staff members who qualify for enrollment upon retirement are those who were enrolled in a UN Medical Insurance Plan at the time of separation from service. Family members who enrolled with the staff member at the time of separation were eligible for continued coverage under the ASHLI program. The UN Joint Staff

Pension Fund provided information on retirees' entitlements/benefits from the Fund, the available benefit options and the actions that staff were required to take for the payment of their benefits. Human Resources Officers (HROs) outlined the detailed administrative procedures for separation from the service of the United Nations and the clearances required for exit from the host country.

The briefing on Life after UN was very revealing and perhaps explains why the thought of retirement is often a cause for much anxiety and uncertainty even sometimes for staff who have prepared for this moment. Among the issues discussed under this topic included what the staff member can expect on relocation, adjustment for relocating families, re-entry shock, reactions relating to leaving work, coping, and relationships in retirement.

They were told that the choice of the geographical place they move to after retirement matters because there, they would find a sense of belonging. Relocating families have a lot of adjustments to make because after retirement, staff members feel a sense of loss—loss of international privileges, loss of self-worth when they no longer feel special or elite, loss of values when those relocating no longer feel their personal choices match with those of old friends and family and there could also be a loss of hope for the future; loss of innocence—when they realize that life has changed while they were away and that home is not always as perfect and as comfortable as they imagined; loss of financial benefits and the expatriate lifestyle and loss of mixing and exchanges with different nationalities.

They learned that for these and other reasons, the returning retired staff members and their families will experience re-entry shock, and it could take anywhere from eighteen months to three years to get over it. Difficulties in coming home were something most staff members don't anticipate and are often inadequately prepared for. The extent of the shock, they were told, would depend on the amount of time spent away, how different the culture they had been living in was, and how well they adjusted to it. This could lead to emotions like anger, exhaustion, depression, confusion, bargaining, guilt, blame, panic, fear, acceptance. These emotions are experienced in a roller-coaster fashion. And depending on how the concerned staff members handle these emotions, they may become angry, ill due to high stress, or withdrawn. The rational response would however be to accept the emotions as natural and adopt coping mechanisms to enable them make the necessary adjustments in relocation.

The briefing and seminar also touched on relationships (between spouses) and self-worth (of the retiree). It was interesting and surprising to learn that retirement could affect the relationship between the retiree and his/her spouse. How couples fare during the transformation depends, in part, on how well they have planned how to live their life together in retirement. It was stressed that during retirement it was important for couples to talk to each other, spend time together, make room in the relationship for differences and value those differences, set goals for the relationship and plan a future life together; they should try not to judge, criticize, or blame each other, be sexually considerate of each other, and express and demonstrate a commitment to the relationship.

Much importance was also attached to the issue of the self-worth of the retired staff members. They were told that it is they who determine their self-worth. In this connection, so much of who they are, is tied with what they do. They have to decide what they want to do in retirement. They can choose to be active learners interested in new things or spend their time complaining about different things. If they choose to be active learners, they can learn new things, develop lots of interests, find useful ways to connect to the world, cultivate important family relationships and friendships and take steps to protect their health.

Definitely, few retirees would want to spend their time in retirement complaining about different things. Rather, they would want to learn new things. In view of this, the seminar had a detailed presentation by an ECA senior professional on 'A Second Career: Opportunities for Paid and Voluntary Work'.[100] Topics discussed included life at the UN and skills acquired and the opportunities and the will to apply them; life after the UN and opportunities to keep mind, body, and soul engaged; opportunities for paid and unpaid work; career in politics, academia, arts, sports, business, etc.; case studies of successful and 'failed' second careers; lessons from case studies and importance of decision-making; and toward the development of a career strategy for the future.

With regards to the development of a career strategy, the crucial issue was what precise skills the retiring staff members have and how these prepare them for the challenges ahead. Can they acquire new skills and can they reinvent themselves? If so, when did they hope to get started after relocation?

The need to protect their health was paramount during retirement. Thus, in addition to being encouraged to enroll in the UN After-Service Health and Life Insurance and taken through the process of enrollment in the program, one of the physicians in the UN Health Center and Clinic made a presentation on 'Keeping Healthy in Retirement'.

The doctor explained the aging process which everybody who lives long passes through and how all organ systems—circulatory, respiratory, digestive, etc., are affected by the aging process. Some of the major geriatric conditions which retirees should be aware of were discussed at length. These included intellectual impairment (delirium, dementia, depression), genitourinary (urinary incontinence, prostate enlargement, menopause, vaginal-urethra mucosal atrophy), falls, immobility, and drug reaction. In order to prevent any of these geriatric conditions, it was important to keep healthy. They were told that health is not just the absence of disease, but a condition of physical and mental wellness and consists of physical wellness, mind/body wellness and social wellness. To maintain physical wellness, it was important to avoid immobility and seclusion. Mobility and physical and mind body exercises (walking, jogging, tai chi, akido), good nutrition, safety, and prevention of diseases were paramount.

Friends and family as well as social commitments were important in maintaining social wellness while activities that keep the mind intellectually active (reading newspapers, magazines, academic reports), spiritually alert (meditation, prayers), avoid stress, and promote mind and body wellness. After the age of forty and particularly in retirement, certain periodic medical tests were invaluable. These include eye examination after fifty years every three years; tests for diabetes, hypertension, cholesterol—every year; dental examination—once a year; heart (blood pressure, cholesterol) tests at least yearly; colon (rectal, gastric)—yearly; prostate (PSA test)—yearly; testicular (self-examination); breast (self-examination and mammogram)—every year; gynecological (pap smear, etc.)—at least once a year.

Participants at the seminar acknowledged with appreciation the pains taken by the HROs to walk them through the many administrative and clearance forms involved in the process of separation from the UN and exit from the host country. In fact, the Human Resources office at the ECA always advised retiring staff members to start clearance formalities three to six months before retirement!

The first important decision which Dorothy and Don took many years before Don's retirement was where they were going to relocate. Over the years, they have had friends who had, for various reasons, decided on retirement to relocate in the United States, the UK, and France. A few, especially those married to Ethiopians, had chosen to remain in Ethiopia. Don and Dorothy's decision to return to Cameroon was a bygone conclusion. However, where to relocate in Cameroon was not as easy as the decision to return to Cameroon.

Initially, they had decided they would relocate in Yaounde, the political capital of Cameroon, where they thought there was a large international community and many opportunities for consultancies with international and regional institutions and government ministries. However, by 1999, they had started to have mixed feelings about relocating in Yaounde. The need for consultancies was no longer paramount. Even if it was, it was not incumbent on one to live in Yaounde to have access to consultancies. With the advances in ICT, one could engage in consultancies from any town or city where ICT facilities were available. Rather, the need to relocate in a place where one had a sense of belonging, where they had family and friends and where the culture was familiar, was more compelling. So also was the need to relocate where the climate was friendly and the cost of living is low, a place characterized by peace, serenity, and little hustle and bustle.

With these considerations in mind, they chose the town of Buea, the Headquarters of the Southwest Region of Cameroon and the capital of the former State of West Cameroon. With this choice made, they decided to start building their retirement home there in 2000, three years to Don's retirement with the assistance of his brother, Mr. Joseph Ako Oben (now Dr. Joseph Ako Oben), and his brother-in-law, Dr. Bernard Nzo-nguty. They completed it just after Don retired when he used a little part of his lump sum to put the final touches to the house. Their next major decision was what Dorothy would be doing after Don separates from the UN. It was he, not Dorothy, who would be retiring. Although she had short-term consultancies with the ECA, they agreed that they should both return to Cameroon.

The question then was, what she would be doing in Cameroon. In this connection, they agreed that she should apply to join one of the faculties of the (Anglo-Saxon) University of Buea (UB). With a Master's degree in Gender and Development from the Institute of Development Studies of the University of Sussex in 1992 and her experience as a teacher in the 1980s and a consultant with the UN in the 1990s, she could find a place in the Department of Women and Gender Studies of the Faculty of Social and Management Sciences.

Considering that she had sacrificed her own career to follow Don all through his own career wherever he went for the sake of keeping the family together, Don was ready to do all he could to stay by her while she engaged in teaching and research at UB if she was offered a position. Their next consideration was the children. By the time of Don's separation, Valentina and Vanessa would still be in secondary school and university respectively in the UK.

Don's Retirement

November 30, 2003, the day Don was due to retire finally came. By then he had completed all the administrative formalities and submitted the clearance forms necessary for the payment of his benefits by the Pension Fund and enrolled himself, his spouse, and dependent children (now only two—Vanessa and Valentina) in the After-Service Health Insurance Plan. The other clearances could be completed only at the point when he was ready to leave the country. The Division gave them a farewell reception to which all the other Divisions were invited. Then followed a flood of farewell luncheons and dinner parties given in their honor by family friends.

The climax came when the Cameroon Community of which he was the president, organized a send-off party for them and showered them with gifts in appreciation for their true friendship and contribution to the growth of the Community. It was the 'mother' of all send-off parties and like typical Cameroon parties, no national from the other communities wanted to be left out. Friends were really emotional at their impending departure, and the appreciation which Don and Dorothy expressed to them from the bottom of their hearts could never be enough.

While arrangements were being made by the ECA for packers to come in and pack their things, Don and Dorothy made a quick trip to Dubai where they purchased and shipped some household goods which would be invaluable in their retirement. These were shipped to Addis Ababa for inclusion in their other personal and household effects which the UN was going to ship to Cameroon as their entitlements.

Part 4
The End of the Search and Journey

Chapter 16
Homeward Bound: Returning
from the Search and Journey

Repatriation and Relocation

Don had shipped two 40-foot containers. The first, which was at Don's expense, had been shipped earlier in the year and contained some personal effects and their old Mercedes Benz car which they had ordered from Germany after Don took up service with ECA in Addis Ababa in 1982 and which was still in excellent condition. The second container was shipped in December at the expense of the organization. This one carried most of their personal effects and household goods as well as a new Toyota Land Cruiser Prado station wagon, which Don had ordered from Japan several months earlier in preparation for his retirement. A four-wheel-drive vehicle was an absolute necessity in Cameroon where most parts of the country are characterized by very difficult terrain and poor road infrastructure.

Don left Addis Ababa at the end of December 2003 after the shippers had packed and moved their personal effects and household goods to their warehouse in preparation for shipment. Since Dorothy was just a few months into a renewed consultancy contract with the ECA, they arranged that she joins Don in Cameroon when her contract comes to an end in July/August 2004. Don arrived in Buea and moved straight into their new retirement house while it was being completed. He used a portion of his lump-sum to complete the house during his first few months in Buea.

The first container had been cleared by his brother Joseph before his arrival. With the contents of this container, Don partly furnished the house after it was completed. Dorothy made a short trip to Buea to attend an interview at the University of Buea on April 2, 2004 in response to her application for a teaching position, and she returned to Addis Ababa to continue her consultancy assignment at ECA. The second container was delivered by the shipper, Panalpina Sarl, to their home in Buea on June 30, 2004 through a door-to-door delivery arrangement between the ECA and the shipper. With the delivery of their other personal effects and household goods, the house soon became perfectly functional.

Don then began to plan for a life in Buea. The first priority was to set up a consultancy office in the upper floor of the house, which Dorothy will also use as her office when she took up her teaching job at the university. Don furnished the office with two large tables and executive chairs, one desk and chair, one wall-to-wall bookshelf, and two small bookshelves-on-desks. These three bookshelves took most of their books, reports, papers, and personal files. For ICT, Don installed a desktop computer and two laptops, a landline telephone link, and a fax and photocopy/scanning equipment. Considering the poor performance history of the utility companies—electricity and water—he had built a tall 2000-liter water tank and installed a 7.5 kw generator which they had purchased in Dubai.

All was soon ready for private consultancy services in agriculture, food security, and sustainable development. Don had decided to spend some of his time, whenever convenient, doing what he does best and had done for most of his life—undertaking studies, preparing policy papers, and providing advisory services. It was not long before international calls and emails started to come in. Dorothy had sacrificed her career to be with him throughout his journey. He was going to devote as much time as possible now to be with her while she taught. He would provide consultancy services only when it was convenient, especially for her.

After she completed her consultancy assignment in Addis Ababa and joined Don in Buea, he sent evidence to ECA of their relocation—a sworn statement that they had relocated to Buea in Cameroon, away from Addis Ababa, his last duty station. This was in fulfillment of the condition for the payment by the United Nations of a repatriation grant to a retiree. With the payment of the repatriation grant, Don's journey had come to an end.

On Relocation: Don and His Family's Experience

The journey ended with Don's retirement, repatriation, and relocation. Having participated in several preretirement briefings and seminars in Rome and Addis Ababa, Don's experience is that preparation for retirement is not a matter of a few months prior to retirement. It should be a long-term plan. In fact, this message echoed in all the seminars Don attended. The seminars emphasized that potential retirees, whether male or female, should decide in consultation with their spouses well in advance in which country and city/town they will relocate. Considerations for the choice of the country/city of location include availability of family and friends, utilities and services such as electricity, water, transport, telephone, and Internet. They should have personal accommodation where they and their families will live in the country/city of relocation. If they do not have one, they should build and have it ready for occupation by the time of relocation.

A personal accommodation avoids large expenses on rents given that their pension benefits now are smaller than their previous UN income. As much as possible, they should try to ensure that all their children have completed their education by the time of their retirement. Payment of school fees during retirement is a big handicap to a retiree. Prospective retirees should plan to have a functional car during their retirement. They should think deeply and decide on their second careers. In this connection, they should consider their skills and whether those skills have prepared them for these second careers, and if not, whether they are ready to learn new skills.

The 'rule of thumb', so to speak, for a happy and comfortable retirement, is that the standard of living of the retired staff members should be almost at the same level with the standard of living during their service with the UN. For this to be achieved, their net income on retirement should be as close as possible to their net income when they were in service. That is why it is important that a retiree avoids the huge expenses on rents, children's education, and health. A second career was not only necessary to keep the retiree busy but to provide additional resources that would augment the income from his or her pension. And for his/her social and emotional stability and happiness, he/she needs to relocate in an area where he/she has family and friends to socialize with as well as functional utilities and other services (transport, supermarkets, or local food and fruit markets) he/she used to enjoy.

From experiences which they learned during the seminars, retirement seemed to have come 'too soon' to many retirees who had not prepared for it. They had not built a retirement home and had no personal accommodation to which they were going to relocate. Some still had children in school and were anxious at the prospects of paying school fees during retirement. Some feared that their pension income would not be enough to sustain their lifestyle. Some had either not been home in years or had almost cut off ties with families and friends back home. So this fear of disconnect in their home countries haunted some retiring staffers.

Don's case was somehow different. He had fairly prepared for his retirement by May 2003 when he was due separation from the UN. The extension of his contract for a further six months only made him more comfortable and more relaxed as he savored the prospects of going into a life in which he was going to be his own master—no deadlines determined and enforced by other people! He and his family always spent most of their home leave when the children were young in Cameroon, and whenever he was on duty travel close to Cameroon, Don always seized the opportunity to sneak in and out of Cameroon to see family and old folks. So throughout his career with the UN, Don had kept in close touch with family and friends. Coming back home in December 2003 was, for him, not too life-changing although he knew they would be missing a lot of things—the immunities and great privileges, friends, the good life, and to a certain extent, international travel.

There was no re-entry shock for Don on relocation. However, having lived for twenty-one years in countries and cities where people are for the most part disciplined, and the administration/public service, utilities, etc., function efficiently, coming back to Cameroon had its concerns. But one of several things Don was thankful to God for is that, unlike civil servants in Cameroon, he didn't have to go through the indignities of compiling and re-compiling and carrying 'dossiers' around ministries in Yaounde in order to get his pension. It started coming within six weeks of his separation from service—even before he had time to check his account!

At the time of retirement, Valentina was in her final year at Royal Russel School in Croydon, UK, and Vanessa was in her second year in the Faculty of Law at the London School of Economics, University of London, UK. So unfortunately, Don still had many years of school fees to pay at retirement, and in fact, more school fees than they had imagined. After graduating with a

Bachelor of Laws degree at LSE in 2005, Vanessa was to later go on to the School of Oriental and African Studies (SOAS) of the University of London to obtain a Master's degree in International Studies and Diplomacy in 2006. Valentina went to Hillcrest Secondary School in Nairobi, Kenya, for her GCE 'A' Level Course before returning to the UK to enter the University of Kent at Canterbury to obtain a Bachelor's degree in Business Studies.

From there, she went to Canada for a postgraduate diploma in International Business and thereafter to Belgium where she obtained two master's degrees in 2016 and 2017, respectively. So Don was caught up spending a large chunk of his monthly pension on school fees even after having been warned during the preretirement workshops. Dorothy returned finally to Cameroon in September 2004 and they found themselves just alone in the large retirement house. This was not unexpected. While the last two children, Vanessa and Valentina, were in school, the first three children had finished school and were now working and living their lives.

Part 5
Looking Back at the
Search and Journey

Chapter 17
Some Reflections

Looking back at Don's epic journey, there are some crucial issues or questions which the expectant or inquisitive reader would want to know. Did Don achieve his overarching dream of 'broadening his horizons' and finding a future, a place in contemporary mass society? Did he also profit from the benefits and privileges and immunities he had dreamed of? What were his achievements or contributions to development during his long journey to the world in search of a future? Looking back at the work which he and his colleagues did at the ECA, what impact did the Commission make on Africa's socioeconomic development? What opportunities came Don's way and what challenges did he face?

Don's Dream of 'Broadening His Horizons' and Finding a Future

Don nursed a burning desire to undertake his journey when he grew up because he wanted to 'broaden his horizons' like his father had done during his travels in Nigeria. As recounted in an earlier chapter, Don faced a lot of 'opposition' particularly from friends when in 1973, he told them of his decision to resign his appointment as Field Assistant in the CDC and go to graduate school. Those who felt that his decision was ill-advised pointed to the benefits he was enjoying in the CDC, including free housing, free utilities (water, electricity and gas), a high salary relative to the public sector, and a car loan and car allowance. They argued that after graduating from graduate school with a master's degree, where would he find employment that would provide him with such remuneration?

To Don, the issue of returning to work for the corporation with a postgraduate degree was out of the question. He was looking far beyond a

Master's degree and the CDC plantations. He was setting his sights quite high—on a Ph.D. degree that would catapult him into international agricultural research or the universities or the United Nations and its agencies. His goal was not only to broaden his horizons but also to find a place in contemporary mass society – find a future. His only anxiety was whether he would be able to make it in graduate school having been out in the plantations for nearly three years after earning his first degree. During this time, he had grown academically rusty. But he knew he would make it given his historical record. Did he achieve these dreams?

What does 'broadening one's horizon' mean? It means to expand one's range of interests, activities, knowledge, skills and experiences and options. Traveling, meeting people from other parts of the world, learning about different cultures, increasing the range of one's knowledge, understanding and experiences, all help to broaden one's horizons.

From the account of the journey presented in this book, it is self-evident that Don set out to broaden his horizons and he DID! He expanded his knowledge and education and acquired skills, bagging a Bachelor's, Master's and Doctorate degrees; He traveled widely through the length and breadth of the African Continent and parts of Europe and North America; had wide employment options—working in the national civil service, the plantations, in international agricultural research, in the universities, and in international development and cooperation; He met, worked or lived with people from different cultures. It is thus abundantly clear that he fulfilled not only his dream of broadening his horizons but also finding a comfortable future for himself and his family.

Don also fulfilled his passion for dancing by learning ballroom dancing. At a time when ballroom dancing was labeled a colonial and elitist dance, Don socialized and danced advanced quickstep, waltz, slow foxtrot and the tango at the Victor Sylvester Ballroom Circle of the University of Nigeria, Nsukka, the Dancing Club of the University of Ibadan, and at the Annual Balls of many Ballroom Circles and Dancing Clubs in Nigeria. In his retirement, two TV programs that give him so much pleasure every season they are aired and bring back memories of his days in the Ballroom, are America's 'Dancing with the Stars' and the UK's 'Strictly Come Dancing'. They are British and American television dance contests in which celebrities partner with professional dancers to compete in mainly ballroom and Latin dance—the quickstep, waltz, slow foxtrot, tango, Argentine tango.

Celebrities or 'Stars' from various spheres of life—film, TV, sports, politics, Academia, etc. fascinated by the dance aspire to also become accomplished ballroom dancers. The prestige and grandeur of the competition, the professionalism in the dancing, and the dancers all resplendent in their designer costumes, always bring back old memories of Don's ballroom dancing era as he sits down with his eyes glued to BBC1 and ABC TV channels which respectively air 'Strictly Come Dancing' and 'Dancing with the Stars'.

Yes, Don did broaden his horizons, and more.

Don's Accomplishments, Contributions, and Footprints

Don's broadened horizons made him a man of many things at different times. As he journeyed farther and farther into the world and acquired more knowledge and experiences, he moved from serving his country to serving the African region and then the entire world. He was a man who was successful and talented in many areas. He was a good civil servant, a hard working veterinarian, an agricultural and socioeconomic researcher, a university don and a development economist. He was a man for all seasons, a man of many parts. He showed great ability in these many different areas. He was versatile. In every area he passed through, he left his footprints.

As far back as a student leader and vice and acting president of the International Students Association at the University of Ibadan in the late 1960s, Don brought about a revolution in the way clubs, societies and associations advertised and marketed their fundraising activities on campus. Small handwritten or typewritten adverts on A-4 printing papers pinned on notice boards and tree trunks or cello taped on walls, gave way to eye-catching and attractive, giant multi-colored printed posters mounted at amphitheaters, halls of residence, cafeterias, and other prominent places on campus.

Don's varied career included a stint as a veterinarian, a technician—the one who does the work and gets his hands dirty in the process. Working with veterinary assistants and technicians, they grazed animals, bathed them; drenched them to remove ticks and other parasites, treated diseases such as foot-and-mouth disease, pneumonia, and streptococcus and performed castrations. He not only worked with Vet Assistants in the field, he also worked in a small animal clinic, treating mainly pets (cats and dogs) and sheep, goats and chickens. He also worked with the director of Veterinary services often going out to the prison farms to treat cows and other livestock and occasionally assisting cows having calving difficulty or dystocia.

In the Cameroon Development Corporation's plantations, where he was placed in charge of 850 hectares of rubber and a labor force of over 200, he planned, directed and supervised all technical operations in his estate including tapping, collection and transportation of cup lumps, polybags and latex to the rubber factory for processing and export. Thus, Don made a contribution to the growth of the economy of Cameroon through foreign exchange earnings from the export of rubber from his estate.

As a socioeconomic researcher at IITA, Don and Ken Menz's work on cassava went a long way in contributing to the expansion and direction of IITA's cassava program in the 1980s and beyond. The decades of the seventies and eighties witnessed IITA playing a leading role in developing improved cassava varieties which are disease- and pest-resistant, low in cyanide content, drought-resistant, early maturing, and high yielding. Don's and Ken Menz's research contributed substantially to an understanding of the patterns in the adoption of improved cassava, improving the quality of cassava preparations, processing traits of improved cassava, and developing more rapid and effective technologies for cassava processing, i.e., technologies which reduced the cyanogenic content and labor requirement, etc. Improved cassava varieties produced at IITA are now used in most cassava-growing countries in Sub-Saharan countries

Don's work with colleagues on hydromorphic toposequences also provided IITA which was working on the design of systems of crop and land management, the much needed information for designing improved technology suitable for the integrated use of such areas by small farmers.

Don's illustrious carrier also took him into Academia and manpower development for tertiary institutions, the civil service, etc. At the IITA, he gave significant support to IITA's Training Program aimed at Manpower development within the National Agricultural Research Centers (NARs), by offering economics-related courses to researchers from the NARS, Research Associates or Assistants who came to IITA for non-degree training to address their individual needs and the needs of their NARs.

More significantly, Don held tenures in two universities, first, at the University of Ibadan, Nigeria, where he made a contribution on behalf of IITA, to teaching in the Department of Agricultural Economics and second, at the Dschang University Center in Cameroon where he held a tenure as Assistant Professor in the Department of Rural Economy in the National Advanced School of Agriculture. Today, his former students having been found 'worthy in character and in learning' occupy high and important positions in the Ministry of Agriculture, the universities, research institutions, regional development authorities and Cameroon's diplomatic missions.

Don spent the last 21 years of his long and versatile career working in the very challenging area of international development, cooperation and diplomacy. Within ECA's Joint ECA/FAO Agriculture Division and later, the Food Security and Sustainable Development Division, he and his colleagues grappled with agricultural development and food security policy issues in Africa and the world. They prepared technical publications on Africa's food and agricultural development for dissemination to member states, contributed the agriculture-related chapters of ECA's flagship publications and reports mandated by various conferences and meetings, and provided Advisory Services to member states, on request, on food and agricultural production, marketing, institutions, service and policies.

Within this broad program, Don carried out some really grueling assignments. As young staffers in ECA in the early 1980s, Don and a colleague Godfrey Coker prepared a Report on the Situation of Food and Agriculture in Africa in 1984 for presentation by the ECA to the 9th Meeting of the Conference of Ministers of Planning. In the Report which they prepared using the most up-to-date data in FAO's database, Don, an Agricultural Economist and Coker, a Statistician, warned of an impending food crisis in Africa and urged African member states and the international community to take all necessary actions to avert it. For this timely warning, supported by concrete analyses, they were berated by a high FAO official who called them 'alarmists' and strongly advised them to delete all reference to a food crisis in Africa.

Don and his colleague refused to back down and took responsibility for the contents of the Report. The ECA accepted and presented it to the 9th Meeting of the Conference of Ministers of Planning. African member states and the international community did not act. It was not long before Africa was engulfed in one of the most devastating food crisis in the continent's history. The African food crisis of the late 1980s and early 1990s and the widespread hunger and starvation captured the attention of the whole world as never before, prompting a global response to save lives.

Another significant assignment was his mission to the University of East Anglia at Norwich, UK, in 1985 to coordinate the preparation of a report requested by the UN General Assembly (UNGA). The UNGA which met On 20 December 1983 had requested the Secretary-General, in consultation with the relevant organs, organizations and bodies of the United Nations system, to elaborate action-oriented proposals in respect of the international year for the mobilization of financial and technological resources to increase food and agricultural production in Africa and to report on the implementation of the present resolution to the General Assembly at its fortieth session, through the Economic and Social Council.

Responsibility for the elaboration of the action-oriented proposals in respect of the international year fell on the ECA and eventually on Don's Division since the Report was in the domain of food and agriculture. This was a huge and important assignment, which unfortunately, could not be handled entirely by the Division considering its heavy workload and other commitments at the time.

Reports to the General Assembly had to be of the highest quality. The Division therefore contracted the assignment, like most UN agencies do, to a consultancy group or institution. In this case, the Division contracted it to the Overseas Development Group (ODG) of the University of East Anglia, Norwich, UK, which had done a lot of work in Africa on agriculture and food security issues. Don was assigned the task of coordinating the preparation of the report at the University of East Anglia at Norwich. Don coordinated the preparation of the Report in addition to drafting parts of the Report and getting and integrating FAO's input into the Report.

It was one of the most engaging assignments Don carried out. After seven weeks in Norwich and three trips to Rome for meetings with FAO to get the latter's input into the draft report, Don returned to ECA with the final Report titled: 'The International Mobilization of Financial and Technological Resources for Food and Agricultural Production in Africa: An Analysis and Action Proposals for the International Year for Africa'. This Report was presented to the Twenty-second Session of the Commission and Thirteenth ECA Conference of Ministers held on April 23–27, 1987, in Addis Ababa before eventually being presented later to the General Assembly through the Economic and Social Council at its Forty-second Session in 1987.

One of ECA's major contributions to the continent's economic advancement in the 1980s as the continent's 'Think Tank' was trying to chart a development path for its member states through developing a number of regional plans and frameworks which were adopted by African member states under the political aegis of the OAU. Three of these include Africa's Priority Program for Economic Recovery (APPER) 1986–1990 which was later converted to the United Nations Program of Action for Africa's Economic Recovery and Development (UNPAAERD) and the Alternative Framework for the Socioeconomic Development of Africa (AAF-SAP) 1986.

Don and his colleagues of the Agriculture Division and later in the Food Security and Sustainable Development Division, made enormous contributions to the development and preparation of the activities, priorities, and policies elaborated in the programs in agriculture and food security within these plans which served as blueprints to guide the socioeconomic development efforts of African member states.

For several years while he was at ECA, Don and his colleagues served as resource persons during the Meetings of the Technical Preparatory Committee of the Whole (TEPCO) and ECA Conference of Ministers of Planning and Development and later, the Joint Conference of Ministers of Planning and Finance. At the World Food Council in Rome, Don and his colleagues serviced annual Meetings of the Council's Ministers of Agriculture. In all these meetings and conferences, they ensured that the Reports of the meetings and any Resolutions requested were well prepared and ready for adoption on the last and final day of the meetings. He represented the ECA in many regional and subregional workshops and meetings at which he presented papers on various aspects of agricultural development and policies on behalf of the ECA. He also organized and coordinated ad-hoc expert group meetings attended by high-level experts and practitioners in the field of food security.

He convened the annual meetings of the Advisory Board on Population, Agriculture and Environment. The Board was made up of eminent persons and experts appointed in their personal capacity with a mandate to bring their expertise to bear on the work of the ECA. As Chief of the Agriculture Planning and Policy Section and later, Team Leader of two successive Teams, he provided professional and technical leadership and guidance to his colleagues as well as supervision of secretarial staff.

Above all, Don was a prolific writer. He has written extensively and consulted on a wide range of agricultural and rural development policy issues reflecting not only his academic but also his career backgrounds. He has published widely in academic and professional journals, journals of research and technology, Bulletins, etc. He has also written many policy papers, issues papers, working papers, and position papers and provided advisory services on request, to African member states.

He was a chairperson or member of many Committees and panels at ECA and WFC. He was also an Assistant Warden for the City of Addis Ababa and the Deputy Warden for the City of Tangiers in the UN security plans of Ethiopia and Morocco respectively.

He was for many years, a Member of the International Association of Agricultural Economists (IAAE), American Agricultural Economics Association (AAEA) and the Canadian Agricultural Economics and Farm Management Society (CAEFMS).

He was listed in 'Profiles of African Scientists' by the African Academy of Sciences, (AAS, 1989) and was a Reviewer of 'Discovery and Innovation' published by the AAS.

His brilliance as a student is reflected in the number of scholarships and fellowships awards that he won during his academic career. These include 1. Mamfe Town and Area Council scholarship (1957–1958). 2. West Cameroon Government scholarship (1959–1964). 3. Cameroon Federal scholarship (1966–1970). 4. Rockefeller Foundation Fellowship (1973–1975). 5. Ford Foundation Fellowship (1975–1978). 6. French Government scholarship for Intensive French Language Course (1999), 7. Post-doctoral Fellowship, IITA (1978–1980).

ECA and Africa's Development

Looking back at his journey, particularly at the work which he and his colleagues and those who had gone before them did at ECA, a question which even Don often asks himself is, what impact did all this work have on Africa's development? At the time of his retirement, was Africa's economic situation better than in the 1980s?

The mandate of the Economic Commission for Africa (ECA) when it was established by the Economic and Social Council (ECOSOC) of the United Nations (UN) at its[101] 7th plenary session held on 29 April 1958, was to promote the economic and social development of its member states, foster intraregional integration, and promote international cooperation for Africa's development. In carrying out this mandate, ECA used its strength as the only UN agency mandated to operate at the regional and subregional levels to harness resources and bring them to bear on Africa's priorities.

To enhance its impact, ECA focused on promoting policy consensus, building needed capacity, and providing advisory services in key thematic fields of focus to African governments, intergovernmental organizations, and institutions. In the 1990s, these key areas included regional integration and trade, social development, natural resources, innovation and technology, gender, and governance. In order to ground its policy research and advocacy on clear objective evidence, the ECA placed a special focus on collecting, evaluating, and analyzing up-to-date and regional statistics.

Equally, if not most importantly, the ECA, as a knowledge-based institution, has played a major role as the 'think tank' of the region and in this connection had been proactive in the search for programs and plans of action for the socioeconomic development of the continent.

To answer the question raised, it is necessary to revisit some of the major initiatives taken by the ECA before and during Don's journey. As mentioned earlier, one of ECA's major contributions to the continent's economic advancement in the 1980s was in developing a number of regional plans and frameworks which served as blueprints to guide the socioeconomic development efforts of African member states. These are the Lagos Plan of Action for the economic development of Africa, 1980–2000, and the Final Act of Lagos, 1980, Africa's Priority Program for Economic Recovery (APPER) 1986–1990, United Nations Program of Action for Africa's Economic Recovery and Development (UNPAAERD) and the Alternative Framework for the Socioeconomic Development of Africa (AAF-SAP), 1986. These plans have been elaborately discussed in chapter 11 and would therefore not be dealt with at length.

The Lagos Plan of Action and the Final Act of Lagos were adopted by African Heads of State and Government meeting in Lagos in 1980. Through this Plan, African leaders sought to use a regional approach based primarily on collective self-reliance to achieve economic growth, promote the economic integration of the African region, and establish the necessary national, subregional and regional institutions which would facilitate the attainment of the objectives of self-reliance and self-sustaining development.

Africa's Priority Program for Economic Recovery 1986–1990 was adopted by the Assembly of Heads of State and Government of the Organization of African Unity in July 1985. In adopting this program, African governments reaffirmed their primary responsibility for the economic and social development of their countries, identified areas for priority action, and undertook to mobilize and utilize domestic resources for the achievement of these priorities. They further committed themselves fully to the implementation of the sharply focused, practical, and operational set of activities, priorities, and policies elaborated in the priority program.

The United Nations Program of Action for African Economic Recovery and Development (UNPAAERD), 1986–1990, was actually an extension of APPER by the UN General Assembly which felt that the international community needed to complement the efforts of African governments in Africa's Priority Program. Thus, noting that it was essentially urgent to develop and implement an international strategy to complement the exceptional efforts that the African countries had themselves initiated by the adoption of APPER to put their economies on course, it adopted the United Nations Program of Action for African Economic Recovery and Development (UNPAAERD), 1986–1990 on June 1 1986, adding a second element to APPER.

This second element was the response of the international community and its commitment to support and complement the African development effort. The first element which embodied the spirit of APPER was the determination and commitment of the African countries to launch both national and regional programs of economic development as reflected in Africa's Priority Program for Economic Recovery, 1986–1990.

In spite of the adoption and implementation of these plans, the Economic crisis in Africa continued unabated, prompting many African countries to adopt and implement IMF/World Bank-sponsored Structural Adjustment Programs (SAPs) for Socioeconomic Recovery and Transformation. Following increasing concerns with respect to their relevance to Africa's long-term development objectives and their social, economic, and financial impacts in the countries, the ECA came up with the African Alternative Framework to Structural Adjustment Programs for Socioeconomic Recovery and Transformation (AAF-SAP). The African Alternative Framework (AAF-SAP) was adopted by the Joint Meeting of African Ministers of Economic Planning and Development and the Ministers of Finance held in Addis Ababa, Ethiopia, in April 1989. It sought to address simultaneously both adjustment and structural transformation problems of the African economies in the face of a dismal economic performance by many African countries in the 1980s.

In its continuing efforts to chart a path for Africa's socioeconomic development, the ECA also strove to lay a strong foundation for infrastructure to support the development efforts of member states. The infrastructure the Commission considered as indispensable elements of development and socioeconomic growth was transport and communication. As engines of economic integration, this infrastructure constituted a precondition for facilitating trade and the movement of goods and people.

It was with this in view and through the Commission's efforts and those of its partners that, at the instance of African countries, the United Nations Economic and Social Council by its Resolution 1980/46 of July 23, 1980, proclaimed two Transport and Communication Decades in Africa (1978–1988 and 1991–2000). These two decades aimed at focusing the efforts of African states and their development partners on the specific issues of transport and communications in Africa. The Trans-African Highways (TAH) system, whose design dates back to the early 1970s and which is composed of about nine main corridors with a total length of 59,100 kilometers, was an integral part of the Decade Program. The TAH aimed at establishing a high-quality road network linking the continent's capital cities, thereby contributing to the integration of the continent and ensuring links between the continent's major production and consumer hubs.[102]

The second important infrastructure considered a prerequisite for Africa's development was industrial infrastructure and facilities. Similarly, through ECA's efforts and at the insistence of African member states, the UN General Assembly adopted a resolution proclaiming the 1980s as the Industrial Development Decade for Africa. In this connection, the General Assembly called upon the United Nations Industrial Development Organization and the Economic Commission for Africa, in close cooperation with the Organization of African Unity, to formulate proposals to implement the program for the Industrial Development Decade for Africa and to monitor its progress.

While sharply focused on the development of regional plans and frameworks to promote the economic and social development of its member states, the ECA also spearheaded the establishment of subregional economic communities to foster intraregional integration and international cooperation for Africa's development. ECOWAS, ECCAS, AMU, COMESA, PTA, CEMAC, etc., were established. It also encouraged member states to create several multinational institutions as centers for stimulating socioeconomic development in Africa. Many of such institutions were established from the 1960s to 1980s covering most of the sectors of social and economic development and intended to serve different groups of countries at subregional or regional levels. These institutions became known as 'ECA-sponsored' institutions even though they were established, owned and run by the member states themselves. By the 1990s, a total of thirty-three such institutions had been established and were at different states of health.

In addition to the Conference of Ministers of the ECA, the Commission used its convening power to organize the African Development Forum (ADF) and several conferences and meetings at which crucial issues of African development were discussed, including those convened as an integral part of the preparatory process for the major international conferences. These included the Regional Conferences on Women, Population and Development, Environment, Industrial Development Decade for Africa, the Transport Decade, African Planners, Statisticians and Demographers, and the ADFs. Resolutions upon resolutions were adopted at most of these meetings and conferences on actions required and agreed to by member states on national, subregional and regional development. The meetings and conferences also provided discussion forums for the key players in national development and a platform for developing an African Common Position on international development issues.

So how has ECA's role impacted the development of the continent? How have African member states responded to their many plans of action, frameworks, initiatives and the numerous resolutions which they themselves passed and committed themselves to implementing? Where is Africa now?

In its evaluation in 'Can Africa Claim the 21st Century?'[106], the World Bank acknowledges that many countries in Africa have made important economic reforms, improving macroeconomic management, liberalizing markets and trade and incomes and reducing poverty. Where these reforms have been sustained and underpinned by civil peace, they have increased growth, raised incomes and reduced poverty. The bank also acknowledges that as parts of the region are making headlines with wars and natural disasters, other parts are making headway with rising interest from domestic and foreign business and higher investment. However, despite gains in the second half of the 1990s, Sub-Saharan Africa (SSA) enters the twenty-first century with many of the world's poorest countries. Average income per capita is lower than at the end of the 1960s. Incomes, assets, and access to essential services are unequally distributed. And the region contains a growing share of the world's absolute poor who have little power to influence the allocation of resources. Other development problems include lagging primary school enrollment, high child mortality, and endemic diseases, including malaria and HIV/AIDs. To make matters worse, Africa's place in the global economy has greatly eroded with declining export shares in traditional primary products, little diversification into new lines of business, and loss of skilled manpower to other regions.[107]

So why, in spite of ECA's efforts, has Africa remained defiant of development? Has the fault been with the ECA or with its member states?

The Solution to Africa's Problems

Don remembers quite well, it was one day in 2003 shortly before his retirement. He was walking toward the library from the New Building (ECA Main Building) when a staff member in the documentation center of the Conference Services Section came up to him and announced: "Mr. Oben, I have found the solution to Africa's problems."

Don took it for one of those jokes they amuse themselves with and was about to brush him aside when he repeated: "Mr. Don Oben, I am telling you that I have found the solution to Africa's problems."

Don stopped and looked at him. "What problems are you talking about?" Don asked him.

"All of Africa's problems," he replied.

Don couldn't help being amused. This was a general service staff working in the documentation center and mainly concerned with the production of documents for conferences and meetings. For him to be telling Don he had found a solution to all of Africa's problems was beyond Don's comprehension. Not even the ECA and the OAU and the ADB working together have been able to find the solution to Africa's problems.

Without waiting for Don to ask more questions, he brought out a book he was clasping under his left arm and thrust it into Don's hands, nodding his head with pride and a sense of achievement as he did so.

"Here is the solution to Africa's problems," he said now with an air of one who had done what Napoleon Bonaparte could not do or, in this case, what the ECA and other African institutions have not been able to do.

With anxious hands, Don quickly turned over the pages of the book which he claimed contained the solution to all of the continent's problems. It was titled *The Solution to Africa's Problems*. It contained an endless list of 'resolutions'. It turned out that this staff member had painstakingly searched the archives of the ECA for the hundreds of resolutions adopted by the Conference of African Ministers of Planning and Ministers of Finance and approved by the Assembly of Heads of State and Government of the OAU since the establishment of the ECA in 1958 right to the present (2003). He had then listed these resolutions in chronological order by date, subject, and the resolution reference.

African Heads of State and Government had adopted resolution upon resolution on all aspects of Africa's socioeconomic development. In particular, they had, by various resolutions, adopted several regional plans and frameworks (the LPA and the FAL, APPER, UN-PAAERD, AAF-SAP, etc.), which they had resolved to implement with a view to achieving the goals of rapid self-reliance and self-sustaining growth and development. They had also adopted resolutions at various regional preparatory meetings of international conferences (International Conference on Population and Development (ICPD), the Transport and Communication Decade for Africa (TCDA), the Industrial Development Decade for Africa (IDDA), the World Conference on Women, etc.) all aimed at fostering the socioeconomic development of the continent.

According to this staff member, the reason why Africa had continued to be plagued by problems of underdevelopment was because African member states had failed to implement the resolutions they themselves had adopted for the development of their countries. It was his conviction that if the countries of Africa had implemented all these resolutions or even just a handful, Africa would have been a developed continent today. Africa had no dearth of policy initiatives nor human resources. What Africa lacked was the 'political will' to implement the hundreds of resolutions that the Heads of State and Government of Member States had adopted over several decades for the socioeconomic advancement of the continent. That was his case. The solution to Africa's problems therefore lay in implementing these resolutions—the resolutions in his book. A credible case, it seemed.

Well, he did not define or explain to Don what 'political will' means. Don suspects, however, that to him it meant just the will power, the strong determination to take a difficult action no matter what the political repercussions may be as a result of taking the action. But 'political will' means different things to different people. Craig Charney once said this of political will: "It's hard to define, harder to grasp, and hardest of all to measure. In a recent paper, three academics took 32 pages just to offer a definition of political will!"[108]

'Political Will' and Africa's Development

Fortunately, we can be informed by the LPA as to what African leaders meant by 'political will' as a prerequisite for Africa's development. In the LPA, this is what was said in the case of agriculture: "As concerns the area of Agriculture, the Plan recognized that the root of the food problem in Africa was the fact that member states had not usually accorded the necessary priority to agriculture, both in the allocation of resources and in giving sufficient attention to policies for the promotion of productivity and improvement of rural life. For an improvement in the food situation in Africa, the fundamental requisite was a strong political will to channel a greatly increased volume of resources to agriculture, to carry through essential reorientations of social systems, to apply policies that will induce small farmers and members of agricultural cooperatives to achieve higher levels of productivity with increased real incomes."

Thus, in the LPA, political will is defined in terms of the allocation of sufficient resources for the implementation of the various policies and programs agreed to in the various resolutions adopted by African heads of state and government over the years. A strong political will was a fundamental requisite not only for agriculture but also for all the other sectors of their economies. In spite of this recognition, African leaders failed to show the political will necessary even in the resolutions they tried to implement.

The issue of 'political will', while credible, has, however, remained an unsettled issue among policymakers. In the context defined above, yes, one might agree that there was a lack of political will by member states. Why, however, did African member states lack this political will, which they themselves had underscored as a prerequisite for development? Some policymakers have argued that there was no lack of political will. Rather, there were other interests (neo-colonial?) or currents that presented impediments to the implementation plans of member states. Some others argue that there were inherent shortcomings in the programs and plans that constrained their implementation such as the absence of 'special mechanisms' for the implementation, coordination, and monitoring of the programs, which are deemed important for implementing the resolutions. This lack of unanimity on this issue, like in many other issues of African development, is a subject of continuing debate.

Concerning the ECA itself, it is important to acknowledge one of its major constraints. The ECA was and still is a knowledge-based institution with some of the best brains in the continent. It served as the 'think tank' of the continent and had a huge convening power. But unlike the financial institutions and other organizations such as the FAO, it was handicapped by lack of financial resources to back its plans and assistance programs to member states. This is understandable because it was not established as a financing institution.

The Journey: Opportunities and Challenges
Did Don Live His Other Dream?

While an undergraduate student at Ibadan, he had come across some World Bank and United Nations vacancy announcements and read the duties and responsibilities of the posts and the remunerations, privileges, and immunities attached thereto. When he was nursing plans to return for graduate study, he was dreaming big. He dreamed of opportunities for working in international organizations and enjoying these benefits, privileges, and immunities which were by far greater than those that his friends were recounting—of living with people of different cultures in various countries; of travel to broaden his horizons; of participation in international conferences and meetings; and of duty-free shopping, etc. It was within this mindset that, upon graduation with a doctorate degree, he submitted his resume to the International Institute of Tropical Agriculture (IITA), Ibadan, the Economic Commission for Africa, and the Food and Agriculture Organization of the United Nations (FAO).

And did his dreams come true? Did going to graduate school and getting a Ph.D. degree open up the opportunities he had dreamed of? Much of this book has been about his journey in the institutions he had dreamed of. As is now known, after graduation, he had tenures at IITA and in two universities and finally crowned his career with a 21-year service with the United Nations—at the ECA and the UN World Food Council Rome, a part of his journey that lasted altogether twenty-six years.

And did he enjoy those benefits and remunerations, immunities, and privileges that he had dreamed of? The answer is 'yes' and much more. They received education grant and education grant travel for the children's education, travel tickets for himself and family for home leave every two years or yearly in the case of hardship duty stations, health and life insurance, rental subsidy in some cases, highly competitive salaries, and good pensions. Through the assistance provided by education grant and education grant travel, they were able to pay the fees to educate their five children (four of them to the master's degree level) without them resorting to taking student loans.

Page 347: Photos: Children's graduation. Left: Lilian, Right: Lorraine.
P.348, Top: Valentina. Left: Vanessa, Right: Don Jr.

But some of these benefits should not be looked at in isolation. They should be viewed vis-à-vis the cost of living as well as the state of the socioeconomic infrastructure in the duty stations. The cost of living in Rome in the 1990s, for instance, was so high that most staff members could barely break even at the end of each month. In fact, most of their accounts at the Banca Commerciale Italiana were perpetually in the red. House rents and school fees in international schools were particularly high. So although they received education grant, what they paid from their pockets to make up the fees was much more than they would have paid if the children were schooling in their home countries. In effect, although the education grant allowance was helpful, it was intended to assist international staff defray some of the astronomically high fees charged by international schools. In Addis Ababa, because of poor school infrastructure in the 1980s, international staff had to send their children after fifth grade to begin secondary school either in Kenya but mostly in Europe.

They also enjoyed some immunities and privileges including tax-free purchases and duty-free monthly shopping and the use of VIP lounges in most African countries. Don remembers the exclusive 'Commissary' (duty-free shop) at FAO Headquarters in Rome and the duty-free shops in Addis Ababa where they, the UN international staff, did their shopping. He remembers also that throughout his twenty-one years of service with the UN, he was never harassed by any cops or an immigration or customs official in any country. There was only one occasion when he was pulled aside by cops on a highway in Spain for speeding. He was only cautioned upon his identification. Certainly, immunities come with responsibilities. The only other occasion was an incident with a customs official in Lagos which is recounted in the last chapter of this book under the title: 'Enforcing the Law'.

Don had dreamed of international travel on missions and of participation in international meetings and conferences. Did that dream come true? Yes, it did, much more than he could have imagined. As discussed in the relevant chapters, the ECA and WFC used their convening power to bring together in various forums, member states, the international community, eminent personalities, etc., to discuss, exchange views and experiences, and adopt resolutions and take required actions respectively on Africa's and developing countries' daunting problems.

The ECA organized every year the Conference of African Ministers Responsible for Economic and Social Development and Planning, which it used to report on its work to the UN Economic and Social Council (ECOSOC). It also organized various sectoral ministerial conferences and meetings, regional conferences, workshops, and seminars, many of which were hosted outside Addis Ababa in member states. While Don was at the World Food Council secretariat which serviced the thirty-six-member ministerial-level World Food Council, it organized the Sixteenth and Seventeenth Sessions of the Ministerial Meetings of the Council in Helsingor, Denmark, and Nairobi,

Kenya, respectively. It also organized preparatory workshops including the WFC/UNDP Interregional Consultation on 'Meeting the Food Production Challenges of the 1990s and Beyond' convened in Cairo, Egypt, in April 1991.

Their attendance at these meetings was imperative; they serviced the meetings, acted as resource persons, drafted the resolutions, and prepared the reports, making sure that they were ready for adoption by the close of the meetings. Don remembers those early years as a young staffer. They would stay up all night working with the secretaries, drafting and reading the corrected drafts and putting the reports together, and all the while drinking hot black coffee to keep awake. Yes, Don traveled widely across the continent and in Europe. He must have traveled to more than forty-five African member states and many European countries during his twenty-one years with the UN, not counting his travels while he was at IITA, Ibadan.

Traveling could be fun. Whenever possible, he tried to mix work with a little adventure while on mission. He would go sightseeing or visiting tourist sites, attractions, and landmarks, and collecting works of arts and crafts as souvenirs. He remembers his tours to the pyramids of Giza in Egypt where he learned to ride a camel, and the candlelit dinner cruises on the Nile. He also remembers his tours of Soweto and Mandela's family house, of Sydney Harbor in Australia, of the long road trip from Wellington to Auckland in New Zealand and the visits to some of NZ's fascinating and remarkable landmarks such as the Huka Falls, the Wairakei geothermal area in Taupo, and the trout pools in Rotorua; of the underground tunnel roads in Gibraltar, of Ellis Island and the Statue of Liberty in the USA, of the Niagara Falls in Canada, of the city of Mamfe in Ghana (a town in Ghana with a similar name to his birth place in Cameroon), of Copenhagen (Denmark), to name just a few.

He also remembers with nostalgia, his holiday in the Town of Okrika and the visits to Degema, Buguma and Abonnema in the Rivers State of Nigeria and his experience traveling in large canoes at a tender age of 15 in his early years in secondary school in Owerri in Eastern Nigeria.

And as recounted in some of the chapters, whenever possible, he took his family on weekend trips and vacations, visiting tourist resorts and landmarks. He remembers their travels in Spain and Gibraltar and their trips to Sion in Switzerland, Asmara and the Red Sea resort and port city of Masawa in Eritrea. He cannot forget the numerous picnics in Tangier, Morocco, and the beautiful lakes of Langano in Ethiopia, their trips to Marrakech (Morocco), Florence

(Italy), and to Falmer (Sussex) and Middlesex in the UK. While serving in Rome, visiting friends would always want Don and Dorothy to take them on sightseeing tours of the city and they would often oblige. They would visit the Vatican, Sistine Chapel and St. Peter's Basilica, the Colosseum, forum Fomanum, Piazza di Spagna, Basilica di Santa Maria Maggiore, the Pantheon, Trastevere, Trevi Fountain, and many other Rome landmarks.

Don notes, however, that traveling was not always fun especially when one's flight is delayed or canceled without notice and one has to spend long hours at airports or if one's itinerary is too long and complicated due to difficulties with flight connections like in Central Africa. One of Don's experiences in this regard is reported in chapter 18, the last chapter of this book under the title: 'Air Travel in Africa'.

Traveling was almost always for duty. Thus, it was often accompanied by hard work, frustration, inconveniences, and stress. It was quite common for Don to arrive in a member country very early in the morning after a long and tiring overnight flight and barely have time to clean up, change clothes, and rush to a 7:30 a.m. meeting with officials in a member state. Neither was it rare for him to confine himself to the hotel every day after work throughout the duration of the mission without having the opportunity to do some shopping or go sightseeing. It is probably to make life a bit less difficult that the UN accorded its staff some of the privileges and immunities Don mentioned above.

In view of the foregoing, it is evident that at retirement, UN staff would definitely experience some losses such as international privileges and courtesies. Don remembers, for instance, his several missions to Central Africa when he transited through Cameroon. He would use the VIP lounge in Douala, and when it was time to take his flight to Addis Ababa around midnight, he and other VIPs would be chauffeur-driven to the plane by the young hostesses in the lounge after all the other passengers had boarded. There is also the loss of financial benefits, high standard of living, the expatriate lifestyle, the international, diplomatic and multicultural environment, and above all, cherished relationships and friendships.

A recurring situation throughout their service with the UN was the frequency with which they made new friendships and lost old ones as they moved from country to country and from one duty station to another. As busy as they often were, and with information and communications technology not as developed in those days as it is now, keeping in touch with old friends and sustaining old relationships was not easy, and sooner than later, they lost touch. Almost all the friends and colleagues whom they had, have also retired—returned to their home countries—Malawi, Kenya, Tanzania, Uganda, Nigeria, Togo, Ghana, Liberia, Sierra Leone, Senegal, the Gambia, Burkina Faso, Mali, Morocco, Italy, the USA, China, the Netherlands, etc.

Some relocated to the United States while a few remained in Ethiopia. Even though they try to keep in touch by email, it is not the same as with those face-to-face interactions—like the discussions and arguments with colleagues and friends, the family visits, house parties, the luncheons and cocktails at the OAU and the embassies, the sports and games they played, the picnics and weekend trips to Lake Langano and the Saturdays at the Kenyan and Tanzanian Embassy compounds unwinding after a hard week, socializing and eating barbecued goat meat ('nyama-choma') and drinking beer. All Don has now are memories. These memories are not only memories of old friends and colleagues at the UN. They are also memories of old school and classmates in secondary school and universities in Nigeria and the United States from whom there has been a disconnect since they all parted in the 1960s and 1970s, at the early part of Don's journey.

In his retirement, Don sees old schoolmates from Sasse, Bali, Okoyong, Saker, and a host of other educational institutions in Cameroon, organizing alumni meetings, planning projects to improve their alma maters, or simply celebrating, socializing, and helping one another. Don has been opportuned to meet only five classmates since he left Government Secondary School Owerri in 1964—Dr. Morrison Amaeshi, a dental surgeon whom he met in Lagos in 1978, and Frederick Uzoma Chinakwe, a naval/marine engineer whom he visited in Warri when he was undertaking a study on cassava and cyanide in the mid-west state of Nigeria in 1979. It was he who took Don to visit Dr. Dan Egbuna, another classmate, a petroleum engineer and Head of a Department at the Petroleum Training Institute at Effurun in Warri.

The other two whom Don met were Felix Chukwuemeka Mbadiwe and Francis Chinedu Akpuaka, both medical students who returned from the east to Ibadan in January 1970 to continue their studies after the Biafran civil war. A third medical student and classmate, Zedekiah Chukwujama, also returned but Don never saw him. Don was to read in a Nigerian magazine while in Addis Ababa in the mid-1990s that Francis Akpuaka, now an eminent Professor of Plastic Surgery, was the Provost of the College of Medicine of Abbia State

University. Apart from these five, Don never ran into or met any former classmates during his entire career in Nigeria and the UN. For those he never met, he still visualizes them as he last saw them in his mind's eyes—as teenage boys! Yet, they should now be in their late seventies.

As mentioned earlier, there were four Cameroonian students in Owerri—Michael Ndip of the Class of 1959, Don himself of the class of 1957, Shadrack Ndam, Class of 1956, and John Agbor of the Class of 1952. Shadrach Ndam and Don met in Addis Ababa in the early eighties when Shadrack came on mission from Vienna, Austria, where he was working with the UN Industrial Development Organization (UNIDO). He henceforth became their guest each time he came on mission to Addis Ababa. Don was opportuned to meet John Agbor in his Bota middle farm's office in the late seventies and a few times subsequently, while he was a senior civil engineer in the Cameroon Development Corporation (CDC). Unfortunately, Michael Ndip and Don never met. The only other schoolmate Don met was Ernie Allison of the Class of 1952 and who was the cricket captain when Don got into form one in 1957. He was working with the UN High Commission for Refugees, and they met in Addis Ababa when he was transferred from Kenya to Ethiopia. He and his wife, Yinka, and Don's family soon became good family friends, and they met in the US many times and still keep in touch.

A remarkable handicap which most staffers, especially Africans, faced and which needs to be mentioned was the difficulty in undertaking projects in their home countries from far off-duty stations. One of the most common projects that the majority of staffers wanted to undertake was to build their personal houses in their countries especially before retirement, at the latest. Because of the distance between their duty stations and their home countries and the difficulties of traveling home frequently to organize and supervise the projects, most staffers used their relatives—brothers, uncles, cousins, etc.—to undertake the projects on their behalf. They would give them the assignments and transfer the required resources to them for the projects as, and when, these relatives demanded. To assure the staffers that the projects were on course, the relatives would send photographs to show the progress being achieved. To cut a long story short, most of Don's colleagues who used relatives to undertake such projects for them had the most bitter experiences.

On receiving news that the projects had been completed, backed by photographs after years of sending money home, these colleagues have gone home with joy, excitement, and great anticipation with their families only to find, to their disbelief and chagrin, that the projects were still at the foundation level. In most cases, they had not even been started! And worse still, no account was given of the monies transferred and received over the years. The relatives had used the monies to build their own houses or establish their own businesses. How cruel and heartless those relatives could be!

Many colleagues who found themselves in these situations returned to Addis Ababa and never returned to their home countries. Some relocated in Europe or stayed on in Ethiopia after retirement. There were isolated cases where some relatives did realize the projects. But it was not until they had first used the monies to make short—term, high interest loans to generate some capital to finance their own projects. However, while one may blame these relatives, some of the staffers must take some responsibility for these outcomes. They were either too trusting or lacked the common sense that they needed to go home periodically to check on the projects or show some interest in their own projects.

Don's case was different. His brother, Mr. Oben Ako Joseph (now Dr. Oben Ako Joseph), and Brother-in-law, Dr. Bernard Nzo-Nguty, assisted them in building their retirement home in Buea. But unlike the case of the colleagues mentioned above, Don took every opportunity of his missions to West and Central Africa to transit through Cameroon to see the project, make any modifications or corrections necessary, and together, they would discuss/plan the next phase, the financial requirements, and time frame. An engineering company in Yaounde, Solid Maison, was contracted to provide technical backstopping to the project which had been given to a contractor. However, no matter how hard his brother and brother-in-law tried, they could not prevent problems from developing in the project. Solid Maison was inconsistent in providing technical backstopping and even stopped before the project was completed.

At some point, most of the workers abandoned the project and joined a road building project nearby because they were not being paid by the contractor. Even though he was receiving his payments, as and when due, the contractor used the money to buy himself a new car rather than pay the workers. He eventually abandoned the project when almost all his workers had left. By the time Don retired, the house was livable but there was still much work to be done. The staff ceiling in the dining, two living rooms and the study was still to be completed; the wardrobes and some doors were still to be fabricated and fitted; aluminum door and window frames and protectors were still to be fitted; the chandeliers and other lamps had not yet been mounted on the ceilings and walls and the whole house was still to be painted. The concrete fence which had been built had to be remodeled into a high, well-tiled concrete fence with one small and two large gates.

With the contractor gone having taken more money than the work accomplished, Don and his collaborators now had to complete the project by employing technicians for specific jobs. By the time the project ended, Don had learned a hard lesson about Cameroonian technicians—there should be no sentiments in business. A technician who had a big workshop in Douala and who was given the contract to fabricate and fit the bedroom doors and wardrobes asked for, and was paid his last installment of 1.2 million CFA before completing his work. Once he received the money, he never showed up again and all efforts to get him complete the work or return the money failed. Another technician who was doing an excellent job fitting the aluminum doors and windows was given an advance payment of 800,000 CFA for another contract to fit protectors on the doors and windows after executing the current contract. He too never showed up to even complete the work he was doing. When he was finally trapped after several months, he said, "I am just waiting to go to prison. I don't have the money to pay back. I gambled it away."

By the time the house was completed, it had cost more than 1.5 times the estimated cost in the plan. Given his hard experience during the few months he took over the house project after his retirement, Don cannot thank his brother and brother-in-law enough for the assistance they gave him and his family in building their retirement home. Don and Dorothy also express their profound gratitude to those who gave them a helping hand in one way or the other in this regard, including their young nephews.

Thus, Don would say that to a great extent, he lived his dreams. But this came at some cost, not only to him, but also to his spouse and children as well as to relatives he left behind at home in Cameroon.

At his retirement and relocation, Dorothy and their children also experienced a sense of loss similar to Don's. Dorothy is much more outgoing than Don, and she made an incredible number of friends in Addis Ababa, Brighton (Sussex), Rome, and especially in Tangier, where she had a group of close friends from Spain, Eastern Europe, France, Italy, and the UK that met informally and regularly and brought their families together to socialize and be there for each other. She did her best to maintain the relationships, but no matter how much one may try, time and distance have a way of actualizing the sayings 'Out of sight, out of mind' and 'Time changes everything'. While she still communicates with some of her friends, most of the others are just mere memories now—memories of the good old times!

Apart from loss of friendships, Don's career abroad had other impacts on Dorothy—positive and unfavorable. During their time abroad, she was able, with Don's support and encouragement, to study for, and obtain a Diploma and a Bachelor's degree in Education in 1979 and 1981 respectively, and a Master's degree in 1992. While in Morocco, she and Don attended French language classes for two years at the Alliance Francais, sitting in the same class. They passed the examinations for the Diplome d'Etudes en Langue Française (DELF) and were awarded the DELF Certificates for Unités A1, A2, A3, A4, A5, and A6, by 'le Ministère de l'Éducation Nationale, Republique Française' in 1995 and 1996 (see an earlier chapter for details of Unités A1–A6). Their stay in Morocco not only enabled them achieve this, but also helped them improve their spoken French. For her, these were positive impacts. Their stay in the various countries certainly broadened her horizons, as it did to Don's.

But her career suffered. Just one month after she was employed by the Ministry of Education in Yaounde in 1982, she had to resign and follow Don with the children to Ethiopia. Again in 1990, she had to leave her teaching job at the International Community School of Addis Ababa (a.k.a. the American School of Addis Ababa) and follow Don to Rome with the children when Don got a position at the World Food Council, Rome, Italy. Although she did some consultancies with the ECA in the later part of the 1990s, she was not able to develop her own career because she followed Don throughout his career path. She thus sacrificed her career for the sake of keeping the family together. This is a sacrifice most spouses cannot make, and Don remains indebted to her.

Don did, however, make a promise to her—that after his retirement, he would accompany and be with her wherever she finds employment. So back in Cameroon and while she was still completing her last consultancy in ECA, Don assisted her to file her application in the University of Buea (UB) for a teaching position. Things worked out well. She got the position. Don tried his best to be a 'house husband' while she taught at UB. He traveled out on international consultancies only when it was convenient for her. In the course of her career in UB, she was required to enroll full time in the Ph.D. program in Women and Gender Studies.

Teaching full-time and studying full-time while still playing the role of a full-time housewife, she struggled with a crushing workload in her last 6 years in UB. She carried a workload that was heavy, unhealthy, stressful, and unsustainable. It was only her resolve, Don's support and her trust in God that saw her through. In April 2020, she was awarded the degree of Doctor of Philosophy (Ph.D.) in Women and Gender Studies by the Anglo-Saxon University of Buea, Cameroon.

Thus, Don fulfilled a pledge he had made to her before they got married. In Chapter 8, it is reported that when Don proposed to her before she completed secondary school and sat for her GCE O-level examination, she said 'yes' but with a proviso that Don does not let their marriage stop her from getting a post-secondary education. In the course of their journey together, with a characteristic determination and Don's encouragement and strong support, she studied and was awarded the Nigeria Certificate in Education (NCE), and a Bachelor of Arts Degree in Education (B.A. Hons) by the University of Lagos, Nigeria, a Master of Arts (M.A.) Degree in Gender and Development by the Institute of Development Studies, University of Sussex, Falmer, UK and finally a Doctor of Philosophy (Ph.D.) Degree in Women and Gender Studies by the Anglo-Saxon University of Buea, Cameroon.

And the children, what benefits did they have and what challenges did they face? They benefited from a good education as the education grant and education grant travel provided by the UN enabled Don to send them not only to some of the best international schools, but also to some of the best universities. Their challenges were similar and formidable and stemmed mainly from being moved from one country to another and having to integrate into and live in different cultures from a young and tender age.

None of their five children was born in Cameroon. Lilian, Lorraine and Don Jr. were born in Nigeria and Vanessa and Valentina in Ethiopia. Lilian and Lorraine went to primary school in Ethiopia, secondary school in the United Kingdom and Kenya, higher school in the UK, and university in the UK and United States. Don Jr. went to primary school in Ethiopia and Italy, secondary school in the UK and university in the USA. Vanessa had her primary education in Ethiopia, Italy, and Morocco, and went to secondary school, higher school and university in the UK. Valentina, the last of the children, went to kindergarten at the age of three in Italy studying in Italian. She then went on to primary school in Morocco and Ethiopia, secondary school in the UK, higher school in Kenya, and university in the UK, Canada, and Belgium.

Thus, they became what is usually referred to as 'Third-Culture Kids' or TCKs. These are kids who are raised in a culture other than their parents' for a significant part of their early development years. They move between cultures before they have had the opportunity to fully develop their personal and cultural identity. Thus, their children have had the unique experience of being exposed to and living in cultures different from their home culture for extended periods of time. There are benefits and challenges to being a TCK. They have an expanded worldview, and with an increased amount of experiences in multiple cultures, they have a *higher* cultural intelligence or the capacity to function effectively across national, ethnic, and organizational cultures. They usually have higher levels of general adjustment as opposed to mono-cultural children.

Their youngest daughter, writing about her experiences as a third-culture kid in a resumé she sent to a university, had this to say:

"My personal background is also one that reflects the international diversity and melting pot of cultures, which your university is renowned for. I am a 25-year-old girl born in Ethiopia of Cameroonian parents and because they worked with the United Nations Organization and in various countries, I, very early in life, lived with people of diverse cultures, nationalities, races, and religious affiliations. Countries in which I have lived and which reflect these diversities include Cameroon, Ethiopia, Kenya, Morocco, Italy, the United Kingdom, the United States, Canada, and Belgium, and I have visited Spain and Switzerland. I have also developed a high degree of inter-cultural communication from studying in most of these countries. My mother tongue is English, but I learned French and Spanish, and in my childhood, I spoke Italian. Thus, my international background will add still more diversity to the university…"

However, third-culture kids who are unable to adjust to the new cultures could experience cultural rootlessness. Don and Dorothy made it an obligation in the 1980s and early 1990s to take their children when they were young on home leave in Cameroon so they may be conversant with their roots. They enjoyed their visits to Sister Eunice[109] and her husband, Dr. Nzo-Nguty, in Yaounde, as well as their visits to Buea and Mamfe, and they enjoyed the company of their aunties, uncles, and cousins.

Above: At the Nzo-Ngutys during home leave in 1988. Sis Eunice is carrying Valentina. Behind her is Dr. Nzo-Nguty.

Going home once every two years when they were relatively young was, however, not enough. They lack a deep identification with their 'home' culture as they have spent little time in their home country. They still lack, to a considerable degree, knowledge about their home town, Mamfe, their country, Cameroon, and their culture, the Banyang culture. For some of them who have not gone home since the age of 7, they could even experience culture shock and identity crises.

One aspect of their lives which they have missed very much is their school days and their old friends. Unlike their parents, they started making new friendships and losing old ones right from a tender age in kindergarten and continued through secondary school to university. The continuous and frequent change of environment and culture led to this disconnect with friends. Unlike the kids of today, they did not have Facebook and the other social media outlets to maintain contacts with friends. Letter writing was the only means of keeping contact then. The frequent movements and changes of environment and schools definitely did have many adverse impacts on them too.

One of the most notable is their exposure to, and conditioning to the patterns or customs of Western and American culture and lifestyles which are quite at variance with, and in some cases, even unacceptable in traditional African culture and values.

Don started the journey as a frail, skinny lad of fourteen and finished as an old man of sixty, still strong and healthy, retired but not tired, with a wife and five third-culture grownup children with whom they made most of the journey together. In the course of the journey, Don lost his father, then his mother and two of her mates (Mama Manyi and Ma Alice Takor), his father-in-law (Mr. James Ako Ako) and mother-in-law (Ma Margaret Enowma), three brothers (Brother Tom Njang Ako, Brother Lawrence Mbi, and Brother James Agbor), as well as a host of relatives and friends.

His loving mother passed away on 28 July 2002. Her death was very abrupt and unexpected. She had collapsed and gone into a coma on receiving news of the death of her dear cousin, Mama Serah Tabi. She never recovered. She died two days later. Don had not seen her for some one or two years. Despite the fact that she had been longing to see Don, his circumstances were such that he could not travel to visit her. The thought that she never got to see him, and he hadn't seen her for long before she died, keeps nagging him. While still mourning his mother, his younger brother, James, her third child, followed her to the world beyond on 21 February 2003. The period 2002–2003 was a very trying one for the family, especially for Don and his sister, Eunice.

In accordance with their tradition and custom, after Brother Tom, the eldest son passed away in 1987, as the next eldest male child of the family Don took over the mantle of leadership as the Head of the Oben Family of Small Mamfe. Throughout his journey, no matter where he was located, he made it a point to keep close to home as much as possible and ensure the family was well.

Photo: Don, then as 'Etuop-Etuop Ntui' during the Ekpe Society funeral ceremonies of their eldest brother, Tom Njang Ako, in 1987. Behind Don is Uncle Tom Tabi, who took him to Owerri, Nigeria, in 1957 as narrated in chapter 3.

I cannot end Don's story without underscoring once again, his appreciation to his father and mother. Don's father suffered from an unusual cough almost throughout his entire post-retirement life. He coughed up only light white phlegm. Doctors could not diagnose what type of cough it was, not even in Lagos, Nigeria. It was alleged that he was poisoned and it disappeared "without notice" after more than three decades of taking hundreds of bottles of the cough syrup "Liqufruta" which he was prescribed in Nigeria. But he did not let the inconveniences and other impacts of this disease affect him or derail his vision for his children and family. Don gives thanks to his father, Ta Ako-Aragbor, for the training he gave him and his siblings during their childhood—a training that underlined hard work, honesty, good behavior, and quality education, qualities that were to make his children and grandchildren some of the most highly qualified professionals and office holders in the country. Any woman would have given up after losing six children. But Don's mother did not give up. She continued until she gave birth to Don and ensured that he survived to undertake the journey.

To her, Don owes a debt of great love and gratitude. His main regret is that he did not start his conversation with her earlier than he did, and so she took away with her when she passed away, a good part of her story—our story. But it is to God Almighty that Don owes the greatest debt. Through His Abundant Grace, He did not only enable Don undertake the journey, but He kept him alive and able to report on the journey more than a decade after it ended.

Would Don do things differently if he went on this journey again? Yes, he says he would, some things. If he had to undertake the journey again, there are things that he would do the same and some that he would address differently, especially, those concerning the children. The fact that they sent their children to boarding school in faraway countries, especially to the UK, at a very tender age sometimes haunts Don. He remembers his own early years in secondary school in Owerri, Nigeria. Even though he was much older, at the age of fourteen, he still felt the cultural differences and the homesickness, because he was far away from home, friends, parents, and family. He had no visitors on visiting days; no family when he was sick. He went home only once a year. He withstood all these because it was his desire to go to Owerri and he was much older. He wanted to study outside the country.

But as a little lad, he did not know the implications and challenges he would face. Why did he not learn from his own experience to know that whatever the case, little children should be kept close to home for as long as possible until they are strong and mature and have formed their character? Actually, he and his wife, Dorothy, did think of sending the children back to Cameroon, but they felt it would be very inconsiderate of them to pass on their responsibilities to other family members and friends who already had their own challenges.

If he were to go on the journey again, he would never send their children away from home early in their childhood, especially to boarding schools in Europe and let them grow with foreign guardians and in 'homes for foreign students'. Children need to grow and mature at home, experiencing and enjoying parental love and guidance and bonding well with their parents and their siblings. Although they were forced by circumstances to send their children to schools away from the duty stations, they should have done all that was possible to send them back to Cameroon instead of abroad. Back home, they would have established stronger, lasting and rewarding friendships, learned their culture and traditions, and known their country better.

An important lesson Don learned, unfortunately quite belatedly, during the journey was the role of 'politicking' and personal connections in one's career growth within much of the UN system. Professional growth did not depend just on doing your job well, being a team player, or meeting all the criteria of professionalism. Establishing friendships and connections with the hierarchy, being their protégé or having a mentor, and most unfortunately, doing favors and passing information around on who is doing what, were important, if not the most important elements in the careers of many lazy, poor performance staff members. They often made faster progress.

Whether rightly or wrongly, Don always believed in pulling himself up by his own bootstraps. He also came to realize the truth about some contradictions in the world as recorded in Ecclesiastes 9:11: In this world, the fast runners do not always win the race, and the brave do not always win the battle. Wise men do not always earn a living, intelligent men do not always get rich, and capable men do not always rise to high positions.

Could he have been less risk adverse? This is in terms of looking for opportunities outside the ECA? A recurrent threat to their jobs throughout his service at the UN was the incessant call by the US, in particular, for a restructuring and downsizing of the Secretariat and some of its organs. They were not just threats. Some of them were carried out, leading to separation of staff from the organization, and suppression or abolition of vacancies.

The ECA was least affected by the restructuring and downsizing exercises that occurred at various times. So jobs were 'safer' there than in other institutions and organizations in the system. But some of these other institutions and organizations had opportunities that Don could have taken advantage of and moved to. However, the situations there were not as stable as at the ECA.

So, a recurring dilemma which Don faced early in his career was whether to remain at ECA where his position was more secure or try to find higher positions in these other agencies and institutions where he could be separated at any time. He was adverse to risk and he refused to take that risk. A few colleagues who were not, took the risks and moved and kept moving from one agency to another, and they rose faster up the ranks. One was, however, caught up in a shake-up exercise at his second move and lost his job. This answers the question which a few colleagues often asked Don, and that is, why he remained in ECA for so long early in his career when there was no vacant higher position in his Division to which he could be promoted.

Well, not only was his position more secure, he also remained long enough to earn his permanent contract in the UN. When he got this permanent status, he made a determined, successful move. And his permanent contractual status paid off. He was able to transfer to the World Food Council (on secondment), taking with him his eight years' service with the ECA. So if he had to do the journey again, he doesn't think he would throw caution to the wind.

During the journey, Don had to make some of the hardest choices or take some of the most difficult decisions of his life. He took five major decisions, four of them life-changing. The first was at high school when he was given two direct entry admissions into the higher school certificate course: at his school, Government Secondary School Owerri, to do the Sciences (physics, chemistry, and zoology), and at Government College Umuahia to do the Arts (history, literature, and Latin). It was a very agonizing decision. He chose to do the sciences at his school.

The second was when early in life he had to change his course at the university from veterinary medicine to agricultural economics. The third was when he resigned from a job many considered lucrative in the Cameroon Development Corporation to go to graduate school. In the fourth, he walked out of a university tenure in Cameroon and took his family abroad. And in the fifth, he had to decide whether to be redeployed to the UN Headquarters in New York or return to the ECA after the abolition of the World Food Council.

In the second instance, he had chosen a course of study that would lead to a career he was not going to enjoy. He had chosen it in order to obtain a government scholarship. But his early experiences as a veterinary officer-in-training provided him with a small window through which he had a glimpse of the realities of a veterinarian's career. What he experienced convinced him that he either had to change his career path or continue and qualify as a veterinarian and have an unhappy, unrewarding career in future. He decided to change. In the third instance, against all advice, he left a supposedly good career in the CDC to embark on a long, difficult, and apparently uncertain journey through graduate school. In the fourth, even after graduate school and getting a tenurial position which had been one of his goals in life, he resigned and took his family to join the UN, against all odds. And in the fifth, he decided that he should be redeployed to the ECA instead of Headquarters in New York after the abolition of the World Food Council, Rome.

Taking each one of those decisions was not easy. Don spent sleepless nights thinking over the issues involved, asking himself questions, examining the pros and cons, agonizing, drained. In the end he had to take those decisions and take responsibility for the outcomes. And did he make the right decisions? Absolutely, he told me—in four out of the five cases.

In retrospect, he often has doubts about the 5th and last decision—his decision to choose to be redeployed to the ECA instead of to New York—to the New Department for Policy Coordination and Sustainable Development (DPCSD). He believes that in taking the decision, he forgot too quickly his 8 years' experience at ECA in the 1980s and did not benefit from hindsight; He relied too heavily on the experiences of staffers who had served in New York as a duty station.

And most importantly, he did not envisage the possibility, however remotely, of being redeployed by the ECA to North Africa or anywhere else except to its Headquarters in Addis Ababa where all his attention had been focused. He admits that although he achieved the primary objective of wanting to be redeployed to the ECA, he concedes that he missed the great opportunities that existed in the new Department for Policy Coordination and Sustainable Development in Headquarters as well as the benefits of working and living in the United States of America, the endless complaints about life in New York by staffers who had served at headquarters and lived in New York, notwithstanding.

Chapter 18
In Search of a Future: Endearing Moments during the Journey

Fascinating Stories and Reminiscences from the Journey

In this chapter, I remember some events or great moments that Don told me he experienced during his journey. I decided to capture and bring them all together in a separate chapter rather than discuss them within the journey in order not to distract the reader but keep him or her focused on Don's journey.

Charles Bukowski110 writing about 'Moments' in his book, War All the Time, says, "Some moments are nice, some are nicer, some are even worth writing about." These reminiscences capture some of such moments during Don's journey that are pleasant memories. As he recalled to me, some were anxious moments and some were light moments too. He remembers them with nostalgia. But there were moments of awe and consternation, and moments that were mind-boggling. They all have one thing in common. They are worth writing about, and in this case, to show the types of terrain Don had to navigate through, and the kinds of human behaviors he had to contend with during his journe – 'the good, the bad, and the ugly' in human behavior and character.

Above all, it is to tell the stories of some accidents and incidents he was involved in and to acknowledge with thanksgiving God's Grace—that incredible, unmerited favor given freely to us by God through His Son Jesus Christ. I have tried to remember and recount these events and moments to the extent possible, as Don narrated to me, starting from the earliest in the 1950s to the latest in the 1990s and 2000s.

"Life is not made up of minutes, hours, days, weeks, months, or years, but of moments," so wrote Sarah Ban Breathnach.[111] "You can enjoy life and treasure the moments—both good and bad for God is with us. You must experience each one before you can appreciate it."

Like Jonathan Huie,[112] Don would say about life, "I receive all of life with Thanksgiving. I have gratitude for everything that has ever occurred to bring me to this moment. I give thanks for the joys and the sufferings, the moments of peace and the flashes of anger, the compassion and the indifference, the roar of my courage and the cold sweat of my fear. I accept gratefully the entirety of my past and my present life."

In the next section, I present twenty-eight (28) great stories of actual events that took place during Don's epic journey. These include four stories which he had recounted to me but had not included in his Book. These four stories are as captivating and hilarious, if not more, as the twenty-four he recounted in his book. These four are: "The Ethiopian Letter," "Credit History," "Declaring His Age," and "Welli Wegbe For PRO."

Each story has its moments. As you read each of them, you may get glued to the book as you experience the story's great moments. In fact, these 28 stories should have been published as a fascinating story book and entitled: 'Reminiscences and Moments from an Epic Journey!' Without question, these stories will be of profound interest to the world's media – radio, TV and movie industry.

1. 'In Accordance With'

The year was 1957. Don had completed standard six in 1956 at Government School Mamfe in the then Southern Cameroons. His First School Leaving Certificate shows that, in order of merit, he emerged second out of twenty-five pupils who sat for and passed the First School Leaving Certificate examination in Government School in 1956. His burning desire had been to continue his education in Nigeria, in one of the three government colleges in the then Eastern Nigeria, preferably Government Secondary School, Owerri, after leaving Government School Mamfe. Admission into these schools was by a competitive common entrance examination administered nationwide in the Federal Republic of Nigeria and the Southern Cameroons. Unfortunately, he missed the common entrance examination in 1956 due to late entry. Determined only to enter one of these colleges, he and his father decided that he waits and sits the common entrance examination in 1957, making sure he applies early.

He eventually sat for the exam and, while waiting for the results, the headmaster of Government School Mamfe, Mr. T. A. Agbor, advised that he should sit for the entrance examination into the Basel Mission College Bali. He, the Headmaster, was recommending his son, Edmund Agbor, who was then in standard six, to sit for the exam also. At that time, Bali was one of the only two secondary schools for boys in the country to which every pupil aspired to enter, the other one being St. Joseph's College, Sasse, Buea (also called Sasse College). Usually to sit for the exam, like other similar exams, pupils in standard six apply through their schools, which then forwarded their names to the college for inclusion in the candidates' list.

Because they had not gone through this formal process and their names were not in the list of candidates to sit the entrance exam, the headmaster gave them an introductory letter in the morning of the exam to take to the invigilator of the examination, which was being held in the Basel Mission School, Besong Abang, some four miles from Mamfe Town.

Armed with this letter and taking with them their writing materials, Don and Edmund Agbor set off early in the morning on the four-mile trip to Besong Abang to sit the entrance examination to the Basel Mission College, Bali, Bamenda. Although the rainy season was approaching, the weather was fine that morning and the two boys were in good spirits, chatting as they went along. Don was carrying the letter and somewhere along the line, they became interested in the letter. What was in the letter? What was its purpose? Why had the headmaster written 'Confidential' on the envelope? Was he writing about them, if so, what had he written? These and other questions raised their interest in the letter to the point where they wanted to know what was in it.

The road to Besong Abang at that time was covered on both sides by forests, bushes, and an occasional farm. There were hardly any houses along the four-mile journey. Banya, the residential neighborhood now in the outskirts of Mamfe Town on the road to Besong Abang, had not developed at that time. Just when they got to where Banya is now located, they could not hold back their curiosity anymore. Don cannot remember which one of them suggested they open the letter. Seeking shelter in a small shed of palm fronds by the roadside to hide (as if they knew they were about to commit a crime), they opened the Headmaster's letter to the invigilator. It was marked 'Confidential' on the envelope and addressed to the invigilator of the common entrance exam to BMC, Bali.

The letter began: "In accordance with _____ I am sending herewith two of our brightest boys, Oben and Edmund Agbor, to sit the common entrance examination into Bali College…" What caught their interest and fascinated them most was the opening phrase, "In accordance with." They had never heard such an expression before. It sounded so intellectual. That was English at its best, they thought, and only the likes of headmasters of Mr. T. A. Agbor's intellectual standing could write it. They immediately started to commit it to memory; They put the letter in the envelope and jumped back on the road to Besong Abang, repeating the expression occasionally to internalize it as they went.

They had not walked up to fifty meters from the shed when the weather which had been so bright, suddenly changed. It started to drizzle. The boys tucked the letter and their writing materials inside their shirts and kept going, thinking it would just be a short drizzle. They were wrong. Within minutes, it was as if the skies had opened, for such torrential rain fell as they had never experienced before at that time of year. There were no houses, and no shacks, no places to hide from the rain. Besong Abang was still some three miles away. So they just kept going. It was not only raining; it was windy, thundering, and cold.

By the time they got to the Basel Mission School where the examination had long commenced, they had been well drenched—soaked to their underpants (that is, if they wore any in those days). They were quivering with cold and were in no condition whatsoever to write the exam even if they had arrived early. So they did not even report at the examination hall. They found a classroom to wait, praying that they do not fall sick. As soon as the downpour showed signs of abating, they set out on their journey back to Mamfe without writing the common entrance examination into Bali College.

It is said that curiosity killed the cat. So, could it be said that the rains had been sent down to punish them for their crime—their curiosity to read the Headmaster's letter? Well, it was a crime. How dare two little boys open and read a 'Confidential' letter entrusted into their care for delivery to an official. In those days, it was unheard of. However, this incident has remained green in their memory; it brought Edmund and Don closer; they have been such great friends ever since. They were so enthralled by the phrase 'in accordance with' that from that day, it became our nickname abbreviated 'IAW'!

P.S. Edmund Agbor later studied medicine in Italy and is now an eminent surgeon emeritus after an enriching career in the Cameroon civil service, the Cameroon Development Corporation (CDC), and Catholic Health Services, Diocese of Buea.

2. Forgetting His Name

As Cameroon government scholars at the University of Ibadan, Don and other students were given air tickets in September to fly from Douala to Ibadan via Lagos at the beginning of the academic year and vice versa in June at the end of the academic year. However, most often, the students did not use the Lagos/Ibadan portion of the ticket because they hardly got a connecting flight to Ibadan on arrival at Ikeja Airport. So they had to complete the journey to Ibadan by road. Since Don often traveled to Lagos either during the short vacations or for other reasons, he would buy the unused tickets from these students who were his friends after their return from Cameroon for use during his many trips to Lagos. He would pay them a 'compensatory' price for each ticket. They recognized that little was better than nothing.

During one of these trips, Don used a ticket he had bought from Augustin Bokwe, a forestry student. After his stay in Lagos, he arrived at the domestic terminal at Ikeja Airport to take his flight back to Ibadan to find a large crowd of passengers not in the departure hall but outside quite close to the plane. It was at a time when Nigeria Airways used to book more passengers than the seats available in the flights. Passengers could also get boarding passes without air tickets. So there was often real confusion when it was time to board the flight as passengers would rush en masse into the plane to secure seats.

This was also the time when the military government at the time decided to instill discipline and orderliness into the Nigerian society by declaring a 'War On Indiscipline'. An important lesson in this war was teaching Nigerians to behave orderly in public places especially where they needed to queue up, like at bus stops, post offices, etc. So on this day, the military was very much present at the domestic terminal supervising the flight to ensure orderly boarding of passengers into the plane.

As soon as it was time for boarding, a fierce-looking military officer with a whip started calling the names of ticketed passengers from the manifest. Don was sitting on something right under his nose with his ticket and boarding pass in one hand and a briefcase in the other, listening attentively. When the officer called a passenger's name, he or she answered, came forward, showed him his or her ticket and boarding pass; they were examined to ensure they were authentic and the passenger was then waved to board the plane.

"Bokwe Augustine," the officer called.

"So Bokwe came to Lagos too," Don was wondering to himself. He looked around, stretching his neck to find where Augustine may be sitting.

"Bokwe Augustine! Is Bokwe Augustine not here?" the officer called out, looking around the crowd of passengers.

"Oh please, let him not miss this flight," Don said, anxiously, still to himself.

It was at the fourth call that it dawned on Don that it is him that the officer had been calling. He was using Augustine Bokwe's ticket!

"Yes, please," Don answered, jumping up with a start. The officer looked at him in disbelief for a while.

"Are you Bokwe Augustine and I have been calling you all this while and you have been sitting right here in front of me?" Don was embarrassed.

Judging from the brutality of the military in its 'War Against Indiscipline', Don guessed what his next reaction would be: use his whip on him before asking for proof of his identity. And if he was found not to be Bokwe Augustine, he would have been held for using someone else's ticket, which was 'nontransferable'. As the officer stood there still stunned that Don was sitting right under his nose and he didn't hear him call his name three times, Don remembered the element of 'surprise' as a potent weapon in war. He rushed forward without giving the officer time to react, said "Sorry, please," waved his boarding pass, and brushed past him and up into the plane. The tactics worked. But that was a close call. Don had to learn never to forget his new names again whenever he used someone else's ticket.

3. Welli Wegbe for PRO

"Welli Wegbe for PRO, Welli Wegbe for PRO, Welli Wegbe for PRO."

At first, the shrill voices sounded quite distant. Then they drew nearer and louder. They sounded like voices of little children crying. But what would little children be doing around here? "This is a university hall of residence," Don muttered to himself as he tried to have some rest in his room in Nnamdi Azikiwe Hall at the University of Ibadan after a grueling laboratory practical. But the shrill voices and sounds continued to draw nearer and louder until they sounded just below Don's room which was above the drive way on the first floor.

At this point, he felt he had to go out and see what the hell was amiss. As he came out of his room to the balcony, many students were already standing on their balconies and looking down at the spectacle while some had gone down. When Don got there and saw what was the source of all the noise, he was stunned and saddened. A small group of some 8 little primary school children were striking empty cans and bottles and shouting with shrill voices 'Welli Wegbe for PRO, Welli Wegbe for PRO'. They must have ranged in ages from 6–8 years and were standing there with Mr. Welli Wegbe campaigning for him for the position of Public Relations Officer in the Students Union Council.

It was really sad to see those young kids, thinly clad and with hardly any shoes on, standing there and shouting the name of Welli Wegbe with their small piercing voices. Don learned they had been going around the Halls of Residence all afternoon, 'campaigning for him'. *Had it come to this?* Don exclaimed.

The Students Union of the University of Ibadan was holding its elections into its Executive Council in 1969. All the positions—President, Vice President, General Secretary, Assistant-General Secretary, Treasurer, Public Relations Officer (PRO), etc. were all up for grabs. Sadly, students' support for candidates in the Students' Union elections, like in elections at the national level went along tribal or ethnic lines. Students from the two main southern tribes, the Yorubas from the West and the Ibos from the East supported the candidates from their respective regions or ethnic groups. It is these candidates who always had the largest followings and who won except unless there was no candidate from these two tribes.

Mr. Welli Wegbe who was contesting for the post of PRO was a student from an Ethnic minority in the Rivers State of Nigeria. The other candidates contesting with him for the post of PRO were from the two majority ethnic groups—Yoruba and Ibo. So as expected during the campaign, the Yoruba and Ibo candidates had large crowds of students at their rallies. Crowds would throng whatever grounds they went to hold their campaigns; they would follow them singing and beating drums and dancing and hailing them as they moved from one hall of residence to another. Their large photos and colorful banners were hung all over the campus and there was hardly any doubt that one of these two candidates would win and by a very slim margin over the other.

Welli Wegbe's candidature was more of a joke than real. Hardly any supporters were seen with him as he went around the campus almost alone campaigning. The few students from his ethnic minority tribe didn't even care to support him as they felt it was a lost battle. Not only did he not have the supporters, he did not have the means to launch a visible campaign like those of the other two candidates. But he was a good orator and an intelligent speaker. Students were, however, not impressed. He did not come from the 'ruling' tribes. They would not gather even to listen to him speak.

In fact, many mocked him and called him the 'one-man' campaign. Thirty-six hours to the day of voting, this was the situation. All over the campus, the arguments and the quarrels and fights regarding the election of the PRO always revolved around who would beat the other—the Ibo or the Yoruba candidate.

Thirty-six hours to the time for voting, the spectacle reported above unfolded. Welli Wegbe appeared on his campaign trail around the campus with a small group of about 8 small primary school children aged between 6 and 8 years. The children were following Welli Wegbe and striking empty cans and bottles and shouting at the top of their shrill voices: "Welli Wegbe for PRO, Welli Wegbe for PRO, Welli Wegbe for PRO…"

It was a sorry and pitiful sight to see these little children, walking bare foot and thinly clad following Welli Wegbe around the large university compound.

It was at this stage of the campaign that Don had heard the shrill voices and he and other students in Azikiwe Hall had come out to find the commotion outside. This is when he had asked "has it come to this?" It emerged that when Welli Wegbe could not get the attention or sympathy of his fellow students, he decided to go to the workers village in Abadina (within the university campus) and 'recruit' these little youngsters to help him with his campaign.

When they arrived at Azikiwe hall, they had been following their candidate all afternoon and they looked tired. Yet they were still singing or shouting their song and beating their empty cans and bottles. Something dramatic happened. The sight of those little children doing what they had to do, invoked in Don and other students standing there and watching, such pity that many of them asked "Has it come to this?" meaning should a candidate be so deprived of support and attention to the extent that he has to get little kids to support him? Should ethnic affiliations becloud their thinking?

Their individual decision to support Welli Wegbe was instantaneous. They joined the children and started singing Welli Wegbe for PRO. They sent the children in front with Welli Wegbe and they followed behind. From Azikiwe Hall, they moved on to nearby Independence Hall. When the students there saw the children, they too joined the campaign. They then moved up to the old Halls and as they moved from Tedder to Mellanby and to Queens Hall, the crowd of supporters grew larger and larger, in fact almost exponentially. By night fall, when Welli Wegbe addressed his supporters, he was addressing almost the entire student body. When the elections were held the following day, Welli Wegbe won by a landslide. He was elected the Public Relations Officer of the 1969/1970 Student's Union Executive Council of the University of Ibadan, Nigeria.

Was it just frustration and desperation that drove Welli Wegbe to decide to go get help from small Abadina school children? Or did he expect the outpouring of sympathy for his campaign by students on seeing the small kids campaigning for him to turn his campaign around as it did?

Unfortunately, Don and those students who first joined the kids and helped turn the campaign around never asked those questions. So nobody will ever know except Welli Wegbe himself. What is known however is that this was the most exciting, dramatic and 'unusual' election in the history of the Students' Union elections in the University of Ibadan. Thanks to the Abadina school kids!

4. Declaring His Age

The court registrar looked up from his desk as Don and his friend, Peter, were ushered into his office by his secretary who introduced Don as the young man who came the previous day to declare his age. "Oh yes, I remember him. I told him to bring a relative or family friend to declare his age," he told his secretary.

"Good afternoon, sir," Don greeted the registrar.

"Good afternoon," he responded, removing his glasses to look at them. He stared at Peter briefly and turning to Don, he asked, "Mr. Oben, is that the uncle you brought to declare your age?"

"Yes sir," Don replied.

"Well, sit down," he said pointing to two chairs some distance away. Still looking at them, he smiled and added: "I will be with you in a minute." He again put on his glasses and continued his writing.

Don had just returned to Cameroon to take up residence and look for a job after a lengthy stay in Nigeria studying. After spending some time in Mamfe, he proceeded to Kumba where his Sister, Eunice, was living. In Kumba, he learned that every Cameroonian citizen carried a National Identity Card (NIC). He was informed that one obtained it from the Police Headquarters in Buea. In addition to completing the relevant form and paying a fee, an applicant for this ID card was required to present his or her birth Certificate. A passport-size photo was also needed but this was usually taken by the police at the police headquarters.

Now, it dawned on Don that he didn't have, and never had a Birth Certificate although he knew his date of birth. His father had told him his date of birth and when he was a little boy in primary school, he had also seen where he had written it—on the frame of one of the doors in his house. Don's father was literate and had traveled widely in Nigeria and Southern Cameroons during his employment in the colonial days. So he knew the importance of keeping records of births, etc. However, for some reasons including the fact that his children were born at home and not in hospitals or maternity homes, they didn't have officially issued birth certificates. So he wrote the birth dates of many of his children in unconventional but visible places such as the door frames of his house.

To apply for a National ID card, Don needed to have a birth certificate. The problem now was how to get one. On inquiry, he was informed that he could establish one by going to the Civil Status Registration Center in Kumba to obtain an age declaration certificate. With this certificate, he could then apply for a birth certificate and a National ID card. It was the quest for this age declaration certificate that had brought Don face to face with the registrar, Mr. Elango (not his real name) the previous day. It was he who had told Don that he needed to bring an old relative or family friend who knew his age to testify before the court when he was born. Such a person could be an uncle or an aunt or a family friend who was present when he was born.

As Don left the court that day, he wondered how and where he would see that 'someone' whom he could take to the court to testify for him. Here he was in Kumba where he knew nobody except his younger sister and her little children.

The day after he met the court registrar, he was walking along Buea Road just looking at places in the manner of an inquisitive tourist when behold, some distance away in front of him, was his old friend Peter, walking toward him. They had not seen each other since they left school. Their 'reunion' there on the street was almost tumultuous. Now Don felt he had found someone who could declare his age at the court. So he asked Peter if he could accompany him to the court to declare his age as an uncle.

"Don, that's no problem," he responded. "When?" he asked.

"Now? The court registrar's office is open," Don told him.

"Okay, I'm quite free now, let's go." And off they went, walking and talking all the way to the courthouse without giving much attention to what was taking them there.

As Don and his friend sat there waiting for the registrar to attend to them, Don was very worried about the way the registrar had smiled when he asked him if Peter was the uncle he had brought to declare his age. *Why did he smile?* And then that question he had asked, "Is this the uncle you have brought to declare your age?" As Don kept thinking about his question and his smile, it suddenly dawned on him that he had forgotten something vital. He turned to whisper to Peter. But it was late, too late! The registrar had finished what he was writing.

"Okay, gentlemen, approach my table; sit in these two chairs in front of me," the Registrar spoke, waving them toward the chairs in front of him as he opened a big register before him. After welcoming them again to the court and reading some texts concerning age declaration in court and his duties as a registrar including the administration of oaths, he asked Don's friend Peter: "Mr. Peter, you have been brought here by Mr. Oben to declare his age, right?" the Registrar asked.

"Yes Sir," Peter replied.

"What is your relationship with him, Mr. Peter?" the Registrar asked again.

"I am his uncle, Sir," Peter replied.

"And you were present when Mr. Oben was born?"

"Yes, Sir," Peter responded.

The Registrar then turned to a certain page in the big register and picking up his pen in readiness to entering the key information in age declaration, he went on: "Okay, now, Mr. Peter, where was Mr. Oben born?" Peter looked blankly at him, then turned to Don and back to him. He remained silent. The Registrar looked at Don and saw the uneasiness and embarrassment on his face. "Okay, now, Mr. Peter, when was Mr. Oben born?" he asked.

This was not an easier question for Don's friend either. He starred at the Registrar and again at Don. He would have wished he had just disappeared, vanished. He turned to the Registrar and remained silent. "If you don't remember the name of the village where your nephew was born, you should at least remember the date he was born. What day? What month? What year?" the Registrar pressed on. Peter raised his head but just stared at him. "If you don't remember the day and month, at least, tell me the year. What year was your nephew, Mr. Oben born?" the Registrar asked, biting his pen.

Peter could not answer this either. He simply just let his head droop. Don felt very sorry and guilty for the embarrassment he had caused Peter. It was while they were sitting waiting for the Registrar that it dawned on Don that he had not briefed his friend Peter on these details. That's when he had wanted to whisper to his friend but it was too late.

The Registrar realized how disconcerted and uncomfortable Don and Peter were. He addressed them, beginning with a little friendly laugh. "You are young boys, just out of school. I understand you well, as an old man and a father. You probably thought that in the matter of age declaration, anybody can come to court to declare someone's age without any proof of truth being sought by the court. You, Mr. Oben and you, Mr. Peter, must be about the same age. If not, the difference in your ages cannot be more than one year, at most two. So how could you, Peter, have been present when Oben was born?"

"When you two entered my office and you, Mr. Oben (turning to Don) responded that you had brought Mr. Peter to declare your age, I knew immediately this was a joke. That's why I smiled. I know that having just left school, you guys have not yet experienced the realities of this world. You will need to open your eyes and ears and use your head. Take government laws, rules and regulations very seriously especially matters relating to the courts of law. It is criminal to make a false declaration in a court of law…"

Then turning to Don, he said, "Mr. Oben, I will exceptionally take the relevant information from you as testimony from your 'Uncle' Peter and use it to establish and issue a Declaration of Age Certificate."

Mr. Elango, the court registrar, was really very kind and understanding and issued Don the age declaration certificate which he signed after attesting as follows:

The undersigned attests the truth of the declaration of the birth of the above mentioned child
Signed: Manasseh Elango

As soon as Don and Peter stepped out of the court premises on their way to town, Peter shot out as expected: "Don, you asked me to go declare your age and you didn't give me the details which I needed. Imagine the embarrassment I suffered. I was like a fool before the registrar."

"But you didn't ask," Don responded.

"I didn't have to ask. You should have told me when you asked me to come declare your age."

"I thought you knew," Don retorted.

"How did you expect me to know. Was I present when you were born?" Peter continued.

"But you always claimed to be older than me; that you were present when I was born and you've wanted me to always call you Big Brother. So, how come you don't know the age of your kid brother? I assumed you did," Don replied with a sneer and a laugh. Then, on a more serious note, he apologized to Peter for not giving him the information he needed before they went to court. He had meant to do so but because they were so excited about meeting each other after such a long time, they talked so much about everything else except what was taking them to court. And in court when it dawned on him that he had not done so and he wanted to whisper to him, the registrar asked them to approach his table. It was too late.

"Birds of a feather," Peter shouted.

"Yes, birds of a feather," Don responded. Then, mimicking the court registrar, Don turned to Peter and asked, "Mr. Peter, where was Mr. Oben born?"

"Get lost, you fool!" Peter pushed him away.

Both of them burst out in contagious laughter!

5. The Accident at Eyang Hill

For those who are familiar with the Kumba-Mamfe road—the highway which links the two towns of Kumba and Mamfe in the southwest region of Cameroon—the Eyang Hill situated along this highway at Eyang Village had, for several decades, presented a formidable challenge to motorists plying the highway. This section of the highway had been constructed between a steep hill on one side and a ravine on the other side.

In the 1970s, a motorist from Kumba bound for Mamfe would, after passing through Eyang Village, descend a small hill, drive over a short narrow timber bridge, and begin a long ascent on the Eyang Hill with a hilly 'wall' on the right and the ravine on the left.

This was the situation at Eyang Hill in November 1972 when Don decided to make a trip to Ibadan in Western Nigeria by road from Tiko through Kumba and Mamfe (in Cameroon) and Ikom and Onitsha (in Nigeria).

He arrived at the Kumba motor park from Tiko close to midday to find that most vehicles had left for Mamfe. Only a lone white, long-wheel-base Peugeot 404 car was at the park and it was loading goods and luggage and preparing to depart. It had a top rack on which was loaded cartons of iced fish, bunches of plantains, yams and other foodstuffs, empty plastic containers, tins of palm oil, suitcases, etc. Its physical condition was not at all inviting, and if Don had a choice, he would not have chosen to travel in this car. But he had no choice so he registered as a passenger, and it was not long before they took off on the trip to Mamfe. Nine passengers crowded into the car. Two sat in front with the driver, four including Don sat in the middle row, and three sat in the back row. It was soon clear that the car was not in good mechanical condition.

It must have been about 4:00 p.m. on that hot afternoon in November when they arrived at Eyang Village. They drove past the village, descended the small hill after the village, passed through the small bridge, and began to ascend the Eyang Hill. All was going on well, but as they were almost getting to the top of the hill, the car began to slow down. The driver changed from the speed gears to the power gears to get the car climb but to no avail. Eventually the engine went off and the car could climb no further. The driver tried to apply the brakes, but they failed and the car began to roll backward down the hill. He applied the foot and hand brakes to bring it to a stop. The brakes continued to fail. Now he decided to control and direct it into the bridge at the bottom of the hill. As the car gathered speed, all the passengers began to panic. They could see the danger coming.

They advised the driver to instead wheel the car to the right so it could hit the hillside, which was like a wall and get wedged. But he refused to listen. The car was now racing down the hill at top speed, and as it was getting to the bridge, the driver feared that he might miss entering the bridge and the car would plunge into the stream. So he wheeled it to the left into the deep ravine. Don remembers that he was quite 'awake' and aware of all that was happening. The car somersaulted about three times in the air, tore through the canopies of some trees, and hit a rocky hill side; the top rack broke off and the car finally plunged to the bottom of the ravine, top down, wheels up, some distance from the top rack!

The passengers found themselves wedged against one another with their heads down and their feet up. There was screaming. Nobody knew the condition of anybody. The doors were jammed and half buried into the ground. The driver forced his door open and crawled out. With his help, another door was forced open, and one by one, all the passengers crawled out. The scene that unfolded in front of them was as if a group of elephants had had a big fight. On its way down, the car had crashed through trees, creating an aerial opening through which the passengers could see the highway far above from where they heard people weeping and wailing in the belief that they all had perished in the ghastly accident. Some passengers had a few bruises and scratches. Some had pains in their necks and heads. Don had a little pain in the neck and a bruise or cut on some part of his face. It was a miraculous escape for all of them. God was merciful. To Him be the glory.

The luggage was scattered all over the accident scene. The torn cartons of frozen fish, the plastic containers of palm oil, the foodstuffs, the suitcases, and other baggage were strewn all over the ravine. As the passengers crawled out of the car, their preoccupation was to get away from the accident scene. Collecting whatever small and important items they could easily lay their hands on, they all started to scramble up the hilly side of the ravine toward the highway. Don picked up his small suitcase, which he found close by the car. Of course, there was no path to lead them to the highway some thirty meters up. From the ravine, they could see and hear people from the village looking down the ravine and weeping and crying. So using them as their direction and going down on all fours, they climbed over small rocks and through trees and bushes until they finally reached the highway.

There they found a large crowd of village people had gathered and more were still running to the scene crying even before knowing what the actual situation was. Apparently, some people walking to the village, whom they had passed on the way after the small bridge and who had seen the car when it crashed into the ravine, had run to the village to raise the alarm. However, tears of sadness gave way to tears of joy as they learned that no lives had been lost. As the passengers waited by the roadside with their scanty belongings, they were picked up by vehicles from Kumba traveling to Mamfe.

It is said that good news travels fast and bad news, like rumors, travels even faster. So it was with the news of the accident. By the time Don arrived in Mamfe, the news of the accident at Eyang was all over the town. At the Mamfe motor park, Don heard some grieving women talking about the car—that it belonged to a young man who turned out to be a younger brother to an old friend of Don. This younger brother was, in later years, to become also Don's close friend. The car had had some small accidents before and had been repaired, panel beaten, and painted, the women continued.

Don's mother had heard the news of the accident too. So when Don arrived unannounced, she asked him whether he had seen the accident that was said to have happened at Eyang. "Yes, I saw it. I was involved in the accident," Don told her. She stared at him in shock and disbelief. Don showed her the cut he had on his face as a confirmation. "By God's Grace, all of us in the car sustained only minor injuries," he reassured her.

After a good bath, Don used some iodine on the cut and massaged his neck with a hot balm. Putting the events of the previous day behind him and giving thanks to God, Don took another car the next day early in the morning to Ikom and thence to Onitsha in continuation of his journey to Ibadan.

6. Credit History

When Don was a young boy growing up in Mamfe in the former Southern Cameroons in the 1950s, some shops had the picture of two merchants hung on their doors. Some other shops pasted this same picture on their walls. The two merchants, one who sold his goods on credit and the other who sold his goods for cash, were sitting in their respective shops. The Merchant who sold his goods for cash was fat, happy and sat relaxing on his chair with one leg crossed over the other, and smiling broadly in contentment. Behind him was a large, open metal safe box stacked with bags and bags of money. Beneath the picture of this merchant was written: "I sold my goods for CASH. For Credit COME TOMORROW!"

The merchant who sold his goods on credit, sat behind a crude table looking miserable, with his hands pulling on his long and disheveled hair. He was thin and haggard and had a look of regret written all over his face. Behind him too was an open safe box. It was EMPTY except for a few coins scattered on the floor of the safe. Beneath his picture was written: "Sorry, I sold on CREDIT."

Don also remembered that some other shops which did not display this picture, had small posters with this advice to their clients: "For Credit Come TOMORROW." The obvious inference which one would draw from the picture of those two merchants is that selling on credit leads to bankruptcy and selling on a cash basis leads to growth and prosperity. Thus, the message behind these pictures appeared to be intended to discourage shoppers from asking for credit facilities when they come to shop.

In fact, people who were known to have a habit of taking goods from shops with a promise to pay were known as 'debtors'. To be called a debtor was humiliating. This was the situation not only in Mamfe where Don grew up but also in the whole country and in most Sub-Sahara Africa countries and it continued even into the 70s and 80s.

Don arrived in America in 1976 to continue graduate studies with this mindset—doing all his shopping as he was used to doing back in Africa without problems until the day when the incident at an electronic shop exposed him to the reality of modern commercial exchange, the credit card and credit history!

It was spring term and Don had moved out of graduate dorm and was sharing an apartment at University Avenue, Davis, California, with Lehman Walker, an African American friend. One afternoon after returning from the city, he breezed into the living room and announced airily, "Lehman, I have some good and bad news."

"First tell me the good news before the bad news. I hate bad news," Leman responded in his usual jovial manner.

"Well, the good news is that I found a fantastic stereo musical set, just the type I have been looking for, and on sale," Don announced, still excited.

"Oh yeah?" Lehman exclaimed with enthusiasm.

"Yes, to say it is fantastic, is an understatement. It's a 3-piece stereo set consisting of a big, heavy amplifier, a cassette deck and 4 large Bose Speakers all going for only $550.00. I listened to a cassette. The sound was as if the amplifier had distilled the music into its component sounds and blended with the bass booming in the background," Don finished presenting the music set.

"That sounds great. Then go ahead and buy it. That's a good deal," Lehman said.

"That's where the bad news comes in." Don said with a sigh.

"And what is the bad news? You can't afford it?" Lehman asked rather confused.

"Yes, I can't afford it. It costs $550.00 and I don't have that kind of money to put cash down," Don replied with a sigh.

"Put $550.00 cash down? What do you mean? Is that what the shop people told you, that you needed to put the money cash down to purchase the music set?" Lehman asked rather surprised.

"No, they didn't say that. We didn't even discuss anything about purchasing it. I just expressed my interest in the set. But how else does one purchase it if not by paying cash in full?" Don asked.

"No Don, you can get it on credit. I mean, on hire purchase—make a small initial payment and then pay the rest by installments," Lehman told Don, rather surprised that Don did not know this. "If you want, I can accompany you to the shop tomorrow to purchase the stereo set as tomorrow is Saturday and I am free. Are you free tomorrow?"

Don was quite excited at the prospect of purchasing the equipment on credit. His mind went back to the situation in his country at that time, not only in his country but in most developing countries, and even up to that time. People shopped with cash for most household goods and services. Shops did not give goods on credit and people who took goods on credit from small shop keepers, vendors, etc. were usually regarded with less respect. To purchase very expensive items such as cars, people would contract loans from the banks, and other lenders, collect the loan and pay for the car or equipment.

Lehman and Don arrived at the shop on the Saturday, saw and inspected the stereo set, and listened to some music played on it. Lehman was also impressed. "Man, I have always known you as a guy with a good taste," he remarked parting Don on the shoulder. The two guys then expressed their desire to purchase the equipment and after discussing and confirming the price at $550.00, the shop assistant opened his books and took down Don's personal details—name, address, telephone number, occupation, etc.

Then looking straight at Don, he asked, "What is your credit history?"

"What do you mean?" Don asked, finding the question rather strange.

"I mean, let me have your credit history so we can proceed with the purchase," the shop assistant continued.

"Yes, Don, he means you should show him some accounts or records of things you have purchased on credit," Lehman explained, sensing that Don did not perhaps understand what the shop assistant was asking for.

"Oh, I never shop on credit," Don replied proudly. "I always pay for my purchases in CASH and I pay IN FULL," he continued with an air of affluence.

"You mean, you have never purchased things using a credit card?" the shop assistant asked, quite stunned.

"No, never. I don't even have a credit card," Don replied, wondering why one must have a credit card.

Lehman was as stunned as the shop assistant. "Don, you mean you really do not have even one credit card? How do you do your groceries and pay your bills?" he asked, rather embarrassed.

"Oh, I do my groceries and pay my bills with cash I always withdrew from the bank," Don explained.

"Then you must be withdrawing large sums of money from the bank and also carrying large sums with you," Lehman remarked, shaking his head.

At this point, the shop assistant looked hard at Don one more time and then closed his books. Putting them aside, he told Don: "Mr. Don, I'm afraid, I cannot sell you the stereo set."

"What did you say, you won't sell me the stereo set?" Don asked, thinking he probably did not hear well or he didn't want to believe what he heard.

"No, I definitely won't," the shop assistant confirmed.

"And why is that?" Don pressed on.

"Because you do not have a credit history," the shop assistant explained again.

"But I'm going to make my installment payments as and when due, you can be sure of that. Lehman here can confirm that my student's monthly stipend is robust enough to pay the installments," Don tried to plead.

"That's not the issue. It doesn't matter how big your stipend is. It is not just a matter of the ability to pay. It is also a matter of trust, that you have the willingness and discipline to honor your commitments as supported by your credit history. You have provided us with no evidence of that and we have none to register in our books. You have no credit history," the shop assistant concluded. It was final.

As Don and Lehman walked back home, Lehman expressed surprise that Don never shopped with a credit card. "Don, in America, people don't make purchases or pay bills with cash. They use credit or debit cards. And the more you use your cards and you make the payments on your cards regularly, the more credit worthy you are. It means any shop can sell to you and have confidence that you will pay your installments. People don't withdraw large sums of money from the bank. In fact, people don't carry much money on them or keep it at home. If I had known this was the case, I wouldn't have bothered to come." Lehman felt quite disappointed for a wasted Saturday morning.

Now, Don understood why people at the bank always cast glances at him or raised eyebrows whenever he made large withdrawals from his account. Yes, he always estimated his weekly expenditures and went to the bank and withdrew enough money that would take him through the week. He would pay for his groceries and other shopping as well as utilities in CASH! Now he realized that was why he received embarrassing glances and raised eyebrows whenever he made his purchases and paid his bills.

Don could still not get himself to believe that he was refused from buying a musical equipment because he had never been in debt before. As he pondered over the events at the electronic shop that day, his mind went back to the situation in his country and most of the developing world. He remembered the picture of the two merchants which he often saw pasted in many shops when he was a young boy in the 1950s and early 60s. These two merchants, one who sold his goods on credit and the other who sold his goods for cash were sitting in their respective shops. He remembered the merchant who asked those who wanted credit to 'come tomorrow' which meant he would never give credit as there was no day called 'tomorrow'. And here, Don was being refused the sale of a stereo set because he had not been shopping on credit. What a clash of cultures, what a shock!

Don eventually built a credit history before leaving America. He however, accepted only one debit and one credit card from the flood of unsolicited credit and debit cards that were sent to him. He also hardly used his cards to shop for goods and services that satisfied his wants rather than his needs. He realized not too long after he joined the rank and file of credit card users that a lot many people were carrying credit cards with unsustainable debt burdens.

7. Trusting 1: A Goat Eats Wher It Is Tied

After their wedding in January 1975, Don's wife moved to Ibadan to join him as he continued his graduate studies. He rented three rooms in a building at Agbowo, opposite the University of Ibadan main gate. They were three of them who took all the nine rooms on the first floor of the building. There was Don, Papa Obehi, a young man about Don's age who worked in the university bookshop, and Peter, who worked at the Secretariat (as the government ministries were collectively called). He was a little bit younger than Don and Papa Obehi. Unlike the latter, Peter was a bachelor. Papa Obehi's wife was a successful seamstress and they had a daughter, Obehi, who was born in the same week in the August of that year as Don's first daughter, Lilian, while they were tenants in that building.

The landlord had installed one electric meter on each floor, and the tenants on each floor were to contribute and pay their monthly bills collectively at the end of each month when the bills arrived.

As Papa Obehi and Don were quite busy, Don suggested that Peter should coordinate the collection and payment of the electricity bills on their behalf. They agreed that they split the monthly bill into three and each of them should pay one-third of the bill since they all had on average about the same number and type of light points and electrical appliances. So on receiving the bill, Peter should collect from Papa Obehi and Don their share (2/3 of the bill) and, together with his 1/3 share, pay the bill at the designated office of the electricity power provider, the Nigerian Electric Power Authority (NEPA). Don and Papa Obehi tried to prevail upon Peter to be prompt in the collection and payment of the bills in order to avoid any levies for late payment. Peter carried out this assignment quite well. Papa Obehi and Don had cause to be happy as they didn't have to worry about the payment of the bills.

However, one day Don's wife, Dorothy, asked him whether he and Papa Obehi had ever asked to see the bill before paying.

"Why, what for?" Don asked her. "The young man is a good guy. We trust him. He is doing a good job," Don assured her.

"How much do you and Papa Obehi know of this guy other than that he is just another tenant? Well, you with trusting people!" she gave up.

Don later told Papa Obehi about the questions his wife had raised concerning the collection and payment of the electricity bills. He was of the same view with Don that they could trust Peter to do a good and honest job. In fact, they should be appreciative for his invaluable assistance.

Several months passed. Then one day, Dorothy again raised the issue about the electric bills.

"D (as she usually called Don), did you and Papa Obehi consider the question I asked you some months ago? Have you been checking to see the bills before you pay to be sure you are not paying more than you should pay?"

"D (as Don also called her), we have not thought it necessary to check," Don replied.

"I can't believe that two old guys like you would be paying bills which you have never seen. A young man tells you how much you have to pay, and you just accept and dish out the money without verification. It is inconceivable. Please, ask to see the bill at least once," she pleaded.

After what Don considered as 'nagging', he decided to check the next time Peter came to announce that the bill had come and payment was due. He always had the habit of cornering Don to ask for payment when Don was about to climb on his motorbike to hurry to school or when he was too busy at home and wouldn't want to be bothered with payment details. Peter had a notebook in which he showed the month, the bill number, the amount of the bill, and each person's share. But the bill itself was never attached.

"Peter, please, can you see me in the evening when I am back from the campus? I am in a hurry, I am running late," Don told him one morning as he came to ask for Don's share to the bill.

When Peter knocked at Don's door that evening and asked for his payment, showing Don the amount in his notebook, Don asked if he could see the bill for the month. Without hesitation, Peter went and brought the bill. Don then asked him if he could see all the previous bills. He obliged. When he returned with them, Don asked him to sit down while he went through his notebook and the bills from NEPA over the past several months.

Don was horrified at what he found. Papa Obehi and himself were each paying 50 percent of the bill every month over the past several months. So Peter had been sharing the bill between the two of them and they had been paying the entire bill each month while he, Peter, had been paying *nothing*! For the current month, he had similarly shared the bill between Papa Obehi and Don, and he was to pay nothing. Don couldn't believe this.

"Peter, you mean that you have been sharing the bills into two parts instead of three and Papa Obehi and myself have been paying the entire bill every month?" Don asked him.

Don called in Papa Obehi and narrated what he had unearthed.

"This cannot be true," he screamed in disbelief.

"But it is true. These are the bills from NEPA, and these are the payments you and I have made to Peter each month." They both stared at Peter. What ingenuity!

What was more agonizing was that Peter looked quite surprised at their reaction. To him, it was like they were making a mountain out of a molehill. With an annoying smile, Peter got up and gave them all the bills and his notebook.

"A goat eats the grass around where it is tied," he told them as he left the room.

Peter quietly checked out of the building the following day while Don and Papa Obehi were not around. Destination unknown.

"Two big, trusting fools," Don's wife sneered at Don when she heard their story. Really, according to Don, she was right. She should have called them 'two big trusting *idiots*'. That's what they were.

8. Trusting 2: Man Must Wack (Survive)

Don says that one of his greatest weaknesses has been trusting people—even people whom one does not have a basis for doing so. He remembers this particular Saturday morning in Ibadan when he had taken a small 'danfo' (bus) to the Dugbe Market to shop for some groceries and food items. This was at the time when his wife was studying at the University of Lagos, leaving him and her mother to take care of their two little girls, Lilian and Lorraine. Since he himself was a graduate student and was busy on weekdays, Saturdays were the most convenient days he could go to the market for shopping, and he did so almost every Saturday.

On this particular Saturday, as Don alighted from the bus at the Dugbe Market bus stop, he was immediately 'accosted' by an elderly man, well-dressed, of average height, and who spoke good English. "My son, I am on my way to my village a few miles from Ibadan, but I didn't know the bus fare was this high. I am short by one naira, 50 kobo (N1.50K). I don't know if you can help me," he said quietly. But before Don could respond, he quickly added, "But don't worry, my son, if you don't have. I will surely find someone else who can help me."

He didn't even need to have added the last statement. Don already felt sorry for him. His quiet, polite manners, dignified comportment and demeanor, and excellent English completely disarmed him. Don thought this man must be some well-off gentleman who had unexpectedly found himself faced with an embarrassing situation. Don's response was very quick because he thought he shouldn't prolong his embarrassment. Don gave him five naira (N5.00K) out of the meager amount he had brought to the market and wished him a safe trip home. Don was sure this small reduction in his shopping money would not significantly reduce his groceries. The way the man thanked Don even made Don more sympathetic and wished he could give him even more.

In about an hour, Don had done his shopping and emerged from the market with one big bag of tinned or packeted foodstuffs slung over his shoulders and a bag of groceries and vegetables in his right hand. As he was pushing his way through the same busy bus stop to board another bus home, somebody tapped him on the back and began to tell him the same story as the man he had encountered not too long ago when he had arrived to shop: he was stranded, he needed only one naira and fifty kobo to make up his transport fare to return to his village, bla, bla, bla. But if Don didn't have, he shouldn't worry… The story sounded so familiar and so was the voice too.

Don turned around quickly to see who it was. Behold, it was the same old man he had given not just the N1.50k he had asked for, but N5.00k. Apparently, he had not recognized Don, probably because Don had not faced him directly and because he was now carrying two heavy bags with all sorts of foodstuffs. Don was furious. He asked the old man if he did not remember that he (the man) had told him that same story and he (Don) had given him not N1.50K but N5.00K. The old man looked at Don straight in the face and smiled very sweetly.

"Man must wack." Then he turned and went on to another passerby.

"A man must eat or a man must survive," Don found himself repeating as the bus sped along the way. He had been fooled by a professional beggar. They come in all forms. So, whom can one trust?

9. Trusting 3: Trusting the AUC

This third episode on trusting happened after the end of Don's journey and should not have been included in this book. But since I am recounting incidents where Don's trust was betrayed, I thought it incumbent on me to include it as the third and most glaring, unexpected example of misplaced trust.

This episode concerns the trust Don had placed in the Department of Rural Economy and Agriculture (DREA) of the African Union Commission (AUC), Addis Ababa, Ethiopia, when he was called upon a few years after his retirement, to undertake a consultancy assignment. The Commission wanted him to undertake a study with the technical guidance and collaboration of the Secretariat of the New Partnership for Africa's Development (NEPAD), on 'Establishing and Formalizing the Conference of African Ministers of Agriculture (CAMA)'.

Due to the need to get the assignment started as urgently as possible, Don was urged to get on board first and commence work without waiting to formalize the contractual agreements. This would be done as soon as possible during the assignment.

To begin with, he was asked to develop a Concept Note/TOR for the consultancy on the need for a formal African Ministers Conference Organ within the formal and protocol establishment of the AU structures. With short notes and pieces of information received by email and over the phone from NEPAD, Don prepared and submitted the Concept Note/TOR document entitled: Establishing and Formalizing the African Agriculture Ministers Conference within the AU Structures and Organs: Concept Note/TOR.

In section 5 of this document, 'Duration of Assignment', Don included some envisaged expenses as well as an indication of his professional fees. This document was accepted. As mentioned earlier, Don was asked to commence the assignment immediately with the promise that the contract would be signed later. Since he had no reasons to doubt the AUC/NEPAD and being anxious to serve this esteemed regional organization, he immediately commenced the assignment with the expectation that issues regarding the contract would be discussed and the latter signed as promised and his professional/consultancy fees paid as soon as the assignment was completed.

Following the approval of the Concept Note/TOR, Don was asked to develop a decision proposal for consideration by the Ministers' Meeting due in April, on the rationale for establishing the African Agriculture Ministers Conference (AAMCo). He prepared this proposal with guidelines provided by the DREA/NEPAD. He was further asked to attend and present this paper entitled 'Establishing and Formalizing the African Agriculture Ministers' Conference within the AU Structure and Organs' to the Joint Conference of African Ministers of Agriculture, Lands and Livestock, scheduled for 20–24 April 2009 in Addis Ababa, Ethiopia.

Don was accordingly sent a return air ticket (Douala/Addis Ababa/Douala) for the meeting, and on his arrival there, he was accommodated at the Addis Ababa Hilton and also paid DSA for the duration of the meeting. While in Addis Ababa, he discussed the paper with the DREA and NEPAD and fine-tuned and retitled the paper: 'Establishing and Formalizing the Conference of African Ministers of Agriculture (CAMA) within the AU Structures and Organs'. He not only made a PowerPoint presentation of the paper on establishing CAMA to the meeting of experts but also attended and assisted in servicing both the meeting of experts and the Conference of Ministers, including attending meetings of the AUC/NEPAD secretariat, discussing the draft reports, and housekeeping matters, etc.

Following the endorsement of the proposal for the establishment of CAMA and, in accordance with the recommendation of the Ministers of Agriculture, Lands and Livestock, Don was now required to propose the functional/operational support systems and relevant structures that would be needed to support the Conference, including the Secretariat and corresponding budget. With this in view, the DREA/NEPAD decided that Don's mission to Addis Ababa be extended for another four days, 25–29 April 2009, for further consultations and discussions at the AU and for collecting any additional data.

Don subsequently had meetings at the offices of the legal counsel; the director of administration and human resources development; the head, human resources development division; the director, human resources, science and technology; head, rural economy division; etc. His stay in Addis Ababa Hilton was accordingly extended for four more days and he was paid additional DSA for those days.

After he arrived in Addis Ababa for the conference, Mr. Bwalya of NEPAD, under whose guidance Don was working, mentioned that the GTZ was raising issues about his consultancy being paid from GTZ funds to NEPAD, which were for a different project. He however assured Don that the matter was being resolved and his contract would be prepared and signed while he was in Addis. This, however, did not happen supposedly, due to pressure of work during the meeting. At the end of the meeting, Don was asked to leave the relevant information needed for preparing the contract with the NEPAD secretariat, which, on arrival back at their Headquarters in Midrand, South Africa, would prepare and mail it to him for signature and return to NEPAD.

While still waiting for the contract to be sent to him as promised, Don went ahead to prepare the final document in which the Ministers of Agriculture, Lands and Livestock required him to propose the functional/operational support systems and relevant structures that would be needed to support the CAMA, including the Secretariat and corresponding budget. This document which he entitled 'Establishing and Formalizing the Conference of African Ministers of Agriculture (CAMA): Institutional Framework and Operational Support Systems' was completed in May 2009 and sent to NEPAD and the AUC for comments before finalizing it. Meanwhile, he continued to work on the document in order to improve it.

After waiting for three months without any comments from either organization in spite of several reminders, Don finalized and transmitted it together with the annexes, to the AUC/DREA and NEPAD in August 2009. During the three months he was improving the document and waiting for their comments, Don continued to make calls and send emails to both DREA and NEPAD reminding them that they had still not sent him the contract documents to sign.

After he had completed the assignment, he wrote to Mr. Bwalya of NEPAD and H.E. Mrs. Tumusiime Rhoda Peace, the Commissioner of AUC-DREA, requesting payment of his professional fees. After several of such letters, he finally received an email from the Commissioner dated Monday 22 August 2011 in which she expressed surprise that the issue of his payment was still pending and directed her Director responsible for technical matters and payments, to ensure that Don's payment was settled. On receipt of this directive from his Commissioner, Dr. Abebe wrote Don requesting him to send him (Dr. Abeb) the details of his contract.

Of course, Don told him he had not signed any contract and explained the circumstances under which he undertook the assignment and the unsuccessful efforts he had made during the past several months to have the contract papers sent to him for signature. Don then referred him to Mr. Bwalya whom he worked with for confirmation and any other information he needed.

On 5 December 2011, Dr. Abebe wrote to inform Don that he regrets that he could not make a request for Don's payment to be processed because Don had no contract with the AUC. In Don's reply to him, Don again reminded him of the circumstances under which he commenced the assignment and the commitment made by the AUC/DREA. He also questioned how the AUC/DREA could pay for his participation at the Meeting of Experts and the Conference of Ministers of Agriculture, Water and Livestock in April 2009 in Addis Ababa at which he made a presentation, and now could not pay his professional fees because he did not have a contract with the AUC. Dr. Abebe was not impressed and he never communicated with Don again.

Don communicated the director's response to the commissioner but never heard from her again either. So, as a last resort, Don decided to bring the matter to the attention of the AUC chairperson, urging her to use her high office to prevail on DREA to meet its obligations.

This letter was mailed by Express Mail Service (EMS) and Don was given a tracking number. It was delivered to Dr. Nkosazana Dlamini Zuma after a long while because she was frequently out of office and the mail had to be delivered personally to her. The delivery was confirmed by EMS, Addis Ababa office to the EMS office in Buea where the letter was mailed. She never responded to the letter.

Don had followed this matter of his payment for four years. He decided to give up at that point. Based on the estimated days he actually worked on the assignment and his charges per day, both of which were accepted by the AUC, Don estimates that he lost USD15,500 in professional fees. With much consternation, Don remembered Shakespeare's Julius Caesar and what Caesar said to his friend, Marcus Brutus, "Et tu, Brute?" So even Africa's esteemed organization could not live up to its promise. Once again, another result of *trusting*! Had Don learned any lessons?

Well, in the three incidents involving 'trusting' recounted above, Don may really be called a fool for trusting especially under circumstances which he should not. His problem with trusting, however, arises from his erroneous assumption or rather expectation that all people should behave the way he does or, should not do things which he would not do. In other words, Don holds everybody to his standards of moral behavior and responsibility. And where he does not have grounds for trusting, he finds it God-fearing to give people the benefit of doubt and assume that they will uphold the trust.

Unfortunately, as recounted above, his trust in all the three incidents was misplaced. The question still is "Has he learned any lessons?" Yes. He recognizes and accepts the fact that among people, there are the good, the bad, and the ugly. One has to use one's intuition to distinguish between these kinds of people and exercise a lot of caution in the degree to which one trusts them. He accepts responsibility for having been deceived. As Shakespeare puts it, "It is not in our stars to hold our destiny but in ourselves."

10. Don and Dogs

Commonly referred to as 'man's best friend', the domestic dog, *Canis familiaris*, is one of the most adorable domestic pets, especially in the Western world. Although they serve many purposes, in sub-Saharan Africa, dogs are kept mainly as guard or watch dogs by individuals, families, and security companies to protect their owners and their property. One of the most popular guarding breeds is the German shepherd. German shepherds are said to be bold, confident, and fearless. They are also said to have a calm demeanor when in a household but can quickly react when their family or home is threatened.

Guard dogs are caged all day and are only allowed out at night to keep watch. This was probably why Don did not know that his neighbor in the other apartment of the duplex in which he was staying had a watch dog—a huge German shepherd that was to attack him just a few days after he moved into an apartment in Tiko, Cameroon.

It was July 1973. Don had arrived in Cameroon to undertake his research on labor absorption in large-scale agriculture in the Cameroon Development Corporation (CDC) plantations. This was in partial fulfillment of the requirements for the award of the degree of Master of Science in the Department of Agricultural Economics of the University of Ibadan. The CDC was generous and allocated him an apartment in a duplex in Tiko where he could stay while undertaking his fieldwork. The other apartment of the duplex was occupied by the Representative of Nigeria Airways in West Cameroon at the time. He and Don had met only once or twice before this incident as Don commenced his work immediately after moving in and only returned late in the evenings.

Shortly after Don's return one evening, the watchman guarding the premises knocked on his door around 7:00 p.m. and announced that a visitor with luggage had just entered the compound and was looking for him. Since he had luggage, he must obviously have come from outside Tiko. Don went outside and welcomed him, and as they turned to walk toward the house, Don heard a sudden movement behind him, then a whine, and before he realized what was happening, he felt a big, sharp bite on the back of his right thigh. Turning around, he saw a huge black German shepherd disappearing behind the house. Unfortunately Don was wearing a pair of shorts so his thigh had been well exposed. It was a deep bite and blood started to flow down his right leg. The pain was excruciating. He received some first-aid treatment that night—cleaning with an antiseptic solution, applying some iodine, and covering with a plaster.

The following morning he went to the Cottage Hospital, the Corporation's hospital in Tiko where Anderson Doh was the Medical Officer. Both he and Don had graduated from the University of Ibadan the same year, and while Don was working as a Field Assistant in Tiko Rubber Plantation, he had been employed and sent to the hospital as the Medical Officer. They were both members of the Tiko Club, and they often played tennis in the evenings at the club. It was the first time they were seeing each other after Don resigned from the Corporation to go for further studies. This first visit to the hospital was the beginning of a month-long agonizing experience with a dog bite. In spite of the antibiotic injections Don was given, the dog bite developed into a big wound that defied the healing process. The pain and discomfort which this dog bite caused him during his two months' fieldwork in the CDC plantations was inexpressible.

It was the height of the rainy season in Cameroon. Don still had to collect data from, among many other plantations, Idenau Palms Plantation located in the rainiest part of West Africa. His daily journeys with his assistants from plantation to plantation in the torrential rain and with a wound that was gnawing him like a toothache made matters continually worse. He had to interrupt his schedule and go for the cleaning and dressing of the wound many times a week. It lasted almost the entire duration of his field trip in Cameroon. This dog bite remains one of his most bitter experiences with dogs because it was very deep. The healing process took so long, and it caused him so much pain and agony over several weeks. He developed a fear for dogs and hoped he would never have to deal with dog bites again. This was not to be.

Eight years later, in 1981, while Don was teaching at ENSA Yaounde, he returned from school after a hard day's work to find a little commotion in front of the house. As he squeezed the car through the narrow gate into the open garage in front of his house and came out, he was told that his neighbor's dog had bitten his little niece, Gwendoline. Don flew into a rage because his mind immediately went back to his own dog bite and its aftermath eight years earlier. It would have been better if the dog had bitten him instead of her because he couldn't imagine a little seven-year-old having to go through the agony that he went through. Don rushed to the neighbor's house and confronted everybody who was standing outside the house. They were Francophones.

In his rage, he forgot almost all the little French he knew and started to upbraid the owner of the dog in a mix of French and English for not securing his dog. The owner apologized that the dog was not a watch dog but a live-in dog and so did not need to be secured. He repeatedly stated that the dog had been given all the necessary vaccinations and so there was no cause to worry. This assurance notwithstanding, Don was not prepared to take any chances. He told the owner he was taking Gwen to the Institut Pasteur in Yaounde for wound cleansing, antibiotics, and a tetanus vaccination and insisted he must accompany him. The owner did. He had to.

The week following this incident was full of much anxiety regarding the condition of the wound. Fortunately, Gwen remained strong. The dog bite was well treated and it healed quickly. Don heaved a big sigh of relief and hoped that he would never have to go down this memory lane again. And again, this was not to be.

It was September 1982, a week after Don took up appointment at the UN Economic Commission for Africa in Addis Ababa. His wife, Dorothy, and children, Lilian, Lorraine, Don Jr., and Gwendoline, were still in Cameroon waiting to join him after he had gotten accommodation. So he was alone. Dr. Lucas Tandap and his wife, Maggie, invited Don for lunch at their home in the Bole neighborhood in Addis Ababa. Don had heard of them while in Cameroon but met them for the first time only after his arrival in Addis. They too had never known Don before. So the lunch invitation was a welcome gesture.

"That's a trendy suit you are wearing. It must be a designer suit," Lucas remarked as Don jumped into his blue luxurious Mercedes 230 to leave the ECA compound for his home that afternoon.

"Yes, it is, thanks. Just bought it in Lagos on my way here. I thought it was important to pick up some new work clothes for Addis," Don explained.

They got to the house, and as soon as the guard opened the gate and they drove in, a huge dog, a great Dane, rushed to greet them or, more rightly, its master, Dr. Tandap.

"Oh, come on out, don't be afraid. It won't bite you," Lucas urged Don out of the car when he noticed Don's apprehension about the dog.

He gently petted the dog to acknowledge its presence. But as they were walking together side by side with the dog toward the house, all of a sudden, Don heard the dog whine just behind him and felt a swift, sharp bite on the back of his right thigh. This time, the dog not only bit him, it made a big hole in his trousers on the spot where it had bitten him. However, the trousers constrained the dog's teeth from piecing deep into his thigh. The wound was nevertheless painful. Don could see the embarrassment on Lucas' face because he had just tried to dispel Don's earlier trepidation. He apologized profusely.

This incident happening within the first week of his arrival in Addis Ababa was not a good welcome. After several visits to the ECA Clinic for treatment, the bite wound healed, but the damage done to his trousers could not be repaired. Don had to discard his suit—a suit he had bought just the week before and had worn that day for the first time. As the wound healed, Don tried to put the incident behind him and keep a distance from all dogs. By this time, he had not only developed a fear for dogs, the fear had developed into a phobia even for small dogs too.

Some years later, after Don had forgotten about the dog bite at the Tandaps, he went to visit Ben and Emma Kasamale at the Chinese Compound in Addis Ababa. They were family friends from Malawi. In fact, they arrived in Addis Ababa to take up their appointments at ECA about the same time in 1982. Ben came to welcome Don when he heard his car drive in. As Don parked and they were about to walk toward the house, their little dog started to bark and run toward them. It was a little brown dog, a mixed breed.

"Oh, don't mind him. He is just a little dog, friendly and playful," Ben told Don in his usual quiet manner and smile. "He is quite harmless," he continued, apparently trying to reassure Don since he knew he had been bitten by the Tandaps' dog some years earlier.

"I don't trust any dog, Ben," Don replied. He couldn't afford to be dismissive of the dog, its small size notwithstanding. Ben drove it away and they turned to go into the house. But as they were about to enter the house, out of nowhere the little dog appeared and before Don knew it, he felt a quick bite up his thigh. It was the same thigh that had been bitten twice before. Taken by surprise and the sharp pain, Don instinctively jumped up and if Ben had not caught him, he would have had a serious fall. The little dog disappeared as soon as it committed the act. Ben could not believe it.

"This dog has never done anything like this before," he lamented. "I am awfully sorry, deeply sorry, and I apologize," he added.

"Well, Ben, no need to be apologetic. You didn't bite me." Don tried to lessen his sense of guilt and cheer him up even though the pain was getting intense.

As Don drove to the ECA Medical Center from the Kasamales' home to have the injury treated, his head was flooded with memories of all the bites he had received from the domestic dog, *Canis familiaris*, 'man's best friend', as it is commonly referred to. So, he and dogs, can they be said to be best friends?

11. Being Mean or Being Just

It was 1987 and Don was on mission to three African countries—Malawi, Lesotho, and Zimbabwe—in connection with a study he was undertaking on *Measures for Improving Credit Facilities and Marketing Services in Africa at the Level of the Small Farmer*. In Malawi, he had visited concerned officials of coffee and other crop marketing boards in Lilongwe and Blantyre. The night before his departure for Lesotho, he was invited by the family of their family friends in Addis, Ben and Emma Kasamale, in Blantyre for dinner. In addition to the dinner, they gave him a plastic bag containing five kilos of pure, white maize flour used for making a traditional maize meal. This maize meal was very popular in East and Southern Africa and also in Cameroon, and Don valued it very much. In Malawi, it is called 'insima', and in Cameroon, 'fufu corn'. Don was to carry the maize flour home to Addis to their friend, his wife.

Don was traveling with one small, hard suitcase and a beautiful pink extendable bag. This bag could be extended upward to make it taller and bigger depending on the amount of stuff one wanted to put into it, by unzipping one, two, or three zips sewn around it. On the other hand, it could be turned into a small portable bag by zipping up all the zips. The only problem with the bag was that one of the four wheels at the base by which one could roll the bag along a tiled or concreted surface had gotten broken and had to be taken off. Therefore, whereas Don used to roll it along when it had four wheels, now he couldn't do so because with three wheels, it would just wobble and tumble over.

Back in his hotel, Don put the five-kilo plastic bag of maize flour into the bag, which he had turned into a small portable bag so he could carry it as a hand luggage. At the Lilongwe Airport, he checked in the small suitcase straight to Maseru (capital of Lesotho) and carried the small pink bag as his hand luggage. In those days when South Africa was under the apartheid regime, travelers to Lesotho by air had to transit through Johannesburg. And if

404

they could not connect their flights on the same day for any reason, they were accommodated at a hotel facility at the airport. Most African travelers, including Don, could not go into Johannesburg because their passports carried the prohibition 'Passport valid to all countries except the Republic of South Africa'.

As Don boarded the South African Airways (SAA) flight which was to take him to Johannesburg, the airline crew insisted on taking the small bag and keeping it with other hand luggage, which they had taken from other passengers, in order to decongest the cabins. They would give them back to the passengers on arrival in Johannesburg. When they arrived at the Jan Smuts Airport, as it was called at that time, Don went through immigration screening and waited for the SAA crew to get his hand luggage. As he waited, he saw a white SAA official approaching him with what looked like his small pink bag now covered with a plastic wrapping.

"Please, is this your bag?" he asked Don directly since he was the only passenger left standing there. Don was surprised at the mess of white 'dust' all over the pink bag and plastic wrapping. The bottom of the bag had given way and some of the maize flour had spilled.

"Yes, it resembles my bag except that it looks funny and messy," Don replied.

"Well, sorry, the bottom of the bag gave way and the plastic bag inside fell out, bursting and spilling some of the powder that was in it. We have tried to clean it up and wrap it with some paper to enable you to proceed on your journey," the official said and proceeded to hand over the bag to Don as if the airline had done him a favor.

"But that isn't how it was when your cabin crew took it from me at the airport in Lilongwe," Don told him.

"Well, the weight was too much for the bag and so the bottom gave way," he explained.

"No, I do not think that the weight of the stuff was too much for the bag. I carried the bag with the stuff in it from my hotel in Lilongwe to the airport, and then to the check-in counter, and to the departure lounge, and on to the flight where your cabin crew took it from me. All along, the bottom of the bag did not give way. How come the stuff became too heavy only when it was in the custody of your airline? The conclusion is inescapable that the bag gave way due to poor and careless handling by your staff. South African Airways must take full responsibility for damaging my luggage," Don argued.

"Okay, the airline will replace your bag. When are you returning from Maseru, Lesotho?" he asked after a short reflection. Don guessed the SAA official couldn't argue against such logic. After Don had told him that he would be in Lesotho for four days, the SAA official took him to an office where Don should check and collect a new bag with his maize flour on his return to Jo'burg.

Don's flight from Maseru to Johannesburg four days later had a delay of one hour, which reduced his connecting time to Harare, the next destination on his itinerary. So on arrival in Johannesburg, he hurried to the office which he had been directed to collect his maize flour and the new bag. After identifying himself, the SAA staff in charge of the office went into an inner room and brought out a bag which he placed on the counter. Opening it, he asked Don if it was not identical to his old bag in terms of color, size, design/model, beauty, etc. It had zips around the body just like Don's old bag, which allowed it to be extended upward when they were unzipped or contracted to a small bag when they were zipped.

Don agreed it was identical to the old bag and was very pleased with himself that his bag had been replaced with a brand-new one. The SAA staff then opened it to show that the content was Don's maize flour. Don was then made to sign a collection register. Since he was in a hurry to catch his flight to Harare, he carried the new bag in one hand and the hand luggage he had brought from Maseru in the other hand.

At Harare, as they descended from the aircraft, they were asked to walk to the terminal building where they would pass through immigration and customs. Since the distance was a bit long, Don decided to consolidate the two hand luggage which he was carrying into one so as to make it easier for him to carry them. He unzipped the zips of the new bag he had collected from South African Airways containing the maize flour so as to extend the bag upward. He then put in the hand luggage from Maseru on top of the five-kilo bag of maize flour. Now, he would be able to walk more conveniently to the terminal building with one hand free and the other hand rolling the new bag along the way.

But as he tried to roll the bag, he noticed that it was wobbling and often tumbled over just like the old bag used to do. But the old bag was wobbling and tumbling because one of the four wheels had gotten damaged and had therefore been removed, leaving only three wheels—two on one side and one wheel on the other side. Don couldn't understand what was going on. Why would a new bag with four wheels behave this way? After trying unsuccessfully to roll the bag on its wheels, he carried it. He would find out what the problem was after he collected his suitcase from the baggage hall.

Don was to receive a most unexpected shock. On close examination of the new bag, he discovered to his chagrin that the South African Airways had decided to replace his bag with a new bag, which was *exactly* like his old bag that they had damaged. After buying a new and identical bag, they had therefore unscrewed and removed one of the wheels, leaving it with three wheels!

Don couldn't believe this—how an airline, a world-renowned airline for that matter, could do this. In Don's experience, any time an airline had to replace a damaged luggage, it simply replaced it with a similar brand-new one—no tampering with it. Don could only guess that their purpose was retaliatory—to make sure that their replacement did not give Don any advantage over the replaced one.

Was the South African Airways' action 'mean' or was it 'just'? That is the question.

12. A Case of Two Cities

Don arrived in Accra, Ghana, during his first mission to that country in the mid-eighties. The Department of Women Affairs was one of the government departments with which his Division at ECA had requested the UNDP to arrange a meeting during his visit. He had arrived the previous night and had been put in a hotel by the UNDP. By 9:00 a.m. the following day, Monday, he was at the office of the Director of Women's Affairs, who was waiting for him.

"Welcome, Brother," she said warmly as Don greeted her courteously and introduced himself as Mr. Oben from ECA.

"Yes, we had been told that you were coming and so had been expecting you," she said as she showed Don to a chair opposite her. "Hope you had a nice flight to Accra. You must be happy to be home again," she continued.

"The flight was okay. Thank you," Don responded without answering the second part of her question.

"When last were you home? I mean, when last were you in Ghana?" she pressed on.

"Sorry, madam, I have never been to Ghana," Don answered. She looked at him, quite surprised.

"What do you mean, were you born outside?" (meaning not born in Ghana.)

"I am not Ghanaian, madam," Don replied.

"What do you mean, you are not Ghanaian? Is your name not Mr. Obeng?" she asked, looking straight into Don's face. Then she shot out, "Oh, so because you have joined the UN, you are now denying your country."

That statement took Don by surprise. He felt uncomfortable, embarrassed. This was at a time when the Ghanaian economy was facing hard times. Things were really tough. Life was hard. Staff going on mission to Ghana used to carry bathing soap, toilet paper, and other simple things which would normally be provided in a hotel. So she must have made the statement against the background of the country's economic situation at the time. At this point, Don felt he needed to assure her that he was not denying Ghana. He was just not Ghanaian, by birth or nationality.

"Yes, madam, my name is Oben and it is spelled without a *g*." In order to leave no room for any doubt in her mind, Don decided to tell her the town he came from in Cameroon. "I am Oben and I come from Mamfe in Cameroon."

Don was mistaken. Instead, she was now even more convinced that Don was a Ghanaian.

"You come from Mamfe and you are Obeng? Then what are you talking about not being a Ghanaian? Mamfe Akwapim is just a few miles from here, on the hills overlooking Accra. So which other Mamfe can you be talking about?" she said, looking up at Don as if she had proven her case.

Her manner reminded Don of his mathematics teacher in secondary school whenever he proved a theorem: 409uode rat demonstrandum, he would write at the end and repeat it loudly.

"I come from a town called Mamfe in Cameroon. Do you mean there is a town in Ghana called Mamfe?" Don asked, really surprised. He was now curious and wanting to know more.

"Of course! And if you doubt it, I can take you there. Ah! Incidentally, I have a meeting there this coming Saturday at 10:00 a.m. It is a meeting of the town's Development Committee. If you are free, I can take you along with me to show you Mamfe. I can pick you up from your hotel."

Throughout the week, each day Don returned to the hotel after the day's meetings, his mind would dwell on the linkage between Oben(g) and Mamfe in both Ghana and Cameroon. Was it just a coincidence or does it have some historical connections, perhaps something to do with migrations, that they both have Mamfe as a place name and Oben (g) as a person name?

Fortunately for Don, his official program ended on Friday afternoon and his flight out of Accra was on Sunday morning. So he was free all Saturday and could therefore go see this Mamfe in Ghana. He called the lady to inform her he would be free to accompany her on Saturday morning.

They arrived at Mamfe just as members of the Development Committee were entering the meeting hall.

"Before we start our meeting, please permit me to introduce to you this gentleman here with me. He is Mr. Obeng and he is on mission from ECA in Addis Ababa, Ethiopia."

There was clapping. "Oh, welcome home," one man said in a loud voice. "You are welcome to our meeting," another said.

"And Mr. Obeng is from Mamfe," Don's host continued.

"Oh, so he is even one of ours. Thank you for bringing him to our meeting."

Some members came forward and started to embrace Don, telling him, "Welcome, welcome." The young people said, "Welcome, Brother." The older ones said, "Welcome, Son." Some were shaking his hands. Don was confused.

"However, Mr. Obeng says he is from Mamfe in Cameroon," Don's host finally ended.

There was an expression of surprise on everybody's face as they shifted their gaze from her to Don and back to her. Then almost in unison two or three people asked: "From Mamfe in Cameroon?"

"How can he be from Cameroon, didn't you say he is from Mamfe?" someone quickly added.

"That is why I brought him to see our Mamfe and I am glad that it so happened that our committee is also meeting today so he has the opportunity of meeting with you members of the Development Committee of Mamfe."

Don was given the opportunity to say a few words. He told them he was happy to be in their midst; that he came from Mamfe in Cameroon and the name 'Oben' spelled without a *g* is found only among the Banyangis who are the indigenes of Mamfe. He was happy to know that some of his ancestors migrated from Mamfe in Cameroon and founded this Mamfe in Ghana and gave their offspring the name 'Oben', to which a *g* was later added and the pronunciation changed a bit to make it sound Ghanaian, he joked. There was laughter and shouts of "No, no, no. It was the other way around," someone added humorously.

The enthusiasm and the friendliness did not diminish. They still referred to Don as 'brother' as they were convinced that some of their ancestors must have migrated to Cameroon and founded Mamfe. The names of the two towns could not be a coincidence. Don was given a guide to take him around the town. His host told him her brother, who is a professor of history, had told her that Mamfe in Ghana was founded in 1492.

Don and his guide went around on foot. Mamfe Akwapim as it is called, is located on the hills overlooking the city of Accra. The town was by far bigger and much more populated than his Mamfe in Cameroon. There was the old (ancient) and the new (modern) town. His guide first took hm through parts of the ancient town and then through some neighborhoods of the modern town. The latter, of course, grew out of the former. Their tour took them about two hours and by the time they returned to the development meeting hall, the meeting had closed and the members were waiting to bid Don farewell.

Since this trip to Mamfe, Don has found himself wondering whether there is a connection between the names 'Obeng' and 'Mamfe' in Ghana and 'Oben' and 'Mamfe' in Cameroon. Experts on African migrations and population movements can have a field day. For Don, this 'coincidence', if he may call it this way, has been quite fascinating and he has found himself going to visit Mamfe in Ghana each time he went there on mission. It became like a pilgrimage!

13. The Misguided Fool

It was around midday on a Sunday in 1983. Don was then a young staffer at ECA. Dorothy, his wife, had just dropped him off at the office on their way from the Lutheran Church in Addis Ababa where they had just attended church service. As it often happened when he had some urgent assignments that he needed to complete, she would drop him off at his office after church service on Sunday and come for him later in the evening. Just as Don was settling down, he heard a knock on his door and the Chief of his Section, the Agriculture Marketing Service, walked in. He was Zohair Abdallah, a Sudanese national.

"What a surprise," Don exclaimed. "This is a Sunday, what's up?" Don asked.

"I just came in to check my mail and I knew you were in. So I thought I should just pop in," he explained.

After exchanging a few pleasantries, he drew up one of Don's guest chairs and planted himself right opposite where Don was seated at his large desk.

"Don, I just want to give you a piece of advice, not as your chief, but as a personal friend. I have observed for a long time that on most weekends when I come in to check or collect my mail, you are in your office, working. That is good and I commend you. We all know that you are a conscientious staffer who has been making immense contributions to the Division's work. But let me tell you, your family is more important than this work. If your family is not happy, you will not be happy and if you are not happy, you cannot even work well. You work so hard during the week that you should spend quality time with your wife and children at home during the weekend."

"In fact, there is no need for anybody who works really hard Monday to Friday to come to the office on Saturday and Sunday except if it is absolutely necessary. I can understand your background given that you came here from the university. But here, you do not need to come in at weekends. I used to do that myself, but I realized it was not necessary."

Wow, such advice coming from one's boss! Never heard it before. *Who can argue against such logic?* Don murmured to himself.

Don understood what he meant by him coming from a university background. Casting his mind back at his tenures at the University of Ibadan and the Dschang University Center, the weekends provided a calmness and serenity on the campus which was conducive to work. Hence, he and a few colleagues often found themselves sneaking into their offices at this time of the week to do some useful work undisturbed—prepare lessons, complete a paper due for publication, or just read some new material.

However, here at the Joint Division in ECA, Addis Ababa, Don's coming to the office on some weekends to work was not as a result of a habit acquired during his tenures at the university. He had cause to do so. Not only was he implementing his personal work program with its deadlines, almost every week he picked up ad-hoc assignments from divisional meetings. Each week, the Division held two to three meetings to discuss issues relating to the work program or assignments from the cabinet office of the executive secretary in the domain of agriculture. At those meetings, each time Don made a suggestion for the way forward on any major issue they discussed, he ended up being asked to take the necessary action to implement the suggested action.

He remembers one occasion when the issue was on 'cooperation' between the ECA and an international organization on some agriculture sector issues. Don had suggested that the Division should prepare a Memorandum of Understanding (MOU) which they would present at the next meeting with that institution, emphasizing that this MOU should, among others, define their working relationship.

"Well, Don, you have prepared a number of MOUs. Can you please help us with this one especially as you came up with the idea? It should be ready by next week. Thanks for your usual understanding," the division's director, Prof. Odero-Ogwel, had asked him.

At various other meetings, when Don had suggested that the Division should prepare a 'position paper' or a 'working paper' or a 'policy paper' or an 'issues paper', which should form the basis for the discussions at an envisaged meeting, the buck had invariable always come back to him.

"Can someone volunteer to prepare this paper? I see no volunteers. I can understand, given your busy schedules. Well, Don, since you came up with the idea of this paper which we all agree is an excellent one, I am sure you have some major issues that you want us to focus on. Can you please prepare this paper and get it ready by our meeting next week?" the director had coaxed him.

That was how Don picked up ad-hoc assignments almost every week, with deadlines that added to his own work program deadlines. And Dr. Abdallah knew this. He sometimes felt concerned that these ad hoc assignments from the Division might constrain the implementation of their Section's work program because they were quite time-consuming.

To prepare a 'position' or 'working' or 'issues paper', some of which were not in Don's area of expertise, required a lot of library research. Unlike now when developments in ICT have made it easy and quick to source information through the Internet, in those days one had to go to the library in search of materials. At the ECA library, one would start by searching through the subject, title or author's catalogue if one knew the subject or title or author of the book or periodical or article that one was searching for. Then armed with the serial number obtained from the catalogue on where to locate the material, one then went to the shelves to start a physical search of the book or paper among hundreds of publications.

So, when Don had these ad-hoc assignments, he often spent an enormous amount of time in the library in the afternoons during the week gathering information and it was at the weekends that he settled down to the nitty-gritty of drafting the paper or document.

When he realized that contributing to the debate and making proposals for action during the Division's meetings was causing him a lot of headache by increasing his workload, Don made a decision to take a back seat at these meetings. But this was not to be for long.

"Don, are you okay?" the Director asked during the first meeting when Don was taciturn.

"Sure, I am okay, Prof. Why do you ask?" Don asked, pretending not to know why the Director had posed the question.

"I thought maybe you're not well today. But I see you do look great. It's just that it is very unlike you to be so silent and seemingly detached," he opined.

Don's strategy didn't work. At the very first meeting, it was with much effort that he restrained himself from talking. At the second meeting, he couldn't help taking the floor several times, no matter how much he tried not to. The discussion at each of these meetings was often so heated and so challenging that Don couldn't help being part of it. The problem only came when colleagues would often not volunteer to take assignments from the meeting.

So in spite of his chief's advice, Don continued to come to the office on most weekends to catch up with his deadlines. But one day, as he reflected on his advice, Don's mind went back to something which his late good old friend, Ignatius Parh, had given him several years earlier to read and take note. Ignatius was a master's student and Don a doctoral student in Ibadan at the time. Don had read and loved it so much that he had memorized it. It seemed to have been tucked away in a remote corner of his memory as he easily recalled it. There it was. After more than four decades, he could still recite it:

The Misguided Fool
He who works himself to breaking point
Under the misguided notion that he is indispensable,
Deceives himself. He is an egotist.
And if he dies tomorrow, he has himself to blame.
He will not be around to read his own obituary.
Vacuum? Nonsense!
His place will be filled the very next day
By an even better talented person.

"How true!" Don muttered to himself.

14. It's a Small World

One Friday evening in 1984, Don had gone to the International Livestock Center for Africa (ILCA) in Addis Ababa to visit Dr. Steve Mbogo, a post-doctoral fellow friend of his whom he had met during his previous tour to ILCA. As he was driving out of the ILCA compound, three young white people (two men and one woman) flagged him down and requested a lift to town some eight kilometers away. They were wearing T-shirts, jeans, and sneakers. By all indications, they seemed to Don to be participants of one of the many ongoing training workshops at ILCA for young professionals from the National Agricultural Research Systems. "Come on in," Don obliged and they came in and Don took off. On the way, Don asked where they were going.

"Oh, just drop us at Revolution Square," one of them replied.

They didn't speak much during the drive as Don left them to chatter among themselves. He was concentrating on the road as it was quite dark now and one stood the risk of hitting a donkey. As they approached Revolution Square, one of them remarked, "You have a luxurious Mercedes. Do you work with ECA?"

"Yes, I do," Don replied, still concentrating on the road.

At the Revolution Square, Don was going to drop them and turn right to go to the ECA. He had planned to go to his office after ILCA before heading home later that evening.

"Here is the Revolution Square where you wish to be dropped, but where are you really going?" Don asked, not directing the question at anyone in particular.

"We are going to the nightclub at the railway station. Just drop us here and we will find our way," one of them told Don.

"I have never been to the nightclub, but I know where the railway station is. I will take you guys there and then come back to ECA."

"No, it's okay, we will find our way. We don't want to derail your itinerary. We appreciate the lift you have given us already."

In spite of their objections, Don took them to the nightclub. As they jumped out of the car, one of them said, "Thank you, Mr.—"

"Don Oben is the name. Nice meeting you. Have fun," Don wished them as they disappeared into the night.

Then it occurred to him that he had not even asked their names nor really looked at them well. So if he were to meet them individually the next day, he would not even recognize them.

Destiny has a way, even with the passage of time, of sometimes bringing us face to face with our past, in ways we would hardly imagine. This was the case with this chance meeting.

In chapter 11, I presented an account of Don's sojourn to Norwich, East Anglia, UK, where he spent several weeks in 1985 coordinating the preparation of the document on the International Year for the Mobilization of Technological and Financial Resources to increase food and agricultural production in Africa in compliance with UNGA Resolution 38/198 of 20 December 1983. On arrival in Norwich, the Overseas Development Group (ODG) of the University of East Anglia arranged a welcome reception in his honor. As the reception got underway, a member of the faculty asked to speak on behalf of himself and two other colleagues.

"Ladies and gentlemen, more than a year ago, I and two of our colleagues here went to Ethiopia for an international conference at the International Livestock Center for Africa in Addis Ababa, Ethiopia. After a very grueling week, it was a Friday evening and we wanted to go out to town some eight miles away and unwind at a nightclub. After trying unsuccessfully to hitch a ride on several cars that were leaving ILCA for town, we flagged down this luxurious Mercedes Benz as it was driving out of the gate. We asked the guy if he could give us a lift to the city. 'Jump on in,' he obliged us."

"On the way, he told us he was bound for the ECA and wanted to know where we wanted to be dropped in town. We told him he should drop us at the Revolution Square. On reaching the square, he again asked us where exactly we were going and when we told him we were going to a nightclub at the railway station, he told us he had never been to the nightclub but he knew the railway station so if we didn't mind, he would go drop us there first before going to his office at ECA where he had planned to go that night."

"Being grateful that he had already given us a lift to town and not wanting to disrupt his evening, we tried to persuade him to drop us at the Revolution

Square. He insisted on taking us right to the nightclub, and as we jumped out of his car into the night in faraway Ethiopia, I just remembered that we had not even asked his name. 'My name is Don Oben. Nice to meet you. Have fun,' was what he said when I asked his name."

"Ladies and gentlemen, the gentleman whom I have been talking about is this Dr. Don Oben whom we are welcoming here tonight. My two colleagues and I are privileged to be part of this occasion."

Don sat speechless because he had forgotten the chance meeting with these guys that took place more than a year earlier. His past had caught up with him but in a way he could have hardly imagined. "It's a small world," was all Don could say amidst the clapping and standing ovation from the faculty and invited guests.

15. Working with Appetite

'Working with appetite' is an expression Don uses to describe a situation where someone is so immersed or engrossed in work that he or she is totally oblivious of the goings-on around him or her. In fact, this expression was coined by their class of 1957 at the Government Secondary School, Owerri, Eastern Nigeria. Many years later, as young school leavers aspiring to enter university, Mr. Henry Agboraw, a mathematician and one-time Director of Audit in the former state of West Cameroon, was to tell them of his experiences at the University College Ibadan, Nigeria: "When you are really studying, even if a fly enters your ear, you cannot realize it." It is true that when one is concentrating on a chore, it is possible to be oblivious of all that is going on around one, but for a fly to enter one's ear and one doesn't realize it, that's bizarre. What Mr. Agboraw said sounded incredible to Don. In Don's own case which I am to narrate here, it was not a fly that got into his ear. It was about how undivided attention to work can cause one to forget time.

An incident happened to him while he was on assignment at the University of East Anglia at Norwich, UK. As described in Chapter 12, he was coordinating the preparation of the report to the UN General Assembly on the International Year for the Mobilization of Financial and Technological Resources to increase food and agricultural production in Africa in compliance with UNGA Resolution 38/198 of 20 December 1983. The Joint Division was preparing this report in collaboration with FAO Headquarters, Rome. The latter's input into the report was to come by way of comments and suggestions on the draft reports, and in order to get these comments, Don had arranged meetings at FAO to discuss these draft reports. For seven weeks while the report was being written, he had to shuttle between Norwich in East Anglia and Rome, arranging and convening meetings of relevant Divisions of FAO to discuss and comment on the various drafts. It was during the first of his shuttle flights that this incident happened.

His flight from Norwich Airport to Fiumicino Airport in Rome was at 11 am that morning. However, since Prof. Belshaw, who was to drop him at the airport, had a 7 am class, they agreed that he could drop Don before going to his class. That would even be good for Don. Getting to the airport as early as 6:45 a.m. would give him quite some time to look through the report (first draft), correct any errors, ensure coherence, etc. It would also give him time to prepare his presentation notes for the meeting. At that time, Norwich Airport was a relatively small airport with the departure hall just a few meters from and directly facing the runway.

As soon as Prof. Belshaw dropped him, he looked around and found the coffee room just besides the departure hall. He took a table, kept his bags, then went for a cup of coffee and some sandwiches since he had not had breakfast. Then returning to the table with his 'breakfast', he spread out his documents and settled down to work.

The atmosphere was very conducive to reading so he worked and worked, sipping his coffee and eating his sandwiches as he did so. He must have had three cups of coffee that morning. Then he felt a need to get up and walk around a bit and stretch his legs before continuing. As he did so, he stopped at the information desk just to make sure his flight was still at 11:00 a.m. as scheduled.

"I hope the flight to Rome is still at 11 am," he asked the lady at the desk.

"Yes. And it took off on schedule—two hours ago, at 11 am," she replied, rather surprised at Don's question.

Don looked at his watch. It was 1:00 p.m. "Oh my God! So I missed the flight?" he asked, rather confused.

"Where were you, sir? We announced the flight so many times," she told Don.

Don couldn't believe he had been working for six hours and had been so absorbed reading the report, making corrections, writing his comments and observations, and preparing his presentation that he was oblivious of all that was happening around him. Don became a bit confused. Whatever the case, he told himself he had to be in Rome that evening in order to be present for the meeting scheduled for 3:00 p.m. at FAO the following day. It had taken a lot of consultation to get the relevant Divisions of FAO to agree on a date and time for this meeting. To miss it would be inexcusable. It would disrupt the day's work schedule of those called for the meeting and disrupt the time table of the drafting group at Norwich. Most damaging to ECA and Don himself, FAO people would say, "That guy, Don Oben from ECA, convened a meeting of various FAO Divisions and never showed up." With such likely sentiments, rescheduling this meeting would not be easy. Come what may, Don had to travel that day.

"Please, is there any other flight to Rome today?" Don asked the lady at the desk. "I have to be in Rome before nightfall," he emphasized, almost pleading.

"Well, let me see. Yes, there is only one more flight to Rome—at 4:00 p.m. Fortunately, it is not full. Would you want me to book you in, sir?" she looked at Don with what seemed like a smile, possibly pleased that she was able to be of help.

"By all means, please," Don replied, much relieved.

Even though the flight was almost three hours away, Don packed all his stuff into his briefcase and came and took a seat right by the door in full view of the few aircrafts on the runway. He couldn't risk missing another flight— not this last one. Four o'clock came and the flight took off promptly to Fiumicino Airport, and by 7:30 a.m. next day, Don was at FAO distributing copies of the report to concerned officials in preparation for the meeting at 3:00 p.m.

Since that incident, if Don has to read or work at the check-in gate at an airport while waiting for a flight, he does so in the midst of other passengers. Or if at a VIP lounge, he sits quite close to the reception desk. And he never forgets to keep at least one ear and one eye open all the while.

16. Attaché Militaire

When Don left Addis Ababa on his mission to Equatorial Guinea in 1987, he had planned to return directly to Addis after the mission. However, while in Malabo, capital of Equatorial Guinea, seeing how close Cameroon was, he decided that he would stop in Cameroon for two days and see his folks before continuing to Addis. He therefore re-routed his flight back to Addis Ababa through Douala. He would arrive in Douala on a Friday and leave two days later, on Sunday at midnight. This would enable him travel right to Mamfe town to see his mother. He did not need to take any leave of absence from the office.

On arrival in Douala on a Friday morning, he proceeded straight to Buea and then to Kumba. Usually when he traveled to Mamfe from Kumba, he would take a salon car and pay for the two front seats so he could sit comfortably during the five-hour trip. On this day, however, by the time he arrived at the Mamfe motor park in Kumba, the few small cars bound for Mamfe had left. Only the seventeen-seater small buses were there loading and taking in passengers. One was ready to leave and needed only one more passenger.

So, Don bought a ticket and took this last seat, which was right at the back of the bus. The park collectors had taken him into the bus with such urgency that Don thought the bus would be leaving within seconds. They were to remain inside the bus for the next forty-five minutes while the collectors and loaders argued and haggled with the bus driver over their commission until the passengers lost their patience. Finally, the bus took off for Mamfe.

An hour into the five-hour road trip, they came to a checkpoint manned by the gendarmerie. The gendarme at the checkpoint greeted the driver and then asked for his car papers and driver's license. Apparently satisfied that they were in order, he demanded to see each passenger's national identity card.

Starting from the front of the bus and moving to the back, he checked and returned each ID card given to him.

Finally, he came to Don right at the back. Because Don had not planned to stop over in Cameroon, he had not brought his Cameroon identity card with him. Instead, he was carrying the red ID card issued by the Ethiopian Government to diplomats and staff of the UN and international organizations. Don handed this to him through the window. He saw him open it and look at it for quite some time. Then he turned to look at the cover page. It read: The Provisional Military Government of Socialist Republic of Ethiopia ID card. Then he opened it again and looked at the left page, where Don's personal information was written. Then he turned to the right page containing Don's photograph and the name and stamp of the Ministry of Foreign Affairs. He turned the card over and over again while scrutinizing it. Then he decided to take it to his superior who was sitting by a rough table in front of a house. Meanwhile, the passengers had become impatient and were grumbling.

"Why is this gendarme delaying us?" asked a passenger, directing the question to no one in particular.

"Oh, you don't know? When they take your ID card to their office, it means there is a problem. And they want the driver to come beg and pay money," opined the woman who had talked almost all the way. She seemed to know almost everything happening around.

"Driver, if you don't go and meet them, we will remain here or they will ask you to put the passenger down," the woman continued.

"Yes, that is true," everyone agreed.

Don himself had been wondering what the problem was. He could see the other officer to whom the first had handed over his ID, still turning it over and over and examining it. Then he held it up above his eyes as if trying to see through it. At this point, Don decided to go down and find out what the matter was. When he stepped down and moved a few steps away from the bus, he noticed that the lace of one of his sneakers was loose. As I bent down to lace the sneaker, he could hear the same woman talking again. "Driver, what kind of man have you carried? Even if he pays them here, that is how he will be paying along the way because he will keep facing this problem."

As Don approached the two gendarmes, he saw the superior officer look at the ID one more time and nod his head. Then looking up at his subordinate with an air of one who had just unraveled a riddle, he declared, "Il est attaché militairè (He is a military attaché)." Apparently, having seen the words 'Military Government of the Socialist Republic of Ethiopia' on the cover page of the diplomatic ID card, he deciphered that Don must be a military attaché. "Il est attaché militairè," he repeated.

"Ah bon (Really)?" the subordinate asked in amazement.

"Bien sûr (Of course)," he assured him, apparently pleased with his ability to read English.

As soon as they noticed Don's presence, the subordinate turned around, stood at attention, and saluted Don. His superior followed suit, handing Don his ID. Don took it with a dignified nod, turned, and started to walk back to the bus. The two gendarmes followed him to the bus, keeping a little distance behind.

The passengers by the door came down to give way for Don to pass on to his seat at the back. As he climbed into the bus and was finding his way to his seat, the superior officer got angry and began to question the driver why he had put Don right at the back of the car. At that time, the law enforcement people, particularly the gendarmes, had arrogated to themselves the right to sit at the front in any commercial vehicle any time they traveled. Their justification was that they were always on duty and had to occupy a comfortable and convenient seat from where they could easily spring into action if and when the occasion demanded. This often caused friction between them and civilian passengers, but the drivers accepted it. This arrangement played to their advantage because vehicles with law enforcement officers seated in front beside them were often just waved past checkpoints, thus saving the driver time and money.

"Why you put this big officer for back moto?" he asked the driver a second time.

"Je voudrais m'asseoir derrière pour bien me reposer. J'étais trop fatigué et j'avais besoin de repos," Don tried to explain to the gendarme officer to save time so they could get on with their journey.

"Bon, mais tu t'es reposé maintenant, Monsieur l' Attaché Militaire. Tu devrais t'asseoir devant," he insisted.

Don told him it was okay. He accepted reluctantly and they took off. As soon as they turned the bend, the driver stopped and begged Don to come sit in front as the gendarme officer had insisted. He asked the passenger who was sitting by the door in front to please, exchange seats with Don.

"Yes, you want him to sit in front because you know now that he is a big military attaché, so the gendarmes will not worry you to give them their five, five hundred francs," the same woman shot out.

"Yes, please, big man, make you go for front so gendarmes no go waste we time for road. Please, help us so we fit reach Mamfe for daytime. We beg you," the woman sitting next to me pleaded.

"No, I am comfortable where I am," Don responded and they took off.

Still, the driver made the best use of Don. At every checkpoint, as soon as he greeted the police or gendarme and they asked him what he was carrying (referring to the luggage up on the vehicle), he would say, "Nothing, only the big military attaché for back moto." Don pretended to be asleep. They would wave him on and he would speed off.

17. The Ethiopian Letter

Don collected the official letters from the Director's office and put them in his brief case as he prepared to set off for the Bole International Airport in Addis Ababa on his mission to Rome, Italy that Friday evening in June 1988. Normally, mail bound for FAO, Rome is sent by pouch but since he was going to get there three days before the next pouch, he was requested to help the Division carry and deliver these letters to FAO.

On arrival in Rome, he checked into his usual hotel at Via Carpo D'Africa and spent the weekend quietly putting his papers together and reviewing his program for the week he would be spending in Rome. Come Monday morning, he was at the FAO. The day went very well and just before offices began to close, he remembered that he had planned to drop by and see Dr. Zohair Abdallah, his friend and the former Chief of the Agriculture Marketing Services Section at the Joint ECA/FAO Agriculture Division at ECA. As an FAO staff, he had been reassigned to Headquarters a few years earlier.

"Hello Don, what a pleasant surprise! You didn't tell me you were coming to Rome. Nice to see you again," Dr. Abdallah exclaimed and embraced him as Don entered his office.

"Nice to see you too again. It's been quite a long while since you left us. We miss you at the Joint Division," Don replied. They asked about each other's family and as they got talking about the happenings in ECA and FAO, a woman knocked at the door and came in with a file.

"Eh! Don, meet Tigist (not her real name), my secretary; Tigist, this is Don Oben from ECA, Addis Ababa, on mission to Rome."

"Oh, how nice to meet you, Mr. Don."

"Thank you. Nice to meet you too," Don responded.

"So you work with ECA. You live in Addis?" Ms. Tigist asked.

"Well, yes," Don responded.

"Please, when are you returning to Addis?" she asked.

"Well, I just started my mission today; I am focusing on what I came to do and to endeavor to complete it," Don told her, not answering her question.

"Don, you don't seem to have changed, never losing focus when work is concerned," Dr. Abdallah cut in.

"But you will be returning to Addis all the same. Please, may I know when you are booked to return?" Ms. Tigist pressed on, this time almost pleading.

"Well, if all goes well, I should be leaving Rome at the end of the week, on Saturday morning," Don got himself to say it.

"Please, can I ask you for a favor? Can you carry a letter to my mother? Oh my old mother, I haven't seen her for ages. How sad, she must really be suffering. Oh that socialist government, denying them everything…" Ms. Tigist suddenly broke down and started to sob or pule.

Greatly embarrassed by the sudden change in Tigist's demeanor, Don had to quickly answer 'yes' to her request to carry her letter to her mother to stop the spectacle. But rather than stopping, she slumped on the chair next to Don and started to wail. "Oh my mother. I wonder how she's been getting along, alone without me there, without a means for me to send her assistance, oh mother, help is coming…" There was nothing Dr. Abdallah and Don could do but to watch. He offered her some tissue and after wiping her face and nose, she stopped.

Don suggested and they all agreed that Tigist should leave her letter with Dr. Abdallah during the week but before Friday and Don would pick it up when he came to bid Dr. Abdallah farewell at the close of work on that Friday.

At the airport in Addis Ababa, Don was used to seeing families sobbing when welcoming relatives with flowers whom they had not seen for long. He has seen them sobbing as well when they are seeing off loved ones who are going away. So it seemed to Don that Ethiopians cry when they are upset or very sad and cry as well when they are over joyed. In effect, there are cries of joy and cries of sadness. But the spectacle Don had just witnessed in Dr. Abdallah's office left him speechless for quite a while. Was it a hoax, a performance?

On Wednesday when Don and Dr. Abdallah were having lunch together in one of the FAO restaurants, Don asked: "Zohair, has Tigist left the letter in your office? If so, I can pick it up after lunch before going to my own office."

"No she hasn't yet. But don't worry, she will bring it before Friday. I don't think she will afford to miss the opportunity of a fast and secure means of sending some money to her mother," Dr. Abdallah opined.

At the close of day on Friday, when Don passed to bid Dr. Abdallah good bye and collect the letter, Tigist had not brought it. "Sorry, Don, Tigist called this afternoon to say she would bring the letter to you at your hotel tomorrow morning, Saturday," Dr. Abdallah told Don.

"But why does she want to bring it all the way to the hotel? I thought that it is easier for her to leave it in your office. And I didn't tell her the hotel where I am staying, so where is she going to find me?" Don asked rather puzzled.

"Well, she asked me and I told her," was Dr. Abdallah's response.

By 8am on Saturday, Don's two pieces of luggage were packed and ready—one suitcase and a carry-on. As Don is one person who would rather check into a flight and wait for hours, if need be, for the flight to take off, rather than race to the airport in an effort not to miss the flight, he was ready to leave for Fiumicino Airport four hours to flight time. Tigist had still not arrived with her letter. The clock ticked and ticked and an hour passed. Don became nervous, nervous about the possibility of missing his flight.

Then as he decided to leave with or without her letter and was about to call a hotel taxi, he heard a knock on the door.

"Sorry for keeping you waiting, the traffic was horrible…bla, bla, bla," she said apologetically, preempting any angry outburst from Don.

"That's okay, just give me the letter, I'm getting late," Don managed to say quietly.

"The letter is in the car. Don't worry, I will drive you to the airport," Tigist announced with a smile.

"But why is the letter in the car? I need to put it in my briefcase. Can you quickly get it from the car? And you don't need to take me to the airport. There are hotel taxis waiting outside," Don told her, barely controlling his impatience. She then left the room and the next thing Don saw was Tigist rolling in a large, heavy, suitcase!

"What's that?" Don asked her, quite confused. "Where is the letter?"

"This is the letter. It's what I wanted to send to my mother," she said rather softly and sweetly. Don didn't find it funny. He was stunned and nearly lost his cool. He wondered whether it was he who didn't know what a letter was. Was his definition of a letter different from hers? According to most dictionaries including the Oxford Learner's Dictionary, a letter is a written, typed or printed communication, sent in an envelope by post or messenger which carries information, news and greetings.

"If this is what you wanted me to carry to your mother, why didn't you tell me in the first place? If you had told me that this is what I was to carry, I would have told you right away that I couldn't carry it. You see my own stuff? I don't have any room to put any of yours inside and I cannot carry an extra bag," Don told her outright.

"Please, let me see what you have in your suitcase. I am sure there should be room enough to put at least a few of my mother's things inside," she suggested. She then opened her own suitcase and wa-o! There were designer clothes, shoes, handbags, jewelry, and an envelope containing two thousand dollars in cash.

Don was quite shocked. He felt lied to. "Is this what you said you wanted to send to your poor, sickly, old mother—designer high-heeled shoes and handbags, to an old woman?"

Before Don knew it, she was rearranging his suitcase and putting in as much of her stuff in. "You see, these two shoes can go in here, this hand bag there, these three dresses in this corner, this small bag of jewelry in this pocket..." she kept telling Don as he stood looking down at her and wishing she would just finish and let him leave for the airport.

Luckily for her, Don had not done much shopping and was carrying his papers and reports in his briefcase. So she was able to put in quite a lot of her mother's stuff in his suitcase. Still insisting on driving Don to the airport, perhaps to placate him, he let her have her way. They got there just on time and checked into the flight. As Don turned to go in, he told her to greet Dr. Abdallah and tell him he had nearly missed his flight. "And you, Mr. Don, greet my old mother for me and tell her I love and miss her so much." And then she began to sob again.

About a year later, Don was returning to Addis Ababa from a mission in Libreville, Gabon, and had to take a connecting flight on Ethiopian Airlines in Douala, Cameroon, in the next hour and a half. In the VIP Lounge where he was sitting and waiting for the flight to take off, there were 5 other passengers—two white couples and one African woman. After the lounge attendant took Don's passport and air ticket and registered him in their register, he sank in a chair quite removed from the other passengers, exhausted and craving for some quiet. Some newspapers on the center table, however caught his attention and so he picked a copy to feed himself with some local news.

The newspaper was the Cameroon Tribune, the Government owned newspaper. As he turned over the pages and scanned the news headlines, he occasionally glanced at his briefcase and his duty-free shopping bag to make sure they were by his side. Yes, he had done a little shopping and picked up a whisky for a friend at the small duty-free shop.

As he was getting to the middle of the newspaper, someone touched him lightly from behind, on his shoulder. He turned and looked up to see who it was. "You are Mr. Don?" a lady asked him.

"Good evening, how are you?" Don greeted her without answering her question.

"Good evening, are you Mr. Don?" she responded to Don's greeting before asking her question again.

"No, I am not Mr. Don," Don responded.

"I mean, you are Mr. Don Oben?" she corrected herself.

"Yes, I am," Don replied, wondering why a lady he has never met should be insisting on finding Don Oben.

"I am Salamawit (not her real name). The station manager told me you live in Addis Ababa," she continued.

"That's right," Don responded.

"Please, I am from Ethiopia and I have my family in Addis. Do you mind carrying a letter for my brother? He lives in Addis."

"Well, I wouldn't mind, provided I see what's in the envelope before you seal it."

"Ok, can we then just go out to the entrance door?" She requested. Thinking maybe that she had some money (American dollars usually) and didn't want the other passengers to see her count it, Don followed her to the door.

"Here are the two bottles of whisky that I want you to take to my brother," Madam Salamawit told Don. Don couldn't believe his eyes and ears. "What did you say?" Don asked her to repeat what she had just told him in case he didn't hear well. But Don knew he heard her very well. "Please, I will be happy if you carry these two bottles of whisky to my brother in Addis," she repeated.

Don was speechless for a few seconds, dumbfounded. "Madam, are you really serious that you want me to carry these two 5-liter bottles of whisky to Addis Ababa and give to your brother?" he asked the lady.

"Of course, I am serious, otherwise I wouldn't be here and I will be very disappointed if you don't," she replied.

These were two giant 5-liter bottles of whisky! The memory of Don's experience with Madam Tigist in Rome a year earlier came back to him immediately and he felt that another Ethiopia woman wanted to use him again. "Well, you will be disappointed. I cannot do what you want me to do," Don told her in no uncertain terms.

"Why can't you help me?" she asked, rather surprised and thinking Don was not serious.

"There are two reasons: Number one, I already have two hand luggage—a briefcase and a duty-free bag containing a 1-liter bottle of Blue Label whisky, so I don't know how I can carry two large bottles of whisky with the two hand luggage I have already even if I wanted to help you. Number two, I cannot import duty-free, 11 liters of liquor into Ethiopia in one go. It's far above my duty-free allowance and there's no way I can pass through customs without declaring these items," Don told her.

"But you work in ECA; you are a senior international staff," she said.

"I know that," Don said simply.

"But you have duty-free privileges," she pressed on.

"I know that too," Don again responded.

"Then what's the problem?" she asked.

For a stranger to be telling Don about himself with such authority was kind of weird. The inescapable conclusion Don could draw was that she got this information about him from the station manager and wanted to use it for her benefit. It reminded him of Tigist who had used him the previous year to carry stuff from Rome to her old mother in Addis Ababa. He felt some revulsion rising within him. *Enough is enough*, Don told himself. He didn't owe her or anybody an explanation if he was unable to give the assistance they ask for. This notwithstanding, he reiterated the two reasons he had given for not being able to carry her two giant bottles of liquor.

"Ok. If you cannot carry the two bottles, can you please, take one bottle at least?" she pleaded.

"No, I'm sorry I can't, for the same reasons I have given you." Then he added that if the two reasons did not make sense to her, then nothing else would do so.

Just as Don finished talking, their flight was called. "Well, I have to go," he said, and turned and entered the lounge. The lounge attendant was announcing that they should remain seated. They would be driven to the plane after all the other passengers had boarded. After dinner that night, try as much as he could to fall asleep, the incident with Madam Salamawit kept resurfacing in his thoughts. He kept wondering whether the word 'letter' had a different meaning in 'Amharic' (the lingua franca in Ethiopia) from its meaning in English or whether the word has any definite meaning at all in that language.

Does the word 'letter' mean different things to different people in Ethiopia, especially the women? Don had to ask himself these questions because in Rome a year earlier, Tigist asked him to help carry a 'letter' to her mother. It turned out to be a large, heavy, suitcase. Now at the Douala Airport, Madam Salamawit asked him if he could help take a letter to her brother and the letter turned out to be two 5-liter bottles of liquor!

Don and some colleagues were having a drink on a Friday evening after work at the ECA Bar a week after his return from his Mission to Libreville. They were about 5 of them. After a hard working week, they were just chatting and cracking jokes and unwinding. At some point in their conversation, the colleague who was the director of one of their divisions said: "Don, I hear you went on a mission to Gabon last week. I am sure you stopped over in Cameroon to see your folks on your way back. Hope they were all well."

"No, I didn't stop over to see relatives this time but I changed flights in Douala," Don responded.

"Oh, in Douala? Is the Ethiopian Airlines Station Manager Ato Girma (not his real name) still there? He knows all the ECA staff who check regularly into his flights. He's quite a friendly guy."

The mention of the station manager made Don recall his meeting with Madam Salamawit and her request for him to carry a letter to her brother in Addis. As Don was recounting his story, three of the colleagues including the director were giggling and Don couldn't understand what was funny. He also recalled his experience with Tigist in Rome and how her 'letter' turned out to be a large, heavy, suitcase. By the time he finished, they had laughed their lungs out. Don was embarrassed, as he thought he was the only one among the 5 of them who had been taken advantage of by Ethiopian women.

"Gentlemen, let me tell you my own story," the director colleague said, pouring himself another drink. And this was his story…

"Two years ago, when I was going on mission to Kenya, my secretary asked me if her brother, Mr. Mulugeta (not his real name), who lived in Nairobi, could give me a letter to bring to her. Of course, you know our secretaries, they always know when we are going on mission. They prepare the PT8 (travel authorization), book the flights, collect the tickets, send the passports to protocol for visas, etc. So I told her yes, provided he left the letter open so I can see what's in it. I told her when the mission would end and the date and time I would be checking into my flight back to Addis. His brother was to meet me just before I checked in and give me the letter. She also gave me her brother's phone number so I could call him if and when necessary while I am in Nairobi."

"My mission took me to several parts of Kenya but I stayed in a hotel in Nairobi. I carried on the mission as planned and arrived at the Jomo Kenyatta International Airport on the specified date, 3 hours to check-in time to take my flight back to Addis. Before leaving for the airport, I called Mr. Mulugeta to let him know I was bound for the airport and he should meet me there as we had agreed. He assured me he would be on his way in a moment. I arrived at the airport and since I had plenty of time, I decided to await his arrival before checking in my luggage."

"However, considering that he was only bringing me a letter which I would just carry in my jacket, I decided after a while, to check in my luggage and wait. With only my briefcase left with me, I found a place where I could see any person coming to the ET check-in counter and waited. Fifteen minutes passed, thirty minutes, then an hour passed; still Mulugeta had not arrived. I called him on his phone and he told me he was quite close to the airport. The flight was going to be called in the next hour and I was still to go through customs and immigration. I was definitely running out of time and I wasn't prepared to miss my flight."

"Just when I picked up my briefcase and turned to go in, I saw someone hurrying toward me. By then, I was almost the only one left hanging around the check-in counter apart from the airline staff. 'Are you Mr. Mulugeta?' I asked. As soon as he said yes, I asked for the letter ignoring all the apologies he was making. 'Sorry, the letter is in the car,' he replied apologetically. 'I wanted to be sure first that you are at the airport before going back to take the letter,'" he continued.

"I couldn't believe what I was hearing. I was so shocked that I almost fell down. How on earth would someone bringing a letter to give to a passenger on a flight that is almost about to take off, leave the letter in the car and first come to check if the passenger is at the airport? Sensing how pissed off I was, he immediately went back to the car to bring the letter while I waited. Two minutes passed, then five minutes and he had not returned. 'What on earth is going on?' I heard myself exclaiming. Then I saw someone carrying a huge object in a carton and coming in my direction, then toward me. That can't be Mulugeta, I thought to myself. Where would he be carrying such a large luggage to?"

"But it was Mulugeta and he put down the carton right in front of me. 'What is this?' I asked him. 'It is a *car windscreen*. My sister asked me to buy a new windscreen for her car and send through you.' How about that, guys?" Don's colleague burst out in laughter as he gulped down a big glass of beer.

Don was so shocked that he felt his own experience with Ms. Tigist and Madam Salamawit was not as troubling as this one. This was hilarious. It was drama at its best. "And what did you do?" Don asked him after their emotions had subsided.

"It was a case in which my secretary tried to take advantage of my relationship with her (as her boss) and my duty-free privilege and to subtly manipulate and present me with a fait accompli—a situation in which I would have no option but to carry her car windscreen to her in Addis. This would entail my paying air transportation for the windscreen from Nairobi to Addis Ababa and clearing it through customs as a duty-free item in my duty-free account," their friend explained, lighting a cigarette. "And talking about the duty-free clearance, 2 or 5 years down the line when you want to leave Ethiopia, you will be required to check out the windscreen from Ethiopia or else pay duty on it; and whether it is in 5 or 10 years' time, you would be paying duty as if the windscreen is new since in this country goods imported into the country duty-free by foreigners do not depreciate!" another colleague cut in humorously.

It emerged that 3 out of 5 of them had had the experience of being asked the favor of carrying a 'letter' to a relative or a loved one by an Ethiopian woman, the reason why some of them were giggling when Don started telling his story. And the modus operandi was the same. "You accept to carry what you know as a letter, It never arrives on time when you are about to leave. Just when you are desperately concerned about missing your flight, the bearer arrives. And the climax—the supposed 'letter' turns out to be something else, anything! And because you are in panic and in a hurry not to miss your flight, you are expected to take and carry whatever the letter turns out to be! An excellent and subtle strategy, isn't it?"

Which brought Don back to the questions he had struggled with during his flight from Douala to Addis. Does the word 'letter' have a different meaning in Amharic from its meaning in English or does it mean different things to different people in Ethiopia, especially the women? But considering that the women concerned were fluent English speakers and the conversations were all in English, the word 'letter' should mean the same thing to all English speaking Ethiopian women. So there was no room for any misunderstanding of the word. The fact that only women seemed to have been making such requests and using the same approach was quite suspect.

18. Dress Code

What makes Don recall this episode is because it was happening in Africa—in an African country, an independent African country—Malawi! But then when one considers that it was happening at a time when Kamuzu Banda was ruling the country, one should not be surprised that this could happen. Though a Malawian, he was an Englishman to the core. He admired British traditions. He built an Eton-style public school in Malawi and even decreed a dress code for women.

It was sometime in 1988 and Don had just flown into Lilongwe, the capital of Malawi, after a long flight from Addis Ababa. The officials from the ministry who picked him up from the airport took him to this posh hotel in Lilongwe, where they had made a reservation for him for one night. Don thinks it was Capital Hotel. It must have been a five-star hotel. He was to spend one night here before continuing to Blantyre. As soon as he checked in, he quickly took a bath to freshen up. Then he put on a nice traditional African short-sleeved shirt popular in West Africa (with embroidery around the sleeves, neck, and side pockets) over a pair of brown pants. To feel still more relaxed, he wore a pair of black leather sandals. He then took the lift to the ground floor and hurried to the restaurant to have dinner. He was hungry.

A tall man wearing a white shirt with a black bow tie, a long, dark tailcoat, and dark pants was standing by the door. The door was closed. As Don stretched his hand to open the door, the man stopped him.

"Where are you going, sir?" he asked courteously.

"I want to go to the restaurant. Is this not the door?" Don asked him.

"Yes, it is, but you can't go in, sir."

"Why?" Don asked, quite surprised.

"Because you are not well-dressed, sir."

"Well-dressed, what do you mean?" Don asked, a little irritated.

"Sir, we have a dress code here. To dine in this restaurant, you have to dress either in a suit and tie or a shirt and tie over pants and a pair of shoes. No sandals or slippers or African wear is allowed, sir."

Don couldn't believe his ears. "Are you serious?" Don asked.

"Yes, sir," he responded, pointing to a notice engraved on a plaque by the door.

"So you are telling me that I am not well-dressed, dressed as I am in African attire? Is it not ridiculous that unless one dresses in a European outfit, one is not considered well-dressed?" Don asked, almost losing his cool.

All pleas for him to let Don go in fell on deaf ears. Don had no alternative but to go back to his room and change his clothes if he wanted to have dinner. He came back dressed in a long-sleeved white shirt and a red bowtie, a pair of dark pants and black shoes. The same waiter was there. He ushered Don in with a bow and led him to an anteroom next to the restaurant. He led Don to a table, drew back a chair, stood behind him, and, after Don sat down, he adjusted the chair. He then served Don some aperitifs, which had been laid out on the table: three different plates of nuts, including macadamia nuts and some champagne, which he served from a champagne bottle that stood in a small ice bucket on a trolley beside the table. He stood a short distance off while Don was eating and drinking.

Don was in no mood for all these pleasantries because he was very hungry. He needed real food. As soon as he finished, the waiter led him to the restaurant where a table had been prepared for him. He was handed the menu, which as expected was overwhelmingly European—aperitifs, dishes, wines, desserts, and digestifs. His dinner came on a trolley. As he dined, he surveyed the surroundings around him. All the diners were dressed in European attire—the men in suits or just shirts and ties, and women in long dresses. They were almost all white. Nobody wore jeans or T-shirts or African wear. The atmosphere likewise was very serene and diners conversed in such low tones as if afraid of their own voices. It was an experience Don had never had in all his travels.

19. Air Travel in Africa

In the 1960s, while Don was a student at the University of Nigeria, Nsukka, and later at the University of Ibadan, he used to think that air travel was fun. As a Cameroon Government scholar, he was issued a return air ticket to travel from Cameroon to Nigeria at the beginning and end of every school year. At the beginning of the academic year, while at Nsukka, he would take his flight from Tiko Airport and in less than thirty-five minutes, the plane would be gliding down to land at Calabar airport. Within minutes, the flight would take off and shortly after, it would land at Port Harcourt and finally at Enugu Airport.

These airports, particularly that at Tiko, were relatively small at the time and check-in formalities were very easy, quick, and less stressful. The planes were also relatively small. The flights were mostly on time, smooth, and relaxing. Even when he transferred to Ibadan and started to fly from Tiko via Douala to Lagos and sometimes to Ibadan Airport, it was still a delight to travel by air even though Douala and Lagos were much bigger airports and the distance by air was now much longer—one hour and thirty-five minutes. Don always looked forward with anticipation to those flights come the beginning or end of the academic year.

However, air travel has witnessed tremendous changes over the last several decades. Modern technology has transformed small planes into roaring giants in the skies that have brought the world much closer together in time and space. Airports have become like sprawling cities within cities, fitted with some of the most advanced facilities for security and processing of passengers and cargo. Advances in airline management have also improved flight scheduling and flight times, making traveling by air less stressful and enjoyable. In general, air travel in many parts of the world is the major mode of international travel. It is fast and even luxurious—but not in Africa, and particularly Central Africa.

Don's experience with air travel in later years, especially since joining the United Nations, has changed the perceptions he had formed about air travel during his early years as a university student. During the last thirty-five years, he has traveled extensively through almost all of Africa and, to a lesser extent, Europe, North America, and East Asia. In Africa and particularly Central Africa, air travel can be a nightmare—delays, cancellations, and late arrivals of flights, lack of information, long and tortuous connections, poor in-flight services, non-arrival of accompanied luggage, etc. And the source? Mainly poor airline management, but also the socioeconomic and political environment where the airlines are located.

Below is an account of just two personal experiences where air travel in Africa was a nightmare and a source of great stress.

In the 1980s, while at the ECA, Don undertook a mission to Freetown, Sierra Leone, and Monrovia, Liberia. He first visited Freetown before proceeding to Monrovia. The night before his departure from Freetown to Monrovia, the Nigeria Airways representative in Freetown told him and other passengers booked to travel on Nigeria Airways to Monrovia the next day at 13.45 pm, that they would be leaving the hotel in Freetown at 6:30 a.m. so as to use the ferry before the arrival of President Momoh from London at 11:00 a.m. This was to enable them be on time for their Nigerian Airways flight at 13:45 p.m. He therefore advised them to check out of the hotel and be ready to board the Nigerian Airways bus that would take them to the ferry and the airport at Langi. At that time, to travel to Freetown, the capital of Sierra Leone, one arrived at Langi Airport on the mainland and either took a helicopter or the ferry to Freetown. Most people took the ferry, which carried passengers, cars, trucks, and everything, including animals.

Accordingly, by 6:30 a.m., all the Nigerian Airways passengers had checked out of the hotel and were waiting for the bus, which came on time and left for the ferry. On arrival there, they met a large rowdy crowd, including passengers of other airlines who were scheduled to travel out of Sierra Leone that morning. The ferry was nowhere to be seen. It had been taken for 'cleaning and decoration' in preparation for the President's arrival at 11:00 a.m. After this, it would then be taken to wait for him at Langi to ferry him and his entourage to Freetown before they could leave for Langi.

The ferry, the main link between Freetown and the mainland, had been closed more than four hours due to the President's arrival and without notice to the public! Don suddenly felt totally drained by the reality that he would have to sit there for the next four hours waiting for President Momoh to arrive and release the ferry for them to cross and take their flight out of the country. As disappointed as he was, his ears could not help catching a conversation between two enraged women. Judging from their English, one of them must have either been a Sierra Leonean or Liberian and the other, a national of some other West African country.

"So the ferry must be cleaned and decorated before Mr. Momoh can be ferried in it? What of the ordinary folks who travel in it daily, they can travel in any shit?" asked one.

"That's even beside the point. Why close the ferry six hours before the arrival of the President? It doesn't take more than an hour to clean it," the other opined.

"This mentality is all over Africa—that roads and streets from the airport through the city to the Presidential palace are closed to traffic several hours ahead of the time a head of state is due to arrive from or depart abroad, causing untold inconvenience and hardship to the public. What is more annoying is that even in the modern era when the police and security people manning those roads have equipment with which they communicate with one another and can know the exact time when the President is due to pass through those roads, they still close them hours before," the first woman said angrily.

"It is not even just closing the roads that is repulsive. You need to see the way the army takes up positions along those streets, with some perched up on rooftops and others in people's backyards staring at people threateningly with their guns at the ready, all because the Head of State is due to pass that way. In Europe and America, one hardly notices when the Head of State is passing," the second woman said as if recounting some past experiences.

"And when Momoh arrives, only God knows how many trips the ferry will have to make to ferry him and his entourage. You know these African heads of state, when they pay an official visit to Europe or America, they carry with them almost their entire cabinet and their aides. That is how they squander the taxpayers' money abroad," she continued.

"God help us if he took only his cabinet and not also his motorcade with him. Otherwise, we will sleep here while the ferry takes him across the channel."

"No, I think that is going too far. How can he take his motorcade with him to Europe?"

"Ah, you don't know our African heads of state. In Europe, only a very short motorcade of one or two motorcycle riders would be sent to receive him from the airport. In their countries, they are used to motorcades of twenty or more motorcycle riders accompanied by all kinds of security cars and vans. Now, some of them have even added white and brown horses and horse-riders to their motorcades. This is unbelievable! Presidential motorcades in the early days of independence used to be small—two riders. They have expanded in leaps and bounds while the countries' economies have shrunk and the populations have grown poorer and poorer."

These women were really angry and were speaking out their minds. However, Don's mind soon began to wander from their conversation and focus on his flight and his concern about the possibility of missing his connection to Monrovia.

President Momoh, as expected, arrived in Langi Airport, fortunately just a few minutes past his expected arrival time. Before long, the ferry arrived Freetown with him and a large entourage, just as the woman above had predicted. After hours of sitting in the small airlines bus, it was such a relief to see the ferry finally arrive. As soon as the president and his entourage had alighted and taken off, the passengers scrambled into the ferry. With such a large crowd that had been gathering at the ferry all morning, it took quite some time for it to load and set off.

Far from expectation, Don and his fellow passengers arrived at Langi Airport within the check-in time and he came out of the Nigeria Airways bus in a lighthearted mood, pleased that he would not miss his flight after all. Many of the passengers who were in the Nigeria Airways bus were also bound for Monrovia. So they all rushed to the Nigeria Airways counter to check in. However, to their utter surprise and dismay, they were informed that the Nigeria Airways flight from Lagos, which was to take them to Monrovia, had not yet arrived. It was expected to have arrived some minutes earlier and be on the ground for forty-five minutes. When they asked when the aircraft was now being expected, the airline staff said they didn't have that information.

However, they were all checked in and taken to the departure lounge to await the arrival of the flight from Lagos. Although it was lunchtime, they were not offered lunch. Many passengers tried to get water and whatever else they could to sustain themselves. It was a very long and uncomfortable wait made worse by lack of information on when their flight would take off. Finally, after five hours of waiting, the flight arrived.

As the flight was about to take off for Monrovia, there was the usual announcement welcoming all embarking passengers on board and wishing them a pleasant flight. They should keep their seat belts fastened until the seat-belt lights go off; but Don was very disappointed and furious when this announcement was over. He had expected the airline to begin by apologizing for the long delay in the flight out of courtesy, as is customary. Nigeria Airways did not. The flight took off as if it was normal for flights to be so delayed. Some twenty minutes into the flight, he called one of the flight attendants, a young man probably in his early twenties, and asked him, "Excuse me, this flight had a delay of over five hours, and Nigeria Airways could not offer an apology to the passengers?"

The guy looked at Don, embarrassed and surprised at Don's question. Then, without responding, he beckoned to another flight attendant who was standing nearby to come. This one was also a young man.

"This passenger say we no make apology for delay," the first flight attendant explained what Don had told him to the second in pidgin English.

"Make apology? Where him from come?" (That is, apologize? Where is the passenger from?), his colleague asked, quite surprised that Don should ask such a question. Then, without a word to Don, both of them just looked at him and walked away, laughing and murmuring "Mr. Apology."

Don couldn't believe what had happened—that two cabin attendants, who are supposed to be as courteous as possible even to misbehaving passengers, could show not only an I-don't-care attitude to a passenger's legitimate concern but to also insult him. Airline crew and staff are supposed to be ambassadors of their airlines. Don had known that Nigeria Airways' reputation was not the best, but he had not expected the type of incident that had just happened. How long could such an airline survive in this era of competition? Well, a few years down the road, Nigeria Airways was no more—it went out of operation!

Coming back to his journey, the incident with the cabin crew spoiled the rest of his flight. By the time they arrived in Monrovia and Don was picked up and checked into a hotel by the UNDP, it was more than twelve hours since he had checked out of the hotel in Freetown that morning. Thus, it had taken him more than twelve hours to travel by air from Sierra Leone to Liberia, two neighboring countries!

Flight routing and connectivity is another major source of frustration and stress in air travel especially in Central Africa. Sometimes, to travel from a city in one country to another city in another country just next door, one has to travel through half the continent before arriving at the destination. Don's flight from Bangui in Central African Republic to Libreville in Gabon some years later is just one of several such tortuous, tiring flights which he had been compelled to take by the airlines.

Don was a member of a team of five Regional Consultants hired by the African Union Commission to undertake a continent-wide or regional study on infrastructure: Improving Rural Infrastructures to Raise Competitiveness of Africa's Agricultural Sector and to Access Regional Markets.[113]

He had responsibility for undertaking the study in the Central African region aimed at examining the state of rural infrastructures in the region as part of a continent-wide rural infrastructure assessment study. It was to identify existing gaps in rural infrastructures in the continent that could help in formulating policy recommendations for developing an effective response to infrastructure development and market access challenges in Africa within the framework of the Comprehensive Africa Agricultural Development Program (CAADP) Pillar II.[114]

Cameroon, Central African Republic (CAR), and Gabon were the countries chosen for the study. Since the study was to review available country data and information provided by Regional Economic Communities (RECs) and other sources, Don was also to undertake missions to the Secretariats of the Economic and Monetary Community of Central Africa/Communauté Economique et Monétaire pour l'Afrique Central (CEMAC) in Bangui, Central African Republic, and the Economic Community of Central African States (ECCAS)/Communauté Economique d'Etats de l'Afrique Central (CEEAC) in Libreville, Gabon that were supposed to be the custodians of data and information on infrastructures in the Central African region.

As he was in Washington, DC during the time of the study, his itinerary should have thus been: Washington-Yaounde-Bangui-Libreville-Addis-Washington. He was provided an air ticket with the following itinerary: Washington, DC-Addis Ababa (Ethiopia)-Douala (Cameroon)-Yaounde (Cameroon)-Douala (Cameroon)-Bangui (CAR)-Lome (Togo)-Lagos

(Nigeria)-Libreville (Gabon)-Addis Ababa-Washington. The flights from Washington to Addis Ababa and from Addis Ababa to Douala and Yaounde seemed quite direct and all right to Don. So also was the flight from Yaounde to Douala and to Bangui. But the one from Bangui to Libreville did not seem right. To travel from the former to the latter, two cities within a stone's throw from each other in neighboring countries, Don was booked to fly as far west as to Lome in Togo before returning east again through Lagos and Douala to Libreville. All efforts to have this leg of his itinerary changed by the airlines failed.

Following the itinerary, Don left Washington on 17 June and by 29 June, he had completed his mission in Bangui and was ready to embark on the long flight to Libreville just next door on Saturday, 30 June. He couldn't wait to leave Bangui. He had arrived there at the time of the political turmoil in the CAR. In fact, some officials privately wondered why he had risked coming there on a mission at that time. The presence of the military was evident everywhere—bands of soldiers speeding through the city streets, some soldiers using small civilian pickup trucks, and some moving on foot. Attacks against two mosques had taken place somewhere close.

On most nights, soldiers attacked many residential neighborhoods and looted people's property. His last two nights in Bangui were particularly frightening—a lot of shooting and gunfire, which could be heard quite close to his hotel. It was therefore a relief when he checked out of the hotel at 6:00 a.m. on June 30 and made his way to the airport to take his flight to Lome by one of Africa's new and emerging carriers. After a delay of maybe an hour, the flight took off for Douala, where it transited for an hour while picking up some passengers for Lagos and Lome. Then it took off again, but this time direct to Lome, its final destination with the Lagos-bound passengers.

In Lome, Don and the Lagos-bound passengers had to check into an Ethiopian Airways flight that was bound for Addis Ababa with stops at Lagos, Douala, and Libreville. The connecting time in Lome was long and stressful as they waited for the Ethiopian Airlines flight to arrive. It was late in the afternoon when they took off for Lagos, Douala, and Libreville. And at each stop, they had to sit in the plane for at least forty-five minutes while cleaners came in to clean and the plane was fueled and dropped off passengers.

It was exactly at 6:00 p.m. when Don arrived in Libreville, was picked up by an official of the Ministry of Agriculture, and taken to his hotel. A direct flight from Bangui to Libreville would have taken him about an hour and thirty-five minutes. His flight this morning had taken him from Central Africa to West Africa and back to Central Africa in twelve hours! To say that he arrived tired and exhausted is an understatement. His experience is not an isolated case. There have been many cases where passengers traveling from Douala to Abidjan in Cote d'Ivoire or to Accra in Ghana have been routed through Nairobi in Kenya (East Africa) and then put on the Ethiopian Airlines trans-Saharan route (Ndjamena, Niamey, Ouagadougou, and Abidjan) to Abidjan.

Air transport faces problems of connectivity between countries due to the collapse of several airlines, the obsolescence of aircraft, and limited airport infrastructure. Other modes of transport have their own infrastructure problems too. Don remember that as a young secondary school kid traveling between Cameroon and Nigeria in the 1950s and 1960s, he experienced the impacts of some of the worst infrastructure on the Cameroon-Nigeria Trans-African highway.

The problem of infrastructure in Africa cuts across all modes of transportation and networks—probable reason why the AUC commissioned the continental study and Don was called to participate in and undertake the study in the most infrastructure-deficient region as if they knew the extent to which he had personally suffered from the lack of sound and adequate infrastructure in Africa in general and Central Africa in particular!

20. What's in a Name?

The power of a name and its value has long been immortalized in prose, poetry, and religious ceremony.[115] A name is composed of a grouping of several letters of an alphabet or other symbols that represent the identification of a person, thus making every person recognized by a name. It is generally believed that a name influences a person's character; it reveals who you are while your date of birth reveals who you should be. It is also believed that names matter because your name creates your personality, the conditions in your life, and your destiny. And for your greatest happiness and success, it should allow the beautiful potential within you to develop through a natural and stress-free expression. Equally important is the belief that there is power in a name.[116] Whether these beliefs are myths or realities, this was not a consideration when Don took the names Don Harris as his first names. And he did not envisage that at some point in the future, he would be asking himself the question, "What's in a name?"

'Don' and 'Harris' were just two separate names that fascinated him, and he took them both. Girls got fascinated with the name. Many friends and family gave the name to their children. It came to a point where people were calling him more by these names than by his surname, Oben. They would either call him Dr. Don or Dr. Don Harris. He would remind them that his name was Dr. Oben. The fascination with his name extended even to people he did not know. Some of these named their business enterprises after him. For instance, they were driving along Main Street in Mamfe in August 2015 when his brother, His Highness, the Paramount Chief of Mamfe,[117] pointed to a stack of old, worn-out signboards outside a sign writer's outfit that had been brought for redecoration. Among them was one that read 'Don Harris Nursing Home and Maternity Center', Kembong (a village in Manyu Division).

"Daddy, so you have a nursing home and we didn't know?" his brother joked.

But Don's problem was with the banks. They just never got his name right. And he has not been able to understand why.

It started from Rome. One of the first things a new staff member does on arrival in a new duty station is to open a bank account. So, shortly after he took up his post at the World Food Council in Rome, he went to the Banca Commerciale Italiana (BCI) at FAO Headquarters to open an account. He completed the form very accurately and passed it to the bank staff concerned. He saw him look through it, cancel something, and then turned to Don and said that he (Don) had made a mistake in his name. It should be Don Juan Oben. And his reason? He had heard of Don Juan and not Don Harris. Don didn't find it funny since he knew the story of Don Juan. It took quite an argument to get the bank staff to write Don's name correctly as he had filled in the forms.

Many years later, after Don's retirement and relocation in Buea, he went to open an account at the Banque Internationale et Commerciale du Cameroun (BICIC). Again, he completed the required forms and opened a checking account to which he made monthly transfers from abroad. The bank mailed him letters showing details of the money transfers received and deposited into his account. Several months later, when the queues at the bank became too long, Don decided to go down the road and open a savings account with Fakoship. When he received his passbook several days later, the name on it was 'Don Charris Oben'. The next time he went to the bank, he queried why his name had been incorrectly written. After verifying from the forms Don had filled, the response was, "We are sorry. We will rectify the mistake."

Out of curiosity, Don decided to check the bank statements he had been receiving from his other bank, BICIC. He had never really looked at the name on the statements, being more concerned with the money aspects of the statements. Behold, his name in the account was 'Don Carlos Oben'. He was stunned. He could not believe it. He went to the bank and complained.

"We are sorry, sir. We will rectify the error," the bank staff apologized.

"Okay, I will sit down here and wait while you do it," he replied, trying to be understanding.

"No, sir, it cannot be done right away. You will have to fill another form and this form will be sent to Douala, the headquarters. It is only there that the name change can be effected." Don looked at her in disbelief, got up, and left the bank. Up to the time of writing this book, his names have not been changed. His account in BICIC still bears the name 'Don Carlos Oben' and that in

Fakoship carries the name 'Don Charris Oben'. Why can't the banks get it right? Don has decided not to bother. What is in a name?

21. Nowhere to Go

One of the most embarrassing moments in Don's life was when he was 'stranded' and had nowhere to go. As mentioned in the account on his time in Rome, his family—spouse and three children (Don Jr. 10, Vanessa 7, and Valentina 2)—joined him in July before schools were to start. With their arrival, he had to move from the hotel in which he had been staying to one which was self-catering and therefore more economical for a family. But this was still a temporary arrangement. Although the hotel was self-catering and comfortable, being a hotel, it was quite expensive and not large enough for a family with three children. It was therefore temporary while they searched for a longer-term residential home. Eventually, they found a nice apartment in a rental property in the same neighborhood.

On the day Don was to sign the lease, he asked his friend and colleague at the World Food Council, James Kanu, to accompany him to witness the transaction with the Italian landlady. The lady was waiting at the apartment when they arrived and copies of the lease were ready on the table for Don to read and sign. The atmosphere was very cordial. They chatted for a little while, and both James and Don went through the lease. But just when the lady was expecting Don to sign it, James whispered to him suggesting that they should take it to show the lawyers at FAO. The Staff Union at FAO Headquarters, which also provided services to the World Food Council staff, had advised its staff to always let its lawyers have a look at any leases and contracts that they had to sign with landlords.

The argument was that since staff were not legal minds, it was possible that landlords and landladies could insert certain clauses in the leases, which could in the future cause legal headaches and prove costly for the staff member. Therefore, at James' suggestion, Don asked the landlady if she didn't mind their taking the lease to show to their FAO lawyer before signing it.

"Oh no, I don't mind. You can do whatever you wish. Just call me when you are ready and we can meet to complete the transaction," she assured them with a smile.

So Don and James left, pleased that she had accepted so easily for them to show the lease to their lawyer. Her attitude was surprising because the prevailing view at the time was that Italian landlords hated more than anything else having their leases scrutinized by lawyers because they always wanted to avoid any publicity on their properties and the possibility of paying property taxes.

James was particularly pleased that they had not rushed to sign the agreement. "Bobo, you never know what 'catches' these landlords can insert in these leases. You sign and you are in trouble when the time comes. The FAO lawyer will tell us if the contract is okay for us to sign."

They did get a feedback from the lawyer. The contract was fine and they should sign it. With this go-ahead, Don called the landlady and got an appointment to meet her at the said apartment to sign and take immediate occupancy of the apartment.

With this arrangement firmed up, Don proceeded to give notice to the proprietor of the hotel where he and his family were staying that they would be leaving the hotel by midday on the day of the appointment with the landlady. The appointment with her was scheduled for 2:00 p.m. Don had figured out that if they moved out of the hotel at noon which was the latest time to check out, by 2:30 p.m. he and James would have completed the transaction with the landlady and he and his family would be able to move into the apartment well before 3:30 p.m. as the hotel was relatively a short distance away.

In the meantime, Don had come in contact with the tenant who was vacating the apartment into which they were to move. He was a young Canadian FAO staff who was returning to Canada after his term of duty. Since he was leaving finally, he was disposing of all his household furniture. This was an opportunity for Don to purchase nice furniture and not have to move it. So he bought the dining table and six chairs, two beds with mattresses and four cotton pillows, and a living room wall unit with wooden and glass-door cupboards, drawers, display areas, and a space for a large TV. Partly because he was running out of time and because Don was a fellow foreign staff member, he gave Don a good bargain. From the look of things, nothing could be better. With this furniture already in place in the apartment and the personal effects Don had at the hotel, they would have almost all they needed when they moved in.

As Don and his family waited for the day of the appointment with the landlady, the proprietor of the hotel came to Don twice to seek confirmation that they would be leaving his hotel on the day Don had indicated. He wanted this confirmation because a group of businessmen in Milan were seeking a booking in the hotel during the same week and he wanted to be sure that Don and his family were definitely leaving before accepting and confirming their booking. Don assured him they would be leaving. The proprietor was a kind elderly man who came to like their three children. Besides, they had stayed in the hotel and had become like a family. So he was concerned that a situation should not arise where their rooms were taken by new clients and they did not have any other rooms into which to move.

On the morning of the day they were to move out, he again came to ascertain that all was as planned and to announce that the businessmen from Milan had arrived. Don could see a lot of hustle and bustle in the hotel lobby with lots of luggage waiting to be moved into the rooms at midday.

At noon, Don's family moved all their belongings out of the hotel and were waiting for Don to come and take them to the new apartment as soon as he completed the signing of the lease and took possession of the apartment.

James and Don left the office and arrived at the apartment at the appointed time. This time, the landlady was with her husband and they had been sitting and waiting for them. As before, she was very welcoming and introduced them to her husband. All the niceties over, Don and James were pleased to announce that the lease agreement was okay with their lawyer and they would now want to sign it and take occupancy of the apartment as had been agreed. As Don spoke, the lady was surveying the living room with her eyes. Then came the bombshell!

"Oh, your lawyer found the contract okay. That is good. Unfortunately, we will not be letting out the apartment anymore," she said, gathering copies of the lease from the table and putting them in her bag. Don thought he did not hear her well, so he asked her what she had just said.

"We have decided not to let out the apartment anymore." The once-beautiful, warm, smiling lady had suddenly transformed into a hard, cold woman without feelings. Don sat there jolted, then transfixed with shock. He could not believe what he had heard. He stared at her blankly. Her husband was absolutely quiet.

"Madam, but you had agreed to let out the apartment to me and we would have signed the lease last week. Besides, it was just a few days ago that we agreed to meet here so I can sign and move in. So what changed so suddenly?" Don managed to ask.

"Our son is returning finally from the UK and will be staying here," she said simply, her gaze now fixed on the wall unit. She was not convincing and Don could sense some indignation in her demeanor. James sat there, too stunned to speak.

Don's mind wandered back to the hotel. His family had moved out and was waiting outside. The businessmen had arrived and should have moved into their rooms. He remembered the concern of the proprietor about the need to be absolutely sure that they had a place to go to because the hotel had been booked to full capacity. Was he dreaming? Was this real?

"Madam, I have checked out of the hotel where I was, in anticipation of moving in here. My family is waiting outside the hotel. Where do you expect us to go now?"

"That's up to you, I don't know," she said without an iota of sympathy. Instead, she asked a question quite unrelated to the issue in the conversation. "Whose furniture is this?" she asked, still with indignation, pointing to the dining table and chairs and the wall unit.

"They are mine," Don told her.

"So you bought them from the Canadian, right?" she asked.

"Yes, I did."

"And you also bought the beds, mattresses, and pillows?"

"That's right," Don answered, wondering how she knew he had bought these items also.

Then it occurred to him that the Canadian must have told her when he was handing back her apartment that the furniture he was leaving behind had been bought by her prospective tenant.

"So you bought all this furniture from the Canadian. Well, you will have to take it out of the apartment. You cannot keep it here."

"I cannot keep it here?" Don said he found himself muttering to himself. This woman was really pouring venom on him. Don told her they don't even

452

have a roof over their heads, much less a place to store such large items as furniture. He tried to explain their situation to her, but she was not listening.

"So it was because of you that the Canadian didn't sell us the furniture. Well, you will have to remove it from the apartment because we want to lock it up now and leave."

So this was the reason why she had changed her mind and decided not to let the apartment anymore. While Don had been convinced that the reason was not because of a son that was arriving from the UK, he had thought it was because they had taken the lease to their lawyer. Now it was clear that she was venting her anger on Don for having bought the furniture she was interested in from the Canadian. Then Don remembered that during his last meeting with the Canadian guy when he issued him the check, the guy had mentioned that the landlady had shown interest in buying all his furniture, but he feared that she was using delaying tactics to put him in a situation where he would have no option but to accept whatever prices she offered.

It was common knowledge that landlords who rented unfurnished apartments like this one in question often bought furniture from departing foreign tenants in order to furnish and rent them out as furnished accommodation. This might have been the intention of the landlady. Don had stood in her way and drawn her ire. He had caused her business plan to fall through, so the contract must fall through also!

"Please, start getting out your furniture because we have to lock up and go now. And don't leave them in the balcony or corridor," she said quietly, getting up and picking her bag. Her husband got up too. He had not uttered a word all this while.

At this point, Don was just barely trying to maintain his cool. Here was a woman who, without warning, had not just rendered him and his family 'homeless', but was now insisting that he take his furniture out.

"Okay, please, give me twenty-four hours to come and collect the furniture," Don asked of her just to have a break even though he hadn't the slightest clue where he was going to find a place in twenty-four hours to accommodate it.

"No, I cannot, because I will not have time to come here again tomorrow. I live very far from here. Besides, I am a very busy person." She and her husband moved to the door.

Don had had enough. She had pushed him against the wall and there was nothing else he could do. So, moving closer to her and looking her right in her eyes, he told her in an unusually calm and soft voice, "Madam, I cannot do the impossible. I will call you to come and give me access to the apartment to collect my things whenever I have a place to store them. Or, if you like, you can confiscate and use them to furnish your apartment and rent it as furnished accommodation and make more money if that is what you have been after. Thank you, fair cruelty."

She stared at Don, speechless. Turning and motioning to James, they stormed out of the room.

As they made their way to the hotel where his family was waiting, James blamed himself for having suggested that they take the lease agreement to the lawyer. He argued that if they had signed it on that first day, maybe what happened today might not have happened. The only option open to Don now, according to James, was to look for another hotel. Visibly moved, he left Don and returned to the office. It was now past 4:00 p.m. The children must have returned from school and must be waiting with their mother to be taken to the new apartment. It had been all excitement the previous night at the prospects of finally moving into an apartment where they would have their individual rooms, have enough room to run around, and feel free. How was Don going to tell them now that they had nowhere to go?

As Don contemplated the next steps, one thing was clear. They could not return to the hotel. There would be absolutely no room there for them. Then, two families in Rome, with whom they were very close, came to mind where they could ask for temporary accommodation. The first was His Excellency, Chief Ambassador Tabong Kima, the Cameroon Ambassador to Italy. But the Embassy Residence was located far away in the outskirts of Rome, on Via Della Camilluccia. Although it was nearer the Marymount International School, it was too far from Don's office at the FAO Headquarters. Commuting daily from the residence to and from work almost across the city of Rome would be a daunting and exhausting task.

The other family was Dr. Namanga Ngongi of the World Food program, and his wife, Becky. A lovely couple with three children, they lived fairly close to FAO. On this score, Don decided to seek his help. By now, it was dark since it was almost winter time. Luckily, Don got him on the phone. Frantically, Don told him he was going to move into his house with his family that evening, that a lease he was to sign earlier that day had fallen through, and that he would explain it to him later; and that at that very moment, they were outside a hotel from where they had checked out at noon that day, and now they had absolutely nowhere else to go. In fact, he was not asking him if he could move in. He was telling him he was moving in. It was a fait accompli.

"Okay-o, if you say so," he replied in his usual quiet, humorous, and sometimes sarcastic manner.

It was marvelous how the Ngongis accommodated Don and his family, how the two wives managed the two families, and how the six children got along with one another so well during this unplanned and unenvisaged 'merger' of the two families. The Ngongis accommodated them for some three weeks before they found a house in Casal Palocco, a residential neighborhood some fifteen miles from the city center. Don and his wife and children will forever be indebted to Namanga and Becky. At a time when they had nowhere to go, they took them in.

22. Cold Beer and Teapots

It was April 1991 and Don and his other colleagues of the World Food Council, Rome, were in Cairo for the WFC/UNDP Interregional Expert Consultation on the Food Production Challenges in the Developing Countries organized by the World Food Council Rome and hosted by Egypt. Members of the Secretariat who were to service the meeting including Don, had arrived a few days earlier to join the Egyptian officials to put finishing touches to the arrangements they had made for the meeting. They were lodged at Hotel Diplomat in the Zamalek neighborhood.

After a hectic first day of the meeting, Don and his friend and colleague, James Kanu, decided to go to a nearby restaurant to have dinner instead of eating at the hotel. Coming from the cool climate in Italy, they found Cairo really hot and uncomfortable. Temperatures were really high. To say they were thirsty would be an understatement. They chose a table by a window at a corner of the restaurant, which offered them some privacy and some air even though the air coming through the window was not as cool as they had expected.

The restaurant was full of clients, mainly Egyptians, as they seemed to be speaking Arabic. So the waiters were quite busy as they took orders and disappeared into the kitchen. After what seemed an endless wait, Don and his colleague managed to catch the attention of a waiter after they had gone through the menu a dozen times.

"Yes, sir, can I take your order?" he asked politely.

"Yes, please, but before ordering our food, we want some cold beer, really cold, two tall cans," they emphasized. "We are dying of thirst," they told him.

"All the same, you can place your order at once," he suggested. They did so, but implored him to get the drinks first. While they were drinking, he could attend to the food. They tried hard to relax as they waited in anticipation for their cold drinks.

All around them, other diners were eating, chatting, and laughing, but Don's and James' orders were not forthcoming. Once when their waiter passed close to them, they waved at him in a manner to let him know they were still there, but he just waved back and hurried away. Finally, when they were almost at their wits' end, their waiter came bearing a tray containing a large teapot and two teacups and saucers, which he placed on their table. James looked at Don and Don looked at him, bewildered. They certainly had not asked for tea. Without uttering a word, the waiter turned to go in a hurry. There was something in his manners that was not quite normal to them.

"What is this? Did you hear what we had ordered?" Don took the question almost out of James' mouth.

"Yes, sir," he replied.

"Then, why have you brought us tea?" Don asked, almost flaring up.

After keeping them waiting for so long, to bring them tea instead of cold beer was more than a provocation. Instead of answering Don's question, he pointed to the teapot and disappeared into the kitchen. At first, Don and James did not understand what his gesture meant. Then James figured it out. He then touched the teapot. It was absolutely cold. They had not noticed that it was even 'sweating'. When they opened it, there was their *cold beer*! They then served themselves with two teacups each before they spoke to each other. Nothing could have been more refreshing than cold beer on that hot Cairo evening.

When the waiter brought the food later, they asked him why he had served them beer in a teapot.

"The sale of alcohol is prohibited in Egypt," was the reply—in a whisper.

Serving beer in teapots! There is always a way to get around the law!

23. A Committee That Never Met Again

While Don was at the World Food Council secretariat in Rome, Italy, there was a P-3 post for an Economic Affairs Officer that had been vacant in the secretariat. The Executive Director decided that it was time to fill the position. This was in 1993. So, he appointed five staff members including Don, to constitute an Appointment and Promotion Committee (APC), which would undertake the process for selecting the most qualified candidate to fill the position in accordance with UN regulations. These five staff members were Uwe, Jan, James, Giuliano, and Don. Giuliano was the executive officer in charge of administration and personnel. It was common knowledge among the staff that Uwe had a preference for one of the two young assistant economic affairs officers who were candidates for the post. This one was German. The other whom most people considered more qualified was Chinese.

Uwe summoned a meeting of the five members appointed to form the Appointment and Promotion Committee. The rest of them were there on time. They waited for him patiently even though none of them could afford the luxury of just sitting there waiting. He finally breezed in with his usual air of one who had the weight of the whole world on his shoulders, clasping a file under his left arm. He went and sat by the table in front of the room facing all the others.

"Sorry, gentlemen, I have been very busy all morning and just when I was about to get myself out of my office, the telephone rang from New York... Well, it is my pleasure to welcome you all to this meeting. You all know why this Appointment and Promotion Committee was formed—to consider and select a candidate to fill the P-3 post now vacant in the secretariat. So, we have just one main item on our agenda to discuss this morning. It is my hope that the meeting will be brisk as we have just two candidates."

He then opened the file that he had brought with him and was turning over the pages. Don glanced at Jan. He looked back at him. Don was sure Jan must have seen the surprise on his face.

"Kindly excuse me, Uwe," Don said just when he was about to read from his file. "I think we are far from reaching this point. We have to start from the beginning…"

"And what is the beginning?" he asked, surprised, looking up from his file.

"Well, I think we are supposed to function as a committee, an APC, and since this is our first meeting, we have to elect a chairperson who will preside over our meetings. We would then review and adopt our terms of reference and rules of procedure. It is after this that we can consider and adopt an agenda and go on to the consideration of the substantive issues in the agenda. As is usual practice, I am sure that Giuliano, as the executive officer, was intentionally appointed into the committee to serve as an ex-officio member and the secretary to the committee," Don replied looking around. He could see the others nodding in agreement. The room was quiet. Uwe looked surprised at what he had just heard.

"Don, but I am the chairperson. By virtue of my being the most senior staff member in this committee, I am invariably the chairperson. It cannot be otherwise. I am a director," he replied with his usual authority.

Don took the floor again. "Uwe, in my experience, Appointment and Promotion Committees or similar committees do not function that way. When members of a committee are nominated or appointed, in their first meeting they elect a chairperson and secretary and then adopt the Rules of Procedure of the committee before the business of the committee starts. And it starts with the consideration and adoption of an agenda discussed and agreed to by the committee. We all, except Giuliano, were appointed members of the committee in our individual capacities. Nobody was appointed the chairperson."

One colleague spoke up, "That's correct."

"Absolutely correct," another colleague supported.

The atmosphere was tense. Sensing that he was not going to have his way, Uwe got up and picking up his file, declared, "In that case, I will adjourn the meeting. You will be informed when the next meeting will take place." Some members were about to get up too when Don raised his hand.

"Excuse me, Uwe, with due respect, you cannot adjourn the meeting either. You do not have the authority to adjourn the meeting because you have not been elected the chairperson. But you can excuse yourself from the meeting, if you so wish, and for whatever reason."

Uwe could not take this anymore. He stormed out of the room visibly upset at the turn of events. The rest, however, remained in the room.

"It is unfortunate that Uwe has chosen to walk out instead of letting us proceed with the meeting in the correct manner. But is it not correct that he has no powers to adjourn the meeting?" Don asked, directing his question to no one in particular.

"No question about that," was the general consensus.

After conferring among themselves for a short while, they decided to allow Uwe to convene a second meeting. During that meeting, they would go ahead and follow the correct procedure with or without him.

As had been mentioned earlier, the WFC secretariat was comparatively small. As such, every staff member, professional or general service staff, knew every other staff member well. And news passed through the offices very quickly too. Everyone was under scrutiny—when one arrived in the morning, when one returned from lunch break, when one left, the quality of one's work, etc., etc. So it was not surprising when a few days after the meeting, Don bumped into the Executive Director at the top of the staircase leading to their offices.

"Don, I heard you had a very productive meeting the other day," he said, patting Don on the back.

"Mr. Trant, I don't think so," Don replied.

"Well, that is what you think," he said as he moved on while Don entered his office.

Sadly, the committee never met again. It was overtaken by the financial crisis that engulfed the UN Secretariat in 1993 and led to the restructuring and abolition of some organs of the secretariat. Later that year, the functions of the World Food Council were taken over by some other departments and agencies of the UN system, followed by staff redeployments and separations and the abolition of the Council.

24. When Not to Tell the Truth

As recounted in chapter 15, Don was nominated by the Executive Secretary to represent the ECA in the World Bank-sponsored study tour of New Zealand for West African senior policymakers on New Zealand's macroeconomic policy reforms. At the end of the tour on 24 April 1997, it was decided that since they all were taking flights home through Sydney in the evening of 25 April, they should spend that day at Sydney Harbor, sightseeing. As mentioned in the account in chapter 15 Don had been issued entry visas not only to New Zealand, but also to Australia. Accordingly, at 06:45 hours, they boarded flight QF40 departing Auckland for Sydney with only their hand luggage. They checked all their other luggage directly to their various destinations.

On arrival in Sydney, They had to go through immigration and customs. As it happened, Don found himself in a different queue from the rest of the group because he arrived at the immigration ahead of the others, and when they arrived later, they went to a different queue. When it was Don's turn to be served by the immigration officer, Don submitted his passport, air ticket, health certificate, and the customs declaration form which they had been given to complete. With just a quick look at the papers, the official kept them aside and asked Don to wait while he proceeded to attend to the passengers who were behind him in the queue.

It turned out to be a long and embarrassing wait during which time all his other colleagues had been cleared and were waiting to leave the customs area. What Don found more annoying was that the immigration officer had given him no reasons for keeping him waiting. Even when Don asked him what the problem was, he just asked Don to exercise patience. Finally, just when Don was almost losing his patience, the officer gave his passport and papers to another officer who asked Don to follow him to a nearby office. At his office, he told Don that he has to be quarantined.

"What did you say?" Don asked, quite astonished.

"You will have to be quarantined before being admitted into Australia," he told Don.

"And why is that?" Don asked still in disbelief of what he had just heard him say.

Meanwhile, Don noticed that his other colleagues were observing the proceedings from a distance and giggling among themselves, which was quite surprising.

"You have to be quarantined because you recently visited a farm as you indicated in the customs clearance form which you filled out," the officer explained.

It was then that it occurred to Don that he had answered 'yes' to a question as to whether he had visited a farm recently. The rest of the group had apparently ticked 'no' to the question, which explained why they had been cleared.

As Don was filling the form and got to that question, his mind went back to their long road trip from Wellington in the south to Auckland in the north and the many farms they visited. He remembered the farm of Phillipa and Hon John Fallon, former Minister of Agriculture in Bideford in the Wairapa, where they raised sheep combined with pasture management and agroforestry. He could not forget especially the farm where they arrived on Id di Fitre Day and the farm owners had given them two fat sheep to celebrate the feast of Ramadan even though they were far out there.

The Muslims among them had slaughtered the two sheep according to their religious tradition, barbecued the meat over an open fire in the garden and they all had eaten with baked potatoes, fresh vegetables, and copious amounts of red wine in celebration of the feast of Ramadan. How could Don forget? In all, they visited over six farms—beef and dairy, sheep and goats, apples and fodder, and they had a tour of each farm after the farm owner(s) had briefed them on their operations and their experiences with the reforms. How could Don, in all honesty, answer 'no' to the question? So, he ticked 'yes'.

Now, however, the issue of honesty or lack of it was not what was at stake. What was at stake and urgent was how to get himself out of the situation which his honesty had put him into. His mind raced away—trying to find a way out.

"Officer, in the 'intent and spirit' of the question, what does visiting a farm mean?" Don asked, looking straight in his eyes.

"Visiting a farm is visiting a farm," he replied.

"And that means what?" Don pressed on.

"Well, it means entering the farm and moving around. It is immaterial whether you mix with the animals or not," he tried to explain.

"In that case, it seems I got it all wrong. We were in a group traveling from Wellington to Auckland in New Zealand. We were supposed to visit a farm along the way, but because we were running late, we could not go on the farm visit as we were already behind schedule. Instead, when we got near the gate to the farm, which was quite close to the highway, the farm owner met us where our guide explained to him that we were running late and would not be able to make the trip into his farm. He was then requested to kindly just give us a brief talk on how the macroeconomic reforms had affected his farm business. We came out of the buses and stood by the fence facing the farm, which was down in the valley below us. We could see the farm buildings and the animals out there at a distance of some one hundred yards. After his talk, we hurried back into our buses and were once more on our way."

"Is that what happened?" he asked.

"Sure. You can even see my colleagues standing over there waiting for me. They know I had made a mistake," Don lied.

"If that is the case, then you should not have answered 'yes' to the question. You are cleared then."

Don heaved a big sigh of relief as he turned and hurried to meet his colleagues. They were still giggling.

"You liars," Don joked, when he joined them.

"You now know when not to tell the truth," one of them responded.

From the airport, they were driven to Sydney Harbor, where they spent a very memorable day visiting tourist sites and attractions around the harbor, including a walk on the harbor bridge and a boat ride along the harbor. Unfortunately, the famous Opera House was closed during that period.

Don had planned to return to Addis Ababa after the study tour through East Asia—through Bangkok and Mumbai (formerly Bombay). So when night fell and the other participants took their flights to West Africa via Perth and Johannesburg (South Africa), he boarded a Qantas Airlines flight to Bangkok.

But his mind would not permit him to forget too quickly the events at Sydney Harbor earlier in the day. The question as to whether he had visited a farm recently again occupied his mind. This incident raised an important moral issue. Should one tell the truth if one will face grave consequences by telling the truth? Should one tell a lie in order to get out of trouble? Is there a time when to tell the truth and when not to?

Many hours into the flight, as the pilot commenced his descent into Bangkok Airport, there came the announcement over the loudspeakers: "Passengers are reminded that the penalty for drug trafficking in Thailand is *death*."

A chill ran down Don's spine. He froze for a while. How cruel the law can be, he murmured to himself!

Don changed flights later that night in Bangkok, taking an Ethiopian Airlines flight to Addis Ababa. As morning dawned and they descended to land at Mumbai Airport, the next day, he saw from his window seat some of the worst slums he have ever seen in his life.

25. Passing Out in the Skies

I'd discussed in chapter 15, the French government's eight scholarships given to the ECA for a one-month intensive French language course in France in 1999. Candidates in the proficiency class competed for these scholarships through a competitive examination, both written and oral. The first eight candidates in order of merit were selected and awarded the scholarships. Don performed extremely well and was one of the eight candidates selected to participate in the one-month intensive French language course. They were to undertake this course at the Centre Audio-visuel de Royan pour l'Etudes de Langues (CAREL), Royan, France, in August 1999. After fulfilling all the visa requirements, they left for Paris and thence to Royan in the Southwest of France.

They were allowed to decide on their itineraries and make their flight reservations individually. Don decided to route his travel through Rome with Alitalia Airlines. He took off from Addis Ababa on 30 July for Rome and then to Paris. He had been reading newspapers throughout the flight from Addis to Rome. Soon after they had taken off from Fiumicino Airport, lunch was served. It was a welcome relief. For aperitif, Don asked for a tall glass of tomato juice spiced with black pepper. For many years up to that date, this had been his most cherished drink during flights. For lunch, he chose fish and pasta with mushrooms and cheese sauce accompanied by a bread roll, butter, and vegetable salad. All this went down well with a miniature bottle of red wine. For dessert, he had a piece of cake. As lunch was ending, tea and coffee were served. He chose a hot cup of cafe macchiato. For whatever reason, he always went for coffee during flights.

By the time he finished lunch, he was so full that he was uncomfortable. He had never eaten so much when flying. He seemed to have had an unusually large appetite that day. Not long after, he began to feel so uncomfortable that he started to sweat. He loosened his tie and unbuttoned his shirt at the neck.

He had a little welcome relief, but it was only temporary. The discomfort soon increased, this time around his tummy, so he loosened his belt a little. Then the plane passed through some turbulence, gaining altitude in the process. The sweating increased and he felt like he did not have enough air to breathe. He began to struggle with himself. His head was beginning to spin. Then he felt like using the toilet—to empty his bladder.

He got up and as he made his way to the back of the aircraft where the toilets were located, his head spun. He staggered and slumped onto the floor just after the last row of seats close to the toilets. Two female flight attendants who had been standing ahead of him rushed to him as he lay on his back. "Are you okay?" one of them asked.

"Any doctor on the flight?" the other asked frantically. Don heard some footsteps. Soon, many cabin crew were all over him as he lay on the floor facing upward. He could feel them raising him, taking off his jacket, and unbuttoning his shirt while all the time fanning him. Then they began to loosen his belt and unbutton his trousers (pants). At this point, he passed out.

He didn't know for how long he remained unconscious, but when he came around, he saw mainly the crew standing and watching over him. He didn't know if there was a doctor among them. "Are you okay? Will you want to use the toilet?" they asked as soon as they saw that he was trying to get up.

"Yes, I think I feel like using the toilet," Don replied.

Two crew members helped him to his feet and led him to the toilet. As he was entering the toilet, they asked him not to shut the door—he should leave it a little open. Apparently, they wanted to make sure they could see if anything went wrong so they could come in unimpeded immediately. When Don came out a short while later, he found them still waiting by the door. "Are you okay?" they asked again. They gave Don his belt and tie and helped him put on his jacket. They had removed and were keeping these items when he passed out.

Don was given some water to drink. He thanked them for their concern and care and told them that he was all right. Even with this assurance, they still insisted on leading him to his seat.

Don must have gotten into some deep slumber during the rest of the flight because when he got up, the pilot was announcing his descent into Charles De Gaulle Airport in Paris. Surprisingly, a flight attendant was sitting close by, probably keeping an eye on Don.

As he was getting out of the plane, he stopped to express once again his sincere gratitude to the crew as they lined up at the doorway to wish the passengers goodbye. "Sir, we trust you are all right?" one of the female flight attendants who had attended to Don most of the time asked again, still with some concern.

"Si, sto bene, grazie mille," Don assured her he was okay while thanking her.

She immediately turned to the others, raising her eyebrows in apparent surprise. "Ciao, ciao," Don added and turned to go.

"Ma lui parla italiano!" Don could hear her exclaiming with excitement that Don speaks Italian as he waved them goodbye and stepped out of the plane.

Don still does not have a clue as to the cause of this malaise. He suspects, however, that it must have been caused by a reaction between the beverages (wine and coffee) and the cocktail of tomato juice and spice (black pepper). He knows that he has a light head for wine and coffee. He had often had a little 'dizziness' whenever he took hot coffee or wine when in the air. So, he had often desisted from taking them especially together during the same meal in flight. He usually either took one or the other, not both. Quite surprisingly, after the incident, he developed a dislike for tomato juice laced with black pepper. For him to have suddenly lost appetite for something he had once cherished so much over the years was beyond comprehension. Was it the cause of his malaise?

Whatever the reason, Don has not taken tomato juice spiced with black pepper since 30 July 1999. He never also takes wine and coffee during a meal when in the skies. It is either one or the other. This experience was not funny. Gladly, it has never happened again, in the air or on the ground.

26. Enforcing the Law

Up to 1960 when Nigeria achieved independence, the country was a leading exporter of many major agricultural commodities. The country was a leading exporter of palm kernel and the largest producer and exporter of palm oil in the world. It was also the second-largest producer of cocoa. During that time, smallholder farmers collectively produced 90 percent of the food needs and 70 percent of Nigeria's export earnings—a dominant share of the country's GDP.[118]

However, when crude oil was discovered in commercial quantities in 1956, it paved the way for the gradual neglect of agriculture by successive governments. The civil war, which lasted from 1967 to 1970 and took place predominantly in Eastern Nigeria in the palm oil belt where the oil palm plantations were established, did major damage to the palm oil sector of the economy. Crude oil became the dominant source of revenue, while agricultural production sharply declined. From over 60 percent in the late sixties, the contribution of agriculture to the GDP plummeted to 22.2 percent in the eighties.[119]

The output of palm oil likewise plummeted to a level where Nigeria went from the largest producer and exporter of palm oil in the sixties to a net importer in the eighties. To put the historical neglect and consequent dismal performance of the palm oil sector in perspective, Malaysia, a country Nigeria gave palm oil seedlings to, had overtaken Nigeria as one of the largest producers and leading exporters of palm oil in the world. Nigeria had become unable to even meet its domestic demand.

The Federal Government in later years strove to sustain the crude palm oil industry of the country. In its efforts to encourage and expand the production of palm oil and other vegetable oils and thus increase their availability to meet domestic consumption and demand, the Federal Government banned all exports of vegetable oils in 1986.

In 1988, Don went on mission from Addis Ababa to Libreville, the capital of Gabon. On his way back to Addis Ababa, he decided to route his flight through Lagos so he could spend a day with his sister and her husband at GRA Ikeja. He had not seen them for some time. He arrived in Lagos on a Friday from Libreville and was to connect with an Ethiopian Airlines flight to Addis just before midnight the following day, Saturday.

International staff from West Africa living and working in Addis Ababa consider it a 'hardship' duty station in the sense that the tropical food crops such as yams, plantains, cassava, cocoyam, palm oil, fresh hot pepper, and most leafy vegetables, which constitute their traditional foodstuff, are not grown in Ethiopia. Thus, whenever most of them travel to West or Central Africa, they usually seized the opportunity to carry some of this foodstuff for family consumption and to share with friends. So while in Lagos, Don decided to buy and carry some foodstuff himself. At the Murtala Mohammed International Airport, he checked in all the foodstuffs but left only a five-liter plastic container of palm oil to carry as hand luggage with his briefcase for fear that the oil might spill in the suitcase if he checked it in.

Just as he was waived through the customs checkpoint, a dark, bulky officer whom Don was later to identify as a senior customs officer who was standing by, intervened and asked Don what he was carrying in his bag. Don told him it was a five-liter plastic container of palm oil and showed him his UN laissez passer. He said that was okay but asked Don to follow him to his office just near the security checks.

"Sorry, sir, you cannot take the palm oil," he told Don, removing the plastic container and placing it on the table.

"Why?" Don asked him.

"Because the export of palm oil from Nigeria is banned," he replied with authority.

"But this is just five liters of oil for home consumption. It is not for sale," Don tried to explain.

"Sir, the decree banning the export of palm oil does not distinguish between commercial exports and exports for home consumption. It bans all exports." He retorted with an air of one very conversant with the decree.

"Well, that may not be true in the letter and spirit of the decree," Don tried to argue.

"Well, sir, whatever the spirit or the soul or the body of the decree meant, all it says is that all exports of palm oil from Nigeria are banned."

At this point, Don was getting frustrated with the officer's uncompromising attitude. He tried to plead with him, explaining that they didn't have palm oil in Ethiopia and they miss it very much. But the officer was adamant and insisted that Don couldn't take the oil with him. Don's flight had been announced many times and the gate was to close soon. In desperation, raising his wrist and showing him that the gate would be closing in less than ten minutes, Don told him:

"Okay, since you don't want me to take the oil with me, I will leave it here." Having said this, Don took his briefcase and turned to leave. He was to get another mind-boggling response.

"I am afraid, sir, that you cannot leave it here," the officer said simply. Don was startled and then thought this must be a joke.

"Why?" Don asked.

"This is a security area. It is not a place for passengers' abandoned goods," he said emphatically. Don was in a fix and getting more desperate. The last call for boarding had been made.

"Officer, you don't want me to take the oil with me and you don't want me to leave it here. So, what do you want me to do?" Don asked despondently.

"Sir, you will have to go out to the check-in area and give it to the driver who brought you to the airport. It is as simple as that," he told Don without the least concern that Don was running out of time.

"It is not as simple as that. The driver should have gone long ago. Even if he were still there, by the time I get out there and find my way back here, my flight would have taken off. Can't you see? The gate should be closing by now, that is, if it has not closed already."

Now, Don was getting really angry and raising his voice. Then, out of the blue, came this question:

"How much money do you have on you? I mean, how much money are you taking out of the country?"

Don had hardly expected or anticipated such a question. However, he answered him, "I think I have about 5,000 naira and 50.00 US dollars." He was sure this was what he had on him because he had counted it after he gave the driver a tip before checking in his luggage.

"Let me see it," the officer asked, stretching out his right hand.

By this time, Don was thinking more about missing his flight than what he was saying or doing. The Ethiopian Airlines flight from Addis Ababa to West Africa was thrice weekly. If he missed this flight, he would have to remain in Lagos for another three days. That was not an option to contemplate. In this state of mind, he obliged the officer, removed the money, and gave it to him. He took it. What happened next was unbelievable. The officer put the money in his pocket, and in the manner of one possessed, he immediately took an old newspaper that was on the table and started to wipe the plastic container of oil as if it was dirty. Then he picked up the bag from the floor, put the plastic container of oil inside, and placed it on the table. As if still in a frenzy, he stepped to the door and started calling out frantically:

"Okoro!…Okoro!" (No answer.)

"Olawole! …Olawole!" (No answer.)

Then he called out more loudly, "Adebayo!"

"Yes, sir," someone answered.

"Please, come…come, come, quickly," he called with urgency.

Don just stood there watching him, stupefied, dumbfounded. As soon as Adebayo came in, the officer turned quickly to him and handed him the bag with the palm oil.

"Take this gentleman straight to the gate where Ethiopian Airlines is boarding. Nobody should stop him. He is a United Nations diplomat. Make sure he does not miss his flight or I hold you responsible. Please, hurry!" he instructed with all the authority he commanded.

Then, probably as an afterthought, he saluted and wished Don a safe trip. Still struggling to recover from what had just happened, Don grabbed his briefcase and rushed after Officer Adebayo who was already racing ahead. It was a long run which left Don breathless by the time they got to the gate. All passengers had boarded and the airline counter staff were just packing up their remaining stuff.

"Mr. Oben/Don, where have you been? We have been calling this flight over and over," the Supervisor asked when Don arrived at the gate. It was more of a guarded scolding than a question that called for a response. Adebayo had raced ahead to alert the airline that one passenger (Don) was still coming. As soon as Don arrived, the Supervisor quickly took his ticket and issued him a boarding pass. She then rushed him to the plane just as the door was closing.

Don was so exhausted and still trying to catch his breath that he just slumped into his seat.

Dinner was served at midnight. As Don wined and dined, it clearly dawned on him that the senior customs officer had intimidated him to the extent that he had to make a choice between arguing to get his money back and missing his flight, or taking his flight and leaving his money with him. In fact, he intimidated Don to the point where Don had only one option, and he knew it—forget the money and take his flight. And the officer succeeded. It was not about enforcing the law—the decree banning the export of vegetable oils. He merely used the decree as a pretext to enrich himself—at Don's expense, through extortion, having failed through bribery!

27. A Silent Listener

Since Don's repatriation and relocation to Buea, Cameroon, in 2004, Saturday seemed the only day of the week when he was able to force himself to remain in bed after 6:00 a.m. to listen to two CRTV Buea radio programs which came up at 7:00 a.m. and 8:00 a.m. These were *Health Update* and *Press Club* respectively. They were two radio programs in which he had taken an interest. In *Health Update*, a medical personnel, usually a physician, presents and discusses a disease or a contemporary health issue led by the host of the program. In this one-hour program, the doctor is given about twenty minutes to present the disease during which he/she is 'guided' or prompted by the journalist and host of the program. In the case of a disease, he/she would present the nature, manifestation, causes, treatment, prevention, and any other aspects of the disease which the host of the program considers of interest to listeners.

After this presentation, the telephone lines are then opened for calls from listeners. In fact, the program, in its current format, made for clarity of presentation and avoidance of repetition by the doctor; there is orderliness in the question and answer session and a clear understanding of the issues by the audience.

This, however, was not the case in 2004 when Don relocated to Buea. At that time, it seemed as if the lines were opened for calls as soon as the program started. As soon as the doctor began his presentation of the disease, the phones began to ring. People started to call and ask questions on aspects of the disease which the doctor would inevitably have dealt with if he/she had been given time to make his/her presentation.

Within minutes into the program, people would be calling and asking such questions as, "How is the disease manifested in patients?"; "What are the causes?"; "How is it treated?"; "Sometime ago, I had symptoms like...can that be the disease?"; "Doctor, how can one consult you?"

The doctor would then stop his presentation to answer the question. And when he had answered the question and wanted to focus on his talk, another caller would be on the line and the doctor is interrupted again. Don could feel the frustration sometimes by the doctor. On resuming his presentation, he would sometimes ask "where were we?"—an obvious indication of a loss of concentration or disconnect in his thoughts. These interruptions at the inappropriate times did not make for smooth and orderly discussions during the program.

Don cannot remember for how long he listened with much unease each week as the program took the same *ding-dong* forward-backward pattern. He decided he would not remain a silent listener. There should be a better way of organizing the program. So one day as the program was about to come to an end, he called and their conversation went along (but not exactly) these lines:

"Hello, who's on the line?"

"I am Dr. Don Oben calling from Molyko."

"Hello, Dr. Oben, what is your question?"

"It is not a question. It is a comment and a suggestion."

"Yes, go on."

Don thanked CRTV Buea for putting up such a useful and educative radio program and commented that in order to make the program more orderly and enable the audience to get a better understanding of the health issue of the day, the doctor should be given some twenty minutes to make a presentation of the subject for the day with only the host intervening if and when necessary to guide the doctor to areas where he/she thinks would be of interest to the audience. After this, the lines could then be opened for callers to ask questions.

The host barely had time to say "Thank you, Dr. Oben." The program immediately went off the air. Now, Don began to worry whether the host really got his suggestion. He had intervened with less than two minutes to go to the end of the program. Surprisingly, during the very next week, the host announced that the program was going to have a different format. It would begin with the doctor presenting and discussing the topic for twenty minutes guided by the host, after which the lines would then be opened to callers. She implored the audience to listen well and not call within those twenty minutes. This would enable the doctor to present the full picture and for the audience to get a fuller understanding of the health issue. And that is how the program has been organized and run since then.

Each time Don listens to *Health Update*, he reminisces about his intervention. It is for this reason that I have selected it for inclusion among his reminiscences. It is also to acknowledge the CRTV female journalist who was the host of the program at the time for her attentiveness and ability to listen, and willingness to accept suggestions and implement them with such immediacy. Kudos to her.

28. Mugged in Washington, DC

It was summer and Don was in the United States visiting their children. His first destination was Washington, DC, where he stayed with their first daughter. On this particular day, as he often did, he had taken Bus 70 at the bus stop at the junction of Georgia Avenue and Webster Street, to Silver Spring in adjoining Maryland to spend the afternoon sightseeing and window shopping. Each year whenever he visited Silver Spring, he saw tremendous changes—new shopping malls and stores, restaurants, apartment complexes, etc.

As he wandered around feeding his eyes with many new changes and taking in the weather, he was oblivious of time. He had planned to take his bus back by 5:00 p.m. when there was abundant daylight so he could see the bus stop where he should alight. But by the time he was ready to return, he realized it was 7:00 p.m. Lights were on and although visibility was still good, it was difficult to see clearly the names of the bus stops except those that were by or near a streetlight. As he took bus 70 back, he missed the Webster bus stop where he was supposed to have alighted. But this was not due to poor lighting. It was because the bus was crowded and his view to the outside was blocked. So by the time he realized where he was, the bus had passed the bus stop where he was to alight and was at Georgia Avenue/Petworth station, about three bus stops farther on. He now had to walk back a distance of three bus stops to get to his daughter's house.

Crossing to the other side of Georgia Avenue, he began to walk along the pedestrian walkway which ran alongside Georgia Avenue. It was a walkway he was used to taking on his way from the Safeway supermarket or the Georgia Avenue/Petworth underground station. There was a restaurant or two, two barber shops, a dental clinic, a laundry shop, a post office, a funeral home, and a few grocery and corner shops along the way on the right before getting to the residential area. Apart from three or four big black boys he saw as he passed by the first barber shop, he met no pedestrians on the walkway. It was a quiet upper middle-class neighborhood so there were not many people around.

Immediately after crossing Shepherd Street NW, which runs across Georgia Avenue, the pedestrian walkway bifurcates, creating a garden in the middle, lined by small trees on both sides. This garden grows bigger along the way; and on crossing Taylor Street NW, which also runs across Georgia Avenue, it turns into a small park on the left, a long narrow lawn in the middle, and a parking lot on the right with trees bordering the park, the lawn, and parking lot, before it ends at the beginning of Ninth Street, which was where he was walking to. As he usually did, he kept on the right walkway which was now farther and farther away from Georgia Avenue and more shaded and secluded by trees than the left walkway.

Don must have been so engrossed in his thoughts after he got to the walkway along the small garden that he did not realize that someone had come close to him, put his left arm gently around his neck, and was poking some object into his lower back with his right hand.

"Don't move and don't shout," the man said quietly but firmly. At first, Don thought it was his son, Don Jr., trying to play one of his pranks. He didn't know why he thought so. Maybe it was because his son often used to pass along this walkway whenever he came to visit them after work, and because he thought the voice resembled his.

Believing it was his son, he replied jokingly, "Don, please, stop those pranks of yours."

But instead of hearing his son's voice, he only heard the order again. "I repeat, don't move and don't shout." The strong arm around his neck began to tighten and so was the poking of the object in his lower back.

It was at this point that it dawned on Don that he was being mugged. He didn't know whether the hard object the mugger was carrying was a knife or a gun. In any case, Don couldn't afford to take any risk. He couldn't see the mugger, but by all indications, he seemed a huge boy or man since he was talking over Don's head and his arm around Don's neck was somehow bulky. So Don kept still and quiet. With his left arm tight round Don's neck, Don could feel the mugger trying to remove his wallet which was bulging in his right back pocket. It was as if he had gone into a trance and a fear had temporarily taken possession of him as the mugger was removing the wallet.

By the time Don came around and realized that the arm was no longer around his neck, he turned around to see a huge fellow running away in the direction from which Don had come. Instinctively, Don began to run after him, but stopped after the mugger turned left into a side street and started climbing up a hill, occasionally looking back to see if Don was following him.

From the look of him, he must have been one of the black boys Don had passed along the way at the barber shop. He had taken Don's wallet which contained two cards—a Mastercard debit card and a Visa credit card. It also contained passport-size photos of some of Don's family, some business cards, and small sheets of handwritten notes. Fortunately for Don and unfortunately for the mugger, the only money in the wallet was just one dime (10 cents). He must have been very disappointed that it contained only a dime. Don believes that he had been deceived by the bulging nature of the wallet because, as soon as he removed it, he stopped searching Don's pockets. Don usually didn't carry his money in his wallet. Little did the mugger know that in Don's left hip pocket, he had some $350.00 in cash in an envelope.

On arriving home, Don's daughter insisted they call the police and report the mugging. Don didn't see the utility of doing so but called all the same. Within five minutes, two police officers arrived in a police car. After taking down Don's statement, they drove around the neighborhood but there was no sign of any of the boys Don had seen at the barber shop, and neither did they see any black boy at all. Don thereafter called the UN Federal Credit Union (UNFCU) to report the loss of his two cards and to ask that they be canceled immediately. As suspected, the mugger had, within such a short interval, tried unsuccessfully to get cash from some ATMs with the cards. Don was told this when he called the UNFCU to report the loss.

Appendix 1

Eyewitness Account of How Pa J. A. Oben Ceded Land for the Construction of Federal Government Bilingual Secondary School, Mamfe

This is an account of how Don's father, Pa Joseph Ako-aragbor Oben (Pa J. A. Oben), of Small Mamfe, Mamfe, transferred part of his farmland to the community for the establishment of the Federal Government Bilingual Secondary School, Mamfe, situated at Mile One in Mamfe. This school is now called Government High School Mamfe. This account was provided by one of Don's younger brothers, now Joseph Ako Oben (Ph.D.). He witnessed the proceedings which he is reporting here as a little boy.

1. My name is Oben Ako Joseph and I am the twelfth out of fifteen children (living) delivered to Pa J. A. Oben by six wives and two mistresses.
2. In technical terms, I was the last child in our father's compound and thus was his attendant, companion, and friend. I accompanied him in almost all his outings except those that came up when I was in school. There were some which were even adjourned awaiting my presence.
3. On the matter of the land for the Federal Government Bilingual Secondary School, Mamfe, situated at Mile One in Mamfe, now called Government High School Mamfe, the event took place sometime in 1968 (I was a little older than six years then and was in primary class three).
4. One late afternoon (about 4:30–5:00 p.m.), I accompanied my father to the compound of Chief Mbeng Besong Michael. I recall the presence of other elders: Pa Lucas Agbor-atah, Pa Enowtanya, and Pa

Ayukegba. There were others, but no member from the Mbiatem family was present. As usual, I was sitting at a corner, ready to observe what was to happen.

5. Shortly after my father and I arrived, some 'big people' (that is how, as children, we addressed high government officials especially if they were dressed in suits) also arrived. They were about five in number and they arrived in a Land Rover wagon. Not this sleeky-shaped models. I mean the original Land Rover 4W drive. I remember that the color was light green. I took note of these because it was rare to see such huge men dressed in suits. I did not know who they were or where they came from.

6. After the initial greetings and serving of some palm wine and cola nuts, the discussions started.

7. One of the 'big people' introduced himself (of course, I could not remember the name) and the others and then asked another 'big man' to speak. The one given the floor said, "We are coming from Buea with some good news for the Mamfe people. President Amadou Ahidjo has approved the opening of a secondary school in Mamfe. The school will be called *Federal Government Bilingual Secondary School, Mamfe.* (There was a little applause.) And this school will be the third *Federal Government Bilingual Secondary School* in Cameroon, citing that one was in Yaounde, one in Buea, and the one in Mamfe would be the third. So Ahidjo has commissioned us to come and meet the natives—the traditional council—for land to be allocated for this school. This is why we have come."

8. There was some whispering among the elders, which lasted for some minutes. I don't know what they whispered about.

9. At the end of their whisperings, Chief Mbeng Besong asked, "How much land would be needed for this school?" It was answered by one of the 'big men': "Much land. It is going to be a big school. Children will come from all over the country. Something like seven to ten acres."

10. Again, there was some whispering among the elders, after which Chief Mbeng Besong said, "I am not sure we have such area of land in Mamfe to give for the school."

11. He had not finished talking when one of the 'big men'—the tallest of them all—stood up and virtually hushed the chief not to continue. He started talking to the chief and elders in Kenyang (our indigenous language), asking them some questions: "Do you want this school to be taken to another division? Do you know what it takes to fight and get this type of school? Do you want to say that the president was wrongly advised? You can't tell us that there is no land in Mamfe." The 'big man' turned to Papa. "Ta'Ako-Aragbor (i.e., Pa J. A. Oben), you have traveled and served under the white man. You know the importance of education. You are the father of this community. Do not allow Chief Mbeng Besong to deceive you. Mamfe people must give land for this school."

12. Chief Mbeng Besong squirmed on his seat. "I have said there is no such land as you need in Mamfe." This statement caused a chill in the room.

13. Then our father, Pa J. A. Oben, asked if he could say something. "If land at Mile One is allocated for this big school, would it be suitable?" The 'big man' who spoke in Kenyang responded, "Land anywhere in Mamfe will be suitable."

14. Our father then said, "In that case, I will give the quantity of land needed for the school from my farmland at Mile One, and I will suggest that there should be no further argument and cracking of heads on this matter." An appointment was taken for the next day at 8:00 a.m. at Mile One.

15. The next day (it was a school day, but I had to be absent in order to accompany Papa to Mile One), early in the morning, Papa and I trekked to Mile One. Later on, the 'big people' from Buea and some other people who were not at the meeting the previous day came. I later on learned that these other people came from the PWD (Public Works Department), the Divisional Officer's Office and the Divisional Department of Education. Papa showed them the area. It was planted with cocoa, bananas, oil palm trees, mangoes, and some pear trees. All the 'big people' agreed that the area was good. This exercise did not last for up to an hour. Worthy of note is that none of the other Mamfe elders was present. Later on, I heard that they (the elders) said Ta'Ako-

Aragbor decided to give his farmland for the school, so that is his problem. That was why they did not show up to witness the exercise.

16. About two weeks later (after the visit to the Mile One site), a team of surveyors went and demarcated the land marked out for the school from the rest of our farmland. Then Caterpillars started bulldozing the area. I saw our cocoa plantation going down, the palm trees, the mango and pear trees. All went down.

17. As a child, I did not notice any expression of regret on Papa's face. Neither did I hear any of our mothers lament the loss of her crops. Activities in the compound continued normally. Till date, I am not aware of any compensation to Papa for the land.

18. So, that is the story of how our father ceded much land for the construction of the Federal Government Bilingual Secondary School, Mamfe.

Later on, Papa told me that the 'big man' who spoke to them in Kenyang was Chief (Dr.) A. D. Mengot. Years later, I read in books that he was the Cultural Delegate of Education in West Cameroon.

I am convinced that the report of that mission can be found in the archives of the Delegation of Education in Buea.

In support of this account, during the twenty-fifth anniversary celebrations of the Grammar School in Mamfe, Chief (Dr.) A. D. Mengot acknowledged that the land for the school was given by late Papa J. A. Oben of Small Mamfe. In recognition of this, he asked the audience to rise for a minute of silence in honor of Papa J. A. Oben. Those who attended the event such as Bro. Oben Simon Besong, Mr. Ayuketah Oswald, etc., are there to testify.

Joseph Ako Oben

Buea, 13 May 2018.

Nota Bene (NB).

I am available to challenge any other version if not told by any of the 'big people' cited in this account.

Appendix 2
ECA-Sponsored Institutions

Cartography, Mapping

1. Regional Center for Training in Aerospace and Remote Sensing Surveys (RECTAS). Established in 1972 in Nigeria with headquarters in Ile-Ife.

2. Regional Center for Services in Surveying, Mapping, and Remote Sensing (RCSSMRS). Established in Nairobi, Kenya in 1995.

3. African Center of Meteorological Applications for Development (ACMAD). Established in 1987 in Niamey, Niger.

4. Center Regional de Teledetection (CRTO). Established in Ouagadougou, Burkina Faso in 1978.

5. African Organization for Cartography and Remote Sensing (AOCRS). Established in Addis Ababa, Ethiopia in 1988 by merger of African Association of Cartography (AAC) and African Remote Sensing Council (ARSC).

Engineering and Industrial Technology

6. African Regional Organization for Standardization (ARSO). Established in Accra, Ghana in 1977.

7. The African Regional Center for Technology (ARCT). Established in Dakar, Senegal in 1977, but became operational in 1980.

8. African Regional Center for Engineering Design and Manufacturing (ARCEDEM). Established in Ibadan, Nigeria in 1980.

9. African Institute for Higher Technical Training and Research (AIHTTR). Established in 1979 in Nairobi, Kenya.

10. African Regional Industrial Property Organization (ARIPO). Established by the Lusaka Agreement of 1976 in Lusaka, Zambia, which came into force in 1978. The ARIPO Secretariat was established in Nairobi in June 1981, but moved to Harare, Zimbabwe in 1982.

11. African Regional Center for Solar Energy (ARCSE). Established in May 1984 with headquarters in Burundi.

C. Economic and Social Development

12. Institut Africain de Developpement Economique et de Planification (IDEP)/African Institute for Economic Development and Planning. Established in Dakar, Senegal in 1962.

13. African Center for Applied Research and Training in Social Development (ACARTSOD). Established in Tripoli, Libya.

14. East and Southern African Management Institute (ESAMI). Established in 1974 as the East African Community Management Institute (EACOMI), it was renamed in 1977 the East African Management Institute (EAMI) when the East African Community broke up. With effect from February 1980, following a unanimous agreement reached at the Third Conference of Ministers of the Lusaka-based MULPOC countries, EAMI was expanded and converted into ESAMI.

15. Regional Institute for Population Studies (RIPS) was created in 1972, within the University of Ghana, Legon, Accra, to cater for the training needs of Anglophone Africa. RIPS was designed to offer graduate programs leading to the award of an MA, MPhil, or PhD.

16. Institut de Formation et de Recherche Demographiques (IFORD). Established in Yaounde, Cameroon in 1971.

17. United Nations African Institute for the Prevention of Crime and the Treatment of offenders (UNAFRI). Established in 1989 in Kampala, Uganda.

D. Finance and Trade

18. Central African Clearing House (CACH). Established in January 1979 in Brazzaville, Republic of Congo.

19. West African Clearing House (WACH). Established in Freetown, Sierra Leone in 1996.

20. African Center for Monetary Studies (ACMS).

21. Association of African Central Banks (AACB). Established on 13 August 1968 in Accra (Ghana), on adoption by a Conference of Governors of African Central Banks of Articles of Association which entered into force on 17 December 1968.

22. Association of African Tax Administration (AATA). Launched about 1982 with Ethiopia as headquarters. Headquarters moved to Yaounde, Cameroon in 1992.

23. Association of African Trade Promotion Organization (AATPO). Established in 1974 and located in Morocco with headquarters in Tangier.

24. Federation of African Chamber of Commerce (FACC). Launched in May 1984 in Addis Ababa, Ethiopia.

E. Minerals and Transport

25. Eastern and Southern African Mineral Resources Development Center (ESMARDC). Established in 1977 and located in Tanzania with headquarters in Dodoma/Arusha.

26. Central Africa Mineral Resources Development Center (CAMRDC). Established in 1983 and located in the Republic of the Congo with headquarters in Brazzaville.

27. Port Management Association of North Africa (PMANA). Established in 1974 and located in Tunisia with headquarters in Tunis.

28. Port Management Association of West and Central Africa (PMAWCA). Established in 1972 and located in Nigeria with headquarters in Lagos.

29. Port Management Association of Eastern and Southern Africa (PMAESA). Established in 1973 and located in Kenya with headquarters in Mombasa.

Some of Don's Other
Publications and Reports

1. Oben, D. H. (1976) "Least-Cost Ration for California Mature Turkeys: An Application of Linear Programming Techniques." Unpublished Special Project Paper on Applied Linear Programming, Department of Agricultural Economics, University of California, Davis, California.

2. Oben, D.H. (1977) "The Impact of Marketing Boards' Pricing Policy on Groundnuts Production and Marketing in Nigeria: A Simulation Approach." Unpublished Special Project Paper on Systems Analysis and Computer Simulation. Department of Agricultural Economics, University of California, Davis, California.

3. Oben, D. (1986) Technical Publication on Agricultural Marketing Training and Manpower Development in Africa. (For distribution to ECA Member States.)

4. Oben, D. (1987) Technical Publication on Measures for Improving Credit Facilities and Marketing Services in Africa at the Level of the Small Farmer.

5. Oben, D. (1988) Report to the Council of Ministers of the Yaounde Based MULPOC Subregion on the Improvement of Food Marketing Institutions.

6. Oben, D. (1984) "The Role of Small Scale Indigenous Entrepreneurs in the Marketing of Food and Agricultural Products in Africa." Prepared for presentation at the Sixth Meeting of the Technical Preparatory Committee of the whole and Eleventh Meeting of the ECA Conference of Ministers of Planning; Addis Ababa, Addis Ababa.

7. Oben et al. (1992) "Toward a New Green Revolution in Africa (follow-up to the Conclusions and recommendations of W F C 18th Session)"; Internal Discussion Paper, UN World Food Council, Rome.

8. Oben et al. (1992) "A New Green Revolution for Africa: Guidelines and Action Plan for the World Food Council"; Internal Discussion paper.

9. Oben et al. (1991) "Meeting the Developing Countries' Food Production Challenges of the 1990s and Beyond: Synthesis of the Regional Overviews of Food-Security Focused Agricultural Research, Technology Transfer and Application." Prepared for the WFC/UNDP Interregional Consultation, Cairo.

10. Oben et al. (1991) "Regional Overview of Food Security-Focused Agricultural Research and Technology Transfer and Application in Asia and the Pacific." Presented at the WFC/UNDP International Consultation on Meeting the Food Production Challenges of the 1990s and Beyond, Cairo.

11. Oben et al. (1997) Facilitating the Demographic Transition in Africa: Issues and Challenges; Vol. I: Main Report Food Security and Sustainable Development Division (FSSDD/UNECA).

12. Oben et al. (1997) Facilitating the Demographic Transition in Africa: Issues and Challenges; Vol. II: Case Studies of Selected Anglophone Countries: Botswana, Egypt, Mauritius, Nigeria. FSSDD/UNECA.

End Notes

---

[1] Sarah Ban Breathnach. Tags: appreciation, experience, life, moments. See Wikipedia: https://www.goodreads.com/quotes/tag/moments and https://www.simpleabundance.com.

[2] Mandu Mandu, Semoh Sengoh, and Mandem Achi are names in Kenyang, the native language of the Banyangis who inhabit Mamfe Town and some of the surrounding villages.

[3] Don was to read many years later [as an adult] from some literature, that the *A.A. Cawan* for example, was a twin screw motor cargo vessel, which weighed 295 tons and had an overall length of 125 ft. It had been designed for trade on the African coast to carry palm oil and was launched in December 1937.

[4] Don's father's wives had the following children: From Ma Alice Takor: Tom Njang Ako (son), Janet Arah (daughter), Lawrence Mbi (son); Don's mother: Don (son), Eunice Besem (daughter), and James Agborta (son); Ma Alice Ayuk Mbuoh: Rosamond (daughter) and Joseph Ako (son); Mama Manyi: Godson Orock (son), Becky Nkongho (daughter); Ma Nancy: Ojong (son); Don's father's sister, Mama Susanah: Theodosia Eyong (daughter), Jedidah Ebanga (daughter), Faustina Egbendiep (daughter), Jasper Ako (son), Cyril Mbiatem (son); Don's father's late wife: Nathaniel Agborta, (son). Altogether, he had about thirteen children.

Among Don's father's nephews, whom he brought from Ntenako village to live with them, was Amos Ayuk Ako. In later life, their father gave him land to build his own house in the compound, and he was to become the caretaker of the family compound and family lands. Don's father's third wife brought children from her previous marriage, namely Godwin Eyong Arreyngang (son), Susan Ebai-enow (daughter), and Samuel Etchinyuo (son) and her brother, Victor Mbu Tarkang. His fourth wife brought two children from her previous marriage, namely Hannah (daughter) and Tambi (son). His first wife,

Ma Alice, had some of her nephews and nieces living with her, and his second wife's two nephews, Samson Ebai Enow-mbi and Samson Mbi Enow-mbi, also came to live with Don's mother. Altogether, they were about twenty children living in the compound.

[5] Joseph Ako Oben was the second child of Don's father's third wife who was present at the time when government officials came to Mamfe to seek land from the Mamfe natives to build the college. At that time, like Don and his other siblings when they were little boys at their own time, their father always took him along when going for important occasions, like traditional celebrations, meetings of elders, etc.

Born in Small Mamfe, Mamfe, in 1962, Oben Ako Joseph attended the Presbyterian Secondary School, Besongabang, Mamfe, and later, the University of Calabar, Nigeria, where he obtained a bachelor of science (BS) degree in agricultural economics and extension in 1986. In 1989, he obtained a master of science (MS) degree in tropical agricultural development from the University of Reading, England. And in 2019, he obtained a Ph. D. degree from the Department of Botany and Plant Physiology (Crop Production) of the University of Buea, Cameroon.

He started his career in 1987 with the "Fond National de Developpement Rural" (FONADER) in Yaounde, Cameroon, as an agricultural economist/cadet officer. He later joined the Cameroon Civil Service in 1990 as an agronomist in the Divisional Delegation of Agriculture in Kumba in the Ministry of Agriculture. He was seconded twice, in 1993 and 2013, to the South West Development Agency (SOWEDA), Buea, where he worked as agronomist/ planning, evaluation and monitoring officer and later as senior monitoring and evaluation officer.

He later rose to the rank of Director of studies and Cooperation in 2014 and in 2017, was appointed the director of the technical department, the main department of the regional agency after the administration. In 2013, Dr. Oben Ako Joseph was elected into the Mamfe Council and a member of its Development Committee. He is also an adviser to the Mamfe Traditional Council. Though the youngest of the Oben first-generation children, Dr. Oben Ako Joseph is the Custodian of the Oben Family Patrimony, a position he holds by virtue of his knowledge of the family patrimony and the Banyangi traditions and customs, which he gained from his long stay with their father, Pa Ako-Arah-Agbor. That knowledge is simply awesome!

[6] Early in 1957 after taking the entrance exam into Government Secondary School Owerri, the Headmaster of Government School Mamfe arranged for Don and his son to go take the entrance exam into Bali College at Besongabang. An account of this is given in "Fascinating Stories from the Journey…." in chapter 18 entitled: "In Accordance With." Also before the results of the entrance exam to the Government Secondary School Owerri were received, Don sat for the entrance exam to Sasse College. During the interview, realizing that he had obtained a very strong First School Leaving Certificate the previous year from Government School Mamfe, the Reverend Father who conducted the interview asked Don if he would want to join the class of 1957 if he admitted him directly. Classes had started in January 1957. To buy time, Don declined, preferring to be admitted with the 1958 class starting in January 1958. Don gave the excuse that he would already be several months behind his classmates. The Reverend Father obliged, even though he tried to convince Don that he would catch up within a short while. Don's admission letter into Sasse came later in the year when he was already at the Government Secondary School, Owerri where his interest had been all along.

[7] Ndiva Kale, 2015 on the occasion of the book launch of Tazoacha Asonganyi's *Cameroon: Difficult Choices in a Failed Democracy*: (Memoir) published by NGT Publishing, 2015, 352pp, Chariot Hotel Muea, Thursday August 13, 2015

[8] William Shakespeare "Twelfth Night, Or What You Will" in *The Complete Works of William Shakespeare*; Act V, p73.

[9] Oben, D.H. (1974) "Labor Absorption in Large Scale Agriculture: The case of the Cameroon Development Corporation (CDC)", (Master's Thesis, University of Ibadan).

[10] Oben, D.H. (1978) "Labor Absorption in the Rural Non-Farm Sector: Evidence from the Kwara State of Nigeria" (Ph.D. dissertation submitted to the Department of Agricultural Economics of the University of Ibadan in partial fulfilment of the requirements for the degree of Doctor of Philosophy (Ph.D.). University of Ibadan.

[11a]Essang, S. M and D.H. Oben (1975) "Labor Absorption in Large-scale Agriculture: A Case Study of the Cameroon Development Corporation Plantations"; Malayan Economic Review, Vol. 20, No 2.

[11b]). Oben, D. H. and S. M. Essang (1981) "Government Policy and Rural Industrialization in Nigeria: The Kwara State Experience." Research for

Development (Journal of the Nigerian Institute for Social and Economic Research), Vol. 1, No. 2.

[12] Nartey, F; Manihot Esculenta (Cassava): Cytogenesis, Ultrastructure and Seed Germination", Munksgaad, Denmark, 1978.

[13] A) Oben, D. H. and K. M. Menz (1980); Sweet versus Bitter Cassava: The Prospect for Low Cyanide Varieties in Nigeria; Discussion Paper No. 8/80, International Institute of Tropical Agriculture, Ibadan.

[13b].b) Oben, D. H. and K. M. Menz (1981); "Prospects for Low Cyanide Cassava in Nigeria; Food Policy (Economics, Planning and Politics of Food and Agriculture), Vol.6, No. 3.

[14] Maduagu, E. N. and D.H. Oben (1981) "A Comparative Assessment of the Effects of the 'Screw Press' and the Traditional Fermentation Method on the Cyanide Content of Grated Cassava Roots." Journal of Food Technology, 16, 299–302.

[15] Moorman, F.R, A.T. Perez, and W.J. Veldkamp (1976) "Potential of Hydromorphic Rice Cultivation in Nigeria," Paper presented, Ibadan, Nigeria.

[16] Lagemann, J. (1977) Traditional African Farming Systems in Eastern Nigeria, (Munich: Weltforum Verlag).

[17] Moorman, F.R. "Agricultural Land Utilization and Land Quality" (IITA, Ibadan, Nigeria, n.d.).

[18] Sonola, S.O. "An Economic Analysis of the Integrated Development and Management of Bottomlands (Bas fonds) and Associated Uplands in the High Forest Area of Western Nigeria," (Master's Thesis, University of Guelph, 1975).

[19] Okigbo, B.N. "Land Use, Soil Fertility and Crop Specialization in East Central State" in Prelude to the Green Revolution in the East Central State of Nigeria, edited by M.O, Ijere.

[20a)] Okali, C., D.H. Oben, T. Ojo-Atere and T. Lawson (1980); Evaluation of Farmers' Knowledge and Use of Hydromorphic Toposequences in the Western State of Nigeria: Findings from Selected Areas of the Oshun River Basin; Discussion Paper No. 4/79, International Institute of Tropical Agriculture, Ibadan, 54p.

[b)] Okali, C., D. Oben and T. Ojo-Atere (1980); The Management and Use of Hydromorphic Toposequences in the Ogun River Basin; The Case of Traditional Farmers in the Ofada Area of Ogun State. Discussion Paper No. 5/80, International Institute of Tropical Agriculture, Ibadan, 54p.

[21a)] Maduagu, E. N. and D.H. Oben (1981) "A Comparative Assessment of the Effects of the 'Screw Press' and the Traditional Fermentation Method on the Cyanide Content of Grated Cassava Roots." Journal of Food Technology, 16, 299-302. [b)] Oben, D. H. and K. M. Menz (1981); "Prospects for Low Cyanide Cassava in Nigeria; Food Policy (Economics, Planning and Politics of Food and Agriculture), Vol.6, No. 3.

[22] See Wikipedia: http://www.icrisat.org.

[23] 23 See www.uneca.org.

[24] United Nations Economic and Social Council (1984); "Situation of Food and Agriculture in Africa." E/ECA/CM.10/19, Prepared for the Fifth Meeting of the Technical Preparatory Committee of the Whole, Nineteenth Session of the Commission and Tenth Meeting of the Conference of Ministers, Conakry, Guinea, 16–30 April, 1984 (Prepared by Oben D, and G. Coker).

[25] United Nations Economic and Social Council; United Nations Economic Commission for Africa (1985–04), Progress Report on the Implementation of the Lagos Plan of Action by the ECA Secretariat, UN ECA Conference of Ministers Meeting, (25–29 April 1985, Addis Ababa, Ethiopia); UN ECA Technical Preparatory Committee of the Whole (6th Meeting, April 15–22, Addis Ababa, Ethiopia); UN ECA Commission (20th Session, 1985, April 13, Addis Ababa, Ethiopia).

[26] Lagos Plan of Action for the Economic Development of Africa, 1980-2000" (LPA). Organization of African Unity, republished by the United Nations Economic Commission for Africa. April 1980. Retrieved 2007-02-02).

[27] Berg, Elliot (1981). Accelerated Development in Sub-Saharan Africa: An Agenda for Action (PDF). Washington, DC: International Bank for Reconstruction and Development / The World Bank. P. 5. Retrieved 13 March 2015.

[28] OAU: The LPA.

[29] OAU: "Lagos Plan of Action.

[30] United Nations Economic Commission for Africa (1982–10), Report of the first meeting of the Technical Committee on Agricultural Cooperation of the PTA for Eastern and Southern African States, UN ECA Technical Committee on Agricultural Corporation of the PTA for Eastern and Southern African States Meeting (1st: 1982, Oct, 26–29: Lusaka, Zambia). Addis Ababa: © UN. ECA. http://hdl.handle.net/10855/8782).

[31] See Wikipedia, the free encyclopedia:

http://www.fao/docrep/w5973e06.htm.

[32] UN. ECA Conference of Ministers Meeting (11th: 1985, Apr. 25–29: Addis Ababa, Ethiopia) UN. ECA Technical Preparatory Committee of the Whole Meeting (6th: 1985, Apr. 15–22: Addis Ababa, Ethiopia), UN. ECA Commission (20th Session: 1985, Apr, 13: Addis Ababa, Ethiopia).

[33] See http://www.un-documents.net/a35r66.htm: Resolution adopted by the General Assembly: 35/66B. Industrial Development Decade for Africa.

[34] See Wikipedia:

https://www.uneca.org/efm1995/pages/transport and communications decade for Africa: UNECA, Transport And Communication Decade for Africa. See Introduction, para 1. Also see

www.un.org/en/sections/observances/international-decades/index.htm: UN International Decades.

[35] See Wikipedia: trove.nla.gov.au/work/6583300?versionId=7587067 National Library of Australia; 1984 English, Conference Proceedings edition; Harare Declaration on the Food Crisis in Africa as adopted by the 13th FAO Regional Conference for Africa on 25 July 1984, Harare, Zimbabwe/ Food and Agricultural Organization of the United Nations.

[36] APPER: These were some of the main areas which it was to focus on.

[37] These issues were to be addressed on the basis of the Kilimanjaro Program of Action for African Population and Self-Reliant Development, adopted by the Second African Population Conference held at Arusha, United Republic of Tanzania, from 9 to 13 January 1984.

[38] UN General Assembly 8th Plenary Meeting, 1 June 1986. See Wikipedia: http://www.un.org/documents/ga/res/spec/aress13-2.htm. Annex: Analysis of Africa's Critical Economic Situation.

[39] UN General Assembly 8th plenary meeting, 1 June 1986. See United Nations; United Nations Program of Action for African Economic Recovery and Development (UNPAAERD) 1986–1990, UN General Assembly A/Res/S-132/2, 8th plenary meeting, 1 June 1986.Wikipedia; http://www.un.org/documents/ga/res/spec/aress13-2.htm.

[40] ECA; AAF-SAP, E/ECA/CM.15/6/Rev 3.

[41] ECA; AAF-SAP, E/ECA/CM.15/6/Rev.

[42] ECA; Rationalization of ECA-Sponsored institutions: Renewal for improved Service. See www.uneca.org/.../rationalization-eca-sponsored-institutions-renewal-improved-service.

[43] UN ECOSOC; International year for the mobilization of financial and technological resources to increase food and agricultural production in Africa; Resolution A/RES/38/198 of 20 December 1983.

[44] United Nations Economic and Social Council; United Nations. Economic Commission for Africa (1987–02). International year for the mobilization of financial and technological resources to increase food and agricultural production in Africa: executive summary. UN. ECA Technical Preparatory Committee of the Whole (8th: 1987, Apr. 13–20: Addis Ababa, Ethiopia); UN. ECA Conference of Ministers Meeting (13th: 1987, Apr. 23–27: Addis Ababa, Ethiopia); UN. ECA Commission (22nd Session 1987, April 23–27: Addis Ababa, Ethiopia). Addis Ababa. © UN. ECA. http://hdl.handle.net/10855/15907.

[45] UNGA: E/RES/1987/67.

[46] "Measures for the Improvement of Cooperatives and Small Farmers' Organizations/Associations in the Marketing of Food and Livestock Products in Africa."

[47] Packard, Phil, D. Oben and E. Zerai (1984); Macro-Economic Review of the Ethiopian Highlands. Prepared for the Ethiopian Highlands Reclamation Study-UTF/ETH/037/ETH, Addis Ababa, March 1984.

[48] Oben, D and H. Ouedraogo (1985) The Formulation, Administration and Management of Prices as an Incentive to Increased Food Production in Africa". Presented at the Seventh Roundtable of the African Association for Public Administration and Management (AAPAM), Accra, Ghana.

[49] UN Economic Commission for Africa; Technical Publication on Measures for the Improvement of Women's Land Holdings and Land Rights in Africa. JEFAD/APISS/89/58, December 1989.

[50] Don Oben; "Increasing food supply and Availability in Africa through Efficient marketing and distribution" in Food and Agriculture in Africa; ECA/FAO Agriculture Division, Staff Papers No. 1, April 1991.

[51] Report of the World Food Conference, Rome, 5–16 November 1974 New York, United Nations, 1975.

[52] See Wikipedia: (http://www.britannica.com).

[53] World Food Council; Food Strategies In Africa: Progress And Critical Issues, 1974–1984.

[54] World Food Council; The Cyprus Initiative Against Hunger In the World; President's Report to the Fifteenth Ministerial Session, Cairo, Egypt, 22–25 May 1989,WFC/1989/2, 3 April 1989.

[55] Oben, D.H, Agricultural Research and Technology Development, Transfer and Application: Issues Note on Africa": Prepared for the Deputy Director of the UN World Food Council for discussion with regional research and Development Institutions in Africa, Rome, June, 1990.

[56] WFC; Toward A New Green Revolution: Perspective for future food production increase in the developing countries with priority to Africa, WFC, Rome, 1991.

[57] See previous reference above: WFC: Toward A new Green Revolution.

[58] WFC; Meeting the developing countries' food production challenges of the 1990s and beyond: summary report of the WFC/UNDP interregional consultation, Cairo, Egypt, 22-24 April 1991; WFC/1991/6 add 1, Rome, April, 1991.

[59] WFC; Report of the World Food Council 18th session, Nairobi, 23–26 June, 1992.

[60] Wikipedia;http://www.nationsencyclopedia.com/United-Nations/Economic-and-Social-Development-WORLD-FOOD-COUNCIL-WFC.html#ixzz4Nkzqn2N4.

[61] See: ECA; The Multinational Programming and Operational Centers (MULPOCS): Strengthening ECA's Subregional Presence. Document E/**ECA**/CM.23/6.

[62] ECA, ibid.

[63].UN ECA Tangier MULPOC, "A Strategy for Sustainable Land Development in North Africa Maritime Areas.

[64] UN ECA MULPOC for North Africa; Follow-up And Monitoring of the Locust and Grasshopper Situation in the North Africa Sub-region and on the Establishment of an Early Warning System, ECA/ TNG/ MULPOC/ ICE/XII/04, October 1994; submitted to the Twelfth Meeting of the Committee of Experts of the North African MULPOC, Tangier, Morocco, 13–16 March 1995.

[65] UN ECA MULPOC for North Africa; The Role of Financial Institutions in the Mobilization of Resources for the Implementation of Multinational Core Projects Within the Framework of the IDDA in North Africa. ECA/TNG/ MULPOC/ICE/XII/Info/01, October 1994; submitted to the Meeting of the

Committee of Experts of the North African MULPOC, Tangier, Morocco, 13-16 March 1995.

[66] UN ECA MULPOC for North Africa; Study on Experiences, Techniques and Know-how of Dates Production in the North African Sub-region, ECA/TNG/MULPOC/IV/95, p.2.

[67] UN ECA MULPOC for North Africa; Study on Experiences, Techniques and Know-how of Dates Production in the North African Sub-region, ECA/TNG/MULPOC/IV/95).

[68] UN ECA MULPOC for North Africa; A Pre-feasibility Study on Efficient and Rational Exploitation of Natural Resources within the North African Sub-region (Energy, Water, etc.) to Support Industrial Development and Industrial Co-operation in the Sub-region, ECA/TNG/MULPOC. September 95.

[69] UN ECA Regional Office for North Africa of the Economic Commission for Africa; The Co-ordination and Harmonization of food and Agricultural Policies, Strategies and Production in North Africa Sub-region, ECA/TNG/MULPOC /AGR/ ICE/XIII/ 8, December 1996; submitted to the Thirteenth Meeting of the Intergovernmental Committee of Experts, Tangier, Morocco, 01–04 April 1997, p.2.

[70] FAO; Follow-up of the UNCED; Integrating Environment and Sustainability into Agricultural Policy Analysis. FAO (ESPC/NE/93/5), Rome, August 1993, p.8.

[71] UN ECA Field Mission on Green Belts Rehabilitation and Conservation. ECA (Output 3b XV); Addis Ababa, 1993, p.6.

[72] United Nations General Assembly; REPORT OF THE UNITED NATIONS CONFERENCE ON ENVIRONMENT AND DEVELOPMENT,**A/ CONF.151/26 (Vol. I),** Rio de Janeiro, 3–14 June 1992.

[73] See also UNITED NATIONS ECONOMIC AND SOCIAL COUNCIL ECONOMIC COMMISSION FOR AFRICA Twenty-eighth session of the Commission/nineteenth meeting of the Conference of Ministers Addis Ababa Ethiopia 3-6 May 1993. REPORT OF THE FOURTEENTH MEETING OF THE TECHNICAL PREPARATORY COMMITTEE OF THE WHOLE, E/ECA/CM.19/26, 2 May 1993, Resolution 3 (XIV): African Strategies for the Implementation of Agenda 21.

[74] Arab Maghreb Union; Charte maghrébine pour la protection de l'environnement et le développement durable, Nouakchott, Mauritania, 11 November 1992.

[75] UN ECA Regional Office for North Africa of the Economic Commission for Africa; Monitoring and Follow-up of Progress in Desertification Control in North Africa. ECA/TNG/MULPOC/AGR/ICE/XIII/5, December 1996; for submission to the 13th Meeting of the Intergovernmental Committee of Experts of the Tangier MULPOC, Tangier, Morocco, 01–04 April 1997.

[76] Report of the Subregional workshop for the North Africa subregion on the preparation of national reports for the Regional and World Conferences on Women, E/ECA/MULPOC/TAN/4Mcw/W/1; 28-30 March 1994, Tangier, Morocco.

[77] The DELF (Diplôme d'Etudes en Langue Française) and DALF (Diplôme Approfondi de Langue Française) are French proficiency certifications for non-native speakers of French awarded by the French Ministry of Education to certify the competency in the French language.

[78] SeeWikipedia:http://www.google.com/url?url=http://*chora.virtualave.net/e conomic-reform-ethiopia.htm* / Economic Reform and Development in EthiopiaByDejene Yirgu, WIC 26/01/2000Jan 26, Dejene Yirgu: Economic Reform and Development in Ethiopia.

[79] ECA; "Serving Africa better: strategic directions for the Economic Commission for Africa (ECA), (ECOSOc, E/ECA/CM.22/2, March 1996.

[80] ECA; "Serving Africa better: strategic directions for the Economic Commission for Africa (ECA)", (ECOSOc, E/ECA/CM.22/2, March 1996.

[81] "Diversification of Food-Based Sectors: The Contribution of Non-Conventional Food Resources" Paper prepared and presented by Don to the Symposium on Food Security: A Recipe for Survival." Pretoria, South Africa from 18 to 21 March 1997).

[82] Economic Development Institute; Reform in the Public and Rural sectors in New Zealand: A World Bank Study Tour for Africans. "Seeing Is Believing". Study Tour Report, April 12–24, 1997, p.2).

[83] See EDI pp 9-11 for the list of participants.

[84] Economic Development Institute; Reform in the Public and Rural sectors in New Zealand: A World Bank Study Tour for Africans. "Seeing Is Believing". Study Tour Report, April 12–24, 1997.

[85] EDI, ibid, Pp 24/25.

[86] For more details see Aritour; World bank West African Governments' Study Tour Of Agricultural Policy In New Zealand, 12–24 April 1997.

[87] For details, see EDI, ibid pp 31–36.

[88] Modeling Population-Environment-Development-Agriculture Interactions for Science Policy Communication and Advocacy in Africa: the PEDA Model, W. Lutz, S. Scherbov, P.K. Makinwa-Adebusoye, and G. Reniers. Paper presented to the XXIVth IUSSP General Conference, Session s-43: the Demography of Sub-Saharan Africa.

[89] The Impact of Policies on Food Security Using the PEDA Model: A Case Study of Botswana, Cameroon and Ethiopia. Kwadwo Tutu, Environment and Development Officer, Food security and Sustainable Development Division, ECA, Addis Ababa, Ethiopia.

[90] "Ensuring Food Security and Sustainable Development in Southern Africa: ECA's New Approach". Prepared and presented by Don Oben at the Fifth Meeting of the Inter-Governmental Committee of the SRDC-SA, Lusaka, Zambia 5–8 October 1998.

[91] UNECA; Mission Report on Workshop 99: The Food chain in Sub-Saharan Africa: Linking Farmers to Markets, ECA/FSSDD/MR/038/99; Bamako, Mali, 14–21 October 1999; Back-to-Office Report by Don Oben; Food Security and Sustainable Development Division, ECA, Addis Ababa, Ethiopia.

[92] See ECA/FSSDD/SH/HU/00/6); ECA; "PEDA Advocacy Booklet: Projections for Ethiopia, Addis Ababa, Nov. 2001; ECA: "PEDA Advocacy Booklet: Projections on Aging for Botswana, Addis Ababa, Nov. 2001; ECA: "PEDA Advocacy Booklet: Case Study: Cameroon, Addis Ababa, Nov. 2001.

[93] Don Oben; Back-To-Office Report On Mission To Windhoek, Namibia, 11–14 April 2000, FSSDD/MR/012/00; UN ECA Food Security and Sustainable Development Division, Addis Ababa, April 2000.

[94] Don Oben; "Poverty, Food Security, and Environmental Linkages: Policy Challenges in Selected Environmentally Fragile Areas in Africa; FSSDD/ECA, 1998.

[95] Don Oben; "Sustainable Food Production and Food Security in the Sahelian Countries: Some Key Issues And Policy Challenges." United Nations. Economic Commission for Africa, Food Security and Sustainable Development Division, Addis Ababa, June 1999.

[96] Oben Don; Forestry, Poverty and Sustainable Development in Africa: FAO/ADB/ECA, Collaboration in The Forestry Outlook Study for Africa; Africa's Population Bulletin No.2, December 2002.

[97] Don Oben; Mission Report To Libreville, Gabon, 25–29 March 2002; FSSDD/MR/008/02, UN ECA, Sustainable Development division, Addis Ababa, 2002.

[98] The Cameroon Community in Ethiopia: Guidelines, April 199.

[99] Ref: HRSS/2003/T4/sg dated 24 January 2003, Notification Of Retirement.

[100] "A Second Career: Opportunities for Paid and Voluntary Work". By Jide Balogun, ECA senior professional, a handout.

[101] Economic Commission For Africa, Sixth session of the Committee on Trade, Regional Cooperation and Integration; 13–15 October 2009 Addis Ababa, Ethiopia E/ECA/CTRCI/5/3, 1 October 2009.

[102] Economic Commission For Africa, Sixth session of the Committee on Trade, Regional Cooperation and Integration; 13–15 October 2009 Addis Ababa, Ethiopia E/ECA/CTRCI/5/3 1 October 2009.

103. UNGA; Res 35/66 B. Industrial Development Decade for Africa, UN General Assembly, Thirty-fifth session Agenda item 61, 5 December 1980.

104. FAO, Harare declaration on the food crisis in Africa; 13th FAO Regional Conference for Africa, 16 Jul 1984, Harare (Zimbabwe), Development Dept. FAO, Rome (Italy).

105.UNGA; The UN Program of Action for African Economic Recovery and Development, UNPAAERD, 1986–1990, A/RES.13/2, 8th Plenary meeting, 1 June 1986.

[106] *The World Bank; "Can Africa Claim the 21st Century?" Washington, DC, 2000.*

[107] *The World Bank; "Can Africa Claim the 21st Century?" Washington, DC, 2000, p1.*

[108] Craig Charney; Political Will: What is it? How is it Measured? Newsletter Clip, May 5, 2009. See Wikipedia

http://www.charneyresearch.com/resources/political-will-what-is-it-how-is-it-measured/

[109] Sister Eunice and Dr. Nzo-Nguty: Don talked much about his sister, Mrs Eunice Nzo-Nguty when I was interviewing him for this book. – especially that time during their childhood when they both struggled to take care of themselves while caring for their mother when she had a most serious eye injury. So it is important to say a few words about her. Mrs Eunice Besem Nzo-Nguty or "Sister Eunice" as Don fondly calls her, was recruited early into the former West Cameroon Treasury Department, Buea on November 25, 1963,

as an accounting machine operator. She was transferred three years later to the newly created Government Accounting Department in the same capacity. In July 1970 she passed the last Public Service Examination for Clerical, Accounting and Judicial staff and was upgraded accordingly. She was transferred from Buea to the Ministry of Finance, Yaounde, in May 1973, and reclassified as Assistant Controller of Treasury. She was later transferred to the Treasury Office, Kumba, where she served until November 1981 when she left on study leave to the USA to meet her husband, Bernard Tarkang Nzo-Nguty, whom she had married in June 1967 when he was a Clerical Assistant in the West Cameroon House of Assembly and Chiefs in Buea. He had left for further studies in Canada in September 1976 and later to the USA after obtaining a Bachelor's and a Master's degree. Their three children joined them two years later. While in the USA, Eunice obtained an Associate Degree in Banking and Finance from the Midland Technical College, Columbia, South Carolina, in June 1987. The family returned to Cameroon in September 1987 and Eunice was re-integrated in the Ministry of Finance, reclassified as Controller of Treasury and served in this capacity until her retirement in June 1993. She is a mother of four children and nine grandchildren.

2) Dr. Benard Tarkang Nzo-Nguty is the husband of Don's sister, Eunice, whom he married in 1967 while employed as a Clerical Assistant in the West Cameroon House of Assembly and Chiefs in Buea. He was later seconded to the National Assembly in Yaounde as an Administrative Assistant in 1973 following the evolution of Cameroon from the federal to the unitary system of government. He holds a Bachelor's degree in political science and library studies from Concordia University, Montreal, Canada, a Master's degree in International Affairs from Charleton University, Ottawa, Canada, and a Ph.D. degree in International Studies from the University of South Carolina, Columbia, USA, awarded in December 1985. On completion of his studies, he was employed by the university to serve as the Director of Study Abroad Programs and Visiting Assistant Professor in the Department of Government and International Studies. He returned home to Cameroon in September 1987 and was appointed to serve as a Research Officer in the National Assembly while teaching part-time in the Institute of International Relations of Cameroon (I.R.I.C). On May 14, 1988, he was appointed Deputy Secretary-General in charge of Administrative Affairs. Subsequently, he was appointed Deputy Secretary-General in charge of Legislative, Linguistic, Research and

Documentation Services cumulatively with the function of Director, Centre for the Promotion of Bilingualism in Parliament—posts which he held until he was retired on October 31, 2002.

After his retirement, he was employed by the Geneva-based Inter-Parliamentary Union and served for 18 months (August 2004–February 2006) in Abuja, Nigeria, as project manager of the European Union/Federal Government of Nigeria Democracy Program Supporting National and State Assemblies. Thereafter, Dr. Nzo-Nguty was retained by the African Capacity Building Foundation based in Harare, Zimbabwe, as an international consultant on governance, and undertook missions of project development, monitoring, and evaluation for the foundation. He is the father of three children and seven grandchildren.

[110] Charles Bukowski. "War All the Time." See Wikipedia: https://www.goodreads.com/quotes/tag/moments.

[111] Sarah Ban Breathnach. Tags: appreciation, experience, life, moments. See Wikipedia: https and https://www.simpleabundance.com.

[112] Jonathan Lockwood Huie. "Jonathan Lockwood Huie's Inspirational Quote About Life." See Wikipedia: https://www.quotes-inspirational.com/quotes/moments.

[113] AUC, 2013. "Improving Rural Infrastructures to Raise Competitiveness of Africa's Agricultural Sector and to Access Regional Markets" Report for Central Africa, By Don Oben, Senior International Consultant, Agriculture, Food Security and Sustainable Development (AFSSD), Buea, Cameroon.

[114] AU/NEPAD (2002). Comprehensive Africa Agricultural Development Program (CAADP) Pillar 2.

[115] See Wikipedia: https://www.kabalarians.com/cfm/whats-in-a-name.cfm.

[116] Wikipedia: https://www.kabalarians.com/cfm/NRMovie-embedded-NR.cfm.

[117] Don's brother, His Highness Nfor Dr. Godson Orock Oben, the eldest child of their father's fourth wife, is a medical doctor and the First Class Chief of Mamfe. Born in 1954 in Small Mamfe, he attended St. Joseph's College, Sasse, Buea; Cameroon College of Arts, Science and Technology, Bambili; Baptist Academy, Lagos; and the University of Lagos, College of Medicine, Nigeria, where he graduated with an MB BS degree. He worked in various hospitals in the Cameroon Civil Service for twenty-five years and retired in 2010 as the Director of the District Hospital, Mamfe, Southwest Province. He

subsequently established and is the Director of the New Life Cottage Hospital Mamfe, a medical foundation engaged in the provision of quality health care services to the less privileged in the community.

In 2017, the Cameroon Medical Council gave him a recognition for his devoted and selfless service to humanity and for upholding the dignity and ideals of the medical profession. The Southwest Regional Delegation of Public Health (Performance Based Financing, PBF) also gave him an Award of Excellence Accreditation "for distinguished quality health care services." In 1992, Dr. Godson Orock Oben was installed the Paramount Chief (First Class) of Mamfe in succession to Chief Mbeng Besong, who died in 1992.

[118] Abiodun, Sulaiman; Nigeria: Palm Oil Importation As Strategic Industry Stabilizer, Opinion, The Guardian (Lagos) 31 December 2014.

[119] Abiodun, Sulaiman; Nigeria: Palm Oil Importation As Strategic Industry Stabilizer, Opinion, The Guardian (Lagos) 31 December 2014.

Milton Keynes UK
Ingram Content Group UK Ltd.
UKHW022323051024
449173UK00003B/37